1 MONTH OF
FREE
READING

at
www.ForgottenBooks.com

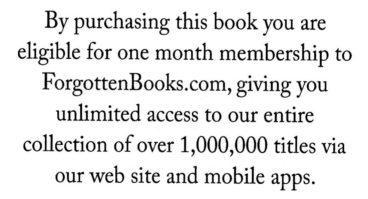

By purchasing this book you are eligible for one month membership to ForgottenBooks.com, giving you unlimited access to our entire collection of over 1,000,000 titles via our web site and mobile apps.

To claim your free month visit:
www.forgottenbooks.com/free149986

ISBN 978-0-365-32985-5
PIBN 10149986

THE SOUTH *in the* Building *of the* Nation

A HISTORY OF THE SOUTHERN STATES DESIGNED *to* RECORD *the* SOUTH'S PART *in the* MAKING *of the* AMERICAN NATION; *to* PORTRAY *the* CHARACTER *and* GENIUS, *to* CHRONICLE *the* ACHIEVEMENTS *and* PROGRESS *and to* ILLUSTRATE *the* LIFE *and* TRADITIONS *of the* SOUTHERN PEOPLE

VOLUME VII

COMPLETE IN TWELVE VOLUMES

The SOUTHERN HISTORICAL PUBLICATION SOCIETY RICHMOND, VIRGINIA

A240335

Manufactured by
L. H. Jenkins
Richmond, Va.

History *of the* Literary *and* Intellectual Life *of the* South

VOLUME VII

EDITOR-IN-CHIEF
JOHN BELL HENNEMAN, M. A., Ph. D.,
Late Professor of English Literature, University of the South

---

CONTRIBUTORS

GENERAL INTRODUCTION

WILLIAM PETERFIELD TRENT, LL.D., D.C.L., formerly Professor of English Literature, University of the South; Professor of English Literature, Columbia University; author of *English Culture in Virginia*, *History of American Literature*, etc.

INTELLECTUAL TENDENCIES IN THE SOUTH

JAMES HAMPTON KIRKLAND, Ph D., LL.D., D.C.L., Chancellor of Vanderbilt University, Nashville, Tenn.

CHARACTERISTICS OF SOUTHERN POETRY FROM THE BEGINNING TO 1865

HENRY NELSON SNYDER, Litt.D., LL.D., President of Wofford College, Spartanburg, S. C.

SOUTHERN POETRY SINCE THE WAR OF SECESSION

EDWIN MIMS, M.A., Ph D., Professor of English Literature, Trinity College, and editor *South Atlantic Quarterly*.

THE FOLK-LORE OF THE SOUTH

ARTHUR HOWARD NOLL, LL.D., Lecturer on Anthropology, etc., University of the South, Sewanee, Tenn.

THE SOUTH'S CONTRIBUTIONS TO THE NATION'S WIT AND HUMOR

GEORGE FREDERICK MELLEN, A.M., Ph.D., formerly Professor of Greek and History, University of Tennessee; now of the *Knoxville Sentinel*.

HISTORICAL STUDIES IN THE SOUTH

COLYER MERIWETHER, Ph.D., Secretary of Southern History Association, and editor Publications of Southern History Association.

CONTRIBUTORS.

ENGLISH STUDIES IN THE SOUTH

JOHN BELL HENNEMAN, M.A., Ph D., Late Professor of English Literature, University of the South, Sewanee, Tenn

THE SOUTH'S CONTRIBUTIONS TO CLASSICAL STUDIES

CHARLES FORSTER SMITH, A.M., Ph D., Professor of Greek and Classical Philology, University of Wisconsin, Madison, Wis.

ECONOMIC AND POLITICAL ESSAYS IN ANTE-BELLUM SOUTH

ULRICH BONNELL PHILLIPS, A M, Ph.D., Professor of History, Tulane University, New Orleans, La

THE SOUTH'S CONTRIBUTION TO MATHEMATICS AND ASTRONOMY

SAMUEL MARX BARTON, A.B., Ph.D., Professor of Mathematics, University of the South, Sewanee, Tenn

THE SOUTH'S CONTRIBUTION TO THE PHYSICAL SCIENCES

FRANCIS PRESTON VENABLE, Ph.D., D.Sc., LL D., President of University of North Carolina, Chapel Hill, N C.

THE SOUTH'S CONTRIBUTIONS TO NATURAL HISTORY

SAMUEL McCUTCHEN BAIN, A D, Professor of Botany, University of Tennessee, Knoxville, Tenn.

THE SOUTH'S CONTRIBUTIONS TO PHILOSOPHY

HENRY CLAY WHITE, Ph.D., D C L., LL.D., Professor of Chemistry, University of Georgia, Athens, Ga.

CONTRIBUTIONS OF THE SOUTH TO THE CHARACTER AND CULTURE OF THE NORTH

H. IRVING BROCK, Editorial Staff of *New York Times.*

CONTRIBUTIONS OF NEW ENGLAND TO THE SOUTH'S CULTURE

GEORGE FREDERICK MELLEN, A.M., Ph.D, formerly Professor of Greek and History, University of Tennessee ; now of the *Knoxville Sentinel.*

LOUISIANA· HER CONTRIBUTIONS TO THE LITERATURE OF THE UNITED STATES

ALCÉE FORTIER, Litt.D., Professor of Romance Languages, Tulane University ; author of *Louisiana Folk Tales; History of Louisiana.*

LAW WRITERS OF THE SOUTH

M. HERNDON MOORE, A.B., LL B., Professor of Law, University of South Carolina, Columbia, S. C

INFLUENCE OF THE BENCH AND BAR OF THE SOUTH

JOSHUA WILLIAM CALDWELL, A.M., Lecturer on the Laws and Constitutional History of Tennessee, University of Tennessee ; author of *The Bench and Bar of Tennessee*

THE SOUTH'S CONTRIBUTIONS TO MEDICINE AND SURGERY

ROBERT MADISON SLAUGHTER, M.D., Member Virginia State Board of Medical Examiners ; Treasurer Medical Society of Virginia ; author of *An Historical Sketch of Medicine and Surgery in Virginia.*

viii

CONTRIBUTORS.

THE SOUTH'S CONTRIBUTIONS TO MUSIC

HUGER WILKINSON JERVEY, M.A'., Professor of Greek, University of the South, Sewanee, Tenn.

THE SOUTHERN PRESS

NORMAN WALKER, Associate editor of New Orleans *Times Democrat,* New Orleans, La.

SOUTHERN MAGAZINES

EDWIN MIMS, M.A., Ph.D., Professor of English Literature, Trinity College, Durham, N. C., editor *South Atlantic Quarterly*

SOUTHERN EDITORS

GEORGE FREDERICK MELLEN, A.M., Ph.D , formerly Professor of Greek and History, University of Tennessee.

SOUTHERN LIBRARIES

EDWIN WILEY, B.A , M.A., formerly Assistant Librarian and Assistant in English, Vanderbilt University ; now in the Library of Congress.

SOUTHERN HISTORICAL SOCIETIES

COLYER MERIWETHER, Ph.D., Secretary Southern History Association, and editor of Publications of Southern History Association.

THE LITERARY AND INTELLECTUAL PROGRESS OF THE NEGRO

H. I. BROCK, Editorial Staff of the *New York Times.*

CONTENTS OF VOLUME VII.

GENERAL INTRODUCTION xv

INTELLECTUAL TENDENCIES OF THE SOUTH.
    I. Material Development................................ xxxii
    II. Educational Progress............................. xxxv
    III. Literature and History............................ xxxviii
    IV Intellectual Independence........................... xl

CHAPTER I

CHARACTERISTICS OF SOUTHERN POETRY FROM THE BEGIN-
    NING TO 1865.
    Southern Poetry of the Colonial Period................... .. 1
    Poetry of the Revolutionary Period........................ 5
    Poetry After the Revolution............................... 6
    Southern Poets and their Poetry up to 1865.............. 8

CHAPTER II

SOUTHERN POETRY SINCE THE WAR OF SECESSION.
    Poets of the War of Secession............................... 25
    Later Poets and their Poetry................................ 31

CHAPTER III

THE FOLK-LORE OF THE SOUTH.
    The South Rich in Folk-Lore............................... 55
    Folk-Lore of the Indians.................................... 61
    Folk-Lore of the Negro..................................... 64

CHAPTER IV

THE SOUTH'S CONTRIBUTIONS TO THE NATION'S WIT AND
    HUMOR 73-87

CHAPTER V

HISTORICAL STUDIES IN THE SOUTH.... 88-114

CHAPTER VI

ENGLISH STUDIES IN THE SOUTH.......................115-134

CHAPTER VII

THE SOUTH'S CONTRIBUTIONS TO CLASSICAL STUDIES.
    The Work of Universities and Professors..... 136
    Schools and Schoolmasters.................................. 160

CONTENTS.

CHAPTER VIII

ECONOMIC AND POLITICAL ESSAYS IN THE ANTE-BELLUM SOUTH.

Theoretical and General Economics 174
Agriculture 175
Mining, Manufactures, Transportation and Commerce... 177
Labor 179
Negroes 180
Slavery 182
Social Surveys........................... 188
Political Essays; Theoretical.............. 189
Constitutional Construction................ 192
Party Politics........................... 195
Sectionalism 196

CHAPTER IX

THE SOUTH'S CONTRIBUTIONS TO MATHEMATICS AND AS-
TRONOMY 200-220

CHAPTER X

THE SOUTH'S CONTRIBUTION TO PHYSICAL SCIENCE.

Contributions in Chemistry................ 222
Contributions in Physics.................. 231

CHAPTER XI

THE SOUTH'S CONTRIBUTIONS TO NATURAL HISTORY.

Naturalists of the Earlier and Later Periods.. 240
Geological Surveys........................ 253

CHAPTER XII

THE SOUTH'S CONTRIBUTIONS TO PHILOSOPHY 259-268

CHAPTER XIII

CONTRIBUTIONS OF THE SOUTH TO THE CHARACTER AND
CULTURE OF THE NORTH.

Beginning of Southern Influence upon Northern Culture.. 272
Influence of Environment 276
Southern Influence in the North Since the War .. 278
Special Contributions to Literature and Science ... 283

CHAPTER XIV

CONTRIBUTIONS OF NEW ENGLAND TO THE SOUTH'S CULTURE

Early Influences.......................... 296
In the Educational Field.................. 298

CHAPTER XV

LOUISIANA'S CONTRIBUTION TO THE LITERATURE OF THE
UNITED STATES

French Poetry in Louisiana 317
French Literary Societies 319
English Literature in Louisiana 321

CHAPTER XVI

THE LAW WRITERS OF THE SOUTH.

Distinguished Southern Law Writers 327
Contributions of Southern Law Writers...... 337

CONTENTS.

CHAPTER XVII

THE INFLUENCE OF THE BENCH AND BAR UPON SOUTHERN LIFE AND CULTURE.

Influence of Southern Lawyers................................ 341
The Lawyers in Literature.................................... 347
The Lawyers and the Aristocracy.............................. 347
Influence upon Culture....................................... 352
The Lawyers and Religion..................................... 354

CHAPTER XVIII

THE SOUTH'S CONTRIBUTION TO THE PROGRESS OF MEDICINE AND SURGERY.

Contributions to Medical Science and Literature.............. 356
In the War of Secession...................................... 368
Since the War.. 369

CHAPTER XIX

THE SOUTH'S CONTRIBUTIONS TO MUSIC.

1732-1800 372
1800-1861 380
Opera in New Orleans... 386
Two Great Composers.. 389
Negro Music.. 392
Patriotic Songs.. 395
The Present.. 897
Institutional Work... 400

CHAPTER XX

THE SOUTHERN PRESS.

Characteristics 402
Early Journalism... 405
Colonial Press Conservative.................................. 409
Journalism in the Southern Colonies and States.............. 409
Date of Establishment of Leading Southern Newspapers........ 426
Journalism and Literature.................................... 427
The Press and Industrial Development......................... 430

CHAPTER XXI

SOUTHERN MAGAZINES..437-469

CHAPTER XXII

SOUTHERN EDITORS 470-483

CHAPTER XXIII

LIBRARIES IN THE SOUTHERN STATES.

Early History.. 485
Destruction During the War................................... 500
Progress Since the War....................................... 501

CHAPTER XXIV

SOUTHERN HISTORICAL SOCIETIES

Early History.. 511
After the War of Secession................................... 513
Special Aid of Southern Associations and Institutions........ 514

CHAPTER XXV

THE INTELLECTUAL AND LITERARY PROGRESS OF THE NEGRO.

The Negro Characteristics and Progress 524
Negro Schools and Institutions............................... 537

INTRODUCTION TO VOLUME VII.

IT is a matter for deep regret that the general introduction to the three volumes of this work which treat specifically of the literary and intellectual development of the South should not have been written by the editor to whom they were intrusted. No other Southerner of this generation was better fitted than the late Professor Henneman, through sympathy, training, and knowledge, to view our literary past in proper perspective, to estimate adequately our current production in all departments of literature and scholarship, and to give the encouragements and cautions likely to be of service to those neophytes of the present who bid fair to become the trained writers and scholars of the future. And apart from his admirable general equipment Professor Henneman was uniquely qualified to furnish an introduction to these volumes because he occupied toward them the position of an architect toward a building. He conceived the edifice as a whole, and it may be almost literally said that he drew the plan of every apartment. Unlike an architect, he would have joined himself to the workmen he had selected and would have made himself responsible for the construction of more than one integral portion of the work he had planned. This was not to be, but the task he left unfinished has been carried on to completion in the spirit with which he began it, and, as far as possible, along the lines he traced.

It is no part of an introducer's duty to attempt to forestall judgments; but I think that in view of the fact that I have no personal responsibility for the chapters that follow, I may venture to point out how thoroughly they cover the field of Southern literature, and how excellently, in some cases, they supply information that will be vainly sought elsewhere. Setting aside the volumes devoted to fiction and oratory, and considering only the papers of historical and critical quality which constitute a coöperative history of the South's intellectual development, we are first impressed by the fact that the range of Southern literary, scientific, and broadly philosophical efforts is far wider than the outside world or most Southerners seem to have thought.

The section has always been noted for its orators, and since the war enough Southern men and women have won reputations by their novels and short stories to make the term "Southern Fiction," both intelligible to the average reader and useful rather than amusing to the student. The phrases "Southern Poetry" and "Southern Poets" also find their way into textbooks and essays on American literature, but they scarcely carry much definite meaning for the reader, and one is sometimes inclined to wonder whether the knowledge and tastes of the professors and critics who employ them might not fairly be described as prevailingly geographical. Yet Poe, Timrod, Hayne, and Lanier form a group that is both distinct and important, and, even though we should consent—as we would not—to pass over in silence their minor contemporaries, we ought to remember that the South to-day can boast of as many true poets as any other section can. This is not the day, and perhaps America thus far is not the country of truly great poets; but surely one of the best ways to speed the coming of great poets is to give reasonable encouragement to such poets as we have and, if Southerners do not specially encourage their own versifying compatriots, it is quite certain that these servants of the Muses will receive scant consideration in other quarters. A recent manual of American literature, the hospitable catholicity of which verges in some respects upon the ridiculous, does not include in its elaborate index any reference to Randall and his "Maryland, My Maryland," or to Father Ryan, Dr. Ticknor, and Irwin Russell among the dead, or to Father Tabb and Mr. Madison Cawein among the living. The two chapters in the present work which deal with Southern poetry are, I submit, neither superfluous nor unduly sectional.

Even less superfluous are the chapters devoted to science and scholarship, to the professions, and to the arts other than literature. The notion that the Southerner of the old régime was little more than a gentleman of charming manners and old-fashioned culture has taken such root in the popular mind that but few Southern names not connected with public life or with service in the War of Secession have become familiar to the entire nation. One or two eminent surgeons, a few writers on scientific subjects like Maury and the Le Contes, an occasional editor and professor may be exceptions, more or less, to this general statement; but the fact remains that the South is considered by many to have been a negligible factor in the intellectual development of the country. The most versatile and prolific man of letters produced by what we call the Old South, William Gilmore Simms, has often been confused with the gallant commander of the Alabama. The accomplished historian of Louisiana, Charles Gayarré, escapes notice in books that would certainly have mentioned him if he had treated a New England theme. Not one man in a hundred has any idea of the part played by Southern physicians who have settled in New York. To most persons the elective system is a Harvard discovery and emphasis upon English studies a matter of yesterday; but the Southerner who is at all interested in such matters smiles and recalls the name of Thomas Jefferson.

It would be idle, of course, to suppose that this state of affairs is due entirely to sectional prejudice and conceit on the part of our fellow Americans. Neither the Old South nor the New can fairly be said to have rivalled New England and the Middle States in contributing to the intellectual development of the nation, nor have Southern writers been discreetly zealous in making known what their section has actually accomplished. If less had been claimed for Poe by the South, more would already have been granted him by common consent. If the historical societies and the colleges and universities of the South had been as active in research and publication during the past forty years as they have been during the past ten, the culture history of the section would be far better known to the country at large. It is no reflection on the South to make this statement, for it is only of late that the much harrassed region has attained the degree of social and economic stability that is requisite to scholarly production upon an extensive scale. But it would be unfair to dwell upon the world's ignorance and neglect of Southern achievements—to which Southerners are supposed to be peculiarly sensitive—without bearing in mind our own backwardness in chrouicling what we have performed.

It is the aim of these volumes to remove as far as may be this reproach; and, when the following chapters are duly weighed and are considered in connection with those upon education and the fine arts included in another division of the work, it would seem that at least adequate materials have been gathered to enable all who are interested in Southern culture to make a fair estimate of its breadth and depth. How far a coöperative enterprise on a large scale stimulates and directs interest in such matters remains an open question; but there can be little doubt that henceforward historians, essayists, and critics, whether Southern or not, will draw upon the information here gathered and will devote greater attention to the part played by the section in the intellectual life of America. Through these writers, as well as through students and readers of the volumes so generously planned, the public will in time be reached, and the misconceptions and prejudices which now exist will be slowly dissipated. To have contributed to this salutary result, it will be seen, entitles many men and women of the New South to the gratitude not only of their fellow Southerners, but of their fellow Americans; and the fact that so many competent contributors could have been secured for this undertaking is one of the best proofs that can be given of the widespread intellectual activity of the Southern people at the present time.

The points I have been making might be illustrated from almost any of the chapters that constitute this volume; but two or three may be selected to serve my purpose. The chapter on English Studies in the South, which in the main Professor Henneman contributed originally to *The Sewanee Review,* will convince any reader that the South yields to no other section in the part it has played in one of the most important and interesting educational movements that have taken place in this country. The emphasis that has been laid of late years upon the study of English in our schools and colleges is not merely a sign of our modernity and our utilitarianism, as a people, nor is it a fact of pedagogical importance only. It is in large measure a result of social conditions incident to democratic expansion in a new and unconfined country, and it has been an important factor in the assimilation, through education, of large masses of our alien population. But the South is popularly supposed to have been the home of the aristocrat, not of the democrat, and your Southern gentleman is depicted as an inveterate quoter of Horace and Virgil and an incontinent contemner of the vernacular literature, at least of most English books written since the days of Dr. Johnson and of all American writings whatsoever. Yet, if we turn to Dr. Henneman's chapter what do we discover? Certainly that here, as almost everywhere, the extraordinarily creative and far-seeing mind of Thomas Jefferson is to be found working, and that in a real sense he may be regarded as the pioneer of systematic English studies in America. We find also that perhaps the most important concerted and plainly effective impetus given in the last generation to English study and teaching in this country is to be credited to a Southern scholar and teacher—not a writer of textbooks but a maker of teachers—Professor Thomas Randolph Price, incumbent of the chairs of Greek and English in Randolph-Macon College, Virginia.

Greek and English! the conjunction is auspicious and not fortuitous. A great teacher thoroughly imbued with the spirit of the ancient classics, not merely a walking respository of dead learning, interprets the literature of his own race to young men eager to upbuild the shattered social fabric of their native section, and under his inspiration and instruction a body of trained teachers of English goes forth to labor, not in the South alone but throughout the Union, goes forth to train up teachers who in their turn shall pass on the torch of scholarship to generations yet unborn. No small work this, and the man who deserves most credit for it was honored for his own scholarship by one of our great universities and for his character by all who knew him; yet the far-reaching effects wrought by him, being intangible, have never been understood by the public, and his name, unsupported by a monument of scholarship, will abide with us only in the event of the development of a greater interest in the things of the mind and of a more discriminating spirit of gratitude than a democracy is likely to exhibit. Such, however, has always been the fate of men who have not worked in permanent materials or exploited their own personalities in a dazzling and dominating way. It is almost idle to regret that human nature is what it is, but it is not idle to emphasize the South's part in the spread of vernacular culture— the work of Price, of Lanier, of Baskervill, of Henneman,—or to express the hope that in the future as in the past this democratic culture will never be sharply separated from that aristocratic culture which is generated and fostered by continued study of the literatures of Greece and Rome. If I may judge from my own experience the men and women who know their classics, if only slightly, have an immense advantage in all that concerns literature and humane scholarship over those who know their classics only through translations or not at all. Thus far the classical tradition, if I may so phrase it, has been less questioned in the South than in any other part of this country—whether or not this has involved a truer study of the classics and not mere lip-service; and I cannot forbear expressing the belief that in their classical heritage Southerners possess an invaluable stimulus and aid to the production of a literature of permanent worth. Perhaps the very modern—and shall I venture to say very crude— literary standards and ideals of the country at large are destined to triumph in the South along with "up

to date" business methods and amorphous political
and social conceptions; but, until I am forced to
acknowledge such a deplorable consummation, I
shall cherish the hope that the South will maintain
to a reasonable extent the old standards and ideals,
and that the young country will come in time and
as a whole to recognize that they should be cherished
because they are valid, not discarded because they
are old.

How valid they have seemed to some of the choicest spirits of the South appears abundantly in the
chapter which Professor Charles Forster Smith has
written on "The South's Contributions to Classical Studies." Professor Smith could not point to
the fact that his own career admirably illustrates
what the classics have done for Southern culture and
character and what Southern scholars have done for
the advancement of learning throughout the country; but he could dwell with just appreciation upon
the prevalence of the classical tradition in the intellectual life of his native section and he could point
to an imposing line of eminent teachers of Greek and
Latin the value of whose services it would be difficult to overestimate. This line practically begins
with the founding of the University of Virginia; for,
modern though he was, Jefferson was too wise to
rush in upon those paths of iconoclasm which some
leading educationalists of our own day have so
blithely trod. The advent of George Long as first
professor of the classics in the new institution was
one of the most important events in the educational
history of the South. Recognition of the classics
as a great formative element in culture was part
of the South's heritage; but profound study of them
in the light of continental scholarship might have
been long delayed but for the coming of the Englishman and for his wise choice of Gessner Harrison as

his successor. Of the work of the latter and of the men he trained—work by no means confined to the higher institutions—it is needless for me to speak. Professor Smith has presented the facts without exaggerating their import. It may not be amiss, however, for one whose studies, more by accident perhaps than by choice, have lain in the modern field, to bear testimony to the inspiration he has received throughout his life from his contact with Southern men whose knowledge and love of the literatures of Greece and Rome has been as the breath of their being. To have been taught by Norwood and Price and Peters, to have known Gildersleeve and McCabe and Forster Smith and Bain has meant more to me than any of these accomplished scholars has ever suspected, and I trust that a century hence some teacher of English will be impelled, as I am now, to express his gratitude to the Southern successors of the men I have just named. There should be no rivalry, only the strongest bonds of comprehension and sympathy between students of the humanities whether old or new.

This leads me to remember that history is, or at least always should be, one of the humanities, and that of late there has been great activity throughout the South in historical studies. The allied subjects of political theory and of economics have also received some attention, and, in view of the important part played in the nation's development by the older Southern statesmen, it is much to be hoped that the present interest in this broad group of studies, to which biography should be joined, will be maintained. Many of the ensuing chapters are themselves manifestations of this interest. The public should know more than it does about the *Southern Literary Messenger* and the reviews of the Old South, and it should encourage the men who are conducting the few Southern periodicals of to-day. **It** should also not allow the achievements of such newspapers as the *Enquirer* and *Examiner* of Richmond and the *Mercury* of Charleston to become matters of vague memory, much as the names of their brilliant and once influential editors have become. It is not necessary that we should think and write as those journalists did, any more than that we should produce lawyers of the old time erudition and quaint charm. Our editors need not be fire-eaters, nor our statesmen reactionaries. Neither, on the other hand, need we forget our traditions and bend all our energies toward transforming ourselves into something that approximates the average American of some other section. It seems much more desirable that we should endeavor to comprehend what our fathers stood for, especially in all matters relating to self-government, then study calmly our own situation, and resolutely acknowledge and adopt the principles and policies that seem to be most consonant with our welfare. So far as my own studies allow me to judge, no other people or fraction of a people has a more admirable body of publicists from whose writings inspiration and guidance may be derived. That in many cases these statesmen and publicists of the South—Washington, Jefferson, Madison, Marshall, Calhoun—are the nation's also is a fact for which neither the section nor the union can be too thankful; but there are not a few writers on public matters who are more distinctively sectional than national, Stephens and Davis, for example, whom the Southerner of to-day, and the American too for that matter, may study with great advantage. If I may be so bold as to express an opinion on a topic which has occupied me but little of late years, I should like to suggest that for lessons of constructive states-manship the writings of the older Southern publi-

cists are invaluable, while for lessons of definite and
resolute policy the writings of the later group are
almost equally instructive. The high ideals and the
broad intellectual and imaginative sweep, to say
nothing of the wholesome practicality of the Revolutionary leaders and the Founders of the Union raise
them to the highest place as exemplars, and I cannot but think that their state papers form one of the
most important sections of American literature, a
section which we shall undervalue, if, as is too often
done, we make originality of thought our prime demand, instead of sound validity and wide applicability. Our early statesmen undoubtedly owed much
to the statesmen and publicists of England and
France, but this fact does not lessen the practical
value of their writings. One of the defects of our
present comparative and evolutionary methods of
study is the undue emphasis they give to originality
and priority. On the other hand, we are all, men of
thought and action alike, too prone to make mere
success our standard of value, and judged by such a
standard the writings of the later Southern publicists must inevitably be found wanting, unless one
is careful to define the meaning of success. Much
that they did and wrote is certainly valueless save
as a warning, but I must repeat that the definiteness
and resoluteness displayed by them ought to stand
the present generation of Southerners in very good
stead. The South still has its great problem to solve,
and in the performance of its task it needs the constructive wisdom of the founders and the definiteness and the resoluteness of thought and expression
displayed by men who have been carefully excluded
from certain lists of great American statesmen.
Problems that are solved blindly and indirectly are
often only half solved—if that.

But I am getting into deep water, and I ought in-

continently to retreat toward the safe shores of
literature. Yet no one more than your student enjoys a plunge—that is an occasional plunge—in the
ocean of life; and after all, according to some critics,
when one is dealing with literature, one is really
dealing with life. That means, I suppose, that my
shore is only an illusory one, and that I may as
well continue to make myself as comfortable as I
can in the waves. I proceed therefore, dropping my
figures of speech, to observe that the master problem of the entire country seems to be to-day what it
has always been, the problem of securing to every
citizen equality of opportunity, that is to say, the
problem of establishing a true democracy. This
problem has been at no time near solution, and it
has assumed varying aspects during different periods and in different sections of the country. At
present we are chiefly inclined to envisage three
aspects of it—the relations of capital and labor, the
rights of the public to control combinations of capital, especially such as are invested in so-called natural monopolies, and the status of races and the two
sexes. It is plain that every citizen of the United
States is vitally interested in all these aspects or
phases of our perennial and universal problem, yet
that one aspect or phase is of peculiar moment to
the people of the South. It is equally true, however,
that each aspect is related with every other, and
there is danger ahead for any section that isolates
one aspect and treats it as though it were an integral
and peculiar problem. It is for the Southern people
of to-day and of the generations that follow to ask
themselves whether they really understand the great
problem that confronts every intelligent citizen of
this country, whether they accept the meanings attached by the other sections to the words democracy
and citizenship, and whether, if they do not, they are

sufficiently trained in clear thought and expression and sufficiently bold, to make their political and social ideals prevail, certainly throughout the South, and perhaps throughout the country. This means, in the last analysis, that the leaders of Southern opinion have a tremendous task before them which they must fail of accomplishing if they neglect to cultivate the entire group of the humane studies in the broadest sense of the term. History and literature, economics and sociology and the theory of politics and law must be studied by Southerners with increasing devotion and acumen, and the lessons learned must be applied with ever-greater intelligence and resolution if the section is to maintain its individuality and augment its prestige. In the light of this fact the inception and completion of the present undertaking must be regarded as a phenomenon of unparalleled importance in the history of Southern publications. No such stock-taking, if I may use a commercial term, has ever been known in the South before, and its beneficial results ought to be widespread and lasting.

One of the most interesting disclosures made by this stock-taking is described in Dr. George F. Mellen's chapter, "Contributions of New England and the North to the South's Culture." That the South owed not a little to Northern wealth and intelligence and energy was long ago known to all persons interested in Southern history, and the part played in Southern education by the Northern tutor or schoolmaster has been described in numerous books; but I doubt whether many readers of Dr. Mellen's chapter will be able to affirm that it did not greatly deepen and widen their conception of the essential solidarity of the country. We of the South are not so peculiar a people as we suppose ourselves to be, and, fortunately, the more closely we scrutinize our-

selves the more we perceive that, save in certain restricted circles of society in restricted areas, our
characteristics natural and acquired are those of
our fellow-Americans, at least of those who were
born in the country.

It is sometimes said that the South is really the
most American part of America, and so far as concerns intermixture of races this is probably true.
It is also true in a measure so far as concerns ideas
and institutions. No other section has of late shown
such an interest in public education, and no idea is
more distinctively American than the idea that every
child within the borders of a state should receive at
least the elements of the training that is needed for
the making of good citizens. When we think of education, we naturally think of schools and colleges as
the institutions through which the idea of popular
education is made effective; but the public library
is a scarcely less important institution for the training of citizens, and it may almost be called a peculiarly American institution. It was long before the
library idea, so to speak, spread to the South, not
because the people did not appreciate books, but because the structure of society and the distribution
of wealth were not propitious to the founding and
fostering of public libraries. Even in the Old South,
however, there were good collections of books, as is
shown for example in interesting monographs by Dr.
Stephen B. Weeks and Professor Yates Snowden,
and to-day Southern librarians feel that the cause
for which they have so long been struggling is
practically won. No great collection of books answering the needs of scholars as well as those of the
general public exists south of Washington, and so
long as this is the case the South in a sense cannot
be intellectually independent. But, as a matter of
fact, America as a whole is still, in this sense, more

or less dependent upon Europe, and there is reason to hope that in the course of time the cities and universities of the South will be able adequately to answer the demands of Southern scholarship.

Scholarship, however, though vastly important, is not so necessary to an expanding people as a growing body of creative literature which expresses that people's aspirations, which puts its thoughts into words. Has the South such a literature now? Is it likely to have one in the future? What are the best means to secure it?

Answers to these questions are likely to vary according to the temperaments and literary standards of the answerers. Some persons may even be inclined to doubt whether the South of 1909 has fulfilled the promise of the South of 1880-1890, the South of Cable and Page and James Lane Allen and Miss Murfree. Others may see in the work of this and that younger novelist and poet and particularly in the great increase in the number of men and women who are anxious to win literary distinction the promise of even greater achievements in the domain of letters than the section can yet boast of. It is really astonishing to observe how many volumes of fiction and verse and biography and history have been published by Southerners within the past five years, and it is pathetic also, for one shrewdly suspects that a very large percentage of the writers paid for their own plates. Whether or not, however, this large literary product has been commercially profitable and whether or not the masterly books and writers have been very few in number, it remains clear that, along with the South's great awakeuing to the need of popular education, the spread of public libraries, and the increased study of the section's past, there has developed throughout the xxxINTRODUCTION.

South a spirit of literary activity unparalleled in the
region except perhaps during the feverish and unsettled years that followed the War of Secession. It
is plain, I think, that the average quality of the books
produced to-day is much higher than was the case
between 1865 and 1870, and, as the South seems to
be far more stable, economically, politically, and socially than it was twenty years ago, to say nothing
of the period of reconstruction, there seems to be no
reason why a normal and healthy advance may not
be expected along all the lines of literary production.
How far the literature thus produced will be distinctively Southern, that is how far it will display
qualities which will be at once recognized as not existing in the books written in other sections of this
country is a question which only a rash critic would
care to answer. There will doubtless be many novels
and histories and biographies and even poems written the scenes and themes of which will be Southern
in some senses, yet the treatment may be American,
nay for that matter British, and the question will
remain how far they are truly Southern products,
full of the distinctive features of Southern life and
character, original in form, and fresh and new in
spirit. In other words, we find ourselves confronted
with the old question how far American literature
really is American—a question which some critics
have answered with more patriotic confidence than
a calm analysis of the facts in the case seems to warrant. I have no desire to imitate them, but neither
do I think it necessary or advantageous to exhibit
traces of that spirit of colonialism which has done
so much to retard our national emancipation with regard to the things of the mind. It seems better to
emphasize the advantage the South's classical tradition ought to give its writers and to express the hope

that, when some future generation undertakes, in a work like the present, to survey the achievements of the section, the volumes devoted to literature will register a progress commensurate with all reasonable wishes and expectations.

WILLIAM P. TRENT,

Professor of English Literature, Columbia University.

NEW YORK, April 24, 1909.

THE INTELLECTUAL TENDENCIES
OF THE SOUTH.

THIS brief review is modest in aim and purpose. It cannot be a history of achievement, nor is it a description of a stable condition of life; it is merely a sketch of a passing phase in the development of a new civilization. It is but an effort to voice the thought of the present South, to indicate the trend of its intellectual movements.

It is significant that these movements are in line with the course of thought elsewhere manifested. The Old South had ideas and ideals of its own; the present South shares the thought and life of the modern world. While the peculiar civilization of former days still challenges the admiration of many and possesses the sympathy of all, the present generation is busy with its own concerns and is fighting its own battles. The South is no longer a problem, it is not even the home of a peculiar people. It shares the intellectual movements of the world and responds to the currents of universal history. It is true that there are remote rural and mountain sections that do not answer to these statements, but such sections are not typical. They are back eddies that testify to the strength of the current that has swept by them. Even the negro race, in its progressive elements at least, reflects the spirit of the times. The advanced negro of the new South is eager to learn, ready to change, willing to abandon his distinctive habits, dialect or physical peculiarities. He is wiling to become a part of the larger life in which he moves and figures.

I. Material Development.

It will be generally admitted that the initial impulse in the reshaping of modern thought has come from science. The results of this movement have been the discovery of a mass of new scientific truths, the application of these discoveries to practical life, and the adoption of a scientific method in every field of thought and research. All these influences have been and are at work in the South. It is true that the South has made small contribution to the achievements of scientific research, but the same statement may be made of America as a whole. But in applying the results of science to the materials of life and civilization the South has made and is making rapid progress. A large part of the intellectual activity of the South at present is concerned with the practical problems of a material civilization. It is easy to understand why this should be so. Poverty has been a stern but successful teacher. The war left the South desolate. Accumulated resources had been swept away, means of production destroyed, the labor system overthrown, and the directing, controlling white population had been decimated. The first problem was that of existence. This was simple, but not easy. The soil furnished its contribution, but labor conditions made agricultural operations uncertain and unprofitable. The splendid beginnings of manufacture made between 1850 and 1860 had come to a violent end, and there was no capital to revive them. Opportunities for employment were so scant that the young men of the South moved westward in large numbers between 1865 and 1875. Those who remained learned the details of every form of physical labor and turned their attention to every opportunity for the creation of wealth. Gradually the richness and abundance of natural resources was realized, slowly capital was accumulated and invested in all manner of industries. The decade between 1880 and 1890 marks the turning of the tide and the beginning of all industrial revival. Between 1890 and 1900 the movement had increased in volume and power and since 1900 has taken on dimensions that attract national attention and interest. This revival has been an intellectual as well as a material movement. It has been based on a study of natural conditions, an appreciation of scientific truth, an application of scientific achievements to all phases of life. It has been in the main the achievement of Southerners. Foreign capital played an inconspicuous part in its early beginnings. In recent years, since the industrial movement has become general and profits well established, there has been an influx of funds from all directions seeking investment. There has been also an accession of capitalists and of skilled laborers, and the tide of immigration is beginning to turn southward.

This article is not intended for the recital of statistics, but we may be pardoned for just a few words by way of summary. Manufacturing capital in the South in 1880 amounted to $250,000,000; in 1890, to $650,000,000; in 1900, to $1,150,000,000; and in 1908, to $2,100,000,000. The value of manufactures in 1880 was $450,000,000; in 1890, $900,000,000; in 1900, $1,145,000,000; and in 1908, $2,600,000,000. The diversity of these enterprises is also worthy of note. While cotton mills and iron foundries furnish the largest items, we must not lose sight of the value of finished products in wool, in leather, in stone, marble, wood and metals.

Agriculture is beginning to feel more than ever the quickening effects of a growing intelligence. In some respects the greatest present problem of the South is to elevate rural life, to make farming profitable and attractive—the expression of a higher culture—to bring to its service the researches of chemistry, biology and physics. To this end a new education is called for and not without hope of speedy realization. The farm products of the South had a value in 1880 of $660,000,000; in 1890, of $770,000,-000; in 1900, of $1,270,000,000; and in 1908, of $2,220,000,000.

II. Educational Progress.

The intellectual life of the South is expressing itself further in educational work. This is the outgrowth of definite and prolonged effort on the part of many earnest leaders and workers. In part, it is the working of a law of self-interest, the recognition of an essential relation between knowledge and power, between education and material prosperity. In part it has progressed by the simple process of imitation from one community or state to another. In part, too, it is the expression of a deep sense of justice, an abiding conviction of right, a recognition of the obligation of strength to weakness, an acceptance of the essential spirit of a true and genuine democracy. The forms of this educational work are manifold. Most important of all is the general system of public schools that has been developed in every Southern state since the war. At no time has this movement been so strong, so intelligent as now. Slowly the fight against illiteracy progresses. Year by year the figures indicating the percentage of illiterates lessen. Most notable has been the progress made by the negro race. Instead of more than 90 per cent. of illiterates at the close of the war, the records now show less than 50 per cent. Gifts of private societies or individual philanthropists have contributed to this result. Valuable as these have been, they would have been of little avail by themselves. The great results have been achieved through public taxation, through contributions made by every property holder in the South. These contributions are made without serious protest chiefly for the reason that they are felt to be right and just. The South is not acting so much through any far-sighted policy of self-interest as from a sense of present duty, a feeling of distinct obligation toward a helpless and feeble race.

Public schools in the South still lack much of reaching a satisfactory standard of efficiency, but the present outlook is encouraging. Since 1900 they show great improvement. Annual appropriations from every state are rapidly increasing. Still more rapid is the increase in revenues derived from local taxation. School terms are lengthening, buildings are improving. Teachers are better trained, defects of school legislation are being corrected, proper supervision is now sought and supplied, and interest in public education has assumed the proportions of a great popular movement. Of course, much remains to be done, but if the present rate of improvement continues for one or two decades, startling results will be accomplished.

The significance of recent educational movements is not merely in the results attained, but in the manner by which these have been brought about. Local taxation springs from local appreciation of education and indicates an advance in community life and thought. This has been stimulated by definite educational campaigns, fostered by the Southern Education Board and other agencies. School improvement associations have been organized in almost every Southern state, and these have helped to provide new school houses, better furnished and equipped; tidy grounds, libraries and other apparatus. Educational interests have occupied much space in the public press and have taken an important place in political platforms. The public school system has won recognition as a great civic interest second to none in value or importance.

Mention should be made of the extension of the educational movement into the field of scientific and technical instruction. Every state has builded on foundations laid by the Federal government and is planning large things for the future. This work has been influential in promoting the material development of the South and is a most profitable investment. The undeveloped resources of the South call for the trained worker, the civil, mining, mechanical and electrical engineer. Textile schools now accompany the cotton mills, and overalls have become the symbol of intellectual training as well as the cap and gown.

Colleges and universities were, in the olden days, the only educational institutions expressive of the intellectual life. To-day they share that function with others already mentioned, but they still maintain their primacy. Their work has greatly improved in character. Progress has been as rapid as funds permitted. The limitations of poverty are severe and unrelenting, but the struggle for higher life and thought goes bravely on. The South does not willingly accept a position of intellectual inferiority. This is shown by the fight now nearing a successful issue for high scholastic standards of college entrance and for the maintenance of professional instruction on a plane equal to that adopted elsewhere. We must not claim too much here. But the whole truth includes ideals and efforts as well as realized results. The hopefulnes of the present situation may be seen in the character of college professors. Most of these are young men, specialists, with definite university training. They have not been enticed by hope of material reward, for salaries are pitiably small; but they are inspired by a love of learning and a zeal for culture. They have acquainted themselves with the thought movement of the world, are in touch with scholars in other sections, and are in sympathy with the tides of universal life. In thought they are free, in spirit they are broad and liberal. Academic freedom is no stranger to Southern institutions. Persecution for opinion's sake would be an anachronism to-day. Southern sentiment is still conservative, but it is not tyrannical.

Recent educational movements have affected materially the training of Southern women. A few high-grade colleges for women have been established and most of the state universities have become co-educational. The traditional type of Southern woman is changing. There are not wanting signs that women are more eager for training than men. The higher classes in public high schools enroll generally more girls than boys. Commercial life is opening many avenues of employment to women and some are even training themselves for professional service. Social life—even in the upper circles—has vague impulses toward intellectual attainment. Weekly clubs alternate Shakespeare with cards, sociology with pink teas, and discussions on civic improvement with feminine fashion and gossip. Altogether, the Southern woman is more intellectual than ever before, and this improvement has been of her own striving. No strong arm has aided her in this struggle; greater, therefore, is her credit and praise.

III. Literature and History.

Much has been written of the barrenness of the Old South in the field of literature. Whatever the cause, the fact is undisputed, but the New South has done something to remove this reproach. It would be pleasant if one might trace these new literary performances to the stimulus of literary work in college or university, but such an effort is not warranted by the facts. Undoubtedly colleges are giving an improved training in English, a better appreciation of literature, a juster critical judgment, and this is helpful. Literature must have a soil, the singer an audience, the writer readers of discrimination and appreciation, and books when made must have purchasers. In all these respects the South is improving and the literary movement already under way is not likely to die without permanent results. The South is rich in literary material, and not all of it has yet been exploited. Where the plowshare of war cut deepest, the first fruits of tradition and of story ought to grow. The burden of Southern sorrow and suffering ought to elicit a burst of Southern song. The exuberance of traditional oratory might well be transformed into the more lasting measures of poetry. Even the presence of an alien race should add its picturesque touches and lighten the shadow it has cast over Southern life and history. And so we point with pride to the Southern writers that have appeared in the field of pure literature and we hope for still more worthy achievements in coming years.

The work of Southern students and writers in the field of history is noteworthy. This has sprung out of a genuine patriotism and has been fostered by a desire to publish the truth. It is right that the South should tell its own story, provided always that it is told fairly and squarely. This task has been aided by college professors, by librarians, by public officials and by private students. Patriotic societies have celebrated all manner of anniversaries with addresses of varying merit. Leaders in the great War of Secession like Jefferson

Davis and Alexander H. Stephens have written their stories. Other leaders have had their biographies written for them. The Southern Historical Society has published a mass of material and has stimulated the establishment of dozens of similar societies in every state and in many cities and smaller communities. These in turn have collected and published a great number of studies and papers. A reference to Poole's Index will show how freely the magazines have lent their pages to articles on Southern history. This work once begun has not been confined to the period of the war. It has been carried back into colonial times and into the earliest beginnings of our life as a nation. This is one of the most distinct intellectual achievements of the New South. The task is not yet completed. Much remains for the coming generations and no time should be lost, for valuable material is perishing every year. To the credit of the Southern student be it said that he is not merely a *laudator temporis acti.* He is something of a critic. The Old South was not all good and the present South has many failings. No good can come of unmerited praise. Accurate statements, true and just comparisons, frank confessions, mark the true historian, and the present school of Southern writers is striving to manifest these characteristics and will merit attention in so far as it succeeds.

IV. Intellectual Independence.

The present tendency of Southern thought is toward intellectual freedom. This is, after all, the supreme test of intellectual life and movement. Wherever thought is rife, wherever progress is real, wherever opinions are sincerely formed as the result of intelligent processes of reasoning, there will result not a blind uniformity but a stimulating diversity of conclusions. Uniformity of opinion is the sign of stagnation, of indifference, of mental apathy or mental slavery. For a long time the South has borne the charge of intolerance and unfortunately has too often deserved it. The solidarity of political action has had its counterpart in a certain solidarity of thought. Convictions have been the outgrowth of sentiment and prejudices as often as the deliverances of reason. This solidarity has been something very distinct from provincialism. All people are more or less provincial. Environment colors life in its outward aspects everywhere. New England seems intensely provincial to the Westerner. The true Bostonian is a Brahmin. The New York journals reflect a self-poised, self-centered population, and the insularity of ·Great Britain is frequently noted by citizens of the world. In this sense the South has always been provincial. Its rural life, its plantation homes, its country churches, its musical accent, have been its own. Its hospitality to strangers and to friends, the occupations and amusements of its leisure hours, its oratory and its political leadership have been among its peculiarities as a province. But all this is entirely distinct from that spirit of intolerance of which we now speak.

Southern intolerance was not the result of blood or character. The South was the battleground of Whigs and Democrats, the home of English Cavaliers and French Huguenots, and of the virile, independent, self-reliant Scotch-Irish. Southern intolerance was the distinct legacy of slavery. It is not true that this has always and in all places been the result of such an institution. Quite the contrary. But the peculiarity of the situation in the South was that here slavery was to fight its last great battle. Here was a struggle protracted through many years to maintain itself against advancing enlightenment and a purer moral code. The length and bitterness of the fight attested the intellectual power, the resourcefulness of the defendants. Gradually the voice of the South on this subject sounded as the voice of one man. The many who had no slaves echoed the sentiments of the few who had many. A cause essentially weak was strengthened by considerations of personal liberty, of state rights, of sacredness of contract. So imperious became the domination of this one idea that Southern patriots gave up the national government which they had been instrumental in building and which they had so ably administered for more than half a century. When this fight was over and lost, the South passed at once into a struggle still more bitter and humiliating. This was the struggle of weakness against overmastering savagery, of intelligence against brutal ignorance, of racial purity against racial degeneracy. Here again her foes were her own brothers, and a great ruling political party became the machinery of her persecution. No wonder the South became solid, in thinking as well as in voting. No wonder everything new was regarded with fear and suspicion.

Slowly conditions began to change. After ten years of subjection—an orgy of misrule—the Southern states secured control of their own affairs. This was affected by a revolution—and not entirely a peaceful one. Both force and fraud played their part and left their sting and their curse. But political control cannot rest in the hands of the ignorant and vicious. Such a condition of affairs is anarchy. There was no progress in the South and no hope till this state of affairs was remedied. With the elimination of ignorance and vice from politics, there is some hope of an intelligent division on questions of great civic interest. A change of attitude in the North has helped wonderfully to free the South from its artificial unity of thought and speech. As the

North grows less critical, less fanatical, less severe, the South grows more open-minded, more just and more free. A commingling of population has proven beneficial to both sections. Business interests are joining both sections in all manner of worthy enterprises. Now, too, differences in political views are beginning to appear. It cannot be said now that the South believes in free trade or in free silver. Sentiment is strongly divided on these as on other great governmental questions, such as labor legislation, control of trusts, railroads, and all matters of foreign policy. Gradually there will work itself out a distinct political struggle of conflicting ideas. In that struggle party machinery will give place to party principles and politicians will yield to statesmen. In the realm of national politics also the South will in time have a voice and give free expression of its opinion. The present exclusion will not be permanent. The Southern temperament is suited for political contest. The art and science of government, once so well understood, will again be more than a memory or a tradition. The call may yet come for an Anglo-Saxon leadership, and if so the response can come from no section sooner than from the South.

Thus, it is that political life, as well as the previously noted factors of commerce and education, are working together for the emancipation of the individual. This will come more rapidly as the years go by. It will no more be hindered by sectional strife, by political oppression, by fanatical hate. But the greatest danger to perfect individual freedom comes from the South itself. As the struggle for slavery banished intellectual liberty, so the continued presence of the negro population in the South hinders the formation and expression of free thought. Political issues and civic problems have often been settled on racial lines rather than on economic principles. When the race problem is injected into any other question, there is an end to all discussion, to all differences, to all freedom of individual opinion. This attitude must be overcome by a new appeal to the spirit of fairness and justice. The South does not need to shackle itself or the negro in order to maintain Anglo-Saxon supremacy. The intellectual freedom and efficiency of the white race will be promoted by generous treatment of the negro. Oppression of every kind will work a double woe. In whatever form slavery may be perpetuated, just so far it will put its shackles on the minds of the Southern whites. If we treat the negro unjustly, we shall practice fraud and injustice toward each other. We shall necessarily live by the standard of conduct we apply to him. This is the eternal curse of wrong and injustice, a curse that abides on the ruler as well as the slave. The South will be free only as it grants freedom.

JAMES H. KIRKLAND,
Chancellor of Vanderbilt University.

HISTORY OF
THE INTELLECTUAL LIFE
OF THE SOUTH.

CHAPTER I.

CHARACTERISTICS OF SOUTHERN POETRY
FROM THE BEGINNING TO 1865.

THE transplantation of English civilization to the southern half of this Republic may be said almost to begin with poetry, if R. Rich's *Newes from Virginia,* a stirring account of the "happy arrival of that famous and worthy knight Sir Thomas Gates, and well reputed and valiant Captaine Newport into England," published in London in 1610, by "one who was of the voyage," can be called poetry. A little later, moreover, 1623, pure literature, at least of a secondary kind, begins with George Sandys' translation of the last ten books of Ovid's *Metamorphoses.* Sandys was an Oxford scholar of literary repute at home, whose really creditable piece of work gave William Stith, one of the earliest Virginia historians (1747), a chance to say that "in the midst of these tumults and alarms the muses were not silent," and writers of American literature after him a conventional date, 1626, the date of the publication of Sandys' translation, with which to start the account of the beginning of pure literature on this continent.

But neither these, nor Capt. John Smith's *Sea Marke,* nor George Alsop's part prose, part verse *A*

Character of the Province of Maryland (1666), can
be called distinctively American, or Southern poetry.
Though some of them were written in America, and
all of them had to do with experiences in Maryland
and Virginia, they were written by Englishmen for
Englishmen. They are interesting therefore more
for their connection with the early settlements in the
South than for any literary value they may have.
In 1676, however, there is a notable poem by an unknown hand in praise of Nathaniel Bacon, the leader
of the first organized protest against British oppression, Bacon's Rebellion, as it is called in history.
This poem, the product of a writer who might have
been born in Virginia, is embedded in the *Burwell
Papers,* and if it does not strike the true American
note, it is at least prophetic of the spirit of a hundred
years later:

> "Death, why so cruel? What! no other way
> To manifest thy spleen but thus to slay
> Our hopes of safety, liberty, our all,
> Which, through thy tyranny, with him must fall
> To its late chaos."

The second century of colonial existence begins
with a vigorous, Hudibrastic account of manners and
customs in Maryland, *The Sot-weed Factor; or, a
Voyage to Maryland,* by Eben Cook, Gent. It was
published in London in 1708; but who this Ebenezer
Cook, Gentleman, was that, according to Moses Coit
Taylor, struck "a vein of genuine and powerful
satire," is a matter of conjecture, though his pre-
tence of being an Englishman condemned to emigrate
to the province of Maryland might hint that he was a
Marylander in hiding. Anyway, the poem was
successful enough to win the compliment of a weak
imitation twenty-two years afterwards in the *Sot-
weed Factor Redivivus.* This ends the matter of
poetic literature at the South till the storm of the

Revolution gathers and breaks. Conditions were too crude, the thought, interests and energies of the people were too deeply concerned with other things. The wilderness had to be made habitable, Indian and French wars had to be fought, and, in general, the rough, immediate work of merely getting on in the new country precluded naturally any considerable attention to what is called polite literature. If there is to be a literature at all it must take the shape of sermon, history, or political pamphlet. In New England religion inspired not a few attempts at pious verse-making, and even the "Tenth Muse," Anne Bradstreet, managed to flourish in the chill Puritan air: while by 1765 the Pennsylvania colony could concentrate enough culture in Philadelphia to bring forth a Thomas Godfrey, who, dying in 1763, left behind *The Prince of Parthia*, a tragedy, "the first important dramatic undertaking in the colonies." But to this time the South had nothing to show that poetry was cultivated to any considerable extent. Even the fiery discussions that led up to the Revolution, producing finally no little lyric prose, failed to inspire anything in the way of patriotic verse much above mere doggerel. A typical poem of this kind of verse was published in the Virginia *Gazette*, May 2, 1776, under the title of *Hearts of Oak*. While it is charged with patriotic fervor and interprets the resolute mood of the time, in expression it falls far short of the occasion:

"On our brow while we laurel-crowned liberty wear,
What Englishmen ought the Americans dare;
Though tempests and terrors around us we see,
Bribes nor fears can prevail o'er the hearts that are free.
Hearts of oaks are we still, for we're sons of those men
Who always are ready, steady, boys, steady,
To fight for their freedom again and again."

Poems of this sort, together with a few rude ballads, largely satirical in mood and representing both the loyalist and rebel side in the struggle, were published in the papers of the time. But none of them has any special merit, and they are of such inferior quality that one wonders not only that they were popular but also that the fierce passions of the hour and the high patriotic idealism of the colonies were able to do no better.

Sometimes the admiration for some special Revolutionary hero or the occasion of his death called forth a tribute in verse. For example, Col. Alexander Martin's *Tribute to General Francis Nash* (1777) is not without a certain dignity of thought and expression:

> " On Bunker's height great Warren is no more;
> The brave Montgomery's fate we next deplore;
> Princeton's famed fields to trembling Britain tell,
> How, scored with wounds, the conquering Mercer fell;
>
>   *   *   *   *   *   *   *
>
> Last flow our sorrows for our favorite son,
> Whom, weeping, Carolina claims her own,
> The gallant Nash, who, with fatal wound,
> Though tortured, weltering on the hostile ground,
> 'Fight on, my troops,' with smiling ardor said,
> ' 'Tis but the fate of war; be not dismay'd.' "

A year later, from a Catholic priest of Maryland, Charles Henry Wharton, comes the first poetic appreciation of the character and service of Washington. This poem, *A Poetical Epistle to George Washington,* is no mean performance, as the following lines will show:

> " Great without pomp, without ambition brave,
> Proud not to conquer fellow-men, but save;
> Friend to the wretched, foe to none but those
> Who plan their greatness on another's woes;
> Awed by no titles, faithless to no trust,
> Free without faction, obstinately just."

Even the conventional Eighteenth century heroic couplet cannot quite conceal the discriminating insight and the noble dignity of these lines.

But verse of this serious character was not all. In the very midst of the turmoil of the Revolution (1777) there appeared *The Belles of Williamsburg,* a poem by Dr. James McClurg assisted by St. George Tucker, but to just what extent is not known. The poem is in praise of the fair ladies of that famous old capital and social centre, and is in form and spirit prophetic of the character of much of the later Southern poetry—a more or less light form of *vers de société.* It is a clever imitation of the same type of verse in vogue in England during the Eighteenth century. It was popular enough to call forth a "Sequel" of a dozen stanzas. Each "illustrious maid," under a conventional pastoral name, is described. For example:

> "Aspasia next, with kindred soul,
> Disdains the passions that control
>   Each gentle, pleasing art;
> Her sportive wit, her frolic lays,
> And graceful form attract our praise,
>   And steal away the heart."

Toward the end of the Revolution period the verse-makers began to multiply. In Richmond, Charleston, and Baltimore enough thin little volumes of attempted poetry are published to indicate that the Muses were at least gaining friends if they were not inspiring genuine 'poetry. In 1786, at Charleston, S. C., Joseph Ladd Brown, a transplanted Rhode Islander, gave the public a volume under the title of *Poems by Arouet,* in which he celebrated in the Eighteenth century pastoral manner his mild love for a certain Amanda, and decided that happiness is,—

> " An empty, fleeting shade,
> By imagination made;
> 'Tis a bubble, show, or worse;
> 'Tis a baby's hobby horse,
> etc., etc., etc."

In 1798 William Munford, son of Col. Robert Munford of Revolutionary fame, who was also "author

of two dramas and some short poems,'' published a
volume of *Poems and Compositions in Prose on Several Occasions,* a volume which, besides minor poems
and translations, contained a tragedy, *Almoran and
Hamet.* To his death in 1825 he worked steadily on
a really creditable translation in blank verse of the
Iliad.   To this same period belongs St. George
Tucker, who left behind one lyric which yet manages
to find a place in any anthology of Southern verse.
It is the well known *Resignation; or Days of My
Youth:*

> Days of my youth,
>   Ye have glided away;
> Hairs of my youth,
>   Ye are frosted and gray;
> Eyes of my youth,
>   Your keen sight is no more;—''

and so on with the loss of all the fine things that
make youth glorious.

With the War of the Revolution over and the scattered seaboard settlements organized as part of a
constitutional Republic, the Southern states proceed
rapidly to evolve into the type of civilization already
predetermined by colonial conditions.   The large
plantation, made possible by the system of negro
slavery, is the social, industrial, and economic unit,
and under it the country gentleman develops as the
predominant and dominating class.   Life at the
South, therefore, was that of a rural aristocracy
whose interests were naturally other than literary.
Living in the country upon widely separated landed
estates, the people failed to develop large centres of
intellectual activity.   While the ruling classes were
themselves widely read in polite literature and cultivated in matters of taste, they were too few in number to constitute a reading public large enough to
inspire and support authorship.   Moreover, the general defect of popular education and the lack of an

intelligent middle class hospitable to ideas limited the diffusion of knowledge and rendered the intellectual atmosphere unfavorable to the production of literature and discouraging to authorship as a profession. While it is true that, throughout the period up to the War of Secession, there were in Richmond, Charleston, Baltimore, New Orleans, and other places no inconsiderable groups of cultivated men and women who were interested in literature and attempted to make it, while it is also true that at each of these places many magazines and reviews of high grade did make literature a matter of serious concern, yet the fact is that conditions were not those under which either a vital poetic or prose literature flourishes.

The conditions to which we are referring existed not only in the older states along the seaboard but also, as the Louisiana Purchase and the Mexican War opened up new territory in the Southwest, the conditions in the older states were simply repeated in the new, and the South from 1815 to 1860 was, from a material standpoint, busily engaged in extending without change its civilization into other fields. This expansion assisted in bringing sharply to the front, and keeping them there, those great political issues that absorbed the constructive intellectual energies of the South and produced that wonderful race of statesmen that for so long shaped the political thought of the Nation. It may be said therefore that the really constructive genius of the South expressed itself in terms of statecraft.

A rural aristocracy is naturally conservative, and it was rendered more so by this absorption of the best thought of the people in matters of politics, particularly as political thinking became more and more sectional in character and as political leaders set themselves the task of maintaining and extending the system of slavery by pressing the doctrine of States' Rights. The result was that their thinking and leadership, together with the peculiar form of Southern life and the peculiar nature of Southern conditions, went deeper than mere questions of politics. It all tended to isolate the already conservative South, to shut it in upon itself, to detach it from the progressive thought of the rest of the world, and to prevent its receiving those large, stirring ideas that made, for example, the air of New England so stimulating to every form of literary endeavor.

It is necessary to keep these things in mind if one would understand the character of the poetic product of the South before 1860. The lack of a large reading public, the widely scattered nature of the population, the conservatism of the people, the absorption of intellectual interests in politics, the failure to welcome and appropriate the liberalizing tendencies of Nineteenth century thought—these are sufficient to suggest the nature and amount of Southern poetry. In the first place, the quantity of it is surprisingly large when all things are considered. A list of approximately 250 writers of verse has been made out, and from 1805 to 1860 there is not a year in which numbers of volumes are not published. This list includes verse written in almost every conceivable form, using almost every conceivable sort of material, and for almost every purpose to which poetry may be applied—lyric, descriptive, satiric, dramatic, political, patriotic, religious. In fact, the whole gamut of the muse's lyre was run, accompanied by a multitudinous array of voices. There was, then, no lack of poetic effort, some of it modestly anonymous and some of it boldly challenging the suffrages of the public under both well known and unknown names.

But all this quantity of poetic effort was largely

amateurish in quality because, in the nature of the case, it was so largely the work of amateurs. One may say that among the legion of verse-makers at the South there were hardly more than four at the outside that can be described as professional men of letters—Edgar Allan Poe, William Gilmore Simms, Henry Timrod, and Paul Hamilton Hayne. The rest were lawyers, physicians, ministers, college professors, sentimental men and women who, busy with other things, courted the Muses only at intervals between more absorbing pursuits. It has been said of old time that poetry is a jealous mistress who demands an undivided loyalty, and she does not yield her best to those to whom verse-making is but a more or less superficial accomplishment and no consuming passion. Hence the poetry of the South before 1860 was what it was because it was largely the work of those who would confess to only a mild bent toward it and who regarded it as merely one of the ornaments of their culture. One would naturally expect therefore to find upon it the marks of the mere amateur.

This amateurishness shows itself generally in the imitativeness of much of the Southern verse. The amateur in literature never frees himself quite from his models, and to the end he is likely to remain a remote echo. Men do not uncover and express what is essentially strong and original in their temperament in any art to which they have not given themselves body and soul. Moreover, this is the price which must be paid for excellence of achievement as well as for originality. And this price was not paid by Southern poets as a class, but only here and there by some isolated individuals. The general result was that the limited excellence which Southern poetry had was due mainly to the skill with which it approximated the qualities of its

models—the monotonously smooth Eighteenth century poets, the grace and melody of the Cavalier
poets of love and wine, the mood and sounding rhetoric of Byron, the sentimentalism of Tom Moore, and
the artificial verbal and metrical prettiness of
Tennyson.

These are the qualities which the Southern poets
now and then caught with a considerable degree of
effectiveness—so much so, indeed, that one may wonder what might have been accomplished if the Southern temperament had been nourished under more
favorable conditions, and had been free to receive the
full tide of Nineteenth century thought and ideals. If,
for example, the South had not been so tenaciously
conservative, if its intellectual interests and energies
had not been so completely absorbed in politics, if
the industrial changes, the transcendental movement,
the new social dreams of the rights and privileges
of all men, the radical readjustment of the modern
mind due to the application of the scientific spirit
and method—if these had swept in upon the thought
and genius of the South, things had been quite otherwise with its poetry, one may be sure. But they did
not, and Southern verse remains as the work of the
amateur—imitative, light and lacking in that seriousness of mood and depth of meaning which so largely
characterize both the Victorian poetry in England
and that of the New England school in America. As
it was, the poetry produced at the South, even the
best, was narrow in range, sentimental in mood, lyric
in form, and so far unoriginal and indeed impersonal
that one might almost say that most of it might have
been written by the same hand.

Here and there, however, there projected out of
the general mass of those who essayed poetry the
few who do best what others do but indifferently.
These are they whom both criticism and common con-

sent have agreed to call the representative poets. But even these have won their place, not by the bulk of their work, nor by any considerable portion of it, but by the single poem that has found its way into the anthologies. An appreciation of these few poems of the representative poets, after this general discussion, will be sufficient to bring definitely before us the absolute achievement of the South in poetry.

In the first quarter of the century John Shaw of Maryland (1810), William Maxwell of Virginia (1812), Richard Dabney of the same state (1812), Washington Allston of South Carolina (1813), and Edward Coate Pinckney of Maryland (1825), had published thin volumes of verse from which a poem or two found its way into the early selections from American literature, some of them even surviving to the present time. Those that have survived are light lyrics of more or less sentimental character, and only a certain grace of versification and a mild appeal to the persistent sentimentalism in human nature have kept them from going the way of the merely trivial in literature. For example, John Shaw's claim to remembrance seems to hang by so slender a thread as one poem of three stanzas entitled "A Song"—a really dainty bit of verse-making:

> " Who has robbed the ocean cave
>   To tinge thy lips with coral hue?
> Who from India's distant wave
>   For thee those pearly treasures drew?
>   Who from yonder orient sky
>   Stole the morning of thine eye?"

Again, a stanza of versified trivialty is even yet quoted from William Maxwell:

> " How many kisses do I ask?
>   Now you set me to my task.
> First, sweet Annie, will you tell me
> How many waves are in the sea?"

"How many stars are in the sky?
How many lovers you make sigh?
How many sands are on the shore?
I shall want just one kiss more."

When one reads the few poems selected by the various anthologies to represent the best of Richard Dabney's poems, one need not wonder that the first volume (1812) failed with the public, and that his publisher pronounced his second (1815) "a quite losing concern." Here is a stanza from *Youth and Age*:

"Its quiet beams, in man's last days,
The Hesperus of life displays;
When all of passion's midday heat
Within the breast forgets to beat;
When calm and smooth the minutes glide,
Along life's tranquilizing tide;   ·
It points with slow, receding light,
To the sweet rest of silent night;
And tells, when life's vain schemes shall end,
Thus will its closing light descend,
And as the Eve star seeks the wave,
Thus gently reach the quiet grave."

When we turn to Washington Allston we find that so distinguished a critic as James Russell Lowell said that the really artistic spirit first came to expression in American literature in Allston's *Sylphs of the Seasons* in 1813. Allston was a South Carolinian who achieved exceptional fame as an artist and enjoyed the friendship of Coleridge and Wordsworth. The former declared that Allston possessed "a poetic and artistic genius unsurpassed by any man of his age"; while Southey was no less pronounced in his estimate, affirming that Allston's poems were "among the first productions of modern times." However, the modern reader of his poetry finds it hard to agree with such judgments, feeling that they are extravagant eulogies rather than just appreciations. At the time, however, his poetry was pub-

Washington Allston

lished it was greatly superior to anything America had produced in the quality of the versification, the delicacy and refinement of the sentiment, and in an imaginative touch that suggests the nature treatment of Wordsworth and the romantic mood of Coleridge, together with a certain vague mysticism which was no doubt due to the influence of the latter. Nevertheless, his poetry has had only enough vitality in it to make of the poet-painter an interesting personality in the early literature of the country— the first name to connect in artistic fellowship the New World with the Old. The two following stanzas from *Rosalie* are characteristic, and have, moreover, enough poetry in them to set them quite apart from anything produced at the South before 1813:

> " For all I see around me wears
>   The hue of other spheres;
> And something blent of smiles and tears
>   Comes from the very air I breathe.
> O, nothing, sure, the stars beneath
> Can mould a sadness like to this,—
>   So like angelic bliss.
>
> " So, at the dreamy hour of day
>   When the last lingering ray
> Stops on the highest cloud to play,—
> So thought the gentle Rosalie,
> As on her maiden reverie
> First fell the strain of him who stole
>   In music to her soul."

Richard Henry Wilde (1789-1847), a Georgia lawyer, congressman, and scholar, particularly in the field of Italian literature, owes his literary fame chiefly to one poem, a melancholy lyric on the vanity of life. Few poems written at the South before 1860 are so widely known as his *My Life Is Like the Summer Rose,* and deservedly so, being a lyric of genuine charm both in thought and expression. It is almost too familiar to make a quotation necessary, yet the last stanza should be given if only for the beauty of the second to the last verse:

> "My life is like the print which feet
> Have left on Tampa's desert strand;
> Soon as the rising tide shall beat,
> All trace will vanish from the sand;
> Yet, as if grieving to efface
> All vestige of the human race,
> *On that lone shore loud moans the sea—*
> But none, alas! shall moan for me!"

Wilde's sonnet *To the Mocking Bird* and his *Ode to Ease* also deserve to keep his memory alive. While one misses in them the natural inevitableness of the best lyric poetry, still they have the finished, though somewhat artificial, grace that marks the work of a man of poetic temperament, if not of poetic power, and are not at all discreditable as the work of one who only occasionally essayed verse.

In 1825 Edward Coate Pinckney, lawyer, adventurer, sometime professor of *Belles-Lettres* in the University of Maryland, and editor of a political newspaper, published a volume of poems in which were several that illustrate the persistent tendency of Southern verse to show its best side in the more or less artificial lyric of sentiment. *A Health, A Picture Song* and *A Serenade* are quite worthy of a place in any anthology of American verse. A stanza from the familiar *A Health* will be sufficient to show the quality of his work:

> "I fill this cup to one made up
> Of loveliness alone,
> A woman, of her gentle sex
> The seeming paragon;
> To whom the better elements
> And kindly stars have given
> A form so fair, that, like the air,
> 'Tis less of earth than heaven."

Thus by the end of the first quarter of the Nineteenth century, what we understand as Southern poetry, when it is worthy of consideration at all, is largely of the nature of the sentimental lyric. So generally is this the case that there is a rather monotonous conventionality about the most of it. It lacks, as we have already said, the distinguishing personal note, and fails of the piercing lyric cry that belongs to the final achievement of lyric poetry. There is, however, in no little of it a clever rhetorical prettiness, an ease and grace of versification, and, at times, a delicate beauty of fancy. It would not be quite just perhaps to say that it is defective in sincerity of mood and reality of passion. Still one cannot help feeling that it is chiefly the work of men who are merely playing with an art, or possibly men who have a dash of poetic sentiment in their nature without much of the genius of the real poet. It will be sufficient, therefore, in order to bring out the characteristics of Southern poetry from 1825 on, to go through a process of selection again, and to take for consideration only those who may be truly called representative.

First, there is Albert Pike who, though born in Boston, early identified himself with the Southwest as a lawyer and newspaper editor, and devoted himself largely to the interests of Masonry. At the age of twenty-two (1831) he wrote *Hymns to the Gods*, which, afterwards published in *Blackwood's* (1839), won praise in both this country and England. Three years later (1834) came his *Prose Sketches and Poems.* However, only a poem or two is all that has survived of his literary activity, and even these show no particular originality, being chiefly interesting for the way they echo something of the spirit and manner of both Shelley and Keats. For example,

Shelley was very near to the poet when he penned his *Ode to Spring:*

"O thou delicious Spring!
Nursed in the lap of thin and subtle showers,
Which lift their snowy wing
From odorous beds of light-enfolded flowers,
And from enmassed bowers,
That over grassy walks their greenness fling.
Come, gentle Spring."

In the same way one who reads his *Ode to the Mocking Bird* must think of Keats' *Ode to the Nightingale:*

"Ha! what a burst was that! the Aeolian strain
Goes floating through the tangled passages
Of the still woods, and now it comes again,
A multitudinous melody, like a rain
Of glassy music under echoing trees,
Close by a ringing lake."

One poem, a lyric of disappointed love, suggesting both the mood and manner of Tennyson when he was in the "Claribel" stage of his development, makes Philip Pendleton Cooke (1816-1850), a Virginia lawyer, worthy of mention in any discussion of Southern verse. Cooke contributed frequently to the literary journals of his day, and published in 1847 a collection of his poems, *Froissart Ballads and Other Poems.* The modern reader fails to find in them what Duyckinck (*Encyclopedia of American Literature*) in 1856 found—that they "are in a bright, animated mood, vigorous without effort, preserving the freedom of nature with the discipline of art"; nor indeed does he agree with the same critic that the one poem which serves to keep Cooke in remembrance, his *Florence Vane,* has "the merit of an antique song" in its "rare and peculiar excellence" and in its "delicately touched sentiment." On the contrary, the modern reader is more likely to feel that the poem is artificial in construction and almost mawkish in sentiment. The last stanza will be enough to remind one of what the poem is like:

> "The lilies of the valley
>   By young graves weep,
> The daisies love to dally
>   Where maidens sleep;
> May their bloom, in beauty vying,
>   Never wane,
> Where thine earthly part is lying,
>   Florence Vane!".

John Matthews Legaré, of Charleston, S. C., author of *Orta-Undis and Other Poems* (1848), is another among these minor poets who, by a certain artificial grace and refinement of verse and sentiment, deserves a passing notice. As with the rest, there is wanting with him the swift, sure utterance of the genuine lyric mood, and one feels that the poetry is made, not inspired. Here is a characteristic stanza from the poem entitled *To a Lily:*

> "Go bow thy head in gentle spite,
>   Thou lily white,
> For she who spies thee waving there,
> With thee in beauty can compare
>   As day with night."

A prolific writer on many subjects was Alexander Beaufort Meek (1814-1865), lawyer, soldier, politician, newspaper editor, and author of *Songs and Poetry of the South* (1857), a volume which was popular enough to go through three editions the year of its publication. Nature, love, sectional patriotism, were his prevailing themes, and a smooth fluency and a verbal exuberance were the characteristic qualities. His lyric to *The Mocking Bird,* though an obvious imitation of Shelley's *Skylark* easily ranks with the best of the Southern lyrics:

> "Why is't thus, this sylvan Petrarch
>   Pours all night his serenade?
> 'Tis for some proud woodland Laura,
>   His sad sonnets all are made!"

"But he changes now his measure—
   Gladness bubbling from his mouth—
Jest and gibe, and mimic pleasures—
   Winged Anacreon of the South!"

In James Barron Hope (1829-1887) we find another lawyer and newspaper editor actively concerned in literary matters and now and then publishing a volume of verse that won him a place in the
affection of those who cared for such things. His
Charge at Balaklava challenges comparison with
Tennyson's poem on the same subject, and in swift-
ness and vigor does not suffer greatly; while his
Three Summer Studies is an idyllic picture of rural
life drawn with charm of verse and sentiment. It
deserves the place it occupies in the various selections from ante-bellum Southern poetry.

John Reuben Thompson (1823-1873), one time editor of the *Southern Literary Messenger,* was a
prolific poet, though he is now chiefly known for
one or two stirring war-time lyrics. However, his
Window Panes at Brandon and *A Picture* are both
poems with enough merit in them to make them more
generally known.

Both Hope and Thompson filled no small place in
the literary life of the older South, and both serve
to illustrate how little survives of that large body of
poetic endeavor that marked the period before the
war. It lacked, as we have seen, so generally reality
of thought and feeling, was so defective in the matter
of originality, and, on the artistic side, was so obviously imitative that in the mass it had not enough
vitality to keep it alive much beyond its own short
day. However, when that lyric quality which seemed
inherent in the Southern temperament really took
fire in the flame of war, the result was a few martial

J . M . Legaré.

lyrics of genuine power, perhaps the best in American literature. Already in 1814 Francis Scott Key had given the Republic, with his *Star-Spangled Banner,* its first national ode, and in 1847 the Mexican War had inspired Theodore O'Hara to write *The Bivouac of the Dead.* Nothing better than this last poem has been done by any other American poet in the way of a purely martial lyric. The last stanza of it is almost perfect as an appropriate expression of the elegiac mood:

> " Yon marble minstrel's voiceless stone
>   In deathless song shall tell,
> When many a vanished age hath flown,
>   The story how ye fell;
> Nor wreck, nor change, nor winter's blight,
>   Nor Time's remorseless doom,
> Shall dim one ray of glory's light
>   That gilds your glorious tomb."

With the breaking out of the War of Secession there came a lyric chorus made up of many voices, chanting the fiercely patriotic mood of the hour. Some were simply passionate appeals to state pride; some told in verse the moving stories of both individual and collective heroism; others paid tribute to great leaders; and still others struck the elegiac note of sorrow for those who died in battle. Considering the entire mass of these war-time lyrics, a just criticism will say that they are the best purely lyric productions flung forth out of the hot passions of this war, and that some of them are among the best of their kind.

The martial choir begins with James R. Randall's *My Maryland,* a poem which still has power, from its direct, passionate appeal, to stir the patriotic feelings, even after the occasion that called it forth has long passed into the sober mood of history that is

made. When it was first published it called like a
blast of a trumpet to the soul of the South:

> "The despot's heel is on thy shore,
>   Maryland!
> His torch is at thy temple door,
>   Maryland!
> Avenge the patriotic gore
> That flecked the streets of Baltimore,
> And be the battle queen of yore,
>   Maryland, my Maryland!"

It was followed by many in the same mood at every
stage of the great struggle; some, merely anonymous, were sung from the corners of local newspapers and thence drifted into popular possessions;
others bore the names of already well known poets.
For example, there is Henry Timrod's *Ode to Carolina,* an exceptionally fine specimen of the martial
lyric:

> "The despot treads thy sacred sands,
> Thy pines give shelter to his bands,
> Thy sons stand by with idle hands,
>   Carolina!"

Quite worthy, moreover, to be classed with the best
of its kind is Francis O. Ticknor's *Virginians of the
Valley.* The last stanza will give a good idea of the
stirring appeal of it:

> "We thought they slept!—the sons who kept
> The names of noble sires,
> And slumbered while the darkness crept
> Around their vigil fires!
> But aye the Golden Horseshoe Knights
> Their Old Dominion keep,
> Whose foes have found enchanted ground
> But not a Knight asleep."

Ticknor is also the author of *Little Giffen of Tennessee,* a lyric that tells with piercing pathos the
heroism of a soldier lad from the plain people. So
perfectly is the story told in simple, direct moving
verse and with no little of the dramatic effectiveness of the genuine ballad, that one must class this

poem with the best of its kind in American literature. Equally well known, and deservedly so, are John Reuben Thompson's *Ashby* and *Music in Camp*. This latter poem has won its way into the heart of the nation as well as of the South, because it brings home to a reunited people so beautifully the pathos of war.

The war over, the natural mood of regret for a cause that is lost and the purpose to keep alive the memory of the heroic dead find appropriate and adequate expression in such poems as Margaret J. Preston's *Shade of the Trees*, Father Ryan's *Conquered Banner*, and Henry Timrod's *Ode to the Confederate Dead*. Few poems in American literature that attempt to interpret the same mood can be classed with this latter poem in simple beauty of style and nobility of sentiment. The last stanza fittingly illustrates both the style and the sentiment:

> "Stoop, Angels, hither from the skies!
> There is no holier spot of ground
> Than where defeated valor lies,
> By mourning beauty crowned!"

It now remains to discuss the four poets who are, for the present generation, the really representative men of letters of the ante-bellum South, men who are remembered for the body of their work, rather than simply by an occasional poem—William Gilmore Simms, Edgar Allan Poe, Henry Timrod, and Paul Hamilton Hayne. Yet even in the case of these, it is not certain that any one of them, with the exception of Poe, will live for the future through anything more than a very few poems. Already Simms, as prodigiously prolific as he was, is hardly thought of as a poet, and nobody except some stray literary antiquarian would dare to attempt to read half of what he has written. It is the novelist that we care for, if we care for Simms at all, and it is hardly conceivable to us now that from 1827 to 1860 he brought out as many as fifteen volumes of verse, about one for every two years! In this immense poetic endeavor he used a wide range of material and almost every known form of verse. He turned out with a facility little short of amazing sonnets, satires, lyrics, descriptive sketches, and dramas until there seemed no limit to the fertility of his production, at least in amount. Yet if one were to search through it all, one would find plenty of Byronic declamation, much that is mere rhetoric, a facility of versification, some originality of invention, if not of mood and sentiment, and occasionally a purple patch of what is almost poetry, the patches coming, however, with hardly frequency enough to reward the search. The truth is Simms was a romancer of real power who wrote an immense amount of inferior verse, and one is surprised not only at the sheer amount but also at the distinction and praise it brought the author when it was published. Aside therefore from his stories he simply remains a striking literary figure, the most striking perhaps, in an age, though comparatively recent, yet strangely remote from the present.

But with Timrod and Hayne the case is different. Both are men of exceptional poetic talent, and time will rather add to, than detract from, their fame. Timrod took his art seriously, and under happier circumstances might have made a large contribution to American literature. As it is, he belongs to those whose renown is unfulfilled. Yet, withal, the high seriousness of such poems as *The Vision of Poesy*, *Ethnogenesis, The Cotton Boll*, the charming naturalness of *Katy*, the delicate beauty of *The Lily Confidante*, are sufficient in both distinction of imagery and melody of expression to make for him a secure place in the affection of lovers of genuine poetry.

1 TIMROD MONUMENT, CHARLESTON
2. SIMMS MONUMENT, CHARLESTON.

Hayne, while he lived to 1886, had yet by 1860 published three volumes of verse, and the mood and tone of his work seems rather to connect him with the past. Above all others, if one takes his poetry in the mass and in connection with the singularly winning personality of the man, he is regarded as the most representative Southern poet. Indeed, he has been not inappropriately called the poet-laureate of his section. The gentle, high chivalry in the best Southern character, the Southerner's love of state and section, the romantic color of his imagination, the sentimentality of his temperament, are reflected with grace and charm in the poetry of Hayne. More sympathetically and adequately than any other has he interpreted the moods and aspects of nature at the South. In the outward form of his art he has caught something of the spirit and manner of the best models, in particular of Wordsworth and Tennyson. One may safely affirm that the winnowing processes of time will leave from Hayne a larger amount of what is really excellent in poetry than from any other ante-bellum poet except Poe.

Poe is the one man of genius, though in a limited sphere, whom the South produced before 1860. But while this sphere is, in truth, limited, yet within it Poe's achievement is simply unmatched in American letters both in mood and in artistic perfection of form. The weird uncanniness of some of his poems, the vague, evasive mysticism of others, the strange romanticism, the poignancy of the mood of sorrow and despair with which they are charged—all appropriately and adequately sung with an exquisitely haunting melody—make them easily the best of their kind, and they bear, too, the distinct marks of Poe's own genius. It is futile, as I have said elsewhere, to discuss the question as to whether Poe belongs to the South, or is some rare exotic transplanted from far off realms. His detachment from contemporary ideas, his persistent lyrical mood, the melancholy atmosphere which pervades his art, his sentimentality, the romantic quality of his imagination, are certainly more Southern than anything else.

BIBLIOGRAPHY.—I. *Selections with biographical notes and critical comment.*—Clark, J. T.: *Songs of the South* (Philadelphia, 1896); Duyckinck, E. A. and G. L.: *Cyclopedia of American Literature* (New York, 1855); Eggleston, G. C.: *American War Ballads and Lyrics* (New York, 1889); Griswold, R. W.: *Poets and Poetry of America* (New York, 1842); Holliday, Carl: *Three Centuries of Southern Poetry* (Nashville, 1908): Painter, T. V. N.: *Poets of the South* (New York, 1903); Stedman and Hutchinson: *Library of American Literature* (New York, 1891); Trent, W. P.: *Southern Writers* (New York, 1905); Trent and Wells: *Colonial Prose and Poetry* (New York, 1901); Weber, W. L.: *The Southern Poets* (New York, 1900).

II. *Historical and Biographical.*—Bradshaw, S. F.: *Southern Poetry Prior to* 1860 (Richmond, 1900); Davidson, J. W.: *Living Writers of the South* (New York, 1869); Holliday, Carl: *History of Southern Literature* (New York, 1906); Link, S. A.: *Pioneers of Southern Literature* (Nashville, 1898); Manly, Louise: *Southern Literature* (Richmond, 1895); Onderdonk, J. L.: *A History of American Verse* (Chicago, 1901); Page, T. N.: *The Old South* (New York, 1892); Trent, W. P.: *Life of William Gilmore Simms* (New York, 1892); Tyler, M. C.: *History of American Literature* (New York, 1878) and *A Literary History of the American Revolution* (New York, 1897).

HENRY NELSON SNYDER,
President of Wofford College.

CHAPTER II.

SOUTHERN POETRY SINCE THE WAR OF SECESSION.

WHEN the War of Secession closed there were a number of Southern poets who had, before and during the war, achieved more or less success in the practice of their art. Some of them had written martial strains that were in unison with the heart-throbs of the Confederacy; armies had marched to the inspiring words of *Maryland, My Maryland,* and *Carolina,* and lonely hearts had been comforted by tributes to Southern heroes. The question was, whether these same poets or others could give adequate expression to the tragedy of a desolate people. Certainly there was never a time when a great poet was more needed, one who might have obeyed the same voice that spoke to Israel's prophet of the Exile, "Comfort ye, comfort ye my people." Themes were not lacking for imaginative minds—the sacred memory of the South's dead soldiers, the hallowed presence of her self-sacrificing women, the confusion of an enfranchised race, the overthrow of a picturesque civilization, the glory of human nature as seen in so many examples of suffering, the hope of a new nationalism and a larger freedom—all these might have been sung by those gifted with poetic power. One who achieved success at a later time has said: "Never in the history of this country has there been a generation of writers who came into such an inheritance of material."

So it seems from the standpoint of the present, but conditions were most unfavorable for creative

work of any kind. There was no inheritance of
literary art, no background of artistic traditions.
All the causes that are generally assigned for the
lack of poetry in the ante-bellum South—the lack of
centres of culture, the failure of the people to appreciate literary work, the absence of magazines
and publishing houses—prevailed in the new era;
and thereto were added unexampled poverty, widespread disaster, and an overwhelming confusion of
the public mind. It is needless here to rehearse the
conditions that prevailed from 1865 to 1875. Lanier
tersely expressed the chief limitation under which
the writers labored when he wrote to Bayard Taylor: "Perhaps you know that with us of the younger
generation in the South, since the war, pretty much
the whole of life has been merely not dying."

Of the poets who survived the war, few made any
advance over their previous work, and only one
grew in range and power of inspiration. William
Gilmore Simms, who, in Charleston, had gathered
about him a band of promising men and who had
done so much for the cause of Southern literature,
was an old and broken man. He went to work with
prodigious energy upon some romances, and now
and then wrote a poem that was but a feeble wail of
despair. He edited a collection of Southern war
poems, the introduction of which was characterized
by unselfish interest in Southern literature and by
a new note of nationalism. He wrote to Hayne: "I
am rapidly passing from a stage where you young
men are to succeed me, doing what you can. God
grant that you may be more successful than I have
been." The words which Simms wrote of himself
are a fitting epitaph to his stormy and sad life:
"Here lies one who, after a reasonably long life,
distinguished chiefly by unceasing labors, has left
all his better works undone"—a remark that poign-

1. Residence of W G Simms
2. Residence of J P Kennedy

antly suggests the ungathered sheaves of many another Southern genius.

Margaret J. Preston, who had, before the war, written for the *Southern Literary Messenger,* and during the war had celebrated the deeds of Southern heroes, after the war continued to live in Lexington, Va.—a member of an interesting circle made notable by the presence of the great Lee and by the memories of Stonewall Jackson. After publishing *Beechenbrook* in 1866, she continued to write for Southern and Northern magazines. Her poetry is, however, imitative rather than original; beyond a slender note of pathos in contemplating the conditions in the South and a sort of common-place religious meditation, her poetry is of little enduring value. Her correspondence, recently published, reveals her as a woman of unusual refinement of manners and culture. In 1870 she brought out a volume of poems, comprising legends from Hebrew and Greek poetry; in 1885 a volume of *Cartoons*—sympathetic studies of masterpieces of art which she had never seen; in 1886 *Poems of Faith and Comfort,* and in 1887 *Colonial Ballads.* Like so many Southern poets, she did not take her work seriously enough. Her husband—a gentleman of the old school—at one time objected to her being known as a poet. She herself summed up her own attitude and that of many another Southern poet when she said:·

"Pray remember that I have never given myself up as most women do who have made any name for themselves in literature. It has only been my pastime, not the occupation or mission of my life, which has been too busy a one with the duties of wifehood, motherhood, mistress, hostess, neighbor and friend. Only when the demands which these relations entailed were satisfied did I turn to my pen. I think I can truly say that I never neglected the concoction of a pudding for the sake of a poem, or a sauce for a sonnet. Art is a jealous mistress, and I have served her with my left hand only."

Perhaps the best poem she wrote after the war was *A Grave in Hollywood Cemetery, Richmond*—a sympathetic characterization of John R. Thompson. It is quoted here not simply as her best poem, but as an imaginative expression of the feeling of more than one "exile" from the South:

"I read the marble-lettered name,
    And half in bitterness I said:
'As Dante from Ravenna came,
    Our poet came from exile—dead.'
And yet, had it been asked of him
    Where he would rather lay his head,
This spot he would have chosen. Dim
        The city's hum drifts o'er his grave,
        And green above the hollies wave
Their jagged leaves, as when a boy,
        On blissful summer afternoons,
        He came to sing the birds his runes,
And tell the river of his joy.

"Who dreams that in his wanderings wide,
        By stern misfortunes tossed and driven,
        His soul's electric strands were riven
From home and country? Let betide
What might, what would, his boast, his pride,
Was in his stricken mother-land,
        That could but bless and bid him go,
Because no crust was in her hand
        To stay her children's need. We know
The mystic cable sank too deep
        For surface storm or stress to strain,
Or from his answering heart to keep
        The spark from flashing back again!

"Think of the thousand mellow rhymes,
        The pure idyllic passion-flowers,
Wherewith, in far gone, happier times,
        He garlanded this South of ours.
Provençal-like, he wandered long,
        And sang at many a stranger's board,
        Yet 'twas Virginia's name that poured
The tenderest pathos through his song.
We owe the Poet praise and tears,
        Whose ringing ballad sends the brave,
Bold Stuart riding down the years—
        What have we given him? Just a grave!"

The reference in the last stanza of the poem to Thompson's poetry suggests that from Thompson himself a prophet of Southern literature might have expected development. Before the war he had been the editor of the *Southern Literary Messenger* and the friend of Poe; during the war he had written two noteworthy lyrics, *Music in Camp* and *Ashby*. He was a critic of discernment and a poet of promise. In 1863 he went to London. When he came back after the war he became literary editor of the New York *Evening Post*. It is said that he would never allow a reference to the "Lost Cause," so deeply had the defeat of the Confederacy entered into his soul. Silence was the only language worthy of the theme. He died in 1873 of consumption.

So within a few years a number of other poets passed away. Albert B. Meek, who had before the war written *The Land of the South*, died in 1865. Theodore O'Hara, whose *Bivouac of the Dead* was a dirge for the soldiers in the Mexican War, though it was more often thought of in connection with the Confederate dead, died in 1867. Others lived on, but gave up entirely the writing of poetry. Ticknor, the author of *Virginians of the Valley* and *Little Giffen of Tennessee,* lived the life of a country doctor near Columbus, Ga. Dr. Bruns, who had been one of Simms' circle of poets in Charleston, moved to New Orleans where he became an eminent physician. Albert Pike, who had, in 1839, published poems in *Blackwood's Magazine* and who during the war had written the best poem we have on "Dixie," moved to Washington, where he became absorbed in Masonic work, to which he gave the rest of his life. Barron Hope, who, in 1858, wrote the poem for the unveiling of the statue of Washington in Richmond, was made editor of the *Norfolk Landmark*. Though he afterwards wrote poems for special occasions, he never advanced beyond the work of his youth. William Gordon McCabe, the author of *Christmas Night of '62* and *Dreaming in the Trenches,* became one of the best-known schoolmasters of Virginia— a position that seemed to deaden his poetic inspiration, though he remained an inimitable *raconteur* and the friend of some of the most gifted poets of England and America.

Better than any of these poets were James Ryder Randall and Henry Timrod, both of whom had touched the high-water mark of lyric poetry in their war odes. Randall in *Maryland, My Maryland,* had written what many consider the best lyric called forth by the war, but he never recovered that first, fine, careless rapture, never again felt the inspiration that lifted him for once in a moment of inspired patriotism into the "eternal melodies." He passed the remainder of his days in the drudgery of a newspaper office. Timrod, who had written *Ethnogenesis* and *Carolina*—poems that expressed in imperishable words the spirit of the Southern people— was to pass through one of the saddest struggles recorded in history—poverty, neglect and disease wreaked their utmost upon him. Hayne's account of his last days is enough to melt the heart of the coldest man. Timrod's letters suggest the tragedy of Chatterton or Keats; their melancholy is broken only now and then by a note of grim humor. He lived long enough, however, to write the most beautiful dirge ever written in behalf of the Confederate dead—"as perfect in its tone and workmanship as though it had come out of the Greek anthology." The last stanza merits the praise that Holmes gave to Emerson's *Concord Hymn;* the words seem as if they had been carved upon marble for a thousand years:

I.

"Sleep sweetly in your humble graves,
    Sleep, martyrs of a fallen cause;
Though yet no marble column craves
    The pilgrim here to pause.

II.

"In seeds of laurel in the earth
    The blossom of your fame is blown,
And somewhere, waiting for its birth,
    The shaft is in the stone!

III.

"Meanwhile, behalf the tardy years
    Which keep in trust your storied tombs,
Behold! your sisters bring their tears
    And these memorial blooms.

IV.

"Small tributes! but your shades will smile
    More proudly on these wreaths to-day,
Than when some cannon-moulded pile
    Shall overlook this bay.

V.

"Stoop, angels, hither from the skies!
    There is no holier spot of ground
Than where defeated valor lies,
    By mourning beauty crowned!"

One who wrote such a poem at the age of thirty-seven, and who had written at least six other poems of the highest excellence, might have done much to realize the possibilities already suggested. He died, however, in 1867. Timrod's friend, Paul Hamilton Hayne, was the only poet who continued to do serious work in the new era of Southern life. He was to be the link between Simms and Lanier. Descended from ancestors of great renown in South Carolina, and with possibilities of success in law and politics, he had before the war deliberately chosen literature

as his profession.   In his first poem he announces his
dedication to the poet's life:

"Yet would I rather in the outward state
  Of song's immortal temple lay me down,
 A beggar basking by that radiant gate,
  Than bend beneath the haughtiest empire's crown.

"For sometimes, through the bars, my ravished eyes
  Have caught brief glimpses of a life divine,
 And seen a far mysterious rapture rise
  Beyond the veil that guards the inmost shrine."

The test of the strength of this dedication came
after the war, when he found himself face to face
with a desolated city and an impoverished and
broken-hearted commonwealth.   With magnificent
courage and faith he moved to a small railway sta-
tion near Augusta, Ga., where he lived the remainder of his days in a cabin of his own building.

There have been many notable descriptions of
this cabin, but none more so than that which Hayne
gives in an account of the visit that Simms made
him in 1866.   He refers to it as an "extraordinary
shanty which seemed to have been tossed by a supernatural pitchfork upon the the most desolate of
hills."   The interior accommodations were not un-
worthy of the outside forlornness.   "We had three
mattresses and a cot (if memory serves me right),"
he continues, "and for supplies a box of hardtack,
two sides of bacon and four-score, more or less, of
smoked herring.   Of cooking utensils there were a
frying-pan, a gridiron, with three broken bars, and
a battered iron pot."   The two poets had much
high conversation that suggested, at least, the times
when they had feasted together in the city by the
sea.   Here, also, Timrod visited him in 1867, just a
few months before his death.   In the poem *Under
the Pine* Hayne suggests the conversation they had

and Timrod's exquisite enjoyment of natural scenery:

"When the last rays of sunset, shimmering down,
Flashed like a royal crown.

"O tree! against a mighty trunk he laid
His weary head; thy shade
　　Stole o'er him like the first cool spell of sleep;
　　It brought a peace so deep
The unquiet passion died from out his eyes,
As lightning from the stilled skies."

Years afterward Maurice Thompson visited Hayne to pay his homage to "the king poet of the Old South." The cottage had been somewhat improved by the deft hand of Mrs. Hayne, but it was still "an arid perch for a songbird, that windy, frowsy, barren hill." The chairs, table and shelves had been made out of goods-boxes. The walls and ceiling of the main room were papered to odd effect with pictures from illustrated journals. Hayne's writing-desk, at which he stood to make his poems, had been a carpenter's work-bench.

Here, then, in this simple home—almost as crude as Thoreau's hut on Walden Pond—Hayne spent the remainder of his days, only once or twice going on a visit to his native city, and once as far as New England to see the poets with whom he had such intimate correspondence, and to whom he had written some of his tenderest poems—at once the expression of his interest in poetry and of his broad national spirit. Here he received visits from young poets to whom he gave advice and inspiration.

Although he was well past middle life when he began to live at "Copse Hill," he maintained a steady and persistent spirit of work. In 1873 he wrote an extensive and noteworthy introductory sketch to Timrod's poems, thus serving to perpetuate the fame of his comrade. In 1878 he published lives of his uncle Robert Y. Hayne and of Hugh S. Legaré. Best of all, he continued to write poetry. He wrote to Mrs. Preston some words that ought to be the perpetual inspiration of American poets: "No, no! by my brain—my literary craft—I will win my bread and water; by my poems I will live or I will starve." In 1872 he brought out his volume *of Legends and Lyrics,* in 1875 *The Mountain of the Lovers and Other Poems,* and in 1882 a complete edition of his poems. A complete bibliography of his individual poems would indicate that they appeared in practically every magazine in the country, including the *Atlantic Monthly* and *Scribner's.* Even a partial reading in the files of contemporary periodicals serves to show that Hayne placed his work to the best advantage, although he was at times imposed upon by the editors of Southern magazines, who often appealed to him from the standpoint of loyalty to advance the interests of Southern literature. He was entirely dependent upon his poetic work for a livelihood, and, as has been said before, his single-hearted devotion to poetry gives him a unique place among American men of letters. Two or three of his best poems were written in his last years, notably *A Little While I Fain Would Linger Yet* and *In Harbor.* He came to the end of his voyage on July 6, 1886.

While Hayne did not strike a deeply original note, he cultivated faithfully the talents with which he was endowed. Accepting the results of the war in good faith, he soon manifested a spirit of reconciliation and even of nationalism, especially in his attitude to the poets of New England. Lamar's noteworthy tribute to Charles Sumner was paralleled by Hayne's sympathetic greeting to Whittier and Longfellow. In a poem to Oliver Wendell Holmes he expressed the gratitude of the South to the generous North at the time of the yellow fever scourge that swept the Southwest. More characteristic, however, were his poems revealing the picturesqueness of Southern landscapes and the melody of Southern birds. In *Macdonald's Raid* and *Æthra* he displayed some power of narrative verse, but his muse was at her best in the simpler forms of lyric verse. His best poems are characterized by delicacy of feeling and conscientious workmanship. His mastery of the sonnet, as well as his severe spirit, is evinced in the sonnet *My Study*.

"This is my world! within these narrow walls,
I own a princely service; the hot care
And tumult of our frenzied life are here
But as a ghost, and echo; what befalls
In the far mart to me is less than naught;
I walk the fields of quiet Arcadies,
And wander by the brink of hoary seas,
Calmed to the tendance of untroubled thought:
Or if a livelier humor should enhance
The slow-timed pulse, 'tis not for present strife,
The sordid zeal with which our age is rife,
Its mammon conflicts crowned by fraud or chance,
But gleamings of the lost, heroic life,
Flashed through the gorgeous vistas of romance."

His ability to depict a phase of Southern landscape in a strikingly original way is best seen, perhaps, in his *Aspects of the Pines:*

"Tall, sombre, grim, against the morning sky
They rise, scarce touched by melancholy airs,
Which stir the fadeless foliage dreamfully,
As if from realms of mystical despairs.

"Tall, sombre, grim, they stand with dusky gleams
Brightening to gold within the woodland's core,
Beneath the gracious noontide's tranquil beams—
But the weird winds of morning sigh no more.

"A stillness, strange, divine, ineffable,
Broods round and o'er them in the wind's surcease,
And on each tinted copse and shimmering dell
Rests the mute rapture of deep-hearted peace.

"Last, sunset comes—the solemn joy and might
  Borne from the West when cloudless day declines—
Low, flutelike breezes sweep the waves of light,
  And lifting dark green tresses of the pines,

"Till every lock is luminous, gently float,
  Fraught with hale odors up the heavens afar
To faint when twilight on her virginal throat
  Wears for a gem the tremulous vesper star."

While Hayne was faithfully and courageously giving himself to poetry, there gradually arose a group of younger writers, some of whom had been soldiers in the war. It is not so generally known that there was "an avalanche of poetry" in the South after the war. New magazines sprang up in Baltimore, Charleston and other Southern cities, and these made demand upon poets. There was a wilderness of mediocre poetry. Partly on account of poverty, partly because they felt that the South should properly be interpreted before the world, and partly because they could not but sing, many writers arose in different parts of the South. Davidson's *Living Writers of the South*, published in 1869, gave a list of 241 writers, 112 of whom were poets. The author naïvely remarked that some of the writers "have talent and character, with corresponding results, which enable them to stand in the front ranks of American authorship; some have limited abilities, and some have none." Another collection was entitled *Female Writers of the South*, about which a reviewer in the *Southern Magazine* used the following vigorous language:

"We shall not have a literature until we have a criticism which can justify its claims to be referred to; intelligent enough to explain why a work is good or bad; * * * courageous enough to condemn bad art and bad workmanship, no matter whose it be; to say, for instance, to more than half the writers in these volumes: 'Ladies, you may be all that is good, noble and fair; you may be the pride of society and the lights of your homes; so far as you are Southern women our hearts are at your feet—but you have neither the genius, the learning nor the judgment to qualify you for literature.' "

ABRAM JOSEPH RYAN.

Of all the writers of the first few years after the war the most popular was Abram Joseph Ryan, generally known as Father Ryan. Before Hayne and Lanier and Russell began to do their best work, he was the poet laureate of the South. He voiced the despair of his people and their loyalty to the conquered banner of the Southern Confederacy. There are other notes in his poetry—notably the expression of his religious faith and his strain of mysticism—but that which made him a contemporary influence in Southern life and has caused him to remain the most popular poet of the South was the note of sentiment and melancholy that centered about the overthrow of Southern hopes. While it is easy to see the defects of his poetry, it is also easy to understand why it has such a hold on the average Southerner. He had fluency and clearness of style; he himself wrote the best commentary on his poems, when he said that they were "written at random— off and on, here, there, anywhere—just as the mood came, with little of study and less of art, and always in a hurry." As there is no finality in his art, so there is no outlook, no hope, but a sort of unconquerable loyalty. *The Conquered Banner* and the *Sword of Robert Lee* are so well known as not to demand quotation here. The reader will scarcely do justice to the poet who does not know, in addition to these, *The Song of the Mystic,* a poem rich in its suggestiveness of the deeper realities of life.

Different alike in careful workmanship and in depth of thought and feeling from Father Ryan was Maurice Thompson. Though he is not, by some, considered a Southern writer, because he lived for a long time in Indiana and later in New York, he himself claimed to be a Southerner by reason of his early life in Georgia, his service as a Confederate soldier and his constant return to the South, where he often hunted and pursued the work of a student of natural history. His volume of poems published in 1897 is distinctly Southern—the theme running through the entire volume is that of the melody and spiritual significance of the song of the mocking bird. When his first poem appeared in the *Atlantic Monthly* in 1873, it was at once recognized by Howells and Longfellow as the work of "a new and original singer, fresh, joyous and true." In Thompson's poems there are suggestions of the author's beloved Greek and English writers, but there is an unmistakable note of originality in the Southern landscapes and in the new note of freedom and naturalism. He was one of the first Southern poets to feel that in resisting the stream of national tendency the South was fighting against the stars in their courses. He never apologized for his course in the war, but boasted that he dared to fight for the South from Lookout to the sea, with her proud banner over him:

"But from my lips thanksgiving broke,
As God in battle thunder spoke,
And that Black Hand, breeding drouth
And death of human sympathy
Throughout the sweet and serious South,
Was, with its chains and human yoke,
Blown hellward from the cannon's mouth,
While freedom cheered behind the smoke."

Tender and imaginative is his tribute to Abraham Lincoln, in the poem read before the Phi Beta Kappa Society of Harvard University:

"He was the Southern mother leaning forth,
At dead of night to hear the summon voice,
Beseeching God to turn the cruel North
And break it, that her son might come once more;
He was New England's maiden, pale and pure,
Whose gallant lover fell on Shiloh's plain,
He was the mangled body of the dead."

Jubilant is his prophecy of the New South:

> "The South whose gaze is cast
>   No more upon the past,
> But whose bright eyes the skies of promise sweep,
> Whose feet in paths of progress swiftly leap;
> And whose past thoughts, like cheerful rivers run,
> Through odorous ways to meet the morning song!"

If one characteristic of the new Southern poetry was the nationalism that one finds in Hayne and Thompson, another was naturalism or realism. The ante-bellum poetry was characterized by sentimentalism, by melancholy, by an almost utter absence of Southern landscape or character. Least of all was there any humorous poetry. Even when the poets wrote of the mocking bird there was the echo of English poets rather than the melody that rang through the Southern forests. All this absence of local color passed away with Irwin Russell's delineation of negro types and dialect. Born on a Southern plantation, he understood their character, disposition, language, customs and habits.

> "He couldn' 'a' talked so nachal
>   'Bout niggers in sorrow and joy,
> Widdouten he had a black mammy
>   To sing to him 'long ez a boy!"

His story of how he began to write poetry is so interesting and significant that I quote:

"It was almost an inspiration. I did not reduce the trifle to writing until some time afterwards, and then, from want of recollection, in a condensed and emasculated form. You know that I am something of a banjoist. Well, one evening I was sitting in our back yard in old Mississippi, 'twanging' on the banjo, when I heard the missis—our colored domestic, an old darky of the Aunt Dinah pattern—singing one of the outlandish camp meeting hymns of which the race is so fond. She was an extremely 'ligious character and, although seized with the impulse to do so, I hesitated to take up the tune and finish it. I did so, however, and in the dialect that I have adopted, and which I then thought, and still think, is in strict con-

formity to their use of it. I proceeded, as one inspired, to compose
verse after verse of the most absurd, extravagant and, to her, irrev-
erent rhyme ever before invented, all the while accompanying it on
the banjo and imitating the fashion of the plantation negro. The old
missis was so exasperated and indignant that she predicted all sorts
of dire calamities. Meantime my enjoyment of it was prodigious."

Russell very early attracted the attention of his
neighbors by his poems in local papers, but he first
became widely known in 1876 by his poems in the
bric-à-brac department of *Scribner's Monthly*. His
poems were among the first evidences of the beginning of a distinctively Southern literature. There
was scarcely a phase of the old-time negro that he
did not present. Now it is the trader trying to de-
ceive his master by putting rocks in his bale of cotton; now the preacher taking up a collection or
talking to his wife just before the angels come for
him. In *Nebuchednezzar* we have the story of the
negro and his mule. More indicative of the negro's
feeling for his master is *Mars John:*

> "I only has to shet my eyes, an' den it seems to me
> I sees him right afore me now, jes like he use' to be,
> A settin' on de gal'ry, lookin' awful big an' wise,
> Wid little niggers fannin' him to keep away de flies.
> He alluz wore de berry bes' ob planter's linen suits,
> An' kep' a nigger busy jes a blackin' ob his boots,
> De buckles on his galluses wuz made ob solid gol',
> An' di'mons! dey was in his shut as thick as it would hol'."

In view of such a poem—so clearly the progenitor
of *Marse Chan* and *Meh Lady*—it is no wonder that
Thomas Nelson Page said, "It was the light of his
genius shining through his dialect poems—first of
dialect poems and still first—that led my feet in
the direction I have since tried to follow." It is no
disparagement to the author of *Uncle Edinburg'
Drowndin'* or of *Uncle Remus* to say that their
stories have their complement in poetry in Russell's
Christmas Night in the Quarters. Modeled after

Burns's *Jolly Beggars* and *Tam O'Shanter*, it is a highly humorous and imaginative operetta—a series of brilliant incidents and pictures held together by the music of the old-time breakdown. Short quotations give no idea of the poem as a whole; a typical passage is "Brudder Brown's" blessing on the dance:

"O Mahsr! let dis gath'rin' fin' a blessin' in yo' sight!
　Don't jedge us hard fur what we does—you knows it's Christmas
　　night;
　An' all de balunce ob de yeah we does as right's we kin.
　Ef dancin's wrong, O Mahsr! let de time excuse de sin!

"We labors in de vineya'd, wukin' hard an' wukin' true;
　Now, shorely you won't notus, ef we eats a grape or two,
　An' takes a leetle holiday—a leetle restin'-spell—
　Bekase, nex' week, we'll start in fresh, an' labor twicet as well.

"Remember, Mahsr—min' dis, now,—de sinfulness ob sin
　Is 'pendin' 'pon de sperrit what we goes an' does it in:
　An' in a righchis frame ob min' we's gwine to dance an' sing,
　A-feelin' like King David, when he cut de pigeon wing.

"It seems to me—indeed it do—I mebbe mout be wrong—
　That people raly *ought* to dance, when Chrismus comes along;
　Des dance bekase dey's happy—like de birds hops in de trees,
　De pine-top fiddle soundin' to de bowin' ob de breeze.

"We has no ark to dance afore, like Isrul's prophet king;
　We has no harp to soun' de chords, to holp us out to sing;
　But 'cordin' to de gif's we has we does de bes' we knows;
　An' folks don't 'spise de vi'let-flower bekase it ain't de rose.

"You bless us, please, sah, eben ef we's doin' wrong to-night;
　Kase den we'll need de blessin' more'n ef we's doin' right;
　An' let de blessin' stay wid us, untel we comes to die,
　An' goes to keep our Chrismus wid dem sheriffs in de sky!

"Yes, tell dem preshis anguls we's a-gwine to jine 'em soon:
　Our voices we's a-trainin' fur to sing de glory tune;
　We's ready when you wants us, an' it ain't no matter when—
　O Mahsr! call yo' chillen soon, an' take 'em home! Amen."

Dialect verse and fiction have been greatly over-done in recent years, but the historic importance of

Russell's work cannot be overlooked. For the use
of dialect in verse Sidney Lanier once wrote a sufficient apology. He himself in his early days wrote
poems in negro and "Cracker" dialects. To Charlotte Cushman he said, in defense of the poems:

"Tell me, ought not one to be a little ashamed of writing a dialect
poem—as at least one newspaper has hinted? And did Robert Burns
prove himself no poet by writing mostly in dialect? And is Tennyson's *Death of the North Country Farmer*—certainly one of very
strongest things he ever wrote—not a poem, really?"

But Lanier's true work was not to be in the line
of dialect poetry, though these poems are valuable as
showing one important phase of his character, as
they also show the picturesque life of his native
Georgia. He was to be the Wordsworth or the
Keats of his time, not the Burns. He is the one man
of the period under consideration who deserves to
rank with the greater poets of America. After a
decade of wavering criticism as to his rank, Stedman
seemed to settle the question, at least for the present, when he put Lanier's picture in the group of
seven first poets as the frontispiece to his *American
Anthology*—an opinion shared by Mr. Curtis Hidden Page in his *Chief American Poets*. Lanier and
Whitman stand out as the original poets of the generation succeeding the war. Different in many respects, they were alike in the cosmic range and sweep
of their imagination.

Lanier was Southern, as Poe was not. His home
life in Macon, Ga., and his education at Oglethorpe
University were typical of that region. He fought
with romantic heroism in the war. The story of his
military career reads like that of some knight of
the age of chivalry. As he shared the hopes and the
disappointment of the Confederacy, so he was bap-
tized with the baptism of his people in reconstruction days, and no one suffered more than he in that

Sidney Lanier

Valley of Humiliation. He traveled in all parts of the South in search for health, from San Antonio to Jacksonville, and from Baltimore to Mobile. Though he moved to Baltimore in 1873, the background of many of his poems is that of the Lower South—the marsh, the mountains, the seashore. The birds and the forests of Georgia and Florida stirred his imagination. The song of the river that flowed by his birthplace is reproduced in the *Song of the Chattahoochee;* the robins of Tampa made melody for his weary soul and sing even now in his onomatopoetic lines. For the marshes of the Georgia coast he essayed to do what Wordsworth did for the mountains and lakes of northern England. It is now seen clearly that Lanier, in his poem *Corn* and in his essay on the "New South," was the prophet of a revolution in the agricultural life of his native land. Everywhere the ruined hilltops are blossoming like the rose, fulfilling his daring hope:

"Thou gashed and hairy Lear,
Whom the divine Cordelia of the year,
E'en pitying Spring will vainly strive to cheer—
. . . .
"Yet shall the great God turn thy fate,
And bring thee back into thy monarch state
And majesty immaculate."

Even more significant than the background is the quality of his poetry. An acute critic of New England has pointed out that the tragic convulsion of the war awakened in the South "a kind of passion which America had hardly witnessed before—a lyric fervor." Now this is seen preëminently in Lanier. It is the source of his limitations as well as of his strength, but it is there—enthusiasm, emotionalism, sentiment, lack of restraint. In *The Symphony* he is speaking as a Southerner in his outlook on modern industrial life, which seemed to him to be destroying the finer graces of the soul. It is scarcely fanciful to say that in the words of the horn —one of the instruments in the orchestra—he is interpreting the message of the Old South to the modern world. The age of chivalry is not dead. The modern era of industrialism may be judged in the light of the feudalism which it supplanted. In a letter outlining the poem, Lanier said: "It is now the gentleman who must rise and overthrow trade. That chivalry which every man has, in some degree, in his heart, which does not depend upon birth but which is a revelation from the God of justice, of fair dealing, of scorn of mean advantages * * * must burn up every one of the cunning moral castles from which trade sends out its forays upon the conscience of modern society." Thus, as throughout the poem, does Southern honor speak through him.

It is not well to stress this point too far, however, for in many other things Lanier was anything but a typical Southerner. He was genuinely national. Even from the close of the war he would have the seeds of that conflict utterly buried out of the sight of men. When the opportunity came to him to write the words for the Centennial Cantata at the Philadelphia Exposition, he felt, as few men in the country, the significance of the event. In musical conception, though not in felicitous words, he chanted the triumph of the Union. In spite of all the physical obstacles that had hindered the early settlers, in spite of the distinct individualities of the various sections of the country, in spite of sectional misunderstandings leading to a fierce civil war, the nation had survived. All of these had said, "No, thou shalt not be," but Columbia answers:

"Now praise to God's oft-granted grace,
Now praise to man's undaunted face,
Despite the land, despite the sea,
I was, I am, and I shall be!"

And the very same year he wrote a much better poem, *The Psalm of the West,* in which he sings the triumph of Freedom and Nationalism. In no other American verse is there a more vivid realization of the meaning of the Republic in the larger life of the world than in the Columbus sonnets of this poem.

Lanier was also cosmopolitan as well as national. No other Southerner, except, probably, Thomas Jefferson, was more alive to the life of the world or had a more open and inquisitive mind. The best that had been or was being thought and said and done in the world he aspired to know. There are two striking evidences of the modernity and the progressiveness of his mind—his attitude to science and to music. While many poets had expressed fear on account of the rapid advance of science, Lanier eagerly welcomed it as the handmaid of religion and poetry. "Poetry will never cease, nor science, nor the poetry of science," he says in his earliest book. He himself became an interested student of biology, and in his poems he shows the results of his scientific habit of mind, saturated as they are with at least the largest final conceptions of current science. An outgrowth of this regard for science was his sympathy with scholarship, and even his devotion, as a specialist, to his own chosen branch of English literature. He imbibed the spirit of the newly established Johns Hopkins University, moving with confidence among its great scholars, and with the eager curiosity of a child always finding fresh woods and pastures new. His study of old and middle and Elizabethan English had the same effect on him

that the study of continental literatures had on
Longfellow and Lowell.

That which distinguishes Lanier most sharply
from all other American poets is his attitude to
music. His letters, as well as the recollections of
those who know him best, go to show that music was
the master passion of his soul. First as an amateur
and then as a careful student in Baltimore, he
learned the art of flute playing. Listening to the
great orchestras and operas in Northern cities, and
reading the biographies of musicians, he came to
see the place of music in the culture life of the
modern world. It was to him not a luxury, but a
prime necessity—a source of education and an ally
especially of poetry. What is more important is
that in his poems *The Symphony* and *To Beethoven*
he has interpreted in words the very soul of music.
The line most generally quoted from him is the conclusion of the former poem, "Music is Love in
search of a word."

Nor was the effect of music on Lanier confined to
his remarkable letters or to his poems on music.
Gradually he conceived an idea that it was his distinctive work as a critic to state the relation of
music to poetic form, and as a poet to create real
musical effects with words. After 1875, especially,
we hear much of his plans, and we see in the few
poems that he left behind a partial realization of
his ideals. There is not space here to go into the
discussion of Lanier's theory of verse, nor to point
out in detail the original work he did as a poet in
the field he laid out for himself. Suffice it to say
that his best poems move to the cadence of a tune.
He probably chanted his words as he composed
them. Sometimes in his briefer poems, as the *Evening Song*, there is a lilt like the singing of a bird,
and sometimes the lyric cry, and yet again in his

longer poems the involved harmony of an orchestra. No other American poet save Poe has such musical effects, and Poe's melodies are simple by the side of the complex and subtle harmonies of Lanier. Lanier did not live to work out his ideas, but who knows but that some poet will make his work the starting point of the greater poetry of the future?

If Lanier and Poe were not far apart in their ideas of the formal side of poetry, they were far removed from each other in the substance of their work, no less than in their lives and characters. Both of them struggled with disease and poverty, both of them died in early life, and both lie buried in the same cemetery in Baltimore. But there the likeness ends. In the complete mastery of his art and of his material, Poe was incomparably greater than Lanier—in this respect there is all the difference of perfection and imperfection, of achievement and aspiration. In purity of character, in a holy regard for the sacred institutions of society, in the love for whatsoever things are excellent and of good report, and in the range and sweep of his mind and imagination, Lanier was immeasurably Poe's superior. In the loftiness of his moral character and in the richness of his spiritual endowment, as well as in his sense of the glory of the poet's work, Lanier takes his rank with Milton and the great modern poets of England and New England. In a memorable passage in the *English Novel* he says:

"Cannot one say with authority to the young artist, whether working in stone, in color, in tones or in character forms of the novel: so far from dreading that your moral purpose will interfere with your beautiful creation, go forward in the clear conviction that, unless you are suffused—soul and body, one might say—with that moral purpose which finds its largest expression in love—that is, the love of all things in their proper relation—unless you are suffused with this love, do not dare to meddle with beauty; unless you are suffused with truth, wisdom, goodness and love, abandon the hope that the ages will accept you as an artist."

His own life and work coincided with the spirit of these words. There was nothing abnormal or Bohemian in his temperament. The story of his relation to his wife suggests that of the Brownings and the Hawthornes. Among half a dozen expressions of his love, *My Springs* is the most notable:

"In the heart of the hills of life I know
Two springs that with unbroken flow
Forever pour their lucent streams
Into my soul's fair Lake of Dreams.

.   .   .   .

"Always when faith with stifling stress
Of grief hath died in bitterness,
I gaze in my two springs and see
A faith that smiles immortally.

"Always, when art, on perverse wing,
Flies where I cannot hear him sing,
I gaze in my two springs and see
A charm that brings him back to me.

.   .   .   .

"O Love, O Wife, thine eyes are they,
My Springs, from out whose shining gray
Issue the sweet celestial streams
That feed my life's bright Lake of Dreams.

"Oval and large and passion pure
And gray and wise and honor sure,
Soft as a dying violet breath,
Yet calmly unafraid of death.

.   .   .   .

"Dear eyes, dear eyes! and rare complete—
Being heavenly sweet and earthly sweet—
I marvel that God made you mine,
For when he frowns, 'tis then ye shine!"

The love that bound him to his family and friends broadened out into a love for mankind. Love was to him the solution of all problems, especially of industrial problems as set forth in *The Symphony*. Against the tyrannies of commerce, love, through the instruments of an orchestra, voices its protest in behalf of human brotherhood. And Lanier came to see that the very essence of Christianity was Love.

He reacted against the Calvinism of his youth to as great an extent as Holmes did. In his letters, as in his poems *Remonstrance* and *Crystal,* we see his hatred of bigotry and narrowness, and his worship of the Master. All art and science and nature were so many roads to God, and Christ was the Incarnate Word. It is not remarkable that the *Ballad of the Trees and the Master* should have found its way into modern hymn-books, or that it should be sung so often during Passion Week:

"Into the woods my Master went,
Clean forspent, forspent.
Into the woods my Master came,
Forspent with love and shame.
But the olives they were not blind to him,
The little gray leaves were kind to him:
The thorn tree had a mind to him,
When out of the woods he came.

"Out of the woods my Master went,
And he was well content.
Out of the woods my Master came,
Content with death and shame.
When death and shame would woo him last,
From under the trees they drew him—last:
'Twas on a tree they slew him—last
When out of the woods he came."*

But the most original poems that Lanier wrote—original alike in art and in conception—are *Sunrise* and *The Marshes of Glynn,* two of a series he planned to write on the marshes near Brunswick, Ga. The former, written when he was in the last stages of consumption, is marked to some extent by Lanier's limitations as a poet, his tendency to conceits, his subordination of poetry to musical effects, his straining after utterance that is beyond him. This criticism does not hold, however, with regard to the passage on the dawn, nor to almost the whole of *The Marshes of Glynn.* One might be sure of Lanier's fame if there were no other poem than this.

*Copyrighted by Mary Day Lanier and Charles Scribner's Sons.
Vol. 7—4.

Here aspiration is achievement. We have something of Wordsworth's spiritual exaltation, of Emerson's optimism, and of Whitman's cosmic imagination:

"The world lies east: how ample, the marsh and the sea and the sky!
A league and a league of marsh-grass, waist-high, broad in the blade,
Green, and all of a height, and unflecked with a light or a shade,
Stretch leisurely off, in a pleasant plain,
To the terminal blue of the main.

"Oh, what is abroad in the marsh and the terminal sea?
Somehow my soul seems suddenly free
From the weighing of fate and the sad discussion of sin,
By the length and the breadth and the sweep of the marshes of Glynn.

"Ye marshes, how candid and simple and nothing-withholding and free
Ye publish yourselves to the sky and offer yourselves to the sea!
Tolerant plains, that suffer the sea and the rains and the sun,
Ye spread and span like the catholic man who hath mightily won
God out of knowledge and good out of infinite pain
And sight out of blindness and purity out of a stain.

"As the marsh-hen secretly builds on the watery sod,
Behold I will build me a nest on the greatness of God:
I will fly in the greatness of God as the marsh-hen flies
In the freedom that fills all the space 'twixt the marsh and the skies:
By so many roots as the marsh-grass sends in the sod
I will heartily lay me a-hold on the greatness of God:
Oh, like to the greatness of God is the greatness within
The range of the marshes, the liberal marshes of Glynn.

"And the sea lends large, as the marsh: lo, out of his plenty the sea
Pours fast: full soon the time of the flood-tide must be:
Look how the grace of the sea doth go
About and about through the intricate channels that flow
        Here and there,
            Everywhere,
Till his waters have flooded the uttermost creeks and the low-lying
        lanes,
And the marsh is meshed with a million veins,
That like as with rosy and silvery essences flow
    In the rose-and-silver evening glow.

            "Farewell, my lord Sun!
The creeks overflow: a thousand rivulets run
'Twixt the roots of the sod; the blades of the marsh-grass stir;
Passeth a hurrying sound of wings that westward whir;
Passeth, and all is still; and the currents cease to run;
And the sea and the marsh are one.

"How still the plains of the waters be!
The tide is in his ecstasy.
The tide is at his highest height:
    And it is night.
And now from the Vast of the Lord will the waters of sleep
Roll in on the souls of men,
But who will reveal to our waking ken
The forms that swim and the shapes that creep
    Under the waters of sleep?
And I would I could know what swimmeth below when the tide
    comes in
On the length and the breadth of the marvellous marshes of Glynn."

Not the least remarkable point about Lanier's poetry is that it was written at a time when, throughout the English-speaking world, the drift was all against romantic poetry. It may be truly said that Lanier was the last of the Nineteenth century romantics. The tendency in fiction, as in poetry, was towards realism—from sentiment to reason. Never has there been a time when so many well-trained poets were writing as during the last quarter of the century. Lanier felt their defects, however, when he referred to "the feeble magazine lyrics —those little diffuse prettinesses and dandy kickshaws of verse. * * * None of them ever attempt anything great."

There is scarcely a Southern state that has not a poet who displays conscientious and skillful workmanship—and occasionally, we have a suggestion of the best poetry. Perhaps the best of all these is Lanier's friend, John B. Tabb. There is scarcely a month that does not bring one or more of his poems, always polished, always clever, and frequently highly imaginative in their conception. There is no better illustration of his work than the lines on Lanier:

"The dewdrop holds the heaven above,
    Wherein a lark, unseen,
Outpours a rhapsody of love
    That fills the space between.

"My heart a dewdrop is, and thou,
Dawn-spirit, far away,
Fillest the void between us now
With an immortal lay."

As Father Tabb celebrated Lanier, so the late
John Henry Boner, of North Carolina, wrote what
is, perhaps, the best tribute to Poe in the poem entitled *Poe's Cottage at Fordham.* Boner likewise
wrote of "the lightwood fire" of his native state,
and a younger poet, John Charles McNeill, of the
same state, who died like so many other poets in
the dawn of a brilliant career, left behind a volume
entitled *Songs, Merry and Sad,* with many exquisite
lyrics of love, and of life on the farm where he spent
his boyhood. In the same state Professor Benjamin
Franklin Sledd, of Wake Forest College, has written
poems characterized by deep and original feeling
and by suggestions of the greater poets of all languages with whom he has a scholar's and a poet's
fellowship. In Alabama Samuel Mintern Peck has
written with decided success the *vers de société, in-*
troducing into this country the forms of verse cultivated so successfully by Dobson and Gosse in England. In Georgia William H. Hayne has followed the
example of his father in cultivating the muses,
though far less industriously; and Robert Loveman
helps to keep the spark of poetry alive in a state
that has, since the war, furnished so large a share
of Southern writers. In South Carolina the late
Carlyle McKinley, in the midst of the busy life of a
journalist, now and then wrote a poem of real worth,
as, for instance, his *Sapelo.*

In Kentucky, too, as if to match the delicate work
of James Lane Allen in prose, Madison Cawein has
enrolled himself among the first of contemporary
poets. Cawein has attracted the attention of William Dean Howells and the English critic, Edmund

Gosse. In his endeavor to capture some hints of the evasive ideal beauty and the truthful impassioned rendition of the actual rich beauty of the world of nature, he has kept up the tradition of Keats and Shelley. Now and then he has expressed with real poetic imagination a childlike sense of the wonder and bloom of the world, as when he says:

"There are fairies. I could swear
I have seen them busy where
Rose leaves loose their scented hair,
In the moonlight weaving—weaving
Out of starshine and the dew
Glinting gown and shimmering shoe;
Or within a glow-worm lair,
From the dark earth slowly heaving
Mushrooms whiter than the moon,
On whose tops they sit and croon,
With their grig-lke mandolins,
To fair fairy ladykins,
Leaning from the window sill
Of a rose or daffodil . . .
Shod with hush and winged with fleetness,
You may see the Little People,
'Round and round the drowsy steeple
Of a belfried hollyhock,
Clothed in phlox and four-o'clock,
Gay of gown and pantaloon,—
Dancing by the glimmering moon."

There is no better general characterization of his poetry than that by Edmund Gosse:

"He brings the ancient gods to Kentucky, and it is marvelous how quickly they learn to be at home there. Here is Bacchus, with a spicy fragment of calamus root in his hand trampling down the blue-eyed grass, and skipping, with the air of a hunter born, into the thicket to escape Artemis, whose robes * * * startle the humming birds, silence the green tree frogs and fill the hot air with the perfumes of peppermint and pennyroyal. It is a queer landscape, but one of new natural beauties, frankly and sympathetically discovered, and it forms a *mise en scene* which, I make bold to say, would have scandalized neither Keats nor Spenser."

In such poetry—notable alike for its artistry and its poetic feeling—one sees the promise of the future of Southern poetry. When the present age of criticism has passed, when the South has become adjusted to its new life, and when again the great poets shall be heard in England and America, we may confidently expect the coming of a great creative era. What Hayne said of Simms is largely true of Southern poets as a whole: "Circumstances were against him. He never spoke out."

The story of their conflicts with adverse circumstances is a sad one, but inspiriting, and prophetic of better days. When there is throughout the South a keener appreciation of literary art, when the perspective of time is brought to bear on Southern romance and experience, great poets will arise to take their place among the great singers of the America of the future. By all considerations of climate, temperament and richness of poetic material, the South is the inevitable home of poetry.

BIBLIOGRAPHY.—Baskervill: *Southern Writers;* Link: *Pioneers of Southern Literature;* Mims: *Life of Sidney Lanier;* Trent: *Southern Writers* and *Life of William Gilmore Simms;* Weber: *Southern Poets;* Poems of Timrod, Hayne, Lanier, Margaret J. Preston, Ryan, Maurice Thompson, Tabb, Madison Cawein.

EDWIN MIMS,
Professor of English Literature, Trinity College, and Editor of the South Atlantic Quarterly.

CHAPTER III.

THE FOLK-LORE OF THE SOUTH.

ROBABLY the oldest legend relating to the history of the United States is that of Virginia Dare, the first child born of English parents on the soil of North America, and one of the colony which so mysteriously disappeared from Roanoke Island between the years 1587 and 1590. It is declared that she grew into fair maidenhood among friendly Indians and was changed by the sorcery of a rejected Indian lover into a white doe. As such she bore a charmed life, until love, triumphing over magic, restored her to human form, when she was slain by a silver arrow shot by a cruel chief. Throughout the South, since then, to see a white doe is an evil omen, and the hunters in regions where deer abound, believe that only a silver arrow will kill a white deer. Furthermore the first Scuppernong vine known to history, found on the mainland of the Carolinas in 1581, bore grapes with white skins, white pulp and white juice from which white wine was made. There are other Scuppernong vines which bear grapes having dark purple skins, yielding a reddish juice and making a red wine. These are said to be seedlings from the mother vine, and the changed color was wrought by the blood of Virginia Dare when slain by the silver arrow.

Perhaps there are few in the South who now believe these legends. Yet the South is rich in folklore of every kind, and when its civilization was at its best, the people held superstitions which were simply and candidly expressed, and beliefs common to most people were held more intensely than in

any other part of our land.   Everything was an omen
of good or bad luck.

They had their ghost tales also.   Hayne, the pa-
triot-martyr of Revolutionary times, on his way to
execution, passed the house of his sister-in-law.
Standing at the window she cried out to him in
agony, "Return, return to us."   He replied, "I will
if I can," and walked on.   At that window at night-
fall one may still hear a ghostly voice, and on the
stairs and in the hall, footsteps as of a man returning, never going down, always going up.   Near the
city of Charleston, South Carolina, is a certain country road on one part of which, it is said, may be
seen in the morning and evening twilight, a big black
dog, bounding along.   He attacks no one, makes no
sound, and disappears at the end of his chosen run,
as mysteriously as he appeared at the beginning.   He
has withstood every effort either to cajole or to shoot
him.

These are typical of the folk-lore of the vicinity
of Charleston with its traditions, chiefly English,
but with enough of the Huguenot to give French
names to most of the old families of South Carolina.   New Orleans with its French and Spanish
traditions, with a history that is scarcely to be differentiated from romance, with its Creole, or white
French-speaking population, how could it avoid being likewise rich in folk-lore?   How otherwise could
it be with a city whose paternal French government
in the old colonial days sent ships freighted with
girls to become wives of the settlers and to "anchor
the roving *courier de bois* into sturdy colonists"?
The folk-tales founded upon the coming of these
ships, first with the "Correction girls" and later
with the "Casket girls," have furnished bases for
many a story of higher literary type.   Haunted
houses are still pointed out in the French quarter,

and ghost stories abound in the minds of the imaginative Creoles. Latin ecclesiastical institutions have persisted, and there are held superstitions galore regarding marriage, the baptism of children and the burial of the dead, as simply and as candidly expressed as those of the Charlestonians. Never will a mother accompany her first born to the church to be christened. Seldom will she accompany any of them. Nowhere are God-parents held in higher regard in the popular mind; and who that has been in New Orleans has not heard of the Church of St. Roch, the shrine to which lovesick girls and young married people make pilgrimages? Is there any city in our country where All Saints' day is so generally celebrated as in the Crescent City? There is among the local folk customs one that is characteristic of New Orleans, if not peculiar to it; that is *lagnappe,* a present proportioned to the value of the purchase, passing from the dealer to the customer. Few indeed are the sales in market or grocery from day to day, that are not accompanied with *lagnappe.*

At a time, not a generation ago, when folk-lore as an aid to the study of anthropology and kindred sciences, was beginning to attract the attention of American students, before it was fully decided what the general term ''folk-lore'' included, and it was supposed that folk-lore was rare if not entirely absent from the texture of American life, a certain writer in a scientific journal, gravely asserted that, with few exceptions, there were neither local legends nor popular superstitions from one end of our land to the other; yet he quickly corrected his hasty statement by admitting the existence of two classes of native Americans who might supply in part these deficiencies: the Indians and the Southern negroes. He overlooked (naturally, for little was then known of them) three millions of white ''mountaineers'' occupying the region sometimes known as Appalachian America, forty thousand square miles of territory included within the states of Virginia, West Virginia, Kentucky, Tennessee, North and South Carolina, Georgia and Alabama. In writing her delightful stories about these mountaineers, Miss Mary N. Murfree (Charles Egbert Craddock) brought these people to the attention of a wide circle of readers but in such a way as to show that there was a reserve of knowledge in her possession, and that she was capable of making a still more valuable contribution to the study of folk-lore and folk customs in America.

These people have a religion, politics, a moral code, folk tales, folk songs, folk customs, and folk ideas, chiefly derived from the old country, even as in their speech (they are the people of the ''we-uns'' and ''you-uns'') are to be found survivals of the English of Chaucer's time. Occupying the same region as that from which the Cherokees were removed about three-quarters of a century ago to a permanent home west of the Mississippi River, they have inherited the Indian's knowledge of woodcraft and folk medicine, to which they have added what they have retained of the pioneer's belief in signs and omens and the practice of witchcraft and whatever traits the pioneers brought over the seas. The rough-and-tumble fight of the Scotch, and the English square stand-up-knock-down boxing match, were resorted to for the purpose of settling disputes until the War of Secession introduced the rifle and pistol. Then arose the ''feud'' in which survives the primitive idea of kin responsibility for the life of the kinsman. Some English ballads survive from three hundred years ago, ballads of lords and ladies, of cuckoos and nightingales, sung by men and women who have no idea that the words used have any meaning and will apologize for their lack of sense. In localities where Scotch family names are common, Scotch ballads are still sung with a Scotch accent to music much like that of Scotland, which frequently drops into a relative minor like the negro plantation music. There are survivals of the wandering minstrels, fiddlers and banjo players who go about making "ballets" to commemorate the deeds of the more notorious feudists, or other incidents of the homely life of the mountaineer, and thus are produced genuine folk songs. The "hymns" they sing at their religious meetings are folk song too, and they have nursery rhymes, folk tales and many proverbs full of home-made philosophy, which would delight the heart of the most ardent collector of folk-lore. "What is to be will be, and that that a'int to be might happen," sums up their fatalism. They do not like to believe of themselves that they are superstitious, but one of them may well say of another "You're as superstitious as some ol' woman that smokes a pipe and don't know the war is over. If the moon knowed what all you-uns hold hit responsible fur, hit'd git scared and fall down out o' the sky." And yet the belief in lunar influences is universal among them. Even their "moonshine" whiskey seems to come within the domain of folk-lore. It originated in the pioneer period at a time when a surplus of corn could not be economically transsported across the mountains unless converted into whiskey, and before the right of a man to manufacture what he pleased was disputed. It is inexplicable to their minds, that the government should have anything to say about it, or should have the right to euforce a tax by drastic measures, involving personal freedom and even life itself.

In their resort to charms and amulets they furnish some choice specimens for the collection of the folk-lorist. The Indian arrowheads found in such abundance in their region are too readily assignable to their true origin to be regarded as "elf-bolts" as in the British Isles, though the more perfect specimens may be worn as ornaments or preserved as relics of some Indian encounter in the early days. But in the mountains of Virginia are found certain cruciform pebbles, a puzzle to geologists and mineralogists, but much in demand by the snake hunters, "moonshiners" and ginseng gatherers, which are worn, not openly by way of ornament, but secretly as a charm against evil of all kinds, for the healing of the sick and by young women as love charms. They must be preserved in secret and to lose one portends evil. There are many legends as to the origin of these "fairy stones" as they are called, though the mountaineers have apparently little recognition of fairies in their folk-lore. The generally accepted one is that the news of the crucifixion was brought to Virginia by supernatural agents who made these stone crosses as mementoes of the event. Another is that in the remote past these stones were showered upon the Indians of the region to turn them from heathenism to Christianity.

They have many signs regarding the weather and implicit faith in the portents of "the ruling days," that is, the twelve days from the 25th of December (Christmas) to Old Christmas (the old English Twelfth Night), each of which rules the weather of a month of the coming year; in the portents of "Ground Hog" day and the prognostications derived from the goosebone, and from the hog milt (or "melt" as it is pronounced). "There will be as many snows in the winter as there were fogs in August." Friday is always the fairest or foulest day of the week; and February always borrows four-teen days from March to pay them back in the same kind of weather in April. The first thunder in the spring awakens the snakes and lizards. Good Friday is the best day for planting beans or garden truck, though it is a wonder that they know when the day comes, as they know nothing of its religious significance. How many of these weather signs have originated among them and how many are traceable to the Indians or to the old country are problems for the scientific folk-lorist.

In many parts of this region there are place names which suggest that they might furnish a clew to some interesting local legends, and many of these clews have been followed up with good success. The names Thumping Dick Hollow, Shake Rag Hollow, Hell-fer-Sartin, and a host of other geographical names in this region suggest volumes that might result from an exhaustive study of the folk-lore of the mountaineers.

The folk-lore of the Indians is of scientific rather than literary interest and as such the richness of the South in material of this characer can be but hastily touched upon. The folk tales of the Indians of the Southland included genesis and migration legends, probably a part of their once complete sacred myths; plant and animal lore, local traditions, with a few songs, chiefly such as had to do with their religious festivals and dances, with perhaps some lullabies. They had, of course, folk customs and games, a wide range of woodcraft and medicine lore, and many superstitions. Most of these were common to the North American Indians everywhere. All of the Indians of the Southland have left traces of their occupancy of the country in an unusually large number of place-names in the Southern states. That local Indian legends were attached to these various places seems evident, for to the Indian mind every feature of natural scenery has been at one time or another suggestive of some story, it may be of some portion of the great original cosmogenetic myth, which thus became expanded and localized and assumed a more definite character. Such an approach to the study of Indian folk-lore is sure to result in interesting discoveries, perhaps in the correction of some popular errors. For example, Port Tobacco, Maryland, seems to have been so named because it was in the midst of a tobacco-growing country, and its name to be of English origin; it is in fact an English corruption of the Indian name "Potopaco." The names of the postoffice towns of Ball, in Louisiana, Mississippi and Texas; Ball Ground, in Georgia and Mississippi; and Ballplay in Tennessee, refer to sites where the Indian ball game was played.

The Cherokees were the mountaineers of the Southern Indians. When, near the middle of the Nineteenth century they were removed west of the Mississippi River, a considerable body remained behind in the Carolina mountains, and now, to the number of about two thousand, scattered in four counties adjacent to their reservation, preserve some of their myths and legends perhaps better than their fellow Indians of the West. When it is recalled that there were about four hundred of these Indians from the mountains of North Carolina in the service of the Confederate army, it will be observed that this remnant of the Cherokees is no negligible quantity in even a hasty survey of the folk-lore of the South. For these Indians, although adopting the dress of the white man and many institutions of the Anglo-Saxons, were still Indians at heart, and the war served to bring out all the latent characteristics of the Indian. They consulted an oracle stone before they set out to the seat of war, to learn if they might expect to return in safety; they celebrated their start with a war dance in which they exhibited themselves in all the characteristic tribal paint and feathers; they repeated the dance from time to time in the course of the war, and held their famous green-corn dance (their great thanksgiving harvest festival), and their ball games; and on one occasion, under great provocation, they scalped one or two Federal soldiers whom they had slain.

It is not remarkable that Indian folk tales galore should be found in the mountains of North Carolina. Those which have been thus far collected and published, chiefly for scientific purposes, have many characteristics that are common to the myths and legends of all Indian tribes, or in fact to those of primitive peoples everywhere, and they are especially interesting as having something in common with the folk tales of the plantation negroes which we shall soon consider. They tell how in the conception of the Indian mind, the world was made; how the first fire originated; the origin of corn and game; of disease and medicine; of the moon and thunder, and so on. For example, take the shortest of them which tells of the origin of the milky way: Some people had a corn mill from which they found one morning that their meal was being stolen in the night. Finding the tracks of a dog nearby, and suspecting who the thief was, they watched the next night, and when the dog came and began to eat the meal from the bowl they sprang out and gave the dog a severe beating. As he ran off howling to his home in the North, the meal dropped from his mouth leaving a white trail where now we see the Milky Way, still called by the Indians, "Where the dog ran."

As in this so in the other Indian myths, animals figure largely, and they are described as possessing very human traits. So it is with the stories of all primitive peoples who are accustomed to observe the characteristics of animals which their religious systems regard as differing in no essential from human kind. They are organized into tribes, and have their chiefs and town houses, their councils and their games. And so rabbit, terrapin, deer, bear, fox and wolf, appear in the animal tales of the Indians to reappear in the tales of the plantation negroes. In the Indian tales of the origin of disease and medicine, and of the ball game of the birds and animals, there is a wealth of animal and plant lore.

Except in a scientific way another remnant of the Indian tribes, the Seminoles of Florida, makes no important contribution to the folk-lore of the South.

Of the negro population of the South three divisions may be recognized, distinguishable chiefly by their dialect. There are the negroes of the uplands of Virginia, the Carolinas and Georgia, extending also into Kentucky, Tennessee and Northern Alabama and Mississippi. This is the region of tobacco and corn. There are the Creole negroes of New Orleans and lower Louisiana. And there are Gullah negroes occupying the Atlantic tide-water region from the mouth of the Chesapeake down to the northeast coast of Florida; the land of rice and sea-island cotton. The folk tales of these three, when fully collated and compared will doubtless show the same general characteristics, but an insuperable bar to the comparative study of these folk tales will be found for some time to come in the difficulties presented by the Gullah and Creole dialects or patois. For the *Negro Myths of the Georgia Coast,* written in the Gullah by the late C. C. Jones, Jr., reached but few readers beyond the region where Gullah is known and understood, while the negro speech of the first division mentioned above has taken its place in the literature of the South and has

been widely read in the stories of a host of Southern
writers. And the Creole or Gumbo dialect is,
through the stories of Mr. George W. Cable, known
to a smaller number of readers. Not unlikely there
is a larger amount of the African surviving in the
folk-lore of the Gullah as there is in their speech,
than in the other two divisions, though the students
who have given attention to the Gullah, claim that
in its vocabulary it is for the most part English
of two centuries ago, with some traces of the Scotch
as found among the white mountaineers. On the
other hand the influence of the French upon the
speech of the Creole negroes is very marked. We
are, however, here concerned with folk-lore and not
with dialect; and while in that of the negro of all
three divisions we find much of the African that survives in their superstitions, in their folk tales there
is another influence quite apparent, and that is the
Indian. And there is no reason why this should
occasion surprise when it is recalled that Indians
were enslaved as well as negroes in the colonies
previous to the Revolution. This was a frequent
casus belli between the colonists and the Redmen,
and in South Carolina as late as 1708 the Indian
population furnished a quarter of the whole body
of slaves. The negroes have a large amount of
the Indian knowledge of woodcraft, weather wisdom
and folk medicine, and in their essential features
the Indian animal myths agree wonderfully with
the plantation tales of "Uncle Remus." The Cherokees said of the rabbit that he was always on hand
whenever there was any mischief brewing. With
the Creole negroes "Compair Lapin" and "Compair
Bouki" furnish the greatest amount of incidents.
With the Gullah, "Buh Rabbit" plans to 'tack upon
"Buh Allegatuh"; "Buh Fowlhawk" lays plans to

catch the sun; and "Buh Turkey Buzza'd" has an important part to play in the drama of life.

It was the opening of a new department in literature when Joel Chandler Harris told his first stories of "Uncle Remus." His was the first attempt at anything like a collection of plantation folk tales "which had become a part of the domestic history of every Southern family"; stories which narrated . contests of wit between the rabbit, the terrapin, the bear, the wolf and the fox. In these contests "Brer Rabbit" and "Brer Terrapin" are the embodiment of weakness and harmlessness, and they triumph, not through virtue but through helplessness, not by malice but by mischievousness. The stories were never intended as contributions to a scientific study of folk-lore, but are nevertheless valuable as such. Variants of these stories are to be found in various parts of the world, sufficient to establish theories for the scientific folk-lorist. Even the famous mediæval folk tale of Reynard the Fox may be regarded as having had its influence on the plantation tales. But the most remarkable number of variants of the stories purporting to be told by Uncle Remus, may be cited from Brazil. The theory that they were obtained by the negroes from the South American Indians seems scarcely tenable, however; it would appear more likely that the South American Indians had obtained them from the negro slaves in Brazil, and both those of the South American and the North American slave states had brought them from Africa. It is even possible that the story of Reynard the Fox had been received from the Dutch in Africa before the coming of the negroes who had heard it, to the western shores.

All these are difficult questions to settle. To one fact, however, these folk tales of the plantation bear testimony, and that is to the childlike happiness of the negro under the slave system. Such humorous stories could never have been told by a people in such oppression as is so often depicted as the lot of the plantation negroes before the war; nor would they be related now by the Uncle Remuses who have survived those days, with such zest and pleasure, did they recall days of sorrow and grief.

Time and space would fail to give any comprehensive view of the superstitions of the negroes. Everything furnishes a sign and a warning for them. An African origin is undoubted in that particular, and there are numberless survivals of actual Fetichism such as may be studied at first hand among the native African tribes. The most powerful implement of the negro superstition is "cunjer," which reaches its acute stage in the system of "Vouhdooh" or as it is usually corrupted "Hoodoo." This was brought to Louisiana from San Domingo, but it may be traced back to the original home of the West Indian negroes in Africa. It was with a knowledge of the superstition of the negro, approaching the scientific, that the "Ku Klux Klan" attempted to terrorize the negroes in the Reconstruction days to prevent the complete subjugation of the white men of the South to their former slaves.

So strong a hold has superstition upon the negroes of the South that it is impossible for his religion to be other than a folk-religion which suggests a wide field for inquiry and research. The chief form of expression for this religion is its hymnody, which has all the elements of folk song. The "hymns," if such they may be called, are never the composition of one man or one mind, but are a collection of separately improvised lines fixed in the popular memory by frequent repetition. Some of their camp-meeting songs, though lacking in dignity, have

strong rhythm and dramatic action, though they all
subordinate sense to sound; and this relation of
sense to sound directs attention at once to the music
to which they are wedded, which is a true folk music.
It has been charged that this music is African and
not American, but upon examination it proves to be
distinctly the result of American surroundings. It
is expressive of the life of the cotton-, rice-, tobacco-,
corn- and cane-field; of the cabin and of the river,
with an ecstatic religious vein far removed from any
African music. Nor is its weird pathos an expression of any sorrow in the slave life, but due rather to
the negro conception of religion.

In 1842 negro minstrelsy had its birth in a northern theatre in a mixed performance made up largely
of songs and dances typical of negro life and character; as a scientific presentation of plantation folk
lore (as was never intended) it was faulty, still it
served to introduce some phases of negro folk-lore
to the attention of a public ready to find amusement
in it; and this prepared the way for the work of
Stephen C. Foster, who is justly considered the
folk song genius of America; and it also prepared
the way for a later popular appreciation of Uncle
Remus when his time should come. Foster, although
born in the North was the son of a Virginian, and he
trained himself for the production of his peculiar
style of song by attending negro camp-meetings.
He wrote in all about one hundred and sixty songs
including "Oh, Susannah," "Old Uncle Ned," "My
Old Kentucky Home," "Massa's in de Cold, Cold
Ground," and "De Ol' Folks at Home," or "Suwanee Ribber," the latter being a negro corruption of
San Juan, the Spanish name for the St. John's River
in Florida. These are not folk-lore, excepting as
they have received folk-adoption, so to speak, but it
would be impossible to complete this survey of the

subject of folk-lore in the South without mentioning this phase, the approximately good imitation of the best folk song of the country. Nor should another folk song by adoption be overlooked. On the Fourth of July, 1861, while the Confederate army in Virginia was drawn up within hearing distance of the Federal army, General Kirby-Smith wrote that the booming of the Federal guns had been ringing a national salute. Powder was too scarce in the Confederate army at the time for any to be wasted in salutes, "but," wrote the general, "our bands have played 'Dixie' from one end of the line to the other." It is evident then that at that early period "Dixie" was the recognized national folk song of the Confederacy. The "Bonnie Blue Flag," though intended for that purpose, never supplanted the other in the hearts of the people. "Dixie" would appear to have all the characteristics of folk song. The name is undoubtedly a negro corruption of Mason and Dixon's Line, and it is a thoroughly negro conception of the land south of that line as a "land of cotton" with "cinnamon seas and sandy bottoms." But the truth is that the senseless words were written by a white man in the North, Dan Emmett, the son of a Virginian, for the use of the negro minstrels of which he was one of the founders; and the tune was probably appropriated from an old negro air. The people and the soldiers of the South liked it. It outlived the Southern Confederacy and now bids fair to become national.

About the time that "Dixie" became the national song of the Confederate army, the South contributed a war song to the Federal army.

> "Say, brothers will you meet us,
> On Canaan's happy shore ?"

with the refrain

> "Glory, glory hallelujah,
> Forever, evermore,"

was written some time before the war by a gentleman in Charleston, S. C., and was used at many
a Southern camp-meeting, and was naturally taken
up by the negro congregations.   It made its way
North and was found in some of the hymn books
there.   A Massachusetts regiment on its way to
the war, took it up and improvising lines to meet
the exigencies of the time, evolved, " John Brown's
Body Lies a-Mouldering in the Grave." It was
after it had spread through the Federal army that
Mrs. Julia Ward Howe was importuned to compose
more dignified words for it, and wrote

"Mine eyes have seen the glory of the coming of the Lord,"

a hymn of high order, of too high an order in fact
for it to supplant anything having the elements of
folk song about it.   For one great peculiarity of
folk song is that it is "of the people, by the people,
and for the people."

ARTHUR HOWARD NOLL,
University of the South, Sewanee.

CHAPTER IV.

THE SOUTH'S CONTRIBUTIONS TO THE NATION'S WIT AND HUMOR.

N 1897, a small volume on "Southern Writers" appeared. It was the work of the late Professor W. M. Baskervill, long professor of English literature in Vanderbilt University. It is a biographical study and critical appreciation of Irwin Russell, Joel Chandler Harris, Maurice Thompson, Sidney Lanier, George W. Cable and "Charles Egbert Craddock." Among these the writer whose work is distinctively humorous is Harris, better known as "Uncle Remus." Introducing his study of Harris, Baskervill said:

"Middle Georgia is the birthplace and home of the raciest and most original kind of Southern humor. In this quarter native material was first recognized and made use of. A school of writers arose who looked out of their eyes and listened with their ears, who took frank interest in things for their own sake, and had enduring astonishment at the most common. They seized the warm and palpitating facts of every-day existence, and gave them to the world with all the accompaniments of quaint dialect, original humor and Southern plantation life."

Twenty-seven years ago Henry Watterson, editor of the Louisville *Courier-Journal,* published a volume entitled *The Oddities in Southern Life and Character.* The extracts selected as most representative of Southern humor were prefaced by brief mention of the lives and works of the writers. In an examination of the entire field the preponderance of Georgia among these is found to be interesting and remarkable. Mr. Watterson secures his extracts from sixteen humorists, viz.: Augustus Baldwin Longstreet, Joel Chandler Harris, William

T. Thompson, Richard Malcolm Johnston, Joseph G.
Baldwin, Johnson J. Hooper, Davy Crockett, J.
Proctor Knott, Charles H. Smith, George W. Harris,
George W. Bagby, George D. Prentice, John E.
Hatcher, Albert Roberts and Alexander E. Sweet.
Of the sixteen, five were Georgians: Longstreet,
Thompson, Harris (Joel Chandler), Johnston and
Smith.   Hooper and Baldwin belong to Alabama;
Crockett, Roberts and Harris (George W.), to Ten-
nessee; Prentice, Knott and Hatcher to Kentucky;
Bagby to Virginia; Sweet to Texas. A complete list
of Southern authors of humor should include Judge
Joe C. Guild, who wrote *Old Times in Tennessee;*
Thomas B. Thorpe, whose home for many years was
in Louisiana, author of *The Hive of the Bee-Hunter;*
and Samuel A. Hammett, whose *Stray Yankee in
Texas* is full of bright humor.

From Mr. Watterson's list, Knott, Roberts and
Hatcher may be expunged. It was a single speech
made in Congress, the "Duluth Speech," that gave
Knott the title of humorist.   Hatcher and Roberts were newspaper paragraphers, whose humorous sketches were widely enjoyed and quoted.
Except as they were gathered into a few pages by
Mr. Watterson, these do not appear in book form.
Prentice belongs to the same class of writers of
witty, pungent paragraphs. During his lifetime they
were published in book form under the title *Prenticeana,* and bear the impress of genuine fun and wit.

The heyday of ante-bellum Southern humor was
from 1835 to 1855. In the first year named Judge
A. B. Longstreet published his *Georgia Scenes.* In
1840 William T. Thompson produced *Major Jones's
Courtship.* This was followed, in 1843, by his *Major
Jones's Chronicles of Pineville,* and in 1848 by his
Major Jones's Sketches of Travel. Though not pub-
lished until 1867, George W. Harris in 1843 began

the writing of his *Sut Lovingood* papers. In 1853
Joseph G. Baldwin published his *Flush Times of
Alabama and Mississippi.* In 1854 Thomas B.
Thorpe brought out *The Hive of the Bee-Hunter*, al-
though some of the same sketches had appeared in
1846 in *The Mysteries of the Backwoods.*

In any treatment of Southern humor, the first
place in rank and time is given to Judge Augustus
Baldwin Longstreet (1790-1870). He was preceded
by two Southern writers whose works, while not
distinctively humorous in character, have a sufficient
quantity of humor in some of their scenes and passages to make this a marked quality of their writings. These are William Byrd and Davy Crockett.
In *The History of the Dividing Line* and *A Journey
to the Land of Eden*, William Byrd (1674-1744), of
Virginia, interspersed his observations with a fine
wit and shrewd humor. Davy Crockett (1786-1836),
of Tennessee, in 1834, published his *Autobiography,*
which is pervaded with a dry wit and quaint humor.
The drolleries and eccentricities of the author are
reflected upon the pages of a book written in self-
defense.

Though he discharged successfully, at different
periods of his career, the offices of jurist, editor,
preacher and college president, it will be as the
author of *Georgia Scenes* that Longstreet will be
best and longest remembered. Riding a Georgia circuit as lawyer and judge, his lively sense of humor
caught the odd and picturesque shades of life about
him. Its humorous incidents were transferred to
the printed page; its eccentric characters were
sketched with a loving, but faithful, portrayal. For
popular appreciation they needed no accessories of
a glowing imagination. Printed first in a newspaper, the Augusta *Sentinel*, which he founded and edited, they appeared in book form in 1835. Without

the approbation of the author, several successive editions were brought out.

In becoming a Methodist preacher and college president, Judge Longstreet practically repudiated the work, regretting that he had ever written it. He came to look upon it as mere bagatelle, the diversion and pastime of some unemployed hours. It rose to plague him somewhat. Behind his back college boys dubbed him "Old Ned Brace." When as political leader in the Democratic party he essayed to instruct and guide voters, his political adversaries of the Whig party avowed that no man from whom emanated so undignified a book and so gross caricatures of his fellowman ought to presume to become a popular adviser. Seriously he contemplated offsetting the influence of the work by writing another *Georgia Scenes,* in which tears should be substituted for laughter. For his name and fame, it is doubtless fortunate that he did not execute the task outlined.

The masterpiece of *Georgia Scenes* is unquestionably "Ned Brace." Ned's drolleries and escapades inevitably provoke convulsive laughter. Though brief, *A Lincoln County Rehearsal* or *Georgia Theatrics,* is one of the happiest sketches. Upon one occasion, from being read in Congress, the story of this mock-fight became a successful substitute for argument. As an answer to a congressman hurling his harmless diatribes at the South, "Sunset" Cox sent to the clerk's desk a copy of the *Georgia Scenes,* and requested that *Georgia Theatrics* be read as his reply. It evoked uproarious laughter. The mad ravings of the combative congressman were effectually suppressed. Another favorite sketch is *The Fight.* Through all the intervening years "Ransy Sniffle" has survived as the most pronounced type of the trouble-maker between individuals or the families of a community. Another admirable sketch is *The*

Debating Society. This is not strictly a Georgia scene. One of the leading characters was George McDuffie, the statesman, while the scene, Willington Academy, was in South Carolina. Though to the refined taste the humor of these sketches may seem too rough and robust, nevertheless, as faithful transcripts of the time, they present the broad humor and fantastic speech of a borderland of civilization.

While Longstreet was a native Georgian and a graduate of Yale College, the most noted humorist of his Georgia contemporaries was born in Ohio and was self-educated. This was William Tappan Thompson (1812-1882). The humorists of the Old South were either lawyers or editors, and frequently were representative of both professions. As a boy in Philadelphia, Thompson became a printer. By way of Florida, where he studied law, he went to Georgia. In 1835 he became identified with Longstreet in publishing the *Sentinel.* The relationship was of brief duration. The success of Longstreet's humorous work is thought to have turned his partner's pen to humorous skits. After publishing the Augusta *Mirror* for a few years, Thompson, in Middle Georgia, began to publish and edit the Madison *Miscellany.* To its pages he committed the sketches, which were published as a book, *Major Jones's Courtship,* in 1840. The scenes and characters therein belong to the delightful rural life of the Old South. Major Joseph Jones is a vigorous, uneducated, unsophisticated product of plantation life. He is wildly in love with Mary Stallings, whose widowed mother owned a joining plantation. Mary has just returned from the Georgia Female College at Macon. The faithful lover is much concerned lest so attractive a young woman, with the acquisition of new ideas, has found new beaux. By the light of a pine-knot fire the major sits in company with Miss

Mary. In his doubt and excitement he spits so excessively and furiously on the glowing knot that there is ever-increasing prospect that the two lovers will be eventually enveloped in darkness—a catastrophe that finally happens. Before the confusion produced by the darkness ensues, Joseph is eager to ascertain whether Mary ''had any bows down to Macon.'' He is greatly perturbed as she confesses, and begins to name ''Matthew Mattix, Nat. Filosofy, Al. Geber, and a whole heap of fellers,'' whose pleasant company she did not hesitate to express her desire to enjoy anew speedily. The most amusing chapter of the book, illustrative of the wholesome merriment that pervades it, is that recounting the device employed by the major in popping the question.

Besides *Major Jones's Courtship*, Thompson wrote two other books of humor, with the same irrepressible major as protagonist. These were *Major Jones's Chronicles of Pineville* and *Major Jones's Sketches of Travel*. They are full of broad and rollicking fun, though unequal to his first work. Hotel experiences in Washington, Baltimore, Philadelphia and New York, with impressions of the sights and historic places of each city, are told in a mirthful and zestful way.

At the time Longstreet and Thompson were affording rich amusement by their sketches, there was a marked intellectual activity in Middle Georgia, of which the works of humor were an expression. After Longstreet had turned his back on the kind of writing that made him famous and that makes secure his name, he was urged to contribute to a literary magazine established in Georgia. In 1838 and 1839 the religious denominations of the state opened their higher institutions of learning. One of these, the Georgia Female College, which claims to be the first institution of the kind in the world, opened for the graduation of young women, it is noted, is referred to by Thompson.

Through Georgia, while Longstreet and Thompson were at work, one destined to take rank with them was pursuing his way from North Carolina to Alabama. This was Johnson Jones Hooper (1815-1862). He was a native of North Carolina and the son of a journalist. Having reached the then capital of Alabama, Tuskaloosa, he tarried only a few months. In Chambers county he began the study of law under a brother, and was admitted to the bar. However, his talents were almost immediately employed in editing the *Tallapoosa Banner,* at Dadeville. It was in this newspaper, published far in the interior, that his humorous articles first appeared. At once they attracted attention, and were copied widely. After a time he was again in Chambers county, where he practised law and edited the Chambers *Tribune.* It was while residing here, at LaFayette, the county seat, that he, in 1845, brought out his most famous work of humor : *The Adventures of Captain Simon Suggs, late of the Tallapoosa Volunteers; together with taking the Census and other 'Alabama Sketches. By a Country Editor.*

The model of Hooper's character, "Simon Suggs," was living at the time the book appeared. He was Bird Young, one of the first settlers of Tallapoosa county. Brewer's *Alabama* says: "The pen-pictures of Mr. Hooper probably have done an injustice to the reputation of Mr. Young. He was a plain man of much vitality and of native talent, but of fair standing as a man." Introducing his subject in the form of a biography, Hooper justifies the act by citing precedents. The biographies of candidates for the presidency, Jackson, Clay, Van Buren, Polk, had been written, for it was said, their "enemies will know enough to attack and their friends must know enough to defend." In the conclusion of the book Hooper takes leave of the wily old reprobate, who is running for office, with this appeal: "He waxes old. He needs an office, the emoluments of which shall enable him to relax his intellectual exertions. His military services, his numerous family, his long residence among you, his gray hairs, all plead for him. Remember him at the polls!"

Hooper finds "Simon Suggs" in his seventeenth year, the son of a "hard-shell" Baptist preacher, back in the red hills of Middle Georgia. The lad's shrewd insight, rascally methods and thorough self-possession are prophetic of his successful career in Alabama as wiry manipulator, pious imposter, venal wretch and imperturbable swash-buckler. After cheating a victim, with cool calculation he exclaims: "Honesty's the best policy. Honesty's the bright spot in a man's character. Honesty's the stake that Simon will allers tie to. What's a man without integrity?" When he has exhibited an unusually good example of brazen dishonesty, he concludes with some moral thoughts. After by foul methods getting an old Indian widow's land he exults: "Yes, there is a Providence. Ef a man says thar ain't no Providence you may be sure thar's something wrong here"—striking in the region of his vest-pocket—"and that man will swindle you, ef he can—certin."

There is sunniness as well as hideousness in the pages of *Simon Suggs*. The grotesque and the amusing are equally presented—a little embellished, but always ridiculous either in scene or in character. Like Longstreet, Hooper came to regret that he had ever turned his pen and talents to depicting the humorous characters and incidents about him. He felt his productions to have been an insurmountable impediment to political preferment, which he coveted.

An Alabama contemporary of Hooper was Joseph Glover Baldwin (1815-1864). He was a native of Virginia, and upon attaining his majority he migrated to Mississippi. After a sojourn of two years in Mississippi he moved to Sumter county, Alabama. In that state he lived and practised law until he moved to California in 1854. His enduring monument is his humorous book, *Flush Times of Alabama and Mississippi,* which was published in 1853. Some of the sketches he had already contributed to *The Southern Literary Messenger,* of Richmond. In literary excellence and sustained vigor, *Flush Times* is superior to Baldwin's predecessors in this species of literary workmanship. The opening sketch, "Ovid Bolus," is a masterly presentation of the dexterous and accomplished liar, a man who drew on his imagination for his facts and on his memory for his flights of fancy. Within recent times, in the national councils, the book has been drawn on for material with which to make a point or to flay an antagonist.

One of the most delightful character sketches in *Flush Times* is the portrayal of the Virginian, haughty, self-consequential, who might breathe in Alabama, but who really lived in Virginia, never was acclimated elsewhere, maintained his citizenship back in the Old Dominion, where his treasure was and his heart also. The conceited lawyer, still a fledgling, has his make-believe skill and learning rudely treated by an old member of the bar. Opposing counsel in a suit for slander, in dismay and disgrace he flies before the withering ridicule of old Cæsar Kasm, known to the wags of the bar as old Sar Kasm. In fact, all the characters commend themselves with overflowing merriment.

As the period around which to weave his sketches, Baldwin chose the so-called shinplaster era, when commerce flourished upon a fictitious basis of universal credit and indefinite financial extension. He introduced pictures of the wildness of speculation and the boldness of adventure that characterized the times. He made disclosures of the frailties of men in selfish indulgence and business peculation. However, above the weakness and wickedness, above the fun and the mirth, there runs through the book the strong, practical insight of the man of the world which the man of letters touches and illumines for the merriment of his fellows. There is genuine sympathy throughout. Satire, ridicule, sarcasm find little place in its pages. It is true, shams and follies, rascalities and villainies are held up to view, but to the touches of subtle humor there are added suggestions of gentle charity. There is an originality and spontaneity about the work which made it immensely popular in its day, and causes it still to be read and quoted.

Baldwin never felt ashamed of his production, and after his removal to California he saw another era of "flush times," and thought to make likewise a faithful and pleasing transcript of them. A beginning was made in a contribution to the same periodical that published his earlier effort. The cataclysm of civil war forbade the carrying out of the purpose.

The London *Westminster Review,* in 1852, had an article on American literature. Speaking of a school of comic writers in the South and West it said: "In this school T. B. Thorpe, of New Orleans, and Johnson J. Hooper, of Alabama, are most conspicuous; and we know not where to turn for anything more rich, original, indigenous than much of the racy mockery and grotesque extravagance of their pages."

Thomas Bangs Thorpe (1815-1878) was a native of Massachusetts. In 1836 he went to Louisiana, as

Thos. B. Thorpe.

he said, in search of health and wealth. In New Orleans at once he became associated with the press, at various intervals, for seventeen years editing newspapers. The strange, wild life about him had a romantic tinge. Its charm appealed to his appreciation of the picturesque, while his sense of humor saw in the odd characters with whom he was thrown in contact excellent material for sketching.

It was while guest of a wealthy planter that he found the subject first utilized. Tom Owen, a lazy, shiftless, eccentric character, withal witty, was pointed out to Thorpe. With axe on shoulder and buckets on arm, he was going in search of a bee-tree with its wild honey. For the novelty of the experience, Thorpe accompanied the man whose intimacy with bee life was so close that, as he declared, ''on a clear day he could see a bee a mile away, easy!'' The result was the sketch *Tom Owen, the Bee-Hunter.* With its publication in William T. Porter's *Spirit of the Times* the writer achieved a remarkable popularity. This, with other sketches, some humorous and other descriptive, appeared in 1846 as a book, *The Mysteries of the Backwoods.*

In 1854 Thorpe published the *Hive of the Bee-Hunter,* a repository of sketches, many of which had appeared in the previous publication. In the main, they are the rich fruit of the pen of a nature-lover whose sense of humor has not been dulled. For delightful humor, *The Big Bear in Arkansas, A Hoosier in Search of Justice, Major Gasden's Story, The Great Four-Mile Day, The Way Americans Go Down Hill* and *A Piano in Arkansas* rank with the best specimens.

Tennessee's representative humorist was George Washington Harris (1814-1869). He was a native of Pennsylvania, whence he was brought a mere lad by his parents to Tennessee. As a mechanical genius he early attracted attention. He became a jeweler's apprentice, a steamboat captain, an inventor and a writer of political articles. The articles were contributed to the Knoxville *Argus*. In 1843 his humorous articles began to appear in William T. Porter's *Spirit of the Times,* over the pen-name "Sugar Tom." When Elbridge G. Eastman, former editor of *The Argus*, became editor of the Nashville *Union and American*, Harris wrote for his friend other humorous sketches. It was in this paper that the "Sut Lovingood" articles for the most part appeared. They ran at intervals until the war. It was not until 1867 that they were gathered together and published as a book.

The local color of the *Sut Lovingood Yarns*, the title of Harris's book, belongs to East Tennessee. The characters are grotesque in their exaggerations. In some of the passages of the work there are suggestions that offend. There is an indelicacy repulsive to those of squeamish tastes. One of Puritanical mould would exclude it as inimical to decency. The ultra orthodox would denounce it as hurtful to religious belief and sentiment. However, between the lids of the book there is many a hearty laugh. There is much sound philosophy. Underneath the bald caricatures and the uncanny situations, there is much of rollicking humor. Here and there are touches of pathos. Despite the coarseness, there is much provocative of merriment. The sketches are not intended to be faithful portrayals of the people among whom Harris dwelt and whom he loved. They are simply the outcome of a riotous imagination, which reveled in a keen sense of the ludicrous and grotesque. They are removed far from delicate humor, taking on its boisterous and outlandish phases.

George Denison Prentice (1802-1870) was known

Geo D Prentice.

as the father of the witty paragraph. In this department he exercised a rare gift. He was a native of Connecticut and a graduate of Brown University. In 1830 he went to Kentucky to write the campaign life of Henry Clay. After its completion he founded the *Louisville Journal*. This meant the abandonment of law, which, like many other contemporary humorists, he had intended to make his profession.

In 1859 he published a volume of his wit and humor, *Prenticeana,* the title selected by his publishers. A second edition appeared the year of his death. Prentice was averse to the publication of his witticisms, some of which were extremely caustic. There was such a popular demand for their permanent preservation that he saw that some other would undertake it unless he took charge. In that event there would appear jests and flings at the expense of former political enemies who, after the lapse of time, had become warm personal friends.

On Prentice's part no word, subject or incident which might provoke mirth escaped his keen sense of the ridiculous. For the sake of a witticism or to render an incident ludicrous he regarded neither wounded pride nor offended feelings. That the expression or the situation was capable of a humorous turn was sufficient excuse for its publication. His witty paragraphs not only gave the *Journal* a national reputation and circulation, but made its editor known and quoted upon two continents. Concerned with the politics, events and personages of a bygone epoch and brought out years after the occasions that called them into existence, they lost much of their directness and flavor. However, they still bear the impress of genuine and refreshing wit.

By reason of their pungency, some came near proving disastrous to this maker of fun. Upon one occasion a Kentucky journalist was cudgeled rather severely by a cane in the hands of one whom he had wantonly attacked. Prentice indulged in ludicrous comment. The contemporary retorted with a scurrilous article upon Prentice's character, closing with the words: "The mark of Cain is upon his brow." The rejoinder of Prentice was: "Mr. George James Trotter says the mark of Cain is upon our brow. We don't know about that; but we do know that the mark of *cane* is upon his back." Thirsting for revenge Trotter, upon sight of Prentice, fired upon him, inflicting a slight wound.

George W. Bagby (1828-1883) was a native of Virginia, and was educated for the medical profession in Philadelphia. The attractions of literature were so compelling that he early abandoned medicine, giving himself to editorial work and lecturing. The humorous aspects of life about him were treated with sympathy, and he injected much wisdom into his intimate interpretations of Virginia character. For the press he wrote over the pen name "Mozis Addums." His sketches found their way into various magazines. In 1860 he succeeded the poet and writer, John R. Thompson, as editor of *The Southern Literary Messenger.* He kept the periodical up to the high standard maintained by his predecessors. That he sustained it almost up to the end of the war will always remain a flattering testimonial to his talents and ability.

After Bagby's death his widow published, in two volumes, *Writings of Dr. Bagby.* Among the humorous sketches that enjoyed wide popularity were *Meekins's Twinses, My Uncle Flatback's Plantation, Jud Brownin's Account of Rubinstein's Playing, Bacon and Greens, or The True Virginian* and *What I Did With My Fifty Millions.* Of his productions it is safe to say that the piano-playing skit is most frequently and pleasantly remembered. Where old-fashioned exhibitions are maintained in the closing exercises of schools, it is probable that few have been held without a happily rendered recitation of "Ruby's Playing." Where elocutionists of approved merit entertain in remote town or village, this is one of the attractive parts of the program. This is a far more finished production than "The Song" in Longstreet's *Georgia Scenes*, though there are passages in the Georgian's sketch which suggest several in the Virginian's more artistic performance.

Charles Henry Smith (1826-1903) was born in Georgia and was a graduate of the State University. He began life as a lawyer, and until near its close practised at the bar. He mingled the occupations of the lawyer with the activities of the politician and of the farmer. Thus he had varied opportunities for careful and critical observation of Georgia life. Smith began his letters of mixed wisdom and humor, wit and sarcasm, scorn and defiance in 1861. The first publication of these in book form appeared in 1866, with the title, *Bill Arp, So-Called; A Side Show of the Southern Side of the War.* Its motto was "I'm a good Union man, so-called; but I'll bet on Dixie as long as I've got a dollar."

In the preface of his book, explaining his pen name, "Bill Arp," Smith said: "When I began writing under the signature of Bill Arp I was honestly idealizing the language and humor of an unlettered countryman who bears that name. His earnest, honest wit attracted my attention, and he declares to this day that I have faithfully expressed his sentiments. Those who know him can see more of him than of me, and in this view of my labors I may be suspected of playing Boswell to an uneducated and humorous man, whose name is not Johnson, but Arp.

Smith's first letter is addressed to Abraham Lincoln in April, 1861. In view of the latter's proclamation calling for troops, "Bill Arp" thought "Abe Linkhorn" ought to be informed of how the Georgian regarded it. He intimated that things were getting too hot for him, and he would like "to slope out of it." Speaking of the boys about Rome, Ga., he says: "Most of them are so hot that they fairly siz when you pour water on them, and that's the way they make up their military companies here now—when a man applies to join the volunteers they sprinkle him, and if he sizzes they take him, and if he don't they don't."

After the war Smith's "Bill Arp" letters first appeared in the Atlanta *Constitution* and in the Louisville *Home and Farm*. These are uniformly full of homely wisdom and piquant humor. Immediately . following the war they were somewhat waspish and mordant. Military government and reconstruction he resented and gave expression to the heart and voice of the South. Many of these were collected and published as books, to wit: *Bill Arp's Letters,* in 1868; *The Farm and Fireside,* in 1882; *Bill Arp's Scrapbook,* in 1886; *Fireside Sketches,* in 1890. As weekly letters these had given the author wide reputation. They are valuable as portrayals of Georgia life.

Next to Joel Chandler Harris (1848-1908), Richard Malcolm Johnston (1822-1898) is the most widely known and appreciated of the Southern school of humorists. In the main, his fame rests upon his *Dukesborough Tales,* the first edition of which appeared in 1864. Subsequently they were enlarged, appearing in the Baltimore *Southern Magazine,* and book form were published in various editions. Having been a lawyer, university professor and a shrewd observer of Georgia "cracker" life, these tales and

JOEL CHANDLER HARRIS

his other books exhibit the fruit of his warm sympathy and lively humor. "Bill Williams," who felt that he had reached the acme of social position in becoming a clerk in a country store, can take rank with Longstreet's "Ned Brace" or Baldwin's "Virginian." Beginning life as a school teacher, he spoke with intimate knowledge of the old-field schools of the South. They are delineated so faithfully and delightfully that interest in their character and operations can never diminish.

As humorist, the work and fame of the late Joel Chandler Harris are so widespread and recognized that mention of his name gives completion to any résumé of the works of leading writers of wit and humor in the South. His mere naming is illustration and verification of the truth that "the last shall be first."

GEORGE F. MELLEN,

Formerly Professor of Greek and History, University of Tennessee.

CHAPTER V.

HISTORICAL STUDIES IN THE SOUTH.

NTEREST in our ancestors is almost a universal passion, but written history is a form of culture too elevated to be pursued until an economic basis has been secured so strong and substantial that there is leisure to record the present, to study the past and to review the progress made. Among nations with a literature, history is usually preceded by prayer, song, story, oration and allegory. But a colony goes forth with all these, and more as an inheritance from the mother country if she possesses them herself. In common with the rest of the country, the South brought over the Atlantic a respectable intellectual baggage from England. As all dreamed of a return to that home, only a few spirits could appreciate the raw materials of the mind around them, or cared to look upon these new shores as anything more than havens of exile from which good fortune was to release them after a short sojourn. Besides, the forest had to be felled and the ground cleared of bush and weed by the most assiduous toil. Logs had to be hewn, riven and split in order to be carried over rough ways and fashioned into rude huts. This heavy drain on the physical powers left but little energy of brain for putting pen to paper beyond meagre letters and bare reports to the masters on the other side of the ocean.

But there were some brave souls that could rise superior to these hardships, and leave for posterity a record of the events mingled with descriptions of the strange nature around them. Thomas Hariot, one of Raleigh's romantic colonizers in the wilds of North Carolina, has left us his account of the experiences of the band he was with, and his impressions of the vast forests and of the life in them, both animal and vegetable, so faithful and true that authors ever since have relied on his views, and on the drawings of his coworker, John White. Their labors, reaching back to 1588, were certainly the first studies of the present region of the South ever made by settlers, temporary or permanent. Of course, explorers—English, French and Spanish—had preceded them, but only to glance at the strange land or wander over it and then return to Europe. The Cabots had sailed along a part of the coast, most likely, and daring gold-hungry adventurers from Spain had boldly plunged into the depths of the wilderness, floundered in the morasses and wandered, half-crazed with fatigue and misery, across the dry plains. Through the patience of chroniclers the tales of their cruelties, their sufferings, and their disasters have been transmitted to us, but these scribes do not come within the scope of this paper.

A little farther northward another figure rises from that morning gloom. In the dimness he has ampler proportions, perhaps, than he is justly entitled to. Of strong personality, roving nature, power of narration and vivid imagination, John Smith fills a wide canvas back there when credulity swallowed marvels with greediness, and when contemporary authors were scanty. Smith used the decorations of fancy rather lavishly, and has projected himself rather richly into the realms of romance and speculation, but nevertheless it is to him we have to look exclusively for many of the facts of that twilight time. For that, if nothing more, he is worth all the controversy that has raged over the

incident he tells of the preservation of his life by
Pocahontas. The dispute may never be laid, but the
thorough searching of his career has brought out the
burden of our obligation to him as the first annalist
of an enduring colony in the South. It remained for
the present to gather his writings, arrange them,
along with other matter relating to him, so that they
can be conveniently consulted. It is to Arber's edition that we can turn for all of Smith's productions.

There were pamphlets, leaflets, broadsides and
reports from Virginia and the other colonies, describing the dangers from the Indians and painting
the beauties of nature, mingled with missionary
prayers for Bibles and tracts, and other aids for
saving the souls of both white and red. The salu-
brity of the climate, the abundance of game and fish,
the quantity of wild honey, the yellow glitter in the
rocks, the fertility of the soil, the easy terms for
acquiring land—in fine, all the delights and tempta-
tions of this region were set forth in all the glowing
seductiveness of the real estate agent of a modern
"boom" town. Usually, a rapid sketch of what had
already been done gave a historical flavor to all.
But it was more the ore of history than the bars
and blocks of the stamp mill that these pioneers
piled up in the shape of memorials, petitions, diaries, letters, official reports and archives of all sorts.
It was at a much later date, even down to the present, that other hands sorted and raked in these
warehouses, turning out monographs and volumes
that are furnishing us a consistent view of those
days. The characters so prominent in those occur-
rences are portrayed for us now in many books.
The resourceful Smith, the unfortunate Raleigh, the
gallant Oglethorpe, and others of less note, are all
honored with dignified biographies. There are four
lives of Oglethorpe, at least half a dozen of Raleigh,

and perhaps more of Smith. College and university students and professors in recent years have carved out theses and studies as requirements for degrees, as basis for desired promotion, as exercises for their talents, as works of love, or as contracts for publishers. Browne, Steiner, James and Randall are examples for Maryland; Bruce, McIlwaine and Latané for Virginia; Weeks and Sikes for North Carolina; Ramage, Whitney and Smith for South Carolina; Jones and Phillips for Georgia. Of course the same ground has been trodden wholesale by the general state histories also, which will be treated more fully.

Passing over the succession of pamphlets, it is about a century after Smith's picturesque utterances that we come to the first formal, ambitious sketch of a Southern colony. Robert Beverly, a Virginia gentleman of considerable means for the time, with a retinue of slaves and with a plantation of several thousand acres, was specially endowed for the task of furnishing a comprehensive view of the locality in the first decade of the Eighteenth century, or nearly one hundred years after a footing had been fixed at Jamestown. He had been educated in the fashion of the day, had traveled abroad, was in close touch with the ruling class, knew the streams and forests, the seasons and the capacities of the land, and was, in truth, a fountain of historical knowledge. He narrated the labors and achievements of the past, painted the natural environment, treated of the Indians and discussed the possibilities of the place. A good all-around account he drew up, permeated with human interest, not a mass of dead documents. He was of the temperament to suit the community, a man of affairs, active, a lover of life in the open air, riding over his broad acres, not a closet student poring over books. But in a score

of years he was succeeded by a man of this type,
naturally a member of the most learned profession
of the time, a man who united two intellectual callings in himself, preacher and teacher.   This was
Reverend Hugh Jones, a professor at William and
Mary College, who composed an account of Virginia
for the home folks in hopes of drawing some religious support.   A half-dozen years later William
Byrd surveyed the dividing line between North
Carolina and Virginia, but his manuscript based on
this task did not become available for students for
a long time afterwards.   It is the highly entertaining views of a superior mind, and altogether worthy
of the reprints with which it has been honored.   On
towards the middle of the century, in 1747, Stith
forged another link in this chain of studies, producing one good volume out of the four that he promised, although Jefferson criticized him as labored
and inelegant.   Like Jones, he was a teacher, and
very likely could not find time to keep his word, as
his days were spent in drilling boys in the essentials
of Latin and Greek.   Another author, John Lawson,
in this half century, had put down his impressions
of the domain southward as far as Georgia, the
lively sense of a traveler contending with the difficulties and mishaps of a journey through the tree-
clad stretches.   Incidentally, also, he tells of the
Indian, and drops bits of history, but mainly he is
the preserver of material for others to work over.

The demands of frontier life with the incessant
perils from the aborigines, with the ceaseless war on
stubborn soil and tangled growth, monopolized the
most of man's strength, bodily and mental. Also, the
contentions and struggles among European nations
for the possession of these virgin kingdoms sent
their echoes across the waves, and the combatants
themselves followed, and the arena of strife was

now along the seaboard, in Canada and up and down the Mississippi valley, turning men from the peaceful paths of the mind. The distant rumblings of the storm between mother and child soon to break began to disquiet the hearts of all the more reflective, and still further drew away thoughts from the muse of history. When the clash came the wild clamor and bitter agony of a family quarrel so concentrated the general attention that all other intellectual activities substantially ceased. There were journals jotted down day by day of the long, fatiguing march, of the little current incidents of the company, regiment or division; there were numberless letters penned, countless dispatches forwarded and received, piles of order books, quantities of military returns and rosters, and, most pathetic of all, there were diaries, missives, depositions, testimonials of the trembling fears, tribulations and indignities suffered by timid women and helpless children. But all these evidences of disorder and upheaval are rather the original material on which the future student was to draw in penning his narrative of these events.

When, however, the soldier returned to the farm, the shop and the marketplace, thoughts were directed to the laying of massive foundations for a great state. How much the domestic productions affected these architects can never be known, but it is undeniable that they looked to the past for examples, for inspiration and for warning. In this important labor a group of men from below the Potomac were leaders for the whole country. In a genuine sense they studied all history and evolved a chart destined to influence all the race. The foremost of this constructive host was Washington, one of the greatest nation-builders of all time. He was alert to the duties and dangers of the path under

his feet, but he also looked to the rear to get bearings
from the road already traversed. Books on agricul-
ture and other practical pursuits preponderated in
his library, but on the same shelves were placed such
American histories as Beverly's *Virginia,* Stith's
Virginia, and geographies and books of travels, like
Gordon and Bartram, with histories of Rome,
France, Prussia and other modern European lands.
Madison, whose pen was so subtle and so convincing
for the adoption of the constitution, showed much
familiarity with the teachings of human experience.
But after the keel was laid and the ship completed,
the real pilot for the destinies of the new-born republic was Thomas Jefferson. He put his own interpretation on the sailing orders, and marked out
the track that was to be the guide-line. He was
steeped in the lore of the past, and saturated with
the current of the times. He dared to formulate his
construction in as exact legal phraseology as he
could, as he was the mainspring in the famous Kentucky and Virginia resolutions that were the starting
point for the "states rights" theory. From a citizen
of South Carolina, Pinckney, came large sections of
our mighty charter. These men and lesser ones
from the South may be said to have had the lion's
share in the framing and working of that powerful
instrument for our civic development. They were
men of culture and of wide reading in history, and
out of their study of the past; and their judgment of
the present, we were launched on the momentous
voyage that has carried us into ever-widening seas.
This resistless passion for expansion certainly received an added impetus from historical study.

In the meantime the Southern states contiguous
to and connected with the Gulf of Mexico had flowed
along a channel almost of their own. Nature's bar-
riers of distance, of river, of mountain and of dif-

ference of climate had made this separation almost inevitable under the industrial conditions of the day. The complications of foreign tongues and customs had made the gap still wider and harder to close for a part of this region. All along the balmy coast of the Gulf the skies were of the hue, and the winds of the softness of those in southern Europe, on another inland sea, the Mediterranean. Peoples from Spain had scattered themselves along the inlets of Florida and southern Alabama, while some from France had grouped themselves at a few convenient spots along the line of surf beats and in the great valley of the Father of Waters. Indeed, many had reached the salt breezes by drifting down from Canada, to be augmented by newcomers direct from France. It was another setting of the elements than in Virginia and the Carolinas, and, consequently, another social growth of darker-eyed men and women, of quicker temper and more picturesque taste. They clung to their speech, too, and whoever wishes to search the original chronicles of their doings will have to learn their idiom, at least, for all the earlier period. Though comparatively of scanty numbers, they have carved indentations in our organic structure.

The Latin races reach back to the ancient city on the Tiber for their principles of government and order. The offshoots transplanted to Louisiana have grafted Roman law on our Anglo-Saxon system. Some of their social usages and amenities have also been domesticated. The ethnological characteristics have engaged the scrutiny of the student of history.

The tangle of diplomacy and geography relative to the boundary lines between us and the French and Spanish has been threaded, in recent years, by careful explorers like Ficklen, Owen and Chambers. The first of these turned out a lasting piece of work as

to the territorial limitations of the Louisiana Purchase agreement, done with all the rigidity and thoroughness of a scientist in his laboratory. Eastward,
some distance from New Orleans, in another early
French centre, Mobile, another patient toiler, P. J.
Hamilton, found leisure from the exactions of law to
trace out all the radiations from the French core
set in the valley of the Tombigbee in his *Colonial
Mobile*. Not with such fulness, but with similar aim,
a trio of investigators have afforded us glimpses of
New Orleans while in the chrysalis stage. These
three, Fortier, Cable and Thompson, may be all the
more attractive to the general reader because they
can impart more literary and philological flavor to
their style. Farther west examples of the same sort
of glances into the corresponding days of Texas are
provided by Garrison, Barker, Bugbee and others.
The granaries of Latin data, while not so extensive
as those for English, were more difficult to explore
as another medium of communication had to be acquired. Journeys had to be undertaken to Madrid,
Paris and the City of Mexico, or expert assistance
obtained at those points, if a comprehensive search
was intended.

But with the migration southward after the general pacification of the country had been assured by
the smooth working of the constitution adopted a
few years after the conclusion of the War of Independence, these Gulf regions, in spite of the alien
tinge of the population, were fast welded to the main
body and intimately linked with their other sisters.
Besides the ties of temperature and of product,
there was a social bond that riveted them together
as by a band of steel. The institution of slavery ran
through them all, and on them all was to wreak its
bloody curse. They had but slight part in the contest with England, and very fittingly none of them

has to its credit any important history of that conflict.

Nor did the Southern states above do very much towards telling the tale of that patriotic era. In his large biography of Washington, Marshall, a Virginian, necessarily had to cover a considerable part of the field as his hero was the central figure through it all, but it was not Marshall's purpose to describe the combats and campaigns as the end in themselves. A South Carolinian, Ramsay, did briefly sketch the chief operations, enlarging, of course, on the rôle that his own state played. A writer in Charleston portrayed Greene, the second military leader of the American side of the clash. There were similar testimonials to the efficiency of other commanders, as Lee, Marion and Washington, but nothing comprehensive for the eight years of strife is the meed of the South, not for several score of years after the surrender of Yorktown.

Some little incidents, however, have given rise to controversies, some of them long and bitter. One of the most fruitful of such topics is the Mecklenburg Declaration in North Carolina at a critical moment at the beginning of the trouble with England. Years after peace had been declared, discussion waxed warm over two sets of resolutions in favor of independence, it being sought to establish priority for this portentous step for North Carolina over the other colonies. A mountain heap of arguments and answers has been accumulated, much of it mere rubbish, but a fair segment of it of a high order of investigation and statement. In this long dispute have figured Graham, Ashe, Goodloe, Cooke, Fries, Hoyt, Salley, and others. The two last are among the latest and among the ablest, with Ashe, who in his monumental history may have said the final word so clear his conception and so strong his grasp.

After passing the colonial and revolutionary eras, historical study in the South seems to have localized itself in the various states, perhaps under the influence of the states rights theory, although all unconsciously we can believe. At any rate, the most imposing memorial of this intellectual pursuit is the long array of volumes composed on the different states. The backbone of all these contributions is the solid series of state histories which began to appear early in the Eighteenth century and continue to the present. They are of very unequal grades as to accuracy and reliability, but all make solid additions to knowledge and stand for painstaking industry and an appalling amount of unremunerative labor. Every one means a noble service, without reward, for the mental uplift of unappreciative readers.

Practically all go through the dreary details of colonial and territorial times, the squabbles and bickerings of jealous contestants for office, the disputes with the superior authority in London or in Washington. They dwell on Indian tribes and their customs, and relate the numerous bloody encounters between the two races. They walk the paths made by new settlers advancing into the mighty forests. They recount the growth of population and the increase in the cities. In the case of the older colonies they expand with great fulness on the state's part in the Revolutionary War. With the irruption of party politics into our national life, they describe the corresponding division among the voters in the local unit, often digressing into an extended general history of each party so as to provide the proper setting for the small body. They also follow the slavery issue, pointing out applications of it in the contracted field they are surveying. Again they enlarge when they come to the doctrine of secession, the terrible shocks of the war and the forces sent to the front. They paint the dark days of reconstruction, and rejoice at the decay of fratricidal animosities and at the mutual understanding and reconciliation of the two sections once so hostile. They also tell of the natural features and resources, of the climate, of the products, and often array the statistics of progress. Not all, in fact only a fraction, tramp this long road, as half, at least, did their tasks before the War of Secession. Even of those since then, some came only to the inception of national consciousness.

Of the authors trying in dignified way to give some important phases of state history, there are not a large number, less than a dozen in some instances, and not very far over that in any, though a bibliography charitably including every publication touching on the state would mount up to a couple of hundred pages for the smallest one. Some of the more ambitious types are all that the limitations here will allow. Burk, Virginia, is among the earliest of this group of general state historians, appearing in 1804 in four volumes, from the dawn to Yorktown. He had access to originals now lost, and hence he is a source in himself. He has been criticized as rhetorical, tedious, disproportioned, giving too much space to Bacon's rebellion, but he has a selection of indispensable documents. Neill has included both Virginia and Maryland in his studies of the colonial period, to which he was much devoted, chiefly emphasizing the documentary side, though he has been much attacked for inaccuracy. Browne (W. H.) has done invaluable work on Maryland, both in monographs, in a condensed, popular history, and in his editing of the records running up to nearly half a hundred volumes. A namesake, but of different family and of different orthography, Alexander Browne, has produced monumental books on

Virginia that can never be superseded, as they are
primary data and studies based on them. He has a
collection of biographies, too, that are very valuable.
Hawks, 1857, brought out a first-class book on colonial North Carolina, conservative, leaning towards
the Tory side, but seeing all faces of the subject.
A little earlier than this, Wheeler surveyed the entire stretch of the same state to his day, but so in-
accurate as not to be used unless verified by other
witnesses. Unfortunately, his biographical sketches
are under the same ban. The latest, and considered
the most comprehensive, and all in all the best of this
class on North Carolina is now (1909) going through
the press by S. A. Ashe, who has put years upon the
task. In South Carolina one of the first to begin
the more serious compilation was Carroll, with his
collection of pamphlets and other illustrations of
the early days. Gibbes did similar labor for the
revolutionary epoch. But Ramsay was the pioneer
to weave a consistent web of the life of the past in
that state. He took in the entire sweep and glanced
over all the forms of activities behind him, as well
as the natural environment. Rivers had done some
of the most careful searching into colonial life.
Simms, the novelist, wrote a very graphic history,
used in schools, full of patriotic fervor. But unquestionably, the one preëminent history of the state is
the four-volume one by General Edward McCrady,
of Charleston, extending from the start to the close
of the revolutionary period. It stands with the very
best of state histories in the United States. All
lines of development were most capably dealt with.
In at least two he was exceptionally strong—social
life and the importance of South Carolina's part in
the fight for separation from England. He was that
very rare instance among military historians; he
had been a soldier himself, having gallantly served

through the war, and he could estimate the weight of the various motives and apportion the value of each. His vast labors got but little financial recompense, but the state legislature rose to the occasion and purchased sets for the schools. The first of these solid productions on Georgia was Stevens' two volumes in 1847, a model, based on first-hand evidence, containing documents and covering the labors of English, French and Spanish in that state. Within a decade he was almost rivaled with a collection of statistics, local and biographical sketches and accounts by White, who, taking a broad view, traversed the entire field. Avery, starting about that time, took similar sweep of vision, but expanded so generously on the career of a prominent politician, Joseph E. Brown, that he is unbalanced. Since the war, Harris ("Uncle Remus") tried the witchery of his pen on short, highly readable descriptions of salient incidents in state history. But, all in all, the latest of these comprehensive efforts is the best, C. C. Jones's *History of Georgia* in two volumes. Although he spent years in amassing and studying his material, the work of composition was remarkably rapid. He was a specialist in Indian antiquities, and an antiquarian of high order, writing a small book on the "Dead Towns" of Georgia, very pleasantly giving a romantic touch to the prosaic facts of decline.

In Florida and the other Gulf states we come to commonwealths younger for their English blood but older for their Latin tinge. The historical literature is not so generous in dimensions as that of the older ones, though it has another flavor, especially in the beginning. In 1859 Brinton did an excellent piece of work on Florida, traveling the entire circle of his subject and holding the interest all the way. The lamented poet, Lanier, undertook a guide book on contract with a publisher, and the result of his labor was better than the average of such hack productions. Fairbanks spent his strength on the colonial times mostly. The work of two authors, Brewer and Pickett, quite capably cover the civic career of Alabama, especially the later edition of Pickett. Just at the middle of the Nineteenth century Pickett issued two invaluable volumes, an authority on all the whole extent of the state history. Brewer, nearly a quarter of a century later, supplemented Pickett by. stressing the local and biographical elements. An admirable addition to Pickett has been made by Owen, extending the narrative to the present. Both of these also lead us into Mississippi history, as the two were under the same boundaries for a season. Two others on Mississippi may be mentioned, Claiborne and Lowry, the former having original data on the territory, mainly the papers of Governor Claiborne. Lowry glances over the whole life. In Louisiana the printed output becomes richer. Hutchins included that troublesome problem of the conflicting claims over West Florida, and is full on Louisiana matters down to American ascendancy. French and Martin compiled documents and facts of importance, but the gigantic task of clearing up the tangled wilderness of the life behind was left to Charles Gayarré, who, in four solid volumes, set forth the relations and achievements of the three races that met in this arena. Of French birth and of American nationality he was well equipped for the heavy burden to be carried. Handsomely he performed the part. A richly illustrated successor is Fortier's history.

In Texas, again, the historical species differs— aboriginal, then Mexican, then independent control, merging into union with the rest of the country. This variety of life, of races, of languages, coupled with the enormous size, renders it an undertaking of magnitude to treat this organism. Necessarily, it has not been accomplished with the minuteness of some of the other states. In fact, only recently have the masses of material been at all available for handy consultation. Nevertheless Yoakum bent himself to the attempt and gave us a good study. Within a few years the edition by Wooten, with careful addenda, has improved the original. Garrison, also, has related the entire story of Texas for the *Commonwealths Series* in a capable manner. Davis, similarly, has a praiseworthy abridgment, dwelling on important and picturesque points. Numerous studies of limited portions have lately been made, especially by the members of the State Historical Society, being published in the *Quarterly* of that body. One of these deserves mention, a critical examination of Coronado's journey of exploration under Spanish dominion at the earliest stage. Other contributions bear on Houston and Austin and the war for independence. Of course, the heroic event of the Alamo has been thoroughly worked over.

North of Texas is the first of the wholly inland states, Arkansas, with nothing very striking in her career, and, consequently, with no abundance of histories. Monette, who treated the valley of the Mississippi under French, Spanish and English influence, included Arkansas along with the other states southward within his scope. Shinn and Hempstead wrote school histories, and Reynolds, in part, covered the ground with biographies. Missouri has fared better. Houck, in three volumes, has gone over the early years with care, and there has been a large crop of books on the military side of the state history. Being on the border there were numerous events to be described during the conflict for secession.

Crossing the Mississippi we are in Tennessee,

whose infancy, as well as that of Kentucky, was
drenched with the blood of pioneers in their grim
dislodgment of the so-called Red man. Boone and
Crockett and Houston and Kenton loom up in the
dust and smoke of this savage conflict. Daring
deeds and reckless encounters were there for the
student to snatch from oblivion. Rather soon did he
begin, too, as in 1823 Haywood published his history, a good, comprehensive volume, especially ex-
pansive on the Indian. So near was he to the period
he treated that he is a source of knowledge for
others. Over half a century later he was, perhaps,
excelled by Phelan, who produced one of the best
local histories of the South. He kept an even balance between the colonial, or territorial, and later
stages. Of special studies there are many, by Mellen, Thruston, Wright and others. Thruston is an
authority on Indian archæology. Garrett did much
for the cause by the publication of a magazine. The
name of the first historian of Kentucky has been preserved in a most unusual yet refined and imperishable way. Filson, a Pennsylvanian, migrated to
Kentucky and published his history of the locality
in 1785. Three years later he disappeared, most
likely at the hands of hostile Indians. His memory
will last as long as typography and libraries do, because of the magnificent publications of the Filson
Club, founded and maintained in Louisville by R. T.
Durrett. Marshall and Butler both turned out histories with much good in them, likewise Connelly,
though largely restricted to the careers of one family. Collins collected a mass of documents and left a
monument to himself by the able way he brought
before us the changing mirrors of the whole past of
the state, physical, political, social, ecclesiastical,
biographical and all. Shaler, a wonderful combination of science and letters, a soldier and student,

prepared the volume on Kentucky for the *Commonwealths Series*.

Beyond Kentucky, West Virginia, which is only part Southern, has been treated by Hale, Lewis and Fast, with other monographers. The segregation from old Virginia has been productive of considerable discussion, some of it acrimonious and of loose phraseology.

But the pride of individuality of these communities was being replaced by a danger facing all alike. The abolitionists were tenaciously forcing their doctrines to the front in the political sphere. The question was complicated with the issue of the tariff and with the theory of state rights. There were stout defenders of the institution of slavery, and some of them did herculean labor, mining in the past for arguments. The Bible was one of the favorite repositories on which to draw. Greece, Rome, and other ancient countries, besides medieval lands, were all ransacked for support. Dew, a college professor in Virginia, was among the earliest prominent advocates for the system of servitude in the South. He was no mean adversary admitting his premises. Just before the bursting of the storm Harper, a jurist of standing in South Carolina, made a similar defense in a collection of papers on the subject. Later, T. R. R. Cobb, of Georgia, a very successful lawyer who rose to the grade of general by the middle of the war, put forth a well-knit plea for his side. His friend, Toombs, of greater oratorical ability but of not half the efficiency of action, laid a cool, logical foundation for the institution in a speech in Boston, one of the most comprehensive briefs ever advanced for the cause. But the giant protagonist of all was Calhoun, who, with powerful subtlety, grasped all three prongs of the matter, fusing them in his glowing intellect into one. With the weapon of state rights which was handed him by a free-thinker and scientist, a strong personality and a vigorous mind, Thomas Cooper, a professor in the state college, Calhoun battered the tariff which he believed would undermine the material foundation of his beloved region. It was for the purpose of preserving this "peculiar good" that he evolved from intense reflection on archaic conditions of mankind the pregnant "contract theory" of government in his profound "Disquisition." It was the wrong conclusion of a mighty and fertile brain, misleading stanch followers into disaster. Perhaps in all the range of literature no historical study has eventuated in more appalling results than the principles Calhoun formulated from the arsenal of the past in order to bolster up the structure based on racial subjection in the South. He had lieutenants, too, and successors. Hammond and Hayne, in South Carolina, Yancey, in Alabama, and Wise, in Virginia, are a few instances, though some of them, like Wise, did not commit their views to paper in the fullest form till after the strife had ceased. To this same stage belong those massive volumes of the *Thirty Years' View* by Benton, a senator from Missouri.

With the call to arms, the vitality of the land was centered on the present. Too much history was being made to allow of its being written. But the material was piled high for the coming pen. No previous war was so well preserved in despatches and reports, in newspapers and archives. Ephemeral histories came out day by day, and week by week, and month by month, but were almost wholly confined to the events and operations immediately preceding, in the field and at home. Every tendon and muscle, every thought and feeling of a proud people were strung to the uttermost to preserve what they considered their sacred rights. But in the very exhaustion of defeat, they began to solace themselves with reviving the four years of marching and charging, of advance and retreat. One of the quickest and most active pens, one that had been busy recording the happenings for daily readers, produced an ambitious volume that was eagerly welcomed by the disbanded soldiers. Pollard's *Lost Cause* had a mournful romance in its very title, and coming so soon after the hush of cannon and musket echoed in responsive bosoms.

The vice-president of the Confederacy, Stephens, frail in health and crippled in body, concentrated all the acuteness of his restless mind on the legal and constitutional defense of secession in his *War Between the States,* an imposing work. It is the most systematic exposition of Southern jurisprudence on this momentous issue. Stephens also later prepared a school history which has long been superseded, though widely used for a time in the section. J. L. M. Curry, towards the close of a long, useful and eventful life, published a small volume on *The Civil History of the Confederacy.* He had been a member of Congress in both the United States and the Confederacy, withdrawing from the latter to do service in the field, and was consequently well qualified to judge and compare the weakness of the legislative branch with the efficiency of the military arm. Although only a small volume, it is the most complete account of this feature of the Confederacy so far written, from an impersonal standpoint.

But on the martial side the output from the press has been overwhelming. The campaigns, the battles, the skirmishes, the occasional encounter, the stray shot, have all been elaborately dwelt upon by officer and private. But the towering figure of all, standing in simple grandeur alone on the eminence, kept a dignified silence through the five years after he laid down his sword till his death. Lee left no memoirs, made no apology, uttered no defense, but left his deeds to speak for themselves, knowing that others would do the drudgery of compiling, collating and commenting. A number of biographies have appeared, some of the latest by Trent, White and Page—the last the famous Virginia novelist. One of Lee's descendants, with rare taste, has chosen from Lee's correspondence a volume of delightful, sensible letters that place Lee on a high pedestal for strength of character and clearness of conception as to his duty in life. His thunderbolt of battle, Jackson, stricken down about the middle of the four years' contest, has fared equally well in the domain of literature. His wife has sympathetically culled from his letters, and an Englishman has made a thorough, highly appreciative study of him, substantially from the Southern viewpoint. A highly eulogistic life came from the pen of another Virginia novelist, Cooke, while the fullest Southern estimate was made by one of Jackson's staff, Dabney.

Of the other prominent generals who committed themselves to paper, Beauregard and Joseph E. Johnston were among those who had commanded large bodies of men during critical campaigns. Longstreet, a fellow corps commander with Jackson, devoted much space in his memoirs to the deplorable controversy over the charge of his responsibility for the loss of the battle of Gettysburg by Lee. He spoke very bluntly to his critics, and aroused such animosity that his wife, after his death, loyally took up the cudgels for his memory and added more fuel to the flame that should never have been kindled, as the residuum of unprejudiced opinion at present on both sides, among those with expert knowledge, seems to be that Longstreet was not to blame for the failure of the Southern force. The man who led the world-renowned charge around which all this war of words has waged, Pickett, has been remembered in at least two lives, one being by his widow. The greatest Confederate general in the West, A. S. Johnston, lives again in our midst through the faithful life of him by his son, for a term of years at the head of Tulane University, in New Orleans.

The organic head of the Confederacy, Davis, a man of great powers and unwavering aim, though of narrow vision at times, spent years of leisure in retirement in Mississippi in preparing a comprehensive survey of his part in the struggle to establish another republic. More of the well-poised judge and less of the zealous advocate would most likely have imparted greater weight to his deliverances. Again have womanly love and tenderness thrown a halo around a husband's career, as his wife, in her declining years, compiled a volume to his memory.

The volumes of personal experiences of the rank and file are almost legion. They are of incalculable value, too, in giving the flavor of the "human interest" element. They deal with every conceivable phase of the conflict. Some of the most realistic are stories of capture and imprisonment, and some of the most thrilling are narratives of escapes. Some of the participants have written very fine accounts of some of their superiors. One of the best of these is Wyeth's portly volume on the remarkable cavalry leader of the Southwest, Forrest.

On the side of the navy, though there is not a fraction of the deeds to chronicle, pens have not been idle or lagging. Scharf put out a general narrative of the navy. Semmes contributes a highly entertaining story of the wonderful cruises of the *Sumter* and *Alabama* under himself, and several of his crew have followed his example. Similar records have been made for the *Florida,* the *Shenan-doah* and other boats, including the adventures of the submarines in Mobile and Charleston harbors. In the latter these strange engines of ocean warfare sank an opposing ship, the only result of note throughout the world to the credit of the submarine to date, as yet.

Numerous ex-Confederates contributed to the series of war papers in the *Century Magazine* and to the volumes of the Century Company on the *Battles and Campaigns of the Civil War.* Both publications created the widest attention through the country, and abroad wherever military history was appreciated. Of expert, dispassionate criticism by the participants not much was to be expected, as their feelings would be too much involved in whatever they might undertake to describe. But an exception seems called for in the case of E. P. Alexander, an artillery officer, for his book lately issued in which he reviews some of the most disputed questions with much calmness and fulness. Not much more work of the kind can be expected as time is laying too heavy a hand on the dwindling number of actors in that mighty drama.

But a new generation of writers is springing up who have turned their attention in considerable part to the tragic results of the war. They are largely the sons of those who fought, and they have done excellent work in treating the baleful policy of reconstruction, which was an effort to reverse all the inherited instincts and accumulated experience of the white race. Garner and Stone for Mississippi, Fleming for Alabama, and Hollis for South Carolina, are first-class types of this new school. Saturated with the ardor to amass the facts and to show their authority, they have built up almost unimpeachable lines of testimony for their statements.

They had been preceded by politicians and public men in such fragments as speeches, interviews and magazine articles, with an occasional volume. One instance of the latter was the compilation edited by H. A. Herbert, who was a cabinet officer under Cleveland for a time. Of the same general character are the concluding portions of many memoirs and reminiscences. Some of the tenderest and most exquisite of these are by women, such as Mrs. Clayton, of Alabama. Bishop Wilmer also has traveled the same path with the tempered warmth of a highminded ecclesiastic.

But of all the reminiscential books, none has made a broader circle than the one showing the innermost thoughts of the Mississippi planter, Dabney, which attracted a glowing endorsement from the great English leader, Gladstone. As through a transparency, the noble, heroic soul of this loyal country gentleman shines in all the integrity which no adversity could affect. There are other records of a past just as sincere, as clear, as strong, but this one stands as a type of the best, giving us pictures which constitute a fascinating historical study of men and manners of a bygone era. It is to his daughter, Mrs. Smedes, that literature stands indebted for this book.

Of the negro who had been the helpless cause of these mountains of historical works, only a comparatively small number of histories are in existence. Brackett made a close study of slavery in Maryland as an institution, and his example has been faithfully and successfully copied by investigators in Virginia and North Carolina and other Southern localities. A most hopeful evidence of the progress of the race itself is the literary work some of its representatives have done on their own people. Du Bois (Atlanta, Ga.) is one of the foremost workers in this quarter, though he is more sociological than historical. The famous educators, Councill and Booker T. Washington, have done much in the same direction. But the most in a historical way has been added and is still being done by A. H. Stone, a Mississippi planter, who has the ability and the leisure to make himself one of the leading authorities, if not the chief, of all the workers in this field.

Other ethnological groups in the South have been treated. Temple, of Tennessee, sought to place the Scotch-Irish on a pedestal as lofty as that the Puritan sits upon. The Creole, in Louisiana, has been gently handled by Gayarré and Fortier and others. The Huguenot, in South Carolina and Virginia, is embalmed in collections of documents, genealogies, wills and other material. The Germans, in Baltimore, in Charleston and other localities have not lacked chroniclers. A sumptuous volume of the highest class of careful investigation is devoted to the Jews of South Carolina by Dr. B. A. Elzas, an eminent rabbi of London, England, and later of Charleston, S. C.

In church history there is a goodly array of investigations, beginning rather early. In the list are Bozman for the Episcopalians, McMahon for the Presbyterians, Russell for the Catholics, Shipp for the Methodists, and Broadus for the Baptists, who are mentioned as mere examples. Others who have delved in the same field are Randall, Ingle, Weeks, Hawks, James, Petrie and numerous others.

Happily, owing to the strength and foresight of N. H. R. Dawson, commissioner of education during Cleveland's first term, and the breadth of view of H. B. Adams, of the Johns Hopkins University, Southern educational history has been quite thoroughly treated. Monographs usually by Southern men cover the field, state by state. There are also college and university histories of high grade. One of the first, and one of the best, was La Borde's history of the state college of South Carolina. All of the better and richer class of the higher educational institutions have comprehensive histories, or at least catalogues and sketches of all the alumni back to the start. Nor have the secondary schools neglected the course of their own development. In some instances the state superintendent, or other public official, has reviewed the past in some formal report.

Perhaps historical study has been weakest on the industrial or economic side in the South. There are short contributions, but no substantial general effort covering the entire scope has yet been placed before readers. The most serious endeavor is that of the Carnegie Institution of Washington, under the direction of A. H. Stone.

On the side of genealogy, a great deal of reliable work has ben accomplished. Nothing better can be found than the pedigrees traced by Hayden, Stanard, Salley and others. The last named published a research into the Calhoun family.

In the allied branch of biography the South is a laggard. Public men and prominent characters that deserve preservation are fading into the past with scarcely more than a few hundred words to retain their impression on their fellowmen. Jefferson and other men of that time have been honored with several biographies, but further south, influential careers have been rather summarily dismissed. Clay has been remembered, Calhoun survives in at least three short lives, but the host of secondary leaders that elsewhere in our land would stand before us in fitting printer's dress are almost obliterated from the realms of literature. And they must usually remain in that oblivion as generally the material was not carefully shielded, or not even collected or saved by the subject himself. The most hardened investigator is balked by dark and empty space. In another respect Southern historical study has failed, in making appeal outside of the region. Even this rough, incomplete summary shows that a mass of good historical work has been done, but it is nearly all limited to the locality. Very little of it has aroused attention beyond the sectional borders. There are some exceptions, not all being natives of the soil. Lieber, the German exile, who taught history in the South Carolina College for twenty years turned out volumes on different aspects of civics or jurisprudence that have been pondered in all civilized lands. Hannis Taylor, a lawyer, diplomat and university lecturer, of Alabama, has written a widely-known study of the English constitution. Woodrow Wilson, a native of the section, though domiciled farther north, is the author of a history of the United States that has been purchased in all quarters.

Such men are opening a new era of Southern historiography; they are leading the way for the broader, more national view, even world-wide probably for those with the talent to command notice. The local field at the same time is being more intensively and more intelligently cultivated. With the economic and industrial growth there are at hand more leisure, more culture and more encouragement for the historical worker, and the brightest future is just ahead.

BIBLIOGRAPHY.—Adams: *Manual of Historical Literature.* Allibone: *Dictionary of Authors* (1891); Holliday: *History of Southern Literature* (1906); Trent, *History of American Literature* (1903); Tyler, M. C.: *History of American Literature* (1897); *Literature of American History* (ed. by J. N. Larned, 1902); library catalogues and the various books mentioned are the best sources of information.

COLYER MERIWETHER,

Secretary, Southern History Association, and Editor Publications of Southern History Association.

CHAPTER VI.

ENGLISH STUDIES IN THE SOUTH.

EFORE the War between the States—that great dividing line which separates every current of thought, historical, political, social, and necessarily too, educational,—the special study of English, in any systematic way, was neglected in most Southern schools, as in fact, pretty nearly everywhere in our country.

Not that composition and the critical study of English style were altogether wanting; but what little training in English was given, was more in the line of a seeming digression, and was classified in most college catalogues—when, indeed, catalogues were published—as "rhetoric and belles-lettres." What grammar was learned was acquired through the medium of Latin, by no means a bad, but sometimes a misleading expedient. A course of rhetoric was associated in some way with logic (the latter being treated, indeed, very much as a form of grammar) and in favored localities the professor of metaphysics was detailed to take charge of the division in the educational forces. The first two years of a college course were devoted wholly to the three studies, Latin, Greek and mathematics. This was so far modified in the third, or junior, year that a place was made for a class in the physical (or natural) sciences. Finally, in the senior year, the principal feature was the lectures on metaphysics by the college president. Sometimes, as in old Washington College, Virginia, this last year was formally called the "English" or "rhetorical" year, as special at-

tention was given to what were then termed the
"English" branches. These were crowned with the
course in "belles-lettres," which was evidently intended as a finishing off or rubbing down process,
and under this foreign appelation, always a little
vague and mystifying as to its exact meaning, was
supposed to lurk the idea of the formal study of
rhetoric (Blair's or Campbell's *Rhetoric* and
Kames' *Elements of Criticism* were long favorite
textbooks), and of literature, specially in its flowery
phases. The old-timed orations and methods in essay writing, all traces of which have not yet disappeared in the South, give perhaps the best evidence
as to the nature of this work.

In most institutions—and these were by no means
the least conspicuous—the chair of metaphysics was
tendered to the gentlemen of the clergy ("moral
philosophy" *par excellence* they naturally called it),
and the conduct of the classes in "rhetoric and
belles-lettres," of course, went with it. It seemed to
be a prevailing notion that the man who could
preach to the community on Sundays, was peculiarly
fitted for expounding the laws of thought and ex-
tracting the beauties of literature on week days.
Once upon a time, indeed, this was true. The system was a relic, in part, of the pioneer days, when
the preacher was missionary in a manifold sense—
the one representative of letters, culture and higher
aspirations in the vicinity. He was preacher and
teacher both, perhaps even more of the latter than
of the former. But, naturally, in a later period of
development, under such a system, not only the
study of philosophy, but especially that of English,
suffered, being not even secondary, but entirely
minor in consideration. The letters and style emphasized were primarily the highly ornamental or
what is known technically as the "rhetorical"—

those which suited best the graces of the Southern orator, whether he chose to imitate his teacher and become a pulpit speaker, or preferred to follow the profession of the law, and develop in due time, as was his natural ambition, into a notable statesman of the republic.

I would not appear to speak slightingly of older methods of education, when we are still so much at sea as to what is soundest and best and most expedient. The minds trained under older systems were of undoubted and uncommon vigor, serving well the needs of their particular day and sphere. But those needs were then fewer; the conditions of life seemingly less complex. This or that system may not meet the demands of our day; that is one thing. But that it did not produce strong men, cultivated men, literary men (as the times allowed), perhaps as efficiently as our more boasted methods, is still to be determined by the measurement of actual results.

Perhaps, at the time this fashion of thus disposing of the English classes came into vogue, it was the best possible; and many of those teachers of the old régime were men endowed with a love for good reading, moved by the study of the best models, and easily capable of stirring the fresh minds of the crude youths in their classes. I look back with peculiar pleasure upon my own experience with one of these—the late Rev. Dr. Whitefoord Smith, a noted Charleston divine in former days, who was for a number of years a professor in Wofford College. I became a member of one of the last classes this aged and worthy gentleman ever had the strength to instruct, and his enthusiasm and the glowing eulogies he bestowed upon his favorite authors and passages inspired not a few among his pupils with a love for reading, and gave them many practical hints where to go for good books and what books were good.

The president of the same institution, Dr. Carlisle, used to give up a portion of his time with his freshman class regularly every Friday afternoon, in order to ask each one of us what we had been reading and had become interested in. Probably we may have acquired less formal mathematics in actual amount as the result, and should not now be able to demonstrate any of those geometrical propositions we were sent to the blackboard to work on. But the habit had the rare merit of broadening the narrow limits and interests of a rigid college curriculum, many of the suggestive thoughts let drop have been treasured up and have constantly borne fruit, and I am sure that we went to the meeting of our debating societies on the same evening better prepared to get and make more out of them. I mention these details, apparently trivial, because they show fairly well the extent and nature of the English course in our colleges up to a very few years ago—and it was not every college that was so fortunate as to have chairs filled by marked personalities like Dr. James H. Carlisle and Dr. Whitefoord Smith. I suspect, too, that the students of the smaller colleges often fared better even than those of the more formal state universities, where there was not the same free, personal contact, which is the greatest factor in college formative influence.

A good deal may be said in support of the claim that English studies received at first more distinct recognition and emphasis in Virginia than elsewhere in the South. Virginia, as the oldest of colonies and mother of states, has been the leader in education, and her English affinities and traditions, comparatively unchanged by mixture with foreign elements, seem to have emphasized not a little the love for

English classic literature specifically, and the more exact study and use of the parent tongue. Her three oldest colleges (and they are likewise the oldest in the Southern states) give evidence of this spirit. The College of William and Mary was founded under the patronage of the Bishop of London, and in direct imitation of English models, emphasized the study of the "humanities"—borrowing the term from English nomenclature—and her linguistic studies, mainly classical, were always directed to this end. Later, Hampden-Sidney and Washington colleges (the latter now Washington and Lee University) were established almost simultaneously under Presbyterian influence, and patterned, naturally, after the Princeton model of those days. In the prospectus of the former, dated Sept. 1, 1775, the debt was frankly acknowledged, with the explicit proviso only, that more attention should be given to English studies.

The first interest in historical English work in America was the offspring of the fertile brain of Thomas Jefferson, constantly active, always investigating, and making some experiment or other. He acquired, as a law student, an enthusiasm for the study of Anglo-Saxon, and continued its advocacy as a definite part of the college curriculum, from 1779, when he was a member of the board for William and Mary, until 1825, when the wishes of a lifetime were at last realized by the opening of his pet creation, the University of Virginia. Jefferson had actually written out, seven years before, what is now a curious synopsis of an Anglo-Saxon grammar with specimen extracts, for his new institution; and this was the first formal incorporation of a course in historical English in an American university, however meagre and defective a course of one or two hours a week in itself was.

It was, likewise, another Virginian, Louis P. Klipstein, a graduate of Hampden-Sidney College, who,
somehow or other, got over to a German university,
and, in order to show his interest in the subject, as
early as the forties began the publication of the first
Anglo-Saxon texts in America—the Gospels, and
two volumes of selections, besides a grammar; but,
it must be added, that scholars in our day pronounce
them uncritical, and those of his own left them to lie
cold on his hands to be disposed of in presentation
copies to his friends.   The truth is, it was too early
for textbooks in Anglo-Saxon in America, whether
good or bad.

Jefferson made it a condition that the occupant of
the chair of modern languages in the University of
Virginia should be an expert in the study of the
early forms of English.   Two scholars, both secured
from abroad, virtually filled this chair during the
first seventy years of its existence; George Blätter-
man, from 1825 to 1840, and M. Schele De Vere after
1844.   There was a slight interregnum between the
two, and the gap of one or two years was filled by
Charles Kraitsir, a curious, all-knowing gentleman,
who (at least so states the catalogue) boldly offered
instruction not only in the whole realm of the Teutonic and Romance languages, but also in the Slavic
and even Magyar tongues.   During the long career
(1844-1895) of Professor Schele De Vere as professor in the University of Virginia he certainly
touched more teachers of language and literature
than any one man in the South, and perhaps in the
whole country.   A very incomplete list would contain the names of Edward S. Joynes, Henry E.
Shepherd, Crawford H. Toy, Thomas R. Price,
James M. Garnett, Rhodes Massie, Thomas Hume,
James A. Harrison, Richard H. Willis, Edward A.
Allen, Henry C. Brock, Alcée Fortier, John R. Fick-

len, Walter D. Toy, F. M. Page, C. W. Kent, W. H. Perkinson, J. D. Bruce and W. P. Trent.

As regards general instruction in English, however, the University of Virginia fared no better than any other institution. Such formal instruction as could be given was left to the tender mercies of the professor of moral philosophy. It was not till after 1857 that this much-abused servant of letters was relieved, and the subjects of rhetoric and literature were transferred to the department of history, just established. This marked the period of the McGuffey's *Readers* and Holmes's *Histories,* conceived for school purposes by the occupants of these two chairs, books which have not yet totally disappeared from our public schools. A distinct chair of English language and literature was first created in 1882, which was filled until 1896 by James M. Garnett, the translator of *Beowulf,* then principal of St. John's College, Maryland. The logical development was still further extended in 1893, when through private munificence the subjects of rhetoric and English literature were definitely awarded a separate foundation of their own, and Charles W. Kent was called for this purpose from the University of Tennessee. In 1898 the English language and German were combined in one chair, whose incumbent was now known as professor of the Teutonic languages. This new chair has been filled ever since its formation by James A. Harrison, the well-known editor and biographer of Poe, and professor of Romance languages in the university from 1895 to 1898. It should be remarked, however, that in 1896—on Garnett's leaving the university—Harrison had already assumed the instruction in the English language.

Such has been the history of the development of the study of English at the one institution commonly recognized as the most prominent of all Southern state universities. She influenced those of other states by her principle of election in studies, by her peculiar system of distinct schools of study in place of the old curriculum, by her rigid and severe standards of examination, by constantly distributing a large and influential number of teachers through the South. On the other hand, it is also very possibly due to the same influence that many of these graduates, using their *alma mater* too rigidly as a model, while they undoubtedly raised the standard of education in other directions, also helped to delay for so long the recognition of English studies as of equal importance with Latin and Greek.

But the need and the feeling was receiving constant utterance. The *Southern Literary Mesenger* is the most characteristic product and faithful exponent of Virginia and the Old South. The first editor, Edgar Allan Poe, emphasized the lack of criticism in America, and forthwith fell to executing a good deal of reckless, but it must be admitted, wholesome slashing. Later, the ardent John R. Thompson frequently pled for a school of letters at the state university, and possibly this had something to do with the changes of 1857. Nor were there wanting attempts on the linguistic side. In the columns of the same magazine appeared two or three articles displaying interest in the origins and development of the language. The number for September, 1848, contained an *Historical Sketch of the Languages of Europe with a Particular Reference to the Rise and Progress of the English Language;* and in that for March, 1856, was a discussion of *English Dictionaries, with Remarks on the English Language,* signed ''A. Roane.'' Continuous evidence of similar interest may be found; for the educated Virginian and Southern mind has always been peculiarly sensitive to the proper understanding and use of the mother tongue. But while something had undoubtedly been accomplished, the dawn of a fuller hope was to arise immediately from another quarter.

It was an institution other than the state University of Virginia, though it was the work of one of her graduates, that was to have the distinction of creating a school of English in the South which should send forth apostles with all the fervor of converts and enthusiasts. Randolph-Macon College would have deserved notice for devoting a separate chair to English literature as early as 1836, almost from its inception; and Edward Dromgoole Sims (a Master of Arts in the University of North Carolina), gave a course on historical English in the year 1839. He was installed in that year as professor of English, after a stay in Europe, where he heard lectures on Anglo-Saxon. Tradition tells how, having no textbooks, he used the blackboard for his philological work. At the end of three years he removed to the University of Alabama in consequence of having contracted a marriage not then allowed under the laws of Virginia. He was preparing a series of textbooks in Old English, tradition again says, when he died in 1845. Had he accomplished his purpose, these works would have preceded Klipstein's in point of time.* It was again at Randolph-Macon College (though now removed from Mecklenburg to Hanover county) that immediately after the war there was founded a distinct school of English, based on historic and scientific principles, and productive of far-reaching results. I believe that I am but paying a worthy tribute to one whom all his pupils have found a helpful guide and inspiring instructor, in making the statement that this movement was

---

* Other occupants of the chair of English at Randolph-Macon were William M. Wightman and David S. Doggett, both afterwards bishops in the Methodist Church South.

mainly due to the inspiration and effort of one man
—Thomas R. Price. I know perfectly well that one
or two institutions assert prior dates for their
courses in English. Perhaps it is the case. Within
the two or three years immediately following the
war—I cannot help repeating the phrase as a constant landmark—the Virginian and Southern institutions were demanding instinctively and almost simultaneously a training course in English, which
should have regard to a knowledge both of the
tongue and of the literature, the former in order to
secure a more thorough appreciation of the value
and spirit of the latter. It was all in the air, as we
say, and two or three institutions were actively responsive. Gen. Robert E. Lee was called almost
from the surrender at Appomattox to the presidency
of the Washington College, at Lexington, and his
sympathy with the study of English was one of the
chief marks of his administration of five years. As
a result, Professor Edward S. Joynes was giving instruction in historical English in connection with the
study of German and French; and Col. William Preston Johnston, afterward president of Tulane University, was called to occupy a newly established Kentucky chair of history and English literature. Dr.
J. L. M. Curry, later Minister to Spain, patron of
letters and life-long devotee of educational interests,
opened a course in English at Richmond College, expressly declared to be of equal importance with the
classics, almost before the smoke of battle about the
Confederate capital had fairly cleared away.
Thomas Hume, not long after graduating at the University of Virginia, had been giving definite instruction in English in a more modest female college.
And I have no doubt there were others still. Everywhere it was a movement essentially of native
growth, and nowhere of foreign importation or imi-

tation. It was a product answering to local needs, as those needs had become intensified through the interruptions and derangements of the war.

The suggestion of the course of English at Randolph-Macon College sprang from the study of the ancient languages. The feeling existed that it was impossible to expect appreciation of idioms in a foreign language, when students knew nothing about those in their own tongue. To quote from Professor Price's own words at the time: "It was irrational, absurd, almost criminal, for example, to expect a young man whose knowledge of English words and constructions was scant and inexact, to put into English a difficult thought of Plato or an involved period of Cicero." The course pursued in consequence was entirely original in its premises, and endeavored to meet these difficulties. Both the disease and remedy were brought out by the condition present; and to this, I think, may be ascribed in large measure the success of the movement and its value as a stimulus. The end set was to place, in the ordinary college course, the study of English on an equal footing with that of Latin or Greek, giving it the same time and attention, aiming at the same thoroughness, and enforcing the same strictness of method. A knowledge of the early forms of English was demanded, not as philology pure and simple, constituting an end in itself, but as a means for acquiring a true, appreciative knowledge of the mother tongue, and thereby for understanding its literature and other literatures all the more. It now seems almost incredible that it required so great an effort at the time to take this step or that old traditions could become so firmly crystallized.

Professor Price's efforts succeeded all the more easily in that they were seconded by his presiding officer, the Rev. Dr. James A. Duncan, a man of singular breadth and sympathy of mind, who had grouped about him, irrespective of church and denominational ties, a band of worthy associates. Price, as professor of Greek and Latin, gave up the latter to his colleague, James A. Harrison, who had charge of the modern languages, and taking control of the English, developed it side by side with his Greek, so as to cover a course through four continuous years. This was the result of the work of two sessions, 1868-70. The movement soon spread far and wide. Other institutions, impelled by the same needs, either imitated it outright—some of them actually going so far as always to unite the English department with the Greek, as if there were some subtle virtue in the connection (building possibly even wiser than they knew)—or developed out of their own necessities, similar arrangements. Indeed, with the courses at the State University under Professors Schele De Vere, McGuffey and Holmes; at Washington College under Professors Joynes and W. P. Johnston, and later James A. Harrison; at Richmond College under Dr. Curry, and at Randolph-Macon under Professor Price, it almost seems that the colleges in Virginia were paying at this time far more attention to the study of English than many of their sisters of like and even more advanced standing in the North and West.

After the men at Randolph-Macon had been drilled in the rudiments and given their primary inspiration, many of them were dispatched to Europe for further training, and returned Doctors of Leipzig and fired with a new zeal. In mere appearances, it should seem as if this Randolph-Macon migration to Leipzig was the beginning of the attraction exerted by the university on young Southern scholars, an attraction which has been rivaled in recent years only by that of the neighboring Johns Hopkins. The land lay open before these young men and they proceeded to occupy it. Robert Sharp returned Doctor from Leipzig and was soon called to Tulane; the late William M. Baskervill returned Doctor from Leipzig and started an impulse at Wofford College, in South Carolina, which he broadened and deepened after his transfer, in 1881, to Vanderbilt; Robert Emory Blackwell returned from Leipzig and succeeded Professor Price in his work at Randolph-Macon; Frank C. Woodward succeeded Baskervill at Wofford, in 1881, and removed to the South Carolina College, in 1887; W. A. Frantz has built up a following in Central College, Missouri; the late John R. Ficklen, having followed Dr. Price to the State University, became associated with Sharp at Tulane. The English fever at Randolph-Macon became epidemic. Dr. James A. Harrison accepted a call, in 1876, to Washington and Lee as professor of modern languages, and formed a new Virginia centre for specialists. Even Price's successor in the Greek Chair at Randolph-Macon, Charles Morris, soon resigned to go to the University of Georgia as professor of English. Nor has the manufacture of Randolph-Macon professors of English ever entirely ceased. Howard Edwards, formerly of the University of Kansas; John L. Armstrong, late of Trinity College (N. C.) and now of the Randolph-Macon Woman's College; John D. Epes, subsequently of St. Johns College (Md.); John Lesslie Hall, Ph.D. (Johns Hopkins), of William and Mary—are later accessions to a list by no means complete.

At the same time that Price left Randolph-Macon to succeed Dr. Gildersleeve in Greek in the University of Virginia (1876), his colleague, James A. Harrison, as we have seen, became successor to Joynes, who had gone to the new Vanderbilt. There has always been something in the quaint, picturesque town

of Lexington, high among the mountains at the head
of the Valley of Virginia, that has fostered education
and letters.   For more than a century it has been the
intellectual centre of the Scotch-Irish population of
the valley, just as Williamsburg, the seat of William and Mary, was the corresponding pole for the
pure English stock in the east.   Rich memories cluster about the historic town.   Here are the graves of
Stonewall Jackson and Robert E. Lee, and here died
Commodore Maury. The presence of General Lee for
the five years of his life after Appomattox, made it
for the nonce typical as a Southern institution.   The
college, first called Liberty Hall in the throes of the
Revolution, was named after Washington, who tendered it its first considerable donation, and the name
of Lee was added after the latter's death—the two
names that appealed most to Southern youths with
a sentiment for history.

This was the natural atmosphere for the academic
career of Thomas Nelson Page.   There were others,
too, inspired with kindred tastes.   Of six graduates
in the school of literature in 1869, all ultimately
M.A.'s of the institution, five became professors—
William Taylor Thom, Duncan C. Lyle, Charles A.
Graves, professor of law; Dr. John P. Strider, professor of moral science and belles-lettres—the last
two at their *alma mater;* and Milton W. Humphreys,
now professor of Greek in the University of Virginia.

The *Southern Collegian,* the student periodical,
took at once a creditable place among the best of similar productions, and ranked with the *Virginia University Magazine* in volume, and perhaps excelled it
now and then in grace and form.   Col. John T. L.
Preston had been professor of belles-lettres at the
adjoining Virginian Military Institute since its foundation, and his wife, Mrs. Margaret Junkin Pres-

ton, was the characteristic woman singer of the South.

Dr. Harrison must have found his new atmosphere congenial, as he set to work to build up a definite English course. He was handicapped, however, by the fact that he was teaching French and German too, and only English philology; but he was gifted with the literary feeling, and it came to expression in his class-room. A course looking to the Ph.D. was offered, and nearly all the candidates for "Doctor" could choose English. Many of them did so, and their influence has extended itself in all directions.

It is very curious to trace these various ramifications of mutual influences, and to see them acting and interacting, crossing and recrossing. Three main lines may be detected. Just as the University of Virginia, through its graduates, became the pattern for many, especially state institutions; and Hampden-Sidney, Davidson, Central, and particularly Presbyterian colleges felt the influence of the course at Washington and Lee; so Randolph-Macon affected among others, Wofford, and then Vanderbilt, which, in turn, has become a new centre of activity.

The transmission of this spirit to Wofford College, and thence to Vanderbilt University at Nashville, is peculiarly instructive. W. M. Baskervill, trained under Price and Harrison and in Leipzig, came to Wofford, in 1876, where he met with a sympathetic circle. The president, Dr. James H. Carlisle, had always been interested in English work, and was a close student of the history and meaning of words. Charles Forster Smith, since called to Wisconsin, was for many years fellow-professor with Baskervill, and James H. Kirkland, first an appreciative pupil, was afterward colleague as Smith's

successor. All three of these young scholars ultimately took their degrees in Leipzig and were called
to Vanderbilt University, of which Dr. Kirkland is
now chancellor. The English language and letters
were steadily emphasized by the close sympathies
uniting these three men in their common work in the
department of languages. Kirkland's Leipzig dissertation was on an English subject, though he afterward became professor of Latin; Smith, the professor of Greek, was a constant contributor on English
points; and Baskervill was specifically professor in
charge. Through the standard which their fortunate circumstances allowed them to set, a new centre
of influence was formed in Nashville.

It was this Wofford influence, if I may be personal
for a space, that had much to do with sending me to
the University of Virginia to hear Price in Greek,
and I but echo the feeling of many in Professor
Price's class-room, that it was hard to know to which
of the two languages his class leaned the more, Greek
or English, so intimately upon one another, especially in the work of translating, did the two depend.
At any rate, it is singular that his pupils, stirred by
the Greek just as at Randolph-Macon, have used this
classical impulse to enter upon the keener study of
their native language and literature. I was priv-
ileged to be in the last Greek class which Professor
Price taught at the University of Virginia; and contemporaneous with me at the university were other
pupils; Charles W. Kent, Ph.D. of Leipzig, now
Linden Kent professor of English literature in his
alma mater; James Douglas Bruce, of the University
of Tennessee; and Professor W. P. Trent of Columbia University, New York. Eventually Professor
Price's strong predilections for English, and the
memory of the work wrought while at Randolph-
Macon, led in 1882 to his acceptance of a call to the

chair of English in Columbia University, New York, which he filled until his death.

The interest in the early forms of English, strengthened by further study at German universities, led to a revival of interest in the Old English texts themselves. I have already adverted to the unfulfilled project of Sims's and Klipstein's early performances. Nothing more of importance appeared in America until 1870, when Professor March, of Lafayette, Pa., published a grammar and specimens, which remained in general use until Sweet's *Reader* appeared. Before this, Professor Schele De Vere had written his *Studies in English,* followed a year or two later by his *Americanisms.* Professor James M. Garnett produced, in 1882, a line-for-line rhythmic translation of *Beowulf,* the first American rendering of the ancient epic, an achievement based upon his class-work in St. John's College; the book has since passed through a fourth edition. In 1889, he added a version of the *Elene,* the *Judith, Athelstan,* the *Fight at Maldon,* in the same form. The "Library of Anglo-Saxon Poetry" was undertaken, in 1882, by a Boston publishing house, with the general editorship in the hands of Professor James A. Harrison, then of Washington and Lee. The first volume to appear was the text of *Beowulf,* with an English glossary, edited by Dr. Harrison himself in conjunction with a former Randolph-Macon pupil, Dr. Robert Sharp, of Tulane. Professor Hunt, of Princeton, furnished the second volume; Dr. Baskervill, of Vanderbilt, added the *Andreas* as third, and Dr. Kent, then of the University of Tennessee, edited the *Elene* as the fourth in the series. Old English poetry has exercised further fascination for Virginians, and one of the latest books is another translation of *Beowulf,* in a free-flowing metrical form, by Professor Hall, of William and Mary, making the second version of this stirring Germanic epic by an American scholar.

It has been seen that the necessity for a complete course in English was felt and received full development in Virginia and the South before the Johns Hopkins University in Baltimore affected the movement. We cannot too strongly emphasize the fact of this native growth, this development from the needs of the country just after the interruptions and distractions occasioned by the war. Nor should we forget that it was an offshoot from the study of the classic tongues, especially Greek—the love of the grandest of ancient literatures naturally giving birth to a desire for a closer knowledge of the spirit of our own, a literature which so many of us would place in the forefront of all modern expressions of life.

The English course at the Johns Hopkins was developed later than some others, and is still partial and incomplete on the side of literary history and criticism. Since, however, under Dr. James W. Bright, the philological course has attained its high degree of scientific accuracy, the tide, which formerly swept across the seas to Leipzig, has been steadily flowing thitherward. Many of Dr. Bright's best pupils it seems, come from Southern colleges, with a love for their special study already implanted in their hearts. Morgan Callaway, Jr., in Texas; the late Charles H. Ross, in Alabama; St. James Cummings, in South Carolina; C. A. Smith, dean of the graduate department at Chapel Hill, and T. P. Harrison in North Carolina, Lesslie Hall in Virginia, and many others— are Hopkins men. Some have preferred the more distant Harvard for the sake of the literary atmosphere, as in the case of John M. Manly, of South Carolina, now the distinguished head of the English department in Chicago University, and W. P. Few, dean of Trinity College, South Carolina. Among

Cornell graduates the most distinguished English student in the South is Edwin Mims, also of Trinity.

I have made no attempt to furnish a full account of all the workers in the South and the work done. I am simply marking out a few distinct lines, along which, it seems to me, this movement has progressed. Of course this body of teachers, most of them comparatively young men, have to confront peculiar conditions in every case, and the work of each must be adapted to these accordingly. Every kind of method must be used, every kind of predilection may find its scope. I am not sure that this is in itself to be deplored. I cannot believe that any iron-clad method, however approved, may suit all times and stages of development, every class of students, and (a very important matter, too) the different temperaments of individual teachers.

Nor do I maintain that the output of professors and teachers in a special department is the sole or even main test of a man's work. It might, on the contrary, be the evidence of narrowing influences and a cramped environment, the mere reflection of academic dexterity. I believe that the broadest and most helpful work is often that which inspires with a profound love for culture and letters, and informs the soul with the instinct and the passion for truth. Everything depends so much on the ends in view and the character of the work. Looking over different college catalogues, I see some lean to æsthetics, some to historical methods; some show enthusiasm for Shakespeare (whatever else may suffer), some treat specifically of prose style, and some of verse as a science of forms; some instruct by periods and topics, and some lay stress on philology and etymologies. I observe the greatest diversity, and I confess, with a certain equanimity; there is no opportunity for dogmatizing too rigidly anywhere. No one is altogether right, we may be sure—the study of a language and its literature has so many facets. Let us also trust that no one is altogether wrong. The work is diverse, but, it is believed, not chaotic. I am satisfied that there is turned out each year a body of students from these colleges with appreciation of the spirit of their mother tongue and its native literature. And may not the several enthusiasms and interests each awaken its own peculiar discipleship?

I believe so intensely in the personality of both teacher and pupil and in the sympathy existing between the two at certain stages in this development, that I trust that by all of these ways the spirit of inquiry, of study, of creation, is awakened. For, after all, it is this spirit, the instinct for creative work, which will lead to that future of education, of scholarship, of literary excellence, toward which, to judge from expression, we are all striving.

There are those who believe always in new possibilities in educational and literary movements, who delight in tracing conditions to effects, and in forecasting events and portraying the tendencies of the future. What is to be the result in the course of time of all this instruction in English, this endeavor, this straining to get and give an exacter knowledge of the native tongue and literature? It is just as characteristic, too, of England as it is of America. It seems to mean, at least, that the literature of the past will be studied, annotated, edited—no name being too poor for reverence. But will it result in broader views of life, in a conscious criticism, in strengthening the personal attitude, so that it may produce an era of its own, with new sources, new aims, and a new fulfillment? It would almost be a pity to close with a query.

JOHN BELL HENNEMAN,

Late Professor of English Literature, University of the South.

CHAPTER VII.

THE SOUTH'S CONTRIBUTION TO CLASSICAL STUDIES.

IT is impossible to make as good a showing for classical studies in the South as the facts would warrant, if one could get at them. The best Southern teachers, in higher institutions of learning as well as in lower, have, as a rule, put themselves more into the making of men than of books; partly because they considered the former more important, still more because heavy teaching left little energy for writing. The records of their work made upon human minds and hearts, rather than on printed pages, have, for the most part, passed away with the fleshly tablets on which they were inscribed. Hence, the major part of the material used in this paper has been gathered from the letters of classical scholars embodying either facts from their own experience or recollections of what they had heard from others. Doubtless wrong has been done unintentionally to the memory of many a good scholar by omission, simply because there was no record which the compiler could get at.

In the space at my disposal it seemed necessary to restrict attention chiefly to the main epoch beginning with the opening of the University of Virginia in 1825, and to illustrate the work in general and the spirit of the whole by a few representative scholars as typical of the many. Before the opening of the University of Virginia there were few colleges in the South besides William and Mary, and the centres of classical influence were private schools; and the important work of the preparatory schools has received considerable attention in the latter part of this paper.

The Work of Universities and Professors.

The opening of the University of Virginia was an event of prime importance for the higher education in the whole country, and really marks a new era. In the South this university completely dominated the situation down to the war and for some time afterwards, being the model for most that was best in the colleges everywhere, setting the standards to which they aspired, and being the source of constant stimulus and inspiration. The University of Virginia, says Professor Trent, "for a long time sufficed for the whole South, and the wideness of the field from which it drew its students is a partial explanation of the wide-reaching character of the influence which it exerted." This remark as to the dominance of the university in general is quite true of its influence in the field of the classics in particular.

George Long, M. A., of Trinity College, Cambridge, was the first professor of ancient languages (1825-1828) in the University of Virginia, being recalled at the end of three years to England to the chair of Greek in the new University of London. It is said that when he first appeared before Mr. Jefferson, the latter betrayed surprise at his youthful appearance, whereupon Mr. Long said, "Sir, it is a fault for which I am not responsible, and which time is sure to remedy." "He fixed," says Professor Trent,* "the standard of requirement in his classes at a higher point than was then known in this country, and he was the instructor and life-long

---

* *The Influence of the University of Virginia Upon Southern Life and Thought* (p. 160); in H. B. Adams's *Thomas Jefferson and the University of Virginia*, U. S. Bureau of Educational Circulars of Information, No. 2, 1888.

friend of his successor, Gessner Harrison." In England Professor Long lived and worked to a good old age, regarded on two continents as a classical authority of great weight. Of his numerous works it will suffice to mention only his *Classical Atlas* and his translations of Marcus Aurelius and Epictetus. A few words of praise of him from Matthew Arnold must command universal assent: "He treats Marcus Aurelius' writings as he treats all the other remains of Greek and Roman antiquity which he touches, not as a dead and dry matter of learning, but as documents with a side of modern applicability and living interest, and valuable mainly so far as this side in them can be made clear; that as in his notes on Plutarch's *Roman Lives* he deals with the modern epoch of Cæsar and Cicero, not as food for schoolboys, but as food for men, and men engaged in the current of contemporary life and action, so in his remarks and essays on Marcus Aurelius, he treats this truly modern striver and thinker not as a classical dictionary hero, but as a present source from which to draw 'example of life and instruction of manners.' "

Gessner Harrison, the successor of Professor Long, was, says Professor Trent, "the man who, of all others, had, so far as I am able to see, the greatest influence upon the university, and through his students upon Southern life and thought"; and was, as Dr. Broadus thinks, "more closely connected than any other with the history of the university and the constitution of its prestige." Born in 1807—the same year with Robert E. Lee—he was, in 1828, one of the three graduates in Greek in the University of Virginia, and also one of the three in medicine, these being the first men regularly graduated from the schools of the university. Mr. Long, on being recalled to England, had been asked by the visitors to name his successor. To the surprise of all he named Gessner Harrison. The visitors gave him the appointment, first for one year, but the next made it permanent. It was an instance of remarkable acumen and prevision on the part of the young Professor Long; and one of his chief titles to esteem and gratitude on the part of the University of Virginia and of American scholarship is that he discovered, trained, and nominated to succced himself this young Virginian. "In the opinion of many,"? says Professor Trent, "who from a long life and distinguished position have had opportunities of judging, Gessner Harrison achieved a remarkable triumph over his difficulties, and without invidiousness he may be said to have done more than any one man, with the single exception of Mr. Jefferson, in raising the standard of education throughout the South."

On an important point I may quote a remark of my own from an article on "Southern Colleges and Schools" (*Atlantic Monthly,* December, 1885): "So far as I can learn, no American institution before the University of Virginia had ever properly emphasized ability to turn English into Greek and Latin, as well as *vice versa,* as an absolute prerequisite to a thorough mastery of those tongues. But from the time of Gessner Harrison, who never graduated a man in ancient languages who could not put a blackboard of English into Greek and Latin without dictionary or grammar, down to the last year's senior Latin paper * * * the University of Virginia has led all our institutions in attention to this subject."

"From 1828 to 1859," says Professor Trent, "he labored zealously and successfully; then worn out, and fearing that he could not make proper provision for his large family, he resigned his professor-

ship and opened a classical boarding-school. Attracted by his reputation, pupils came from all parts
of the South. But the war broke out and Gessner
Harrison did not survive it. From nursing a son
who had sickened with camp-fever, he contracted a
modification of the disease and died April 7, 1862.
A more fitting end to his career could not have been
wished: he lived for others, he died for another."

As a fit and just estimate of his worth and his
work, I may quote from a personal letter lately received from a distinguished pupil of Gessner Harrison's, Dr. Edward S. Joynes, emeritus professor of
modern languages in the University of South Carolina, whose connection with classical work ended as
the war began, when, for a short time, he was professor of Greek in William and Mary College. He
says: "But my own classical life was chiefly, and
most honorably, as assistant professor for three
years (1853-1856) with the illustrious and really
great professor, Dr. Gessner Harrison. He was the
pioneer of true philology and classical education in
the South—the first to abandon the old superficial
system and to lay the foundation, against prejudice
and difficulties almost insurmountable, of new and
profounder methods, for which not only classical
philology, but all branches of education in the South
will ever owe him lasting obligations. None can
ever take his place, either in the veneration of those
he taught or in the enduring merit of his work. I
have heard all the greatest scholars at the greatest
university in Germany, yet I can say that Dr. Harrison's thorough teaching, his independent thought-
producing method, will always remain the solid
groundwork of my own philological training and
my model of language teaching." * * * "I
quote," he adds, "from a letter written soon after

his death in 1864, and now, in 1908, I see no reason to modify that opinion."

"He seems to have had positive genius for language," writes Dr. Humphreys. "He inspired many of his students with zeal, and his influence is felt in the South to-day. * * * His book on *The Greek Prepositions and Their Cases* was a great contribution to Greek grammar. His only Latin work, *An Exposition of the Laws of the Latin Grammar*, was, for its day, a very scholarly work, but not free from errors."

Lewis Minor Coleman, founder of Hanover Academy, had already made an enduring reputation as head of that school, when he was called to succeed Gessner Harrison as professor of Latin in the University of Virginia in 1859. A still greater career seemed to be opening before him in his new field, but he soon went with his students to the war and met his death at Fredericksburg.

In 1856, three years before Gessner Harrison's retirement, came one greater even than he—Basil L. Gildersleeve. Born in Charleston, S. C., in 1831, he was graduated from Princeton in 1849, studied then for four years in the universities of Berlin, Bonn and Goettingen (Ph.D., 1853), was professor of Greek 1856-76, and of Latin 1861-66, in the University of Virginia, since 1876 professor of Greek in Johns Hopkins University. His chief published works are a *Latin Grammar* (1876-1894) *Persius, Justin Martyr, Odes of Pindar, Greek Syntax* (Vol. I of a compendious work, 1900), and a volume of *Essays and Studies*. But as the editor, since its foundation in 1880, of *The American Journal of Classical Philology*, he is still more widely known. It is a delicate matter to write discriminatingly of the services of one who still survives, but Professor Goodwin, the other chief of our Trojan heroes expressed himself on this very point of the *Journal* work as long ago as 1890 (preface to *Moods and Tenses*), and this I may quote: "It is with pride and pleasure that I acknowledge my deepest in-indebtedness to an American scholar, whose writings have thrown light upon most of the dark places in Greek syntax. I need not say that I refer to my friend, Professor Gildersleeve, of Baltimore. As editor of the *American Journal of Philology,* he has discussed every construction of the Greek moods, and he has always left his mark. His two reviews of Weber's work on the final sentence in Vols. III and IV of his *Journal* may well save many scholars the trouble of reading the book itself, while they contain much new matter which is valuable to every one. The acute observation that the use of ἄν and κέ in final constructions depends on the force of ὡς, ὅπως, and ὄφρα as conditional relative or temporal adverbs, explains much which before seemed inexplicable. His article on πρίν in Vol. II stated important principles of classic usage which were confirmed by Sturm's statistics; and this, with the later review of Sturm's volume, has done much to correct current errors and to establish sounder views about πρίν. His article on the Articular Infinitive in the 'Transactions of the American Philological Association for 1878' and in the third volume of his *Journal,* practically anticipated the results of Birklein's statistics. I can mention further only his article in Vol VI of the *Journal* on the Consecutive Sentence, which gives (it seems to me) the clearest statement ever made of the relations of ὥστε with the infinitive to ὥστε with the finite moods. I have expressed my indebtedness to these and other writings of Gildersleeve as occasion has required; but I have also often referred to his articles in his *Journal* by the simple mention of that periodical. I have also sometimes omitted a reference where one might seem proper, lest I should appear to make him responsible for what he might deem some dangerous heresy."

"Where did you study under Gildersleeve?" some one asked me one day. "I was never under him directly," I replied, "but we have all gone to school to him in the *Journal* and in his books." Indeed, I am fond of saying, "Gildersleeve's greatest pupil never sat on the benches before him, yet he made him." I refer to Humphreys of the University of Virginia, who, even while a student at Washington and Lee, was, perhaps unconsciously, modeling himself on Gildersleeve's published doctrines. Yes, we have all been to school to Gildersleeve. Two of my recent letters tell the common story. One is from Prof. W. H. Bocock, of the University of Georgia, dated Nov. 20, 1908: "I shan't begin on Gildersleeve; I'd write a book." The other letter is from Prof. Chas. W. Bain, University of South Carolina (Dec. 2, 1908). He says, "I have never had the good fortune to study under Professor Gildersleeve, but he has been uniformly kind and helpful to me on all occasions, and, of course, all of my Greek syntax that was worth knowing was culled from the notes on Justin Martyr and Pindar, and from his wonderful articles in the *Journal.*"

William E. Peters, born 1829, was a graduate of Emory and Henry College and of the University of Virginia, and became, first, professor of Latin and Greek, Emory and Henry College, 1852-1866, then professor of Latin, University of Virginia, 1866. He returned from a sojourn of two years in Germany to enter the war in the Confederate service, in which he rose to lieutenant-colonel. He was the officer who refused to obey General Early's order to apply the torch to Chambersburg. General Lee ordered his release from arrest. "He was brave to a fault. It is said that on one occasion he remained and fought with his pistol after his whole regiment had fled." He was for forty years one of the great intellectual forces of the University of Virginia, and consequently of the South, but a great teacher who published little; so we may well let his pupils state the case for him. Professor Bocock writes me: "His *Latin Case Relations* and *Syntax of the Latin Verb* contain one of the best first-hand collections of examples in existence; a collection which, by examples, silently corrects a good many misstatements of standard grammars. He was a thorough drill-master, and his men 'knew the facts of the language,' to use one of his favorite phrases." "Of Colonel Peters I hardly know how to speak," writes Professor Bain. "He, too, was a very great teacher, full of enthusiasm, and the deepest read man in Latin I have ever studied under or read after. It is, perhaps, due to Colonel Peters to say that, while he states in his *Syntax of the Latin Verb* that he does not believe any accurate historical syntax has been written, he did not neglect it, and always taught it where he believed it had been carefully worked out. He thus saved himself the horror of perpetuating the numerous errors of historical syntax in Schmalz and in the *Antibarbarus*. I remember very well, in fact I have the note made then, that in 1883 he taught us that the impf. subjv. in an unreal condition in *oratio obliqua* became *-rum fuisse,* not *-rum esse,* as was taught, and is generally taught to-day. The article in the *Journal of Philology* by Terrell was inspired by a letter from Colonel Peters to Professor Morgan, of Harvard, about this very subject. There are many points of this kind that I could mention that Colonel Peters taught us who were fortunate enough to sit under him, long before they found their way into books. In matters of syntax I would give him an equal place in Latin with Gildersleeve in Greek, though they worked in an entirely different manner. Perhaps I should mention, too, that he made a very thorough study of metres, and this was one of the most delightful and instructive courses he gave. In later years I had the privilege of discussing nearly every construction of Latin syntax with him, and I never wrote him about a point that I did not find he had a full supply of cogent examples on every stand he took, and you could be pretty sure that, when he said this or that occurred or did not occur, he was absolutely correct, for he made such statements only on his reading and not another's. I know it was this constant and careful investigation that led him to make his statements about historical syntax.'' ''Colonel Peters trained more men in Latin,'' says Professor Humphreys, ''than any other Southern teacher, and exercised an enormous influence through the men who went from here to teach Latin or Greek elsewhere. * * * I never knew a man so completely absorbed in anything as he was in Latin grammar and Latin metres. He required his graduates to know every little detail of both. * * * He read Cicero, Cæsar, etc., to teach grammar, Horace, Virgil, Plautus, etc., to teach metres. The subject matter and the literary effect he ignored and despised.''

The chair of Latin is now held by Professor Thomas Fitzhugh, M.A. (University of Virginia), formerly of the University of Texas, selected, it is said, by Dr. Peters to be his successor.

Along with the earlier professors of the University of Virginia it seems proper to mention one who spent his life mainly in a theological seminary, but knew his classics well and was, during all his career, a potent classical influence, Dr. John A. Broadus, of the Southern Baptist Theological Seminary. He was one of the greatest scholars and one of the most inspiring teachers whom the South has produced.

Professor Thomas R. Price, Dr. Gildersleeve's successor in the chair of Greek at the University of Virginia (1876-82), has left nothing in print to show his classical scholarship except reports in Gildersleeve's *Journal,* and he is chiefly known by his phenomenal success and influence as teacher of English at Randolph-Macon College (1868-76), and afterwards at Columbia University (1882-1903). He was a great teacher, whether in Greek or English, and I have never heard a living teacher so praised, I think, as he used to be by his old Randolph-Macon pupils. A large number of the important chairs of English in Southern colleges were filled by old pupils of his, and the new style of teaching English in the South is often called ''Price's method.'' ''Professor Price I knew personally,'' writes Professor Bain, ''who did splendid work at Randolph-Macon College, and filled with brilliant success the chair of Greek at the University of Virginia. Few men have had a harder task and have acquitted themselves with a more brilliant record. As you know, perhaps, he followed Gildersleeve in that chair. * * * He was a superb teacher, most careful, accurate and painstaking. My brothers and two cousins were under him in Greek, and I got my instruction in Greek from one of his pupils, so I know from them how inspiring he was. A glance at his reports in the *Journal* will show what a great teacher he was.''

John H. Wheeler (professor of Greek, University of Virginia, 1882-87) lived only five years, but the testimony of his old pupils is that he was a remarkable man and brilliant scholar. "That highly gifted man," says Professor Trent, "Dr. John H. Wheeler, a graduate of Harvard and Bonn, a pupil of Gildersleeve and the successor of Dr. Price as professor of Greek in the University of Virginia, was one of the very few of whom it may be said that outside and inside the teacher you found the whole-souled man." Professor Bocock says: "I trust you will pay due tribute to John H. Wheeler, a thorough scholar and inspiring teacher, a lecturer of exquisite good taste, a man of personal charm, who worthily upheld the traditions of a chair that had been occupied by George Long, Gessner Harrison, Basil L. Gildersleeve and Thomas R. Price. * * * I owe my first love to Kemper and Johnston [who prepared him for college], my great love to Wheeler —he made me go out into the night and recite a chorus from the *Antigone* to the stars. * * * To me he is one of three: Wheeler, Gildersleeve, Vahlen—though I was never under Gildersleeve."

Professor Bain writes: "I am delighted to say that, as I had not the good fortune to study Greek under either Dr. Gildersleeve or Professor Price, I was so fortunate as to be under Dr. Wheeler, who, had he lived, would have had no superior anywhere. It was from him that I first learned what Greek really was, what the study of language meant. He was a superb scholar, full of inspiration, and accuracy itself. His notes are to-day, twenty-three years after taking, full of inspiration and helpful points and valuable suggestions. Much of his work stands out in my mind as clearly to-day as when I was under him. His life was short, sacrificed to his work, and to his desire to keep that chair unspotted and unpolluted as it had been handed to him; but no man could have had more influence upon his students. Out of seven men whom he graduated in 1884, six became teachers of Greek.''

Milton W. Humphreys, occupant of the chair of Greek in the University of Virginia since 1887, is a very interesting figure. Born in Clarksburg, Va. (now West Virginia), in 1844, he was a student in Washington College when the war broke out, and promptly entered the Confederate service in the artillery. His active and versatile brain, drawn even then as much toward mathematics and physics as toward linguistics, was much interested in experiments to determine the range of the enemy. Student tradition had it that he had some of his Greek and Latin classics constantly with him at the front, beguiling therewith the intervals of camp leisure. He reëntered college in 1866 and had the great privilege of graduating and of serving as assistant and adjunct professor of ancient languages under Gen. Robert E. Lee.

Washington and Lee University was the first institution in this country to adopt the Roman pronunciation of Latin. This was in 1868, and due to Humphreys. The head of the department (Professor Harris) had told him he might investigate the subject and adopt what he should believe to have been the pronunciation of Cicero. Humphreys did so, but when the professor attended an oral at the intermediate examination he was amazed, and wanted Humphreys to abandon the ''new-fangled pronunciation.'' But this Humphreys refused to do. He had already met ridicule enough from his students, e. g., the nickname of ''old Keeckero Kaisar.'' He taught all the students of the first two years, i. e., four-fifths of those who went on into advanced Latin, and these, having become accustomed to the Roman pronunciation, refused to change when they reached Professor Harris. ''I

have had some fights in my life of which I am wont
to boast," says Humphreys, "as when, from sunset
till dark, with one three-inch rifle I fought at 400-500
yards range nine pieces of artillery under Colonel
DuPont(five of them belonging to the regular army);
but the fight of my life that required most moral
courage was c=k, j=y, v=w in Latin, with the influence of my full professor against me."

In 1872 he went on leave of absence to Germany,
and studying there first in Berlin, then in Leipzig,
took his Ph.D. at the latter place in 1873. Part of
his thesis appeared as his *Doctor-Arbeit* in 1873, all
of it in the "Transactions of the American Philological Association" from 1876-79. The immediate effect upon American classical scholars was to
make him at once the acknowledged classical metri-
cian of America and to bring him to the presidency
of the American Philological Association before he
was forty years old. Thirty years later at the
Washington meeting of the Philological Association (January, 1907), a New York scholar referred
to these very papers as exhibiting profounder metrical knowledge than that shown by the great English Homer scholar, Monro. His name has long been
a by-word among American scholars for acumen,
exhaustive erudition and accuracy—"One of our
two most accurate American scholars," Professor
Seymour once remarked. Of course, the old students of Dr. Humphreys, whether from Vanderbilt,
or Texas, or the University of Virginia, have un-
bounded confidence in his omniscience, and will tell
wonderful stories of what he knows about metres
and mathematics, physics and botany—and most of
it will be true. This ripe scholar has published only
two books (editions of the *Clouds* and of the *Antigone*), and a few other papers besides those above
mentioned—notably, *A Contribution to Infantile*

Linguistic (1880)—a very careful and interesting study recording, step by step, the process of development made by his own first child in learning to talk. Nor must his reports for Gildersleeve's *Journal* on *Philologus* and the *Revue de Philologie* be overlooked. In connection with his review of Zielinski's *The Agon of Old Attic Comedy* (*American Journal of Philology,* Vol. III., 179-206) there hangs a tale at once interesting and pathetic. Humphreys, then professor in the University of Texas, was himself preparing a paper upon this very subject, in blissful ignorance of Zielinski's forthcoming work. But the University of Texas was just established and without books. I remember Humphreys writing to me to verify some things in the library at Vanderbilt, for still other points he had to wait till books could be ordered from Germany. Before he had been able—for lack of books—to verify all his conclusions and appear in print, he saw one day an announcement of Zielinski's book, *Die Gliederung der Alt-attischen Komödie* (1885), with a feeling of sickening certainty that all his labor of years had been anticipated. When he got Zielinski's book he found that he himself had worked out every point made by the German scholar, and even more fully in some cases. The German work was a brilliant study—quite as much so was that of Humphreys— but nothing was left for the latter but to review Zielinski's book for Gildersleeve's *Journal.*

Next to the University of Virginia the University of North Carolina is, of all Southern institutions, doubtless entitled to consideration in the ante-bellum period, though its success in the line of making strong public men was much more marked than in that of literature or of pure scholarship in general, or of the classics in particular. Indeed, it might easily be inferred that at the beginning—the university was opened in 1795—the atmosphere was anti-classical. "When Dr. Caldwell came to the university the trustees and the public were prejudiced against the classics, and it was owing to his efforts that Greek was finally given its just recognition in the curriculum."* Greek was first required for a degree in 1804. After it was introduced, it was evidently not taught so as to make it an attractive study; e. g., Dr. Battle in his history quotes the following from Dr. Hooper's reminiscences: "Greek, after its introduction, became the bug-bear of college. Having been absent when my class began it, I heard, on my return, such a terrific account that I had no more durst encounter the Greeks than Xerxes when he fled in consternation across the Hellespont after the battle of Salamis. Rather than lose my degree, however, after two years I plucked up courage and set doggedly and desperately to work, prepared hastily thirty dialogues of Lucian, and on that stock of Greek was permitted to graduate." But this must not be taken too seriously, for he mentioned that the terror of chemistry was quite as great. He was more in fun than in earnest, a clever fellow, the "best scholar" in his class, and became eventually "professor of humanity."

Prof. Manual Fetter, the first Professor of Greek after the "chair of humanity" was divided, was, according to Dr. Battle, "well versed in the reading and parsing of Greek, but had the defect of most classical teachers of his day, that of not calling attention to the literary excellence of the books he taught. * * * Those who studied Greek for the grandeur of the thought and beauty of imagery were not pleased; but those who wished familiarity with the grammatical structure of the language, the

* C. L. Smith in *Circular of Information of Bureau of Education*, 1887, p. 68. Dr. Caldwell was a Princeton man, and Princeton influence was in that early day in North Carolina exerted in the good cause, as it is to-day in a wider field.

declensions and tenses, dialects and derivations of words, obtained as much as they could carry off.''

This same Professor Fetter seems to have had a kind heart and a sense of humor, for it is related that when he found once a student of Scotch descent seated helpless by an empty jug, he asked: ''Haven't you been drinking?'' ''Yes, sir, a little.'' ''How much?'' ''About a gallon, I reckon.'' We may infer from the record that the Scotchman was ''rusticated,'' for we read that ''he was allowed to return, graduated, and became eminent in his profession.'' The students had wit enough, of course, after that to speak of a Scotchman that drank, in Tacitus' phrase as *capacissimus vini.*

If the classical professors had only been as wise as Prof. C. F. Deems, adj. prof. of rhetoric and logic —afterwards the noted pastor of the Church of Strangers in New York—who, besides the work in his own department, had a class in Horace and one in the Bible! ''He did not care,'' says Dr. Battle, ''for the niceties of parsing and grammar, but he brought out the literary power of the work studied remarkably. * * * Of all the teachers of Latin I have known he was the most happy in showing the force and beauty of the poetry of Horace.''

There were some good classical scholars at the University of North Carolina from the time of the first professor of humanity, Rev. David Kerr, graduate of Trinity College, Dublin, to the present, including William Bingham, the first of that family so noted for several generations in secondary school work in North Carolina, and Dr. Andrews, a graduate of Yale, who, after his return to New England, prepared the well-known series of Latin textbooks. When we come to the eighties I can speak from my own knowledge, for I recall the great impression made instantly by George Taylor Winston when he became professor of Latin, and I remember Maj. Robert Bingham writing me, about 1885, that he was the strongest college professor he knew. But executive work soon claimed him, first as president of the University of North Carolina, then of the University of Texas, and finally of the Agricultural and Mechanical College of North Carolina.

Those who know Dr. Eben Alexander, professor of Greek in the University of North Carolina since 1886, regret that a personality so rich and rare, of scholarship so sound and stimulating, has not made itself felt in print as strongly as in the classroom. But nearly all of his life he has been cumbered about much serving, early in his career as chairman of the faculty of the University of Tennessee, then—after seven years as professor of Greek in the University of North Carolina—for four years as United States minister to Greece, more recently as dean of the University of North Carolina. He still holds his professorship of Greek, but in off hours must interview bad boys instead of writing classical papers or books.

Returning to Virginia, reference may be made to college work there. William and Mary College, Virginia, chartered Feb. 19, 1693, hence, the second in age of all the colleges of the country, and mother of statesmen in the Revolutionary period, was also in that period a centre of classical learning. "The country gentleman of Virginia prior to the Revolution knew his classics well (not critically, of course, but in mass), and could cap a fellow Burgess' line from Virgil or Horace as neatly as any M.P. over seas of his time. * * * The plays of Plautus and Terence were repeatedly acted by the students of William and Mary College to the great delight of the Burgesses and the gentry of the colony, so many of whom were educated in the great public schools of the mother country."* This good old college, which saw evil days for a very long period, has in recent years been renewing her youth and has now one of the most scholarly classical professors in the country, C. E. Bishop, M.A., Ph.D. (one of "McCabe's boys," I think), author of important philological monographs on the Greek verbals, etc.

It was hoped to make some fuller mention of Professors J. J. White and C. J. Harris, who held the classical chairs at Washington and Lee University in General Lee's time. Professor Bocock says they "produced little or nothing, but were inspiring teachers and men of scholarship." But my efforts to get facts have failed.

Addison Hogue, now of Washington and Lee University, has been recognized, ever since his early work at Hampden-Sidney College, as an excellent teacher—"a teacher of the same type as Peters," some one said of him. What he modestly says of his work now—"In a modest and conscientious way we try to give sound undergraduate instruction, good as far as it goes"—was true also of his University of Mississippi service. So conscientious has been his teaching all these years that he has found time for only one book—*Irregular Verbs of Attic Prose* (1889).

Professor E. W. Fay, while at Washington and Lee, had already attracted considerable attention by his etymological studies. He continues, at the University of Texas, to give published proof from time to time of his acumen and of his devotion to pure scholarship. He is a constant contributor to various classical journals in the United States and England, on Latin and Sanskrit, as well as etymological subjects. His colleague in the Greek chair at Austin,

---

* Private letter from W. Gordon McCabe.

Dr. W. J. Battle, is well fitted by training at home and abroad to further the cause of Greek by writing as well as teaching; but by accepting a deanship he has doubtless signed away most of his time to executive work. These two men hold chairs of which scholars have a right to expect much, for their predecessors have been such men as Humphreys, Sterrett and H. N. Fowler.

"Walter Blair, of Hampden-Sidney College" (now retired), writes Professor Bocock, "was one of the most polished and scholarly teachers of the South. Like Peters and Price, he came back from his German university course to enter the Confederate army. His book *On the Pronunciation of Latin* was, I think, a pioneer in this country."

I cannot refrain from mentioning here two or three classical professors who were deservedly eminent as teachers, but left little or nothing in print. One of these was Prof. John Henry Neville, head of the department of ancient languages in the University of Kentucky, who died Sept. 28, 1908, at the age of eighty-one. He was, beyond question, an extraordinary teacher and a man of ripe culture. I have heard and read of his classroom method as described by enthusiastic pupils, and I recall at the moment at least five remarkable men, products of his teaching. I had a letter from him once, of the most remarkable and beautiful penmanship I have ever seen and long as a magazine article, and which, indeed, published as such, attracted wide attention and commendation. "His latinity was exquisite," said an old pupil, "and when called upon for a recommendation of a student he would, perhaps, write it off in the language of Livy." I know that is true, for I saw once such a testimonial of his in exquisite Latin and beautiful as the writing of a mediæval monk on parchment. I have known two of his pupils who were masters of English styles very remarkable, but entirely different—James. Lane Allen, and Prof. W. B. Smith of Tulane University—who, I must believe, owe it above all to him. Another is a scholar of distinctly literary bent, who edits, translates and writes for the journals on Greek subjects, Prof. John Patterson, of Louisville. He made men, not books, and who will say he was not wise? Most books soon become antiquated; teachings implanted in a human soul live longer and with greater vitality. "As a teacher," writes Prof. W. B. Smith, "he was not surpassed by anyone I have ever known, and under other conditions he might have left behind him some enduring literary monument."

Another great teacher is W. S. Wyman, professor of Latin in the University of Alabama (now retired). Over fifty years professor in the same institution, he has been nearly all that time its chief figure, having acted several times as president and as often declined the tender of the office. He was wise in declining the office; most of the presidents are already forgotten, but "old Wyman" is one of the abiding traditions of the campus and the state.

In Tennessee the highest order of classical work done, before the time of Humphreys at Vanderbilt, was, doubtless, that of F. D. Allen, who was for a few years professor in the University of Tennessee, whither he had come from Oberlin. But his reputation belongs mainly to Harvard. Since his day the classical tradition at the University of Tennessee has been worthily sustained in various hands—Alexander, Jordan, Mellen, Shannon.

Dr. M. W. Humphreys, first professor of Greek in Vanderbilt University, set the classical pace in that young institution. He was succeeded by the writer of this monograph, who, while there (1882-94),

edited two books (*Thucydides* III and VII), and
published numerous philological papers. He was
followed by the present incumbent, Dr. H. C. Tol-
man, a Yale man, who is as well known for his ac-
quaintance with Sanskrit and old Persian as for
Greek, and is the author of nine different volumes
on Greek and Latin, Greek history, mythology,
archæology, Persian, etc., as well as numerous occasional articles. Dr. J. H. Kirkland, who became
professor of Latin in 1886, had already won an eu-
viable reputation as scholar and teacher, and with
his excellent edition of Horace's Satires and
Epistles had given an earnest of his productive capacity, when he was drafted into the chancellorship.
"I lament, as you do," writes Professor Fay,
"Kirkland's loss to productive Latin scholarship.
His few articles and his Horace seem to represent
some of the best Southern work in Latin." University presidencies these days allow no leisure for
either teaching or writing classical books, and Dr.
Kirkland has had to turn over his Latin chair to
another, Dr. R. B. Steele, who is a very prolific contributor to classical journals, chiefly on subjects in
Latin syntax.

A playmate of Dr. Kirkland's from the town of
Spartanburg, S. C., has spent all the years of his
manhood in the neighboring University of the South
at Sewanee. He succeeded Prof. Caskie Harrison
in 1883, and ten years later Professor Trent wrote
of him: "Professor Wiggins, when he took the chair
of ancient languages just vacated by Prof. Caskie
Harrison, was, perhaps, the youngest professor in
the United States. His chair had long been the most
important in the university; a natural result of
church control and of the avowed following of English traditions. Under Professor Wiggins it has
lost none of its prestige, although the growth of the

university has brought other chairs into prominence. It is safe to say that there are few better teachers of the classics anywhere than Prof. Wiggins, and it is equally safe to say that no institution in the South turns out more well-equipped classical scholars than Sewanee." But soon after that was written Dr. Wiggins, too, was drafted into the chief executive office, that of vice-chancellor, and has had gradually to turn most of his teaching over to others.

Tulane University, one of the best endowed and strongest institutions in the South, opened at New Orleans nearly at the same time with Vanderbilt at Nashville. Dr. Richard H. Jesse was the first professor of Latin and was fast establishing University of Virginia traditions on the banks of the Mississippi, when he was called away to the presidency of the University of Missouri. His successor, Professor Dillard, has lately been called to executive work elsewhere. But the classical work continues in competent hands, Prof. Walter Miller especially upholding the best traditions of both classical and archæological erudition.

One is tempted to pass over into Missouri and speak of classical and archæological conditions at the State University, but that, perhaps, is Western territory.

In the classical work of the University of Georgia the descendants of its sometime great president, Moses Waddel (see below), have been especially conspicuous. Of one of these Professor Bocock writes: "I fancy the most accomplished man who ever held the chair of ancient languages in the University of Georgia was William H. Waddel (1860-1878)." He was author of a Greek grammar. Concerning Professor Bocock, the present incumbent of the Greek chair, Professor Bain writes: "Of the younger generation, and I am excluding, of course,

Dr. Humphreys, of the University of Virginia, the best Greek scholar is unquestionably Professor Willis H. Bocock, of the University of Georgia. Mr. Bocock has published little in a classical way, though he has contributed much to various magazines; but he is a deep and accurate student, full of enthusiasm, and a most capable teacher. I have known him for years, and it has been my good fortune to have him enlighten me innumerable times, and I know that he has collected vast material in both Greek and Latin that contains many new points. I do not know of any man in the South who is his equal. You may, perhaps, recall that when Dr. Gildersleeve reviewed Fuchs' article on the 'Temporal Sentence of Limit,' Mr. Bocock sent in many examples which had either been omitted by Fuchs or which corrected him in his interpretation or conclusions. I have discussed with him hundreds of matters in Greek and have never failed to be enlightened by his thorough knowledge, accurate scholarship, breadth of vision, and thorough grasp of his subject. There has been no knotty point of syntax on which he has failed to throw some light. We have discussed together nearly every article in the *Journal of Philology* and many notes and questions of grammar, so I feel that I can speak personally and, hence, strongly of his work. He is now engaged in editing Pliny's Letters for the Gildersleeve-Lodge series. Though his specialty is Greek, and he has worked in that field for more than twenty years, yet, when he took this work up he brought to it the same methods, and by his fine scholarship, keenness of vision and accurate work has already corrected many details of historical syntax.''

Of Prof. Charles W. Bain, of the University of South Carolina, I am so fortunate as to be able to give an estimate by a scholar who knows him well.

"There is," Professor Bocock says, "no better Latinist in the South, *quod sciam,* than Bain. Charles Wesley Bain, born 1864, one of 'McCabe's boys,' University of Virginia, 1883-85, M.A.; University of the South, first classical master in Mc-Cabe's school, 1891-95; head master Sewanee grammar school, 1895-98; professor of Ancient Languages University of South Carolina since 1898, contributor to the *Nation, American Journal of Philology,* article on 'Classical Literature' in *Encyclopædia Americana,* editor of Homer's *Odyssey* VI. and VII., First Latin Book (Gildersleeve-Lodge series), *Ovid* (selections)." "Bain is one of the best men we have in the South now," writes Alexander. Of Bain's colleague Fay writes, "Greene, of South Carolina, is mentally vigorous."

If space permitted it would be a pleasure to go into some detail about the conscientious scholarly work done in some of the smaller colleges, as, *e. g.,* Davidson (North Carolina), Randolph-Macon (Virginia), Wofford (South Carolina), Georgetown (Kentucky). No less a pleasure would it be to tell of the work of some of the Southern scholars whom the South has given to Northern universities, notably, Professor Sterrett, M.A. of the University of Virginia, who, after taking his Ph.D. at Munich and making a name as an archæologist at Athens and in Asia Minor, taught for a while at the University of Texas, then at Amherst, and now is head of the department of Greek at Cornell. He is the editor of *Inscriptions of Sebaste, Assos,* and *Tralles* (1885), author of accounts of his epigraphical journeys, editor of Homer's *Iliad.*

Except as to Dr. Gildersleeve, no claim has been made for the South to Johns Hopkins University, for that institution, though located at Baltimore, is national.

Schools and Schoolmasters.

In several of the older states good classical schools flourished in the colonial period long before the era of colleges. This was notably true of South Carolina, as shown by Edward McCrady, Jr., *Colonial Education of South Carolina* (United States Bureau of Education, 1889); of North Carolina (see C. L. Smith in United States Bureau of Education, 1888), and of Virginia. Confining our attention to the Nineteenth century, especial mention may be made of a great school in South Carolina.

Moses Waddel (1770-1840) was president of the University of Georgia, 1819-29, but his name is chiefly connected with the deservedly famous academy which he founded at Willington* in Abbeville district (county), S. C. His father and mother had emigrated from County Down in Ireland, and were settled at the time of his birth in Rowan county, N. C. A cousin of his was the blind man who preached the sermon on the agony and death of Christ, described by William Wirt as rivalling the sublimity and grandeur of Massillon or Bourdaloue. Graduating from Hampden-Sidney College, Virginia, he taught for a time at Wrightsborough, Ga., but in 1804 opened the Willington Academy near his country seat in Abbeville county, S. C. Far from the noise and dissipation of town or city, and anxious to merit the praise of their great preceptor, the students, as a rule, worked as hard as health would permit. "Their life was simple and industrious, and their food was Spartan in its plainness—corn-bread and bacon. Instead of using gas and student-lamps they pored over the lessons by the aid of pine torches. At the sound of the horn they retired to bed, except a few adventurous spirits that

---

* See C. Meriwether, United States Bureau of Education, 1889, p. 37ff.

set out in quest of hen-roosts or to unhinge gates. They rose at dawn and resumed their studies." Thoroughness of work Dr. Waddel always insisted on, and the advanced nature of his instruction may be inferred from the fact that so many of his pupils entered the junior class in the different colleges, *e. g.,* Patrick Noble (afterwards governor) at Princeton, John C. Calhoun and Judge Longstreet at Yale, George McDuffie at South Carolina College. He himself was reputed to know some of the Latin authors by heart, and "would hear the classes recite in Virgil with his eyes closed." The drones of the class would prepare one hundred to one hundred and fifty lines of Virgil for a single recitation, while the bright leaders would master one thousand. "The brilliant, ambitious boys would not be held back by the drudges; he would form new classes and push the best students on. * * * George Carey (afterwards member of Congress from Georgia) prepared a thousand lines of Virgil for a Monday's recitation when at Willington. The Virgil class was too large, and its members were of such unequal grades that the teacher announced that it would be divided on the basis of the work done by each one by the following Monday, and it was under this stimulus that Carey did his work. George McDuffie excelled this feat a year or so later with one thousand two hundred and twelve lines of Horace." He was a very hard student and is said "to have devoured his Latin grammar in three weeks." Hon. Armistead Burt says (in an unpublished eulogy of McDuffie), "Within a fortnight after he commenced Virgil, from Friday evening to Monday morning he prepared for recitation eleven hundred lines."

"Men are still living," says C. Meriwether, "who speak with pride of their attendance at Willington, and their children cherish it as an honor to the family. George McDuffie, when a senator, and Thomas Farr Capers in after life revisited the place, and as they walked among the dilapidated houses and recalled their old teacher and his school, they were moved to tears. No other man in the South has so powerfully impressed himself on men who influenced the destiny of the country as this Willington master. He needs no monument, but lives in the great men whom he has trained. There went forth from this school 'one vice-president and many foreign and cabinet ministers; and senators, congressmen, governors, judges, presidents and professors of colleges, eminent divines, barristers, jurists, legislators, physicians, scholars, military and naval officers innumerable.' ''*

Virginia, more than any of the other older Southern states, had good classical schools in the colonial period. W. Gordon McCabe, in his University of Virginia Alumni address (1888), ''Virginia Schools Before and After the Revolution,'' mentions the most important of these, and gives credit to the ''Old Parsons, who, although they had never heard of logœdic rhythms, or the classification of the conditional sentence, could read Homer and Demosthenes without a dictionary and quote Horace with an apt felicity, which seems to have gone out with the last century.'' But the really great classical period of the Virginia schools was coincident with the opening of the University of Virginia. ''The number and character of the preparatory schools in Virginia,'' wrote Mr. Strode, of Kenmore University School, in 1885, ''I have always thought to be due solely to the influence of the University of Virginia. Except under its shadow we could not

---

* I count one vice-president, three members of the cabinet, four United States senators, two foreign ministers, ten members of Congress, six governors (several holding more than one of these offices).   Among these were W. H. Crawford, of Georgia and John C. Calhoun of South Carolina.

maintain the high standards which characterize what we call the University Schools." No better evidence could be adduced of the high character of the classical training given in the schools than the remark quoted by McCabe: "Gessner Harrison during his latter years here was wont to declare that pupils were coming to him from the leading preparatory schools with a better knowledge of Latin than twenty years before had been carried away by his graduates."

Among the Virginia schoolmasters of the Nineteenth century, F. W. Coleman was "the greatest teacher of his time." Born in 1811, he entered the University of Virginia at twenty-one and was graduated M.A. at twenty-four. He was the son and grandson of teachers, and went to the university to fit himself for better teaching. Joining his older brother, who had succeeded his father at Concord, within a year he became sole proprietor of that school, which he soon made famous. That was in 1835. Dr. Joynes, an old pupil of his, describes his impressions of Concord Academy in the late forties.* "Concord Academy was a massive brick building surrounded by a few log-cabins, situated absolutely in the old fields—no inclosures—no flowery walks—no attraction for the eye, such as I had been accustomed to in the academies I had attended in the North. Within all was rude and rough—the barest necessities of decent furniture—the table abundant, but coarsely served; the rooms devoid of all luxury or grace, no trace of feminine art, nor sound of woman's voice to relieve the first attacks of home-sickness—everything rough, severe, masculine.

"I looked and enquired after the 'Rules and Regulations' of the school. I found there were none. To

* Letter to W. Gordon McCabe, see *Virginia Schools*, etc., p 44ff.

my horror I felt deserted even by the eye of discipline. It seemed to me the reign of lawlessness, with utter desolation and loneliness. But I soon found there reigned at Concord the one higher law: *Be a man*—that what I thought solitude and helplessness was the lesson of individuality—*Be yourself*. As for discipline, there was none in the usual sense of the term. *Be a man, be a gentleman,* nothing more. ** * *

"Obedience and truthfulness were the only virtues recognized or inculcated at Concord: obedience absolute to Frederick Coleman—his will was law, was gospel, was Concord. There was not a boy, even of those who loved him most, who did not fear him absolutely. And truthfulness with courage. All else was forgiven but lying and cowardice. These were not forgiven, for they were impossible at Concord."

"The boys studied," says McCabe, "when and where they chose, and the length of time given to a class varied from thirty minutes to three hours, according to the judgment of the instructor. Boys were knocked up at all hours of the night, sometimes long after midnight, and summoned to the recitation room by Old Ben, the faithful negro janitor, who equally feared and worshipped his master. A sharp rap at the door and the familiar cry 'Sophocles, with your candles, young gentlemen,' would send the youngsters tumbling out of bed in the long winter nights, just as they had begun to dream of home or of certain bright eyes that had bewitched them in the 'long vacation.'" "Many and many a time," says Dr. Joynes, "each fellow with his tallow dip, have we read long past midnight, and never a sleepy eye while Old Fred expounded to us *Antigone* or *Ajax*."

"Once the boys, playfully taking advantage of a mistake of the master, who inadvertently announced the wrong day for the next recitation, slipped off and went fishing. They reached the trysting-place two miles away and were just casting their lines, gleefully thinking they had outwitted Old Ben, when the familiar cry was heard, 'Ripides, young gen'l'-men, Mars Fred is waitin'.' " "Frederick Coleman's teaching," says Dr. Joynes, "what was it? Wherein its magic power? Why is it still famous after forty years, so that like Nestor μετὰ τριτάτοισιν ἀνάσσει? Ah! I cannot tell you. I cannot analyze or describe it. I only know that I have seen no such teaching since, and I have sat at the feet of Harrison and Courtenay and McGuffey at home, and of Haupt and Boeckh and Bopp abroad. It was just. the immeasurable force of supreme intellect and will that entered into you and possessed you, until it seemed that every fibre of your brain obeyed his impulse. Like the ancient mariner, he held you with his glittering eye, and like him he had his will with you. * * * He held that the first book of Livy contained all Latinity, and that 'all the glory that was Greece' was to be found in the *Hecuba* of Euripides. These were his *pièces de resistance,* and he taught them as they were never taught before or since. From these as centres or starting points, his teachings of Latin and Greek proceeded. A copy of the *Hecuba,* for instance, as taught by Coleman, would be a literary curiosity. Every line, phrase, idiom, was made a centre of citation ranging far and wide over the plays (we used only the complete texts without 'notes' at Concord). *'Where does this occur elsewhere?'* *'Where otherwise.'* *'What is the difference?'* *'What is the point thus differentiated or illustrated?'* *'Why?'*—until the margin could hardly hold the references. * * * As a teacher he was the greatest of his age; there has been no other like him.''

"His conversation," says another old pupil of his, Prof. Guy Carroll, "was a never-ending pleasure to his boys. Sometimes he would join a knot of them sitting in the shade on a summer evening, and enter with them into the discussion of any subject that happened to engage their attention at the moment. Presently the discussion would become a monologue. Parties at play in different parts of the grounds would drop their bats or their marbles and silently gather around. Before long it would become known from room to room that 'Old Fred is talking,' and the whole school would be collected about him, listening with such charmed intentness to his words that even the sound of the supper bell was regarded as an unwelcome intrusion."

W. Gordon McCabe, the greatest and most widely known of the recent successors of the Colemans, was born in Richmond, Aug. 4, 1841, and now resides there since his retirement in 1901. For an account of the discipline and instruction that obtained in his Petersburg University School in the year 1885, when it was at the acme of prosperity and efficiency, see my article in the *Atlantic Monthly* of December, 1885. I repeat now the estimate then expressed: "I know nothing better that the South can do in her schools than to take this school as a model. * * * The methods and thoroughness of this school, and of such schools, are worthy of imitation anywhere." As to McCabe's scholarship, one of his "old boys," Professor Bain, of the University of South Carolina, writes (Dec. 2, 1908): "One of those who have influenced my own life most is W. Gordon McCabe, formerly headmaster of the University School, Petersburg, Va., now living in Richmond, unquestionably one of the greatest classical scholars in the South or in the country in his day, and the most inspiring teacher I have ever known. I was a student under him four years and taught with him six years, so I feel that I knew him thoroughly. I was with him when the last edition of Gildersleeve's *Grammar* was coming through the press, and I had the rare good fortune to discuss with him nearly every point of Latin syntax, and I can assure you he did much to make the present book what it is. I suppose next to Gildersleeve and Peters he has had more influence on classical scholarship than any man in the South. He is a thorough scholar, and I know he had more influence in shaping my career than any one else.'' Professor Gildersleeve speaks of him in the preface to the revised edition of his Latin grammar, as ''a Latinist of exact and penetrating scholarship''; further as ''a man of extensive and scholarly attainments, the master of an easy and graceful style, an impressive and imposing speaker, accustomed to controlling and guiding young men, himself an energetic and ardent student.'' Professor Peters reckoned him ''one of the most reliable, exact and accomplished Latinists in this country.'' Charlton T. Lewis, ranking him ''among the leading Latinists of America,'' says, ''Second to no American instructor in his personal control over students and in the power to make the routine of the class a stimulus to intellectual ambition, he is also eminent for scholarly accuracy and literary taste.'' Dr. McCosh, of Princeton, said, ''Coit, of St. Paul's School, Pingry, of Elizabeth, and McCabe, of Virginia, are probably the best high school instructors on this side of the water.''

I mentioned in the *Atlantic Monthly* article above referred to other university schools in Virginia worthy to be compared with McCabe's, namely, Hanover Academy, the Episcopal High School at Alexandria, Kenmore Academy, Pantops Academy, and might have added Hampton Academy, Brookland School, and Broun and Tebbs School. "But alas!" writes Mr. McCabe in a letter, Jan. 26, 1909, "owing to the hysteria about practical education and the public school education, that type of 'university school' is fast disappearing and it is not likely that we shall see hereafter any considerable number of lads who can write Greek and Latin prose with correctness and flexibility. Eheu!"

The school in Alabama most noteworthy for classical teaching, as well as otherwise, was that long conducted by Dr. Henry Tutwiler, one of the first M.A.'s of the University of Virginia. He gave up a college professorship in 1847 to open a private school, which was often called the "Rugby" of the South. The extraordinary success of the school— the number admitted was limited and applications were often filed a year in advance—was due, chiefly, to the character, common sense and learning of its founder. It flourished for thirty-five years under its founder, who died in 1884.

Dr. David Caldwell was the most famous name in the early educational annals of North Carolina. The son of a Scotch-Irish farmer, he was born in Lancaster county, Pa., in 1725, and graduated at Princeton in 1761. "It was his practice to study at a table by the window with the sash raised until a late hour, then cross his arms on the table, lay his head on them, and sleep in that position till morning." He established a classical school in Guilford county about 1766 or 1767. "His log-cabin served North Carolina as an academy, a college and a theological seminary." "Dr. Caldwell, as a teacher, was probably more useful to the church than any one man in the United States." Such are some of the estimates given of his work. On the establishment of the University he was offered the presidency, but declined on account of age. He died in 1824 at the age of ninety-nine, "the most illustrious name in the educational history of North Carolina," says C. L. Smith in a monograph of United States Bureau of Education. "Five of his scholars became govern ors of different states; many more members of Congress * * * and a much greater number became lawyers, judges, physicians, and ministers of the gospel."

In North Carolina, as in Virginia, the most nota ble development of classical schools or academies was coincident with the opening of the state uni versity. In January, 1821, the *North American Review* speaks of the influence of the university, viz.: "In an ardent and increasing zeal for the establish ment of schools and academies for several years past, we do not believe North Carolina has been outdone by a single state. The academy at Raleigh was founded in 1804, previous to which there were only two institutions of the kind in the state. The number at present is nearly fifty, and is rapidly increasing."

The greatest of all these North Carolina schools was the Bingham Academy, of which I wrote in the *Atlantic Monthly*, December, 1885, viz.: "The fa mous Bingham School in North Carolina was found ed in 1793 by Rev. William Bingham, grandfather of the present principal. He was followed by his son Wil liam J. Bingham, and he by his sons, successively, William and Robert. The school has seven teachers. Within the past five years twenty-two states of the Union and four foreign countries have been repre sented there, and attendance has increased from 103 in 1876 to 251 in 1884. It is and has been from the beginning, a private enterprise, depending solely on the brains and energy of the remarkable family that has been at its head since the foundation. The pride of the state, as well known in North Carolina as the

old university of that state, and better known
abroad, it finds only a rival or two in the South outside of Virginia, and the name alone is anywhere in
the South a sufficient guarantee for a thorough preparation for college." It was recently transferred to
Asheville, N. C., where it continues under the old
head, Major Robert Bingham. Other classical schools
maintained in North Carolina are the William Bingham School, Mebane, N. C.; The Horner School, Oak
Ridge Institute, The Graham School.

The most important educational influence in the
history of Tennessee has undoubtedly been Vanderbilt University, opened in 1875 at Nashville, Tenn.
It has done for preparatory schools in Tennessee
and the Southwest what was accomplished by the
University of Virginia and the University of North
Carolina for secondary education in those states
early in the last century, and it has done its work in
this direction even better. "The credit for the
happy change in the matter of preparatory training," I wrote in 1891, " is largely due to the example and phenomenal success of the great Webb
School, now at Bell Buckle, Tenn. The name of the
writer of this paper has sometimes been creditably
mentioned in connection with this movement. I have
heard Mr. W. R. Webb, Sr., who established his school
at Culleoka in the early seventies, say that but for the
opening of Vanderbilt University in 1875, when his
first boys were just ready for college, he did not
know what he should have done with them. The
sending of these first well-trained young men to
Vanderbilt was just as important for the inauguration of high standards there. The two institutions
—the university and the school—have always
worked hand in hand, and equal credit is due to both
for the result. W. R. and J. M. Webb are brothers,
graduates of the University of North Carolina, hav-

ing their preparatory training from the Horner School in North Carolina. They are joint-principals. The older—a veteran of the war—is a man of fine executive talent, an excellent speaker, and an inspiring teacher; a great personality; the younger is the best school-teacher and one of the wisest men I have ever known. I used to say at Vanderbilt University, "My hardest task is keeping students up to such love of Greek as they bring with them from John Webb." The seniors in the school are taught by him alone in all the subjects—geometry, Chaucer and Shakespeare, Anabasis and Homer, Æneid and elementary German; and I have never known any combination of teachers in any school to teach these subjects so well. It was a great compliment to these brothers that the late Professor Seymour of Yale once planned to send his son to Tennessee just to be under the tuition of the Webbs. This school has enjoyed phenomenal success for its whole history of forty years—"is every year crowded with students from all parts of the South, and sometimes rejects in one year applicants enough to fill another school." For years the limit of attendance has been fixed at two hundred, though generally a few more than this are admitted; and the school is always full, though since 1900 it has ceased advertising for pupils in any paper.

The following schools that fit primarily for Vanderbilt University and do about the same grade of work as the Webbs, are manned by old Webb pupils: Mooney School, Murfreesboro, Tenn.; Branham & Hughes School, Spring Hill, Tenn. (now the largest preparatory school in the state); Peoples School, Franklin, Tenn.; Morgan School, Fayetteville, Tenn.; Massie School, Pulaski, Tenn.; Robbins School, Mckenzie, Tenn.; Fitzgerald & Clark School, Trenton, Tenn.; Peoples & Tucker School, Springfield, Tenn. Besides these may be mentioned especially: Montgomery Bell Academy, Nashville, Tenn.; Wallace School, Nashville, Tenn.; Bowen School, Nashville, Tenn.; Sewanee Grammar School, Sewanee, Tenn.; Columbia Military Institute, Columbia, Tenn.; Castle Heights School.

Good classical schools, on the model of the Webb School, tributary mainly to Vanderbilt University, flourish in other Southwestern states. One of the best of these is the Clary School at Fordyce, Ark. The following statements, taken from the *Vanderbilt Quarterly* of October, 1908, are significant in this connection: "In the academic and engineering departments 168 new students have matriculated this fall. They have come from forty-one schools and twenty-seven institutions of higher learning. Seventy-six have come from thirteen accredited schools. Fifty-five in all have entered by examination. Thirty-four have come by transfer from colleges and other institutions of higher grade. Practically every private school and a number of the public schools are prepared to give the full course in Greek. There is rarely a school, public or private, that is not ready to give a course in Latin through to the end of its curriculum." The commendation of Professor Hogue, of Washington and Lee University (letter Nov. 7, 1908), seems deserved: "Tennessee seems to be the Southern state in which Greek is most successfully studied."

CHARLES FORSTER SMITH,
Professor of Greek and Classical Philology,
University of Wisconsin.

CHAPTER VIII

ECONOMIC AND POLITICAL ESSAYS IN THE ANTE-BELLUM SOUTH.

IN the ante-bellum period and for a generation afterward the Northern people and
those of many European countries were
profoundly concerned with liberalizing
their social and economic institutions and with
strengthening their national governments. But in
the South the oppressive burden of the great race
problem forced the body politic into social conservatism, and at the same time the necessity of in-
suring exemption from Northern control through
Congressional majorities obliged the Southern leaders usually to antagonize nationalistic movements.
The great world outside was radical in temper and
nationalistic in policy; the South was conservative
and stressed the rights of local units under the general government. The world measured the South by
its current standards and found the South wanting.
The world was not concerned with what the South
had to say in its own behalf; it refused to read
Southern publications and judged the South un-
heard. While alien and unfriendly views of the Old
South abound to-day in huge editions, the conservative writings of Southerners to the manner born are
mostly fugitive and forgotten. Yet on the whole,
the Southern product of economic and political essays was very large, and in the mass these writings
constitute a varied and often excellent body of literature, highly valuable as interpreting and recording
the life and opinions of the successive generations.

As a rule these writings deal not with strictly economic or strictly political themes, but with complex public questions involving economics, politics and society simultaneously. They can be fitted into a plan of treatment only with difficulty and with some danger of slighting significant minor phases in some of the important essays discussed.

Theoretical and General Economics.

Economic theory is, of course, a development of quite recent growth. There was not much discussion of it in America in the ante-bellum period, and few Southerners, in particular, were closet philosophers enough to deal with its refinements. Some of the strongly edited newspapers, such as the *Federal Union* of Milledgeville, Ga., assigned columns regularly to "Political Economy," discussing theoretical questions in them at times, but filling them more generally with concrete items relating to industry and commerce at home and abroad. Among the college professors who wrote on economic themes, Thomas Cooper, long the dominant personality in South Carolina College, schooled a whole generation of budding statesmen in thorough-going *laissez-faire* economic doctrine; Thomas Dew, at William and Mary, and George Tucker, at the University of Virginia, appear to have taught political economy, without special bias, along with various other subjects in social and psychological fields, while J. D. B. DeBow, professor of political economy in the University of Louisiana at New Orleans, probably treated in his lectures more of concrete subjects of American industry and commerce than of unsubstantial theories. Each of these men might well have written general economic treatises, but Tucker and Cooper alone did so.

After a preliminary series of vigorous essays on

banking, public debts, population, etc., written in 1813 and collected into a volume in 1822, Tucker published a scholarly general treatise on money and banking in 1839, and a statistical analysis of the United States census returns in 1843. Cooper's only formal economic writing was his *Lectures on the Elements of Political Economy*, 1826, which embodied the current economic thought of the *laissez-faire* school. He, of course, advocated free trade and free banking. Incidentally, he estimated slave labor, under the existing conditions in the cotton belt, to be more expensive than free labor. Dew apparently published nothing noteworthy except his famous essay on slavery, 1833, while DeBow contented himself with editing his *Review* and a cyclopedic description of Southern and Western resources in 1853-54, superintending the eighth United States census, writing a compendium of that census, 1854, and issuing occasional articles on the plantation system and the project of reopening the foreign slave trade. Aside from the writings of these few professional economic philosophers, the South produced practically nothing in economic theory or in formal statistics. Robert Mills' *Statistics of South Carolina*, 1826, and George White's *Statistics of Georgia*, 1849, were mere historical and descriptive miscellanies.

Agriculture.

Few Southerners were pen-and-ink men by native disposition. Most of them wrote for publication only under the pressure of public emergency. In easy times the reading class of Southerners would read the ancient and modern European classics, and the local newspapers would be concerned mainly with world politics. But in times of industrial crises thinking men would inquire for economic and social treatises throwing light upon American problems;

the newspapers would teem with essays on the causes, character and remedies of the existing depression, and the job-presses would issue occasional books and numerous pamphlets by local authors upon the issues of the day.

In Southern agriculture each occurrence of a crisis brought forth substantial writings, whether soil surveys, descriptions of methods, or didactic essays. Near the end of the Eighteenth century, for example, occurred a severe depression in Carolina coast industry, and in 1802 appeared Drayton's *View of South Carolina,* describing methods and improvements in indigo, rice and cotton, and in 1808 Ramsay's *History of South Carolina* was published, with a large appendix full of agricultural data from and for the sea-island district. During the War of 1812 tobacco was heavily depressed, and John Taylor, of Caroline, began to write his *Arator* essays for newspaper and pamphlet publication. In the late twenties the Eastern cotton belt felt the pinch of Western competition, and in 1828 was established at Charleston the *Southern Agriculturist,* a strongly edited monthly which was well supported by subscribers and contributors for several years until the return of easy times. From 1839 to 1844 was the most severe economic depression in the history of the ante-bellum South. Cotton was principally affected, but all other interests suffered in sympathy. The result was an abundant activity in economic writing, agriculture included. Edmund Ruffin, who had long been conspicuous as a soil and crop expert in Virginia, was employed by the commonwealth of South Carolina to make an agricultural survey of the state, made his first descriptive report in 1843, and published occasional essays and addresses during the next decade upon soils and fertilizers. R. F. W. Allston, a sea-island planter, published in 1843 a memoir on rice planting (as well as a general descriptive essay in 1854 on Southern seacoast crops), and in 1844 Whitemarsh B. Seabrook, president of the South Carolina Agricultural Society, afterward governor of the state, published a memoir upon the development of sea-island cotton culture.

All of these publications were soon eclipsed in importance by the establishment of the famous and invaluable *DeBow's Review* at New Orleans in 1846, which for many years afterward not only abounded in contributed articles and news items upon agricultural and other economic subjects, but also reprinted most of the noteworthy fugitive addresses and essays which appeared in the field of Southern economics during the period of the *Review's* publication. The *Cotton Planters' Manual,* compiled by J. A. Turner, of Georgia (1857), deserves mention as a collection of useful essays reprinted from various sources on cotton culture, plant diseases, manures and commerce. On the sugar industry, nothing was written in the United States of value comparable to several essays in the West Indies: Clement Caines, *Letters on the Cultivation of the Otaheite Cane* (London, 1801), the anonymous *Practical Rules for the Management and Medical Treatment of Negro Slaves in the Sugar Colonies* (London, 1803), and M. G. Lewis' *Journal of a West India Proprietor* (London, 1834).

Mining, Manufactures, Transportation and Commerce.

Upon the subject of mining, all Southern colonial and ante-bellum literature is negligible after the time of William Byrd's excellent description of the Virginia iron mines about 1732. West Virginia salt, Tennessee copper and Georgia gold were neglected by all but newspaper writers, while Carolina phosphates, Alabama iron, Louisiana sulphur and Texas oil did not begin to be mined until after the antebellum period.

On manufactures, William Gregg published a series of articles in the *Charleston Courier* and collected them in a pamphlet, 1845. He described the prior attempts at textile manufacturing in South Carolina, attributing their ill-success to the smallness of the scale of operation and the failure of each mill to specialize in a single sort of cloth; and he urged more extensive embarkation upon manufacturing and the avoidance of past errors. Aside from factory officials in their company reports and occasional descriptive, apologetical and hortatory writers in *DeBow's Review,* Gregg, with his slender writing, seems to have been alone in the field.

In the field of transportation there were innumerable essays and reports upon local problems, projects and progress in the improvement of transit facilities. Among them the treatise of Robert Mills on a project of public works in South Carolina, 1822, is notable for its elaboration and pretentiousness and for the complete impracticability of his plans. Robert Y. Hayne's essays and reports on the Charleston and Cincinnati railroad project, 1837-39, were similarly chimerical, as were also some of the Alabama writings on plank roads about 1850. To offset the recklessness of such writings as these, an anonymous writer published a notable series of ultra-conservative essays in the *Charleston Mercury* and collected them in a pamphlet, *The Railroad Mania, By Anti-Debt,* Charleston, 1848. In the main the Southern essays in the field of transportation were distinctly sane and well reasoned. Some of the official railroad reports are distinctly valuable as noting general economic developments in their territory year by year. Among such are the reports of the Central of Georgia officers, which were collected and reprinted by the company in occasional volumes.

The genius of the Southern people ran very slightly to commerce, and their literature shows little attention to any but a few of its spectacular features. The principal themes attracting the newspaper and periodical writers (and there were practically no others dealing with commerce) were the importance of cotton in the world's commerce, the possibility of cornering the cotton supply or otherwise manipulating its price in the interest of the producers, the project of establishing direct trade in steamship lines between Southern ports and Europe, and thereby attempting to reduce the Northern profits on Southern commerce, and the possibility of reopening the African slave trade. The cotton trade discussions were most conspicuous about 1836 to 1839, the study of foreign commercial relations was mainly in the fifties, and the debate over the slave trade was waged, between a few advocates and numerous opponents, between 1855 and 1861.

Labor.

White wage-earning labor was probably not so extremely scarce in the ante-bellum South as most historians would have us believe, but trades-unions were few, and the labor problems apart from negroes and slavery were not conspicuous enough to occasion the writing of many formal essays. Joseph Henry Lumpkin, later chief justice of Georgia, published, in 1852, an essay, *The Industrial Regeneration of the South,* which gives his interpretation of existing conditions, incidentally, in his somewhat utopian argument in favor of manufactures. He says, in part:

"It is objected that these manufacturing establishments will become the hotbeds of crime * * * But I am by no means ready to concede that our poor, degraded, half-fed, half-clothed and ignorant population, without Sabbath schools, or any other kind of instruction, mental or moral, or without any just appreciation of character,—will be injured by giving them employment, which will bring them under the oversight of employers who will inspire them with self-respect by taking an interest in their welfare."

The pros and cons of employing free labor for plantation work were discussed in newspaper articles, but probably the best journalistic item in this connection is that of the traveler-scientist, Charles Lyell, written in 1846 and published in his *Second Visit to the United States* (Vol. II., p. 127):

"The sugar and cotton crop is easily lost if it is not taken in at once when it is ripe * * * Very lately a planter, five miles below New Orleans, having resolved to dispense with slave labor, hired one hundred Irish and German emigrants at very high wages. In the middle of the harvest they all struck for double pay. No others were to be had, and it was impossible to purchase slaves in a few days. In that time he lost produce to the value of ten thousand dollars."

Negroes.

The Southerners of the plantation districts were as familiar with the typical plantation negroes as they were with typical cows and horses. Thomas Jefferson, in his *Notes on Virginia* (Query 14), characterized negroes as improvident, sensuous, inconstant, well endowed in memory, poor in reasoning power and dull in imagination. Few, aside from Jefferson, thought it necessary to describe the obvious. In the West Indies, where for many decades the volume of slave imports was enormous and where the fresh Africans were representative of all the diverse tribes from Senegal and Abyssinia to Good Hope and Madagascar, the planters were prompted to compare the tribal traits and thus to publish discussions of negro characteristics in general. But in the continental South, in the antebellum period, the tribal stocks, Berber, Coromantee, Ebo, Congo, Kaffir, Hottentot, etc., had become blended into the relatively constant type of the American plantation negro. As a familiar item in the white man's environment, the negro was not to be described or interpreted, but was rather to be accepted and adjusted. Dr. J. C. Nott, of Mobile, at the middle of the Nineteenth century, like Mr. F. L. Hoffman at the end of it, was led to study and publish upon negro traits by reason of his interest in life insurance. Dr. S. A. Cartwright, of New Orleans, in the same period as Nott, was led into a general study of the negro by his interest in negro diseases. Practically all the other writers approached the subject of the negro as a corollary to the question of the perpetuity of slavery. Dr. J. H. Van Evrie, of Washington, later of New York, voiced the dominant opinion when he wrote (1853) that the ills of the South were mainly attributable not to slavery, but to the negro. In 1861 Van Evrie further elaborated his unflattering opinion of the negro in his book, *Negroes and Slavery,* which he reprinted in 1867 with the title, *White Supremacy and Negro Subordination.* Van Evrie, as usual with controversialists, falls into the error of proving too much.

In the case of anti-slavery writers, whether Northern or Southern, it required the abolition of slavery to reveal the negro as a concrete phenomenon. H. R. Helper was the most extreme example of this. His *Impending Crisis* (1857) denounced the institution of slavery with the greatest vigor as the cause of all the Southern ills, but his *Nojoque* (1867) was devoted to a still more absurdly extreme denunciation of the negro as a worthless encumbrance and a curse. It is curious that extremely little was published upon the mulatto element, except a few essays upon the orthodox but indefensible theme that by reason of their shortness of life, their infertility and their moral degeneracy, the mixed breed formed a negligible though vicious fraction of the population.

Slavery.

The economic and social aspects of slavery furnished a bulk of essays only equalled in the South by that upon the political bearings of the same institution of domestic servitude. In the colonial period the discussion was abundant, sane, and matter-of-fact, so far as may be judged from indirect evidence, but little of it went into print. In the period of the Revolution the discussion was so hysterical in tone that it resulted at the South more in reaction than in liberalism.

The great ante-bellum debate on the subject brought forth an extreme variety of essays, both as to scope and tone, but the general inclination of the writers, with the notable exception of Helper, was to confront conditions, not theories. Before 1833 the discussion in the South tended to be a humdrum rehashing of time-honored views, relieved by an occasional reflection of the ideas of the European economists. James Raymond wrote an essay on the *Comparative Cost of Free and Slave Labor in Agriculture* in 1827, which was awarded a prize by the Frederick County, Maryland, Agricultural Society. His argument follows the line of Adam Hodgson's reply to J. B. Say's discarded early views: the farmer needs an elastic supply of labor, and hireling labor is suited for this while slave labor is not; slaves are lazy, slipshod, wasteful, as contrasted with the carefulness, efficiency and frugality of freemen. Raymond, of course, like the typical abolitionist, divorced the slavery issue from the negro issue by ignoring the question of what would become of the great mass of Southern negroes when freed. Raymond also ignored the fact that in the principal Southern industries, under the plantation system, regularity was more to be desired than elasticity in the labor supply, and that slavery secured the desired constancy in the number of laborers available. The publication of Professor Dew's famous essay in 1833, prompted by the debate upon projects for abolition in the Virginia legislature in 1831-32, demonstrated that the slavery question was essentially a phase of the great negro question. After censuring the recklessness of the Virginia debate, and showing that slavery had been a highly serviceable institution in furthering human progress in many countries and in many centuries, Dew analyzes the American situation and the proposals for its betterment. He condemns the several plans, varying in detail, for the emancipation and deportation of the negroes on the grounds of the excessive cost of the process, the threatened paralysis of plantation industry, and the inability of the negroes to maintain their own welfare if deported to Africa. He condemns still more strongly all plans for abolition which do not include provision for deportation, pointing out the social and industrial dangers of freeing an irresponsible population, and pointing to the record of the Northern free negroes and to the chaotic state of affairs in Hayti as warnings. After Dew's essay no writer could secure countenance in the South for any anti-slavery plans unless he could show some means of readjusting the negro population in a way not endangering the security of the whites or threatening the general welfare.

In close harmony with Dew's argument, essays were written in the thirties and forties by Chancel-

lor William Harper and Gov. J. H. Hammond, both
of South Carolina, which were reprinted in 1852
along with Dew's essay and a slender one by W. G.
Simms, in a volume entitled the *Pro-Slavery Argument*. Harper, following Dew's theme in general,
lays main stress upon the civilizing and tranquilizing effects of slavery. Hammond's essay, written
in the form of a reply to Thomas Clarkson's attacks
upon slavery, is an exceptionally strong apology for
the institution. He concedes that slave labor is expensive, by reason of the slave's first cost and the
expense of feeding, clothing and sheltering him and
his family in infancy, sickness and old age, in bad
seasons as well as good; and he prophesies that any
great increase in the density of population will
cause the abandonment of slavery by making free
labor available and cheaper. Meanwhile, in view
of the sparseness of the Southern population and
the unfitness of the negroes for the stress of competition, he deprecates any radical readjustments
and resents extraneous interference.

Numerous other Southern essayists clamored for
public attention, of whom only the more significant
can here be noted. John Fletcher, of Louisiana, in
1851 issued a bulky primer to prove the goodness of
slavery, in easy lessons and with main reference to
Holy Writ. George S. Sawyer, also of Louisiana,
gave an elaborate eulogy of slavery upon historical
and ethical grounds in his *Southern Institutes*
(1859). Henry Hughes, in pamphlets of 1858-59,
tried to bolster up slavery by the euphemistic device
of changing its name to warranteeism, and thereby
indicating that its purpose was to maintain industrial
order rather than to exploit the laboring class; but
Hughes could not get an audience even in the South
for his ineffective plea. Daniel Christy, of Cincinnati, entitling his book *Cotton is King* (1855), mag-

nified the economic efficiency and vital importance of slavery as a divinely established institution. Though Christy may not have been a Southerner, his book was adopted by the Southern ultramontanists as their own. Professor A. T. Bledsoe, of the University of Virginia, in his book *An Essay on Liberty and Slavery* (1856), endeavored to refute seventeen specific fallacies of the abolitionists, and to vindicate slavery and all its works, including the fugitive slave law. In 1860 E. N. Elliott, "President of Planters' College, Mississippi," bought the authors' rights to Christy's and Bledsoe's books, secured new scriptural arguments for slavery from Dr. Stringfellow, of Virginia, and Dr. Hoge, of New Jersey, and an ethnological essay from Dr. Cartwright, of New Orleans, added to these Hammond's and Harper's already standard essays, and the text of the Dred-Scott decision by the United States Supreme Court, printed the whole in one bulky subscription volume, *Cotton is King and Pro-Slavery Arguments* (1860), and sold it in great numbers to the planters and townsmen on the eve of the war. The book, on the whole, compares very unfavorably with the more modest but substantial *Pro-Slavery Argument* of 1852.

More notable as a contribution to thought are the two books by George Fitzhugh, of Virginia, with the curious titles: *Sociology for the South, or the Failure of Free Society* (1854), and *Cannibals All, or Slaves Without Masters* (1857). Declaring himself an outright socialist, Fitzhugh denounces the whole modern system of wage-labor, and contends that laborers on hire are subject to more severe exploitation than laborers in bondage. He advocates benevolent despotism on general principles, and particularly where applied to a class so little capable of selfprotection as the negroes in America. He holds up

the Southern plantation system for the admiration
of all socialists, communists, or other paternalists.
Fitzhugh, however, injures the effect of his books
by his own loquacity. He adds chapters at random
championing the South against the North in every
possible connection, and thereby lets it seem,
whether justly or not, that he is a socialist only for
the sake of the argument.

As an assault upon the general position held by
the whole group of writers above treated, Hinton R.
Helper, of North Carolina, issued his startling book,
The Impending Crisis of the South (1857). He
points out the relative economic stagnation in the
South, asserts that slavery is its sole cause, and denounces the slave-holding class as a cruel and wicked
oligarchy conspiring for the oppression of the negroes and non-slave-holding whites alike. Helper
is a past master in the art of leaping at conclusions
and concealing the feat by outbursts of perfervid
rhetoric. Helper was the spokesman of a group of
radical Southern non-slaveholders, but he secured
relatively little Southern endorsement on the whole
because he failed to meet adequately the vital problem of what to do with the negro population in the
event of the abolition of slavery. But the North
bought fifty thousand copies in three years, and at
the North, where Helper's *Nojoque* has always been
unknown, his *Impending Crisis* is still considered by
thousands to be the soundest of interpretations.

Daniel R. Goodloe, of North Carolina, was a much
more substantial though less glittering opponent of
slavery. In his pamphlet of 1846, *Inquiry Into the
Causes Which Have Retarded the Accumulation of
Wealth and Increase of Population in the Southern
States,* he presented most of the data which Helper
used ten years later, along with some interpretations which were too deep for Helper to grasp. To

the time-honored criticism that slavery hampered industrial progress by stigmatizing labor, Goodloe added a thought which he had worked out that a still more important phase of the burdensome character of slavery lay in its devoting a huge volume of capital to the purchase and control of laborers. He showed that by buying laborers instead of hiring them the South had long been sinking money and depriving itself of resources which might have been used to great advantage in the development of large-scale manufacturing and commerce.

The final ante-bellum word upon the burdensomeness of slavery and its actual and prospective decadence was written by George M. Weston, who seems to have come from Maine and lived mostly in Washington, and at Washington to have gotten into sympathetic touch with the clearest thinkers on slavery, and also to have read well a wide variety of pertinent literature. In his book, *The Progress of Slavery in the United States* (1857), he shows the relatively stagnant condition of the slave-holding communities, discussing the reasons therefor, he points out the encroaching of the free-labor system within the border of the slave-holding section, prophesying a still further restriction by economic process of the area and importance of slave-holding industry, he demonstrates that the then current agitation for the congressional increase of slave-holding territory was purely political in character and offered no economic advantage to the captains of industry in the active plantation districts, and he foretells that the decadence and disappearance of slavery will inure to the benefit instead of the injury of the South. To the careful student of Southern history it may well appear that Weston's little-known book was more representative of the views of well-informed and thoughtful Southerners than were the manifestoes of the politicians. In those years of excited controversy just preceding the war, public opinion in the South, of course, opposed any revision of opinions in the face of the enemy. Public expressions of doubts as to the perfect efficiency and goodness of the slavery system were discouraged at the time. But there is little doubt that many substantial Southerners held many of the views which Hammond, Goodloe and Weston expressed. Among the evidences of this may be cited the essays of representative keen Southern students of the following generation, who it is most reasonable to suppose expressed much of what had existed, even though the ideas may have been latent, in the minds of thoughtful men in the ante-bellum years. Among the essays in point may be mentioned: W. L. Trenholm, *The Southern States, Their Social and Industrial History, Conditions and Needs,* published in the Transactions of the American Social Science Association for September, 1877, and J. C. Reed, *The Old and New South* (1876), reprinted in the Appendix to the same author's *The Brother's War* (1905).

Social Surveys.

As a general treatise upon social types, D. R. Hundley's *Social Relations in Our Southern States* (1860) stands alone among the productions of Southern writers. Born in the South, the author says his education "was chiefly acquired at Southern institutions of learning, in the states of Alabama, Tennessee, Kentucky and Virginia," and was completed by a course in law at Harvard. His collegiate migrations would indicate a waywardness of disposition somewhat characteristic of well-to-do Southern youth in the period, and his waywardness crops out at many places where flippant digressions and gibes at the North mar the character of his book. Nevertheless, Hundley was widely traveled, closely observant, keen in analysis and facile in characterization, and his book is valuable accordingly. His chapters on the Southern gentleman, the Southern middle class, the Southern yeoman, the poor-white and the cotton snob, as he calls the *nouveau riche* of the South, are particularly useful contributions. He gives good fragmentary data, also, upon student dissipation, upon slave traders and upon negro conditions generally, including a notice of the social distinctions which prevailed among the slaves.

William Gilmore Simms, in his *Southward Ho* (1854), gives informal sketches of society in Virginia and the Carolinas, from the point of view of one who was at the same time a middle-class South Carolinian and a citizen of the world. Joseph Baldwin's *Flush Times of Alabama* (1853), a semi-humorous work, is the chief writing upon society in the Southwest.

Political Essays; Theoretical.

Southern writings upon the abstract theory of government were as scarce as we have seen those to have been in theoretical economics. Practically all state papers are negligible as essays in political theory, including Jefferson's Declaration of Independence and Mason's Virginia Bill of Rights, for each of these was merely a brilliantly phrased set of ideas borrowed from current European philosophy, and applied concretely to interpret and justify the American problems and policy of the moment. The writings of Francis Lieber, notable as they are, ought hardly to be claimed as of Southern production, for although Lieber was a professor in South Carolina College for many years and wrote all of his principal books there, he never ceased to be an alien in the Southern country. With his mind always dominated by German idealistic devotion to liberty and revolution, he could feel nothing but repugnance at the conditions in the midst of which he sojourned and at the philosophy of the people who, against his preference, were his neighbors. Lieber's books would indicate that he never confronted any of the distinctive Southern problems of concrete racial adjustments. There remain for mention here only St. George Tucker and John C. Calhoun, each of whom had the United States constitution conspicuously in mind when writing upon government in general, and each of whom was a full-fledged product and a spokesman of the Southern community. Tucker's essay, published as an appendix to his edition of Blackstone's *Commentaries* (1803), championed the Eighteenth century doctrine of inherent rights and the social compact, and applied it elaborately in interpreting the Federal system of the United States. By correlating the position of the states in the Federal compact with the position of individuals in the theoretical social compact, he, of course, provided a basis for reasoning out the supremacy of the states and the subordinate character of the central government. He proceeded to state expressly as an inevitable deduction from his general scheme of political philosophy, that the several states had an indefeasible right of seceding from any Federation or Union which they had entered or might enter.

Calhoun organized his formal writing in political philosophy into two treatises written shortly before his death. Of these, the *Disquisition on Government* (1851), as Professor W. A. Dunning has well said, "is in some respects the most original and the most profound political essay in American literature. It is by no means a complete philosophy of the state, nor is its relation to the concrete issues of the day much disguised; but it penetrates to the very roots of all political and social activity, and presents, if it does not satisfactorily solve, the ultimate intellectual problems in this phase of human existence.'' In bald outline the thread of the essay is as follows: Society is necessary to man, and government is necessary to society; but governments tend to infringe upon the just liberties and rights of individuals, and popular governments are no less prone toward this oppression than are monarchies, for the reason that popular majorities are prone to consider their own interests as the only ones which the government ought to promote, and prone accordingly to ignore and override the interests and rights of minorities.   The suffrage franchise alone will not safeguard the individual against oppression.   Just as governments are instituted to secure the weak against the strong, constitutions are established in large part to restrain the governments when controlled by strong interests from overriding minority rights.   To limit the government properly in this regard without unduly weakening it is a most delicate and difficult problem, and one which the framers of the American Federal constitution did not fully solve.   This is the profound problem as seen by Calhoun.   His prescription of a remedy is less strong than his diagnosis of the trouble.   He proposes a system of concurrent majorities by which each great interest in the country should be put into control of one branch of the legislative power of the government, and thereby be given a veto power upon measures proposed by each other great interest.   Calhoun's plan is not fully adequate for the solution of the problem, but neither is any other plan ever yet devised by any philosopher or any nation.

Constitutional Construction.

Whenever in Federal politics of the ante-bellum period a majority in Congress overrode the opposition, or was about to override it, upon an important issue, it was a fairly constant practice for the spokesman of the minority to appeal to the constitution and declare the programme of the majority to be an exercise by the Government of unwarranted powers. The majority, of course, could often ride rough-shod and had little need of resorting to pamphlets and treatises to defend its constitutional position. Quires were written in championship of broad construction, but reams for strict construction; and it happened that most of strict construction writers were men of the South. Madison's articles in the *Federalist* may be dismissed as being devoted to explanation and eulogy rather than to the construction of the constitution. Madison soon reacted from his nationalistic position and wrote the Virginia Resolutions (1798), which, with Jefferson's Kentucky Resolutions, adopted in minority remonstrance against the Alien and Sedition acts of Congress, served for many years as the official embodiment of constitutional construction for the state-rights school. Shortly afterward, in 1803, John Marshall began his series of vigorous nationalistic decisions which averaged more than one per year for the next thirty years, accompanying the decisions of his court in most of these cases with fulminations from his own pen to preach the doctrines of broad construction. Henry Clay, who, aside from Webster, was the principal other spokesman in the United States for broad construction, contributed no arguments of note upon constitutional topics, but confined himself largely to arguments on the grounds of expediency, making special use of the *argumentum ad hominem*. The several steps taken

by Marshall and Clay gave the chief occasions for
the publication of strict construction arguments by
the opposing school. The principal essayists who
were spurred immediately by Marshall were the
Virginians, Spencer Roane and John Taylor, of
Caroline. Roane, who as chief justice of Virginia
had the chagrin of seeing some of his own state-
rights decisions reversed by Marshall's court on
appeal, resorted to the public press in remonstrance.
His principal series of articles was printed in the
Richmond Inquirer in May-August, 1821, and collected in a pamphlet entitled *The Letters of Alger-
non Sidney.* Taylor issued a succession of polemical
books: *Inquiry Into the Principles and Policy of the
Government of the United States* (1813), expressing
his disrelish of the consolidation tendencies of the
time; *Construction Construed* (1820), denouncing
the McCulloch *vs.* Maryland decision and asserting
the sovereignty of the states; *Tyranny Unmasked*
(1822), denying the power of the Federal Supreme
Court to assign limits to the spheres of state and
Federal authority, and advocating a state veto for
emergency use in curbing Federal encroachment,
and *New Views of the Constitution* (1823), which
reiterated his former contention and stressed the
value of the states as champions of sectional interests against injury by hostile congressional majorities.

Clay's campaign for his "American System"
drew fire mainly from the South Carolinians. In
1827 Robert J. Turnbull, under the pseudonym of
Brutus, published a series of thirty-three articles in
the *Charleston Mercury,* and promptly issued them
in a pamphlet entitled *The Crisis: Or Essays on
the Usurpation of the Federal Government,* which
he dedicated "to the people of the 'Plantation
States' as a testimony of respect, for their rights

of sovereignty.'' Turnbull vehemently urged the
people of the South to face the facts, to realize that
the North was beginning to use its control of Congress for Southern oppression by protective tariffs
and otherwise; and he proposed as a remedy that
South Carolina should promptly interpose her own
sovereignty and safeguard Southern interests by
vetoing such congressional acts as she should decide
to be based upon Federal usurpations and intended
for Northern advantage at the cost of Southern oppression.   McDuffie and Hayne promptly assumed
the leadership of the state-sovereignty-and-South-
ern-rights cause in Congress and many other prominent South Carolinians fell in line, including the
editors R. B. Rhett and J. H. Hammond, and including most conspicuously John C. Calhoun, who
drafted nearly all the state papers of South Carolina during the nullification episode, and who, in
addition, issued powerful memorials upon the issues
of the day over his own signature.   These writings
are too prominently a part of American history to
require any detailed discussion here.

The final issue prompting state sovereignty expressions was that of negro slavery.   The principal
work in this group was Calhoun's *Discourse on the
Constitution and Government of the United States*
(1851), which supplements his *Disquisition on Government,* already outlined.   This *Discourse* follows
the theme of his more general *Disquisition,* applying
its contentions more specifically to the American
Federal problem; it champions concurrent majorities again, champions the historical doctrine of
state sovereignty and defends, in somewhat subdued
phrase, his former pet plan of nullification.   The
Discourse and the *Disquisition* were Calhoun's political testament; the great obituary of the state
sovereignty and secession movement was Alexander

H. Stephens' *Constitutional View of the War between the States,* which, as a post-bellum work, falls beyond our present scope.

Party Politics.

It was the custom of but a few leaders to address their constituents for party purposes through essays instead of from the hustings. One of these was Robert Goodloe Harper, who, upon his retirement from Congress in 1801, addressed to his South Carolina constituents a eulogistic but sane and vigorous memoir upon the constructive work of his party: *A Letter Containing a Short View of the Political Principles of the Federalists, and of the Situation in Which They Found and Left the Government.* Another was Edward Livingston, who, when asking for reëlection to Congress in 1825, issued an *Address to the Electors of the Second District of Louisiana,* which is notable for his attempt to reconcile the desire of the sugar planters for protection to their own industry with the disrelish of the cotton planters for the policy of protection in general, by the device of calling the duty on sugar a revenue item and not a protective item in the tariff schedules. Various other candidates, of course, issued electioneering pamphlets, practically all of which are negligible as essays. On a plan combining an historical sketch with political propaganda were several writings such as Thomas Cooper's *Consolidation: An Account of Parties in the United States, from the Convention of* 1787 *to the Present Period* (1824), written, of course, with a state-rights purpose; Henry A. Wise's *Seven Decades of the Union,* eulogizing John Tyler and the policy of the state-rights Whigs, and such biographies as J. F. H. Claiborne's *Life and Correspondence of John A. Quitman* (1860), which contains secession propaganda on the au-

thor's own account along with the biography of
Quitman.

Sectionalism.

Instead of making a catalogue of the many essays
which deal with petty sectionalism within the several states and with grand sectionalism between the
North and the South, we will conclude our view of
economic and political writings by presenting the
theme of William H. Trescott's *The Position and
Course of the South* .(1850), as an embodiment of
the soundest realization of the sectional conditions
and prospects of the Southern section in the closing
decade of the ante-bellum period.   The author, a
leading, experienced, conservative citizen of South
Carolina, states in his preface, dated Oct. 12, 1850,
that his purpose is to unify the widely separated
parts of the South.   He says his views are not new,
but they are characteristically Southern: "We are
beginning to think for ourselves, the first step toward acting for ourselves."   The essay begins with
an analysis of industrial contrasts.   He says that
in the slavery system the relation of capital and
labor is moral—labor is a duty, in the wage-earning
system the relation is legal—the execution of contract.   The contract system, he says, promotes constant jealousy and friction between capital and
labor, while the slavery system secures peace by
subordinating labor to capital.   The political majority of the North represents labor; that of the
South, capital; the contrast is violent.   Free labor
hates slave labor, and will overturn the system if it
can.   The two sections with many contrasting and
conflicting characteristics are combined under the
United States constitution, but they are essentially
irreconcilable.   Even in foreign relations the North
is jealous of foreign powers for commercial and
industrial reasons, while Southern industry is not

competitive with, but complementary to European industry and commerce, and the South, if a nation by itself, would be upon most cordial terms with foreign powers. "The United States government under the control of Northern majorities must reflect Northern sentiment, sustain Northern interests, impersonate Northern power. Even if it be conceded that the South has no present grievance to complain of, it is the part of wisdom to consider the strength and relations of the sections, and face the question, what is the position of the South? In case our rights should be attacked, where is our constitutional protection? The answer is obvious. If the expression of outraged feeling throughout our Southern land be anything but the wild ravings of wicked faction, it is time for the South to act firmly, promptly and forever. But one course is open to her honor, and that is secession and the formation of an independent confederacy. There are many men grown old in the Union who would feel an honest and pardonable regret at the thought of its dissolution. They have prided themselves on the success of the great American experiment of political self-government, and feel that the dissolution of the Union would proclaim a mortifying failure. Not so. The vital principle of political liberty is representative government, and when Federal arrangements are discarded, that lives in original vigor. Who does not consider the greatest triumph of the British constitution the facility and vigor with which, under slight modifications, it developed into the great republican government under which we have accomplished our national progress. And so it will be with the United States constitution. The experiment of our fathers will receive its highest illustration, and a continent of great republics, equal, independent and allied, will demonstrate to the world the capabilities of republican constitutional government. We believe that Southern interests demand an independent government. We believe that the time has now come when this can be established temperately, wisely, strongly. But in effecting this separation we would not disown our indebtedness, our gratitude to the past. The Union has spread Christianity, fertilized a wilderness, enriched the world's commerce wonderfully, spread Anglo-Saxon civilization. "It has given to the world sublime names, which the world will not willingly let die—heroic actions which will light the eyes of a far-coming enthusiasm. It has achieved its destiny. Let us achieve ours."

BIBLIOGRAPHY.—Acton, Lord: *The Civil War in America* (1866, reprinted as Chap. IV. of his *Historical Essays and Studies*, London, 1907); Allston, R. F. W.: *Memoir of the Introduction and Planting of Rice in South Carolina* (Charleston, 1843), and *Sea-Coast Crops of the South* (1854, reprinted in *DeBow's Review*, XVI., 589–615); Baldwin, Jos. G.: *The Flush Times of Alabama and Mississippi, A Series of Sketches* (New York, 1853); Calhoun, J. C.: *Works* (Charleston, 1851, New York, 1853–5); Cooper, Thos.: *Consolidation: An Account of Parties in the United States, from the Convention of 1787 to the Present Period* (published anonymously, Columbia, 1824), and *Lectures on the Elements of Political Economy* (Columbia, 1826); DeBow, J. D. B.: *The Industrial Resources, etc., of the Southern and Western States* (New Orleans, 1853–4); Dunning, W. A.: *American Political Philosophy* (in the *Yale Review*, August, 1895); Elliott, E. N.: *Cotton Is King and Pro-Slavery Arguments Comprising the Writings of Hammond, Harper, Christy, Stringfellow, Hodge, Bledsoe, and Cartwright on This Important Subject* (Augusta, 1860); Fitzhugh, Geo.: *Cannibals All, or Slaves Without Masters* (Richmond, 1857), and *Sociology for the South, or The Failure of Free Society* (Richmond, 1854); Fletcher, John: *Studies on Slavery in Easy Lessons* (Natchez, 1852); Goodloe, D. R.: *Inquiry into the Causes which have Retarded the Accumulation of Wealth and Increase of Population in the Southern States* (Washington, 1846). (This essay is said by S. B. Weeks to have been written in 1841; it was published first in the *New York American*, 1844, and in several places thereafter); Gregg, Wm.: *Essays on Domestic Industry, or an Inquiry into the Expediency of Establishing Cotton Manufactures in South Carolina* (Charleston, 1845); Harper, Robert Goodloe: *Select Works* (Baltimore, 1814); [Harrison, Jesse Burton]: *Review of the Slave Question, Extracted from the American Quarterly Review, December, 1832, Showing That Slavery is a Hindrance to Prosperity*, by a Virginian (Richmond, 1833); Helper, H. R.: *The Impending Crisis of the South: How to*

Meet It (New York, 1857), and Nojoqua, A Question for a Continent (New York, 1857); Houston, D. F.: A Critical Study of Nullification in South Carolina (New York, 1896); Hughes, Henry: State Liberties: The Right to African Contract Labor (Port Gibson, Miss., 1858); Hundley, D. R.: Social Relations in Our Southern States (New York, 1860); Ingle, Edward, Southern Sidelights (New York, 1896); Merriam, C. E.: The Political Theory of Calhoun (In the American Journal of Sociology, VII., 577-594); Nott, Josiah, C.: Two Lectures on the Natural History of the Caucasian and Negro Races (Mobile, 1844); Phillips, U. B. The Slave Labor Problem In the Charleston District (In the Political Science Quarterly, XXII., 416-439); The Pro-Slavery Argument, as maintained by the Most Distinguished Writers of the Southern States, Containing the Several Essays on the Subject, of Chancellor Harper, Governor Hammond, Dr. Simms and Professor Dew (Charleston, 1852); Ruffin, Edmund: An Address on the Opposite Results of Exhausting and Fertilizing Systems of Agriculture (Charleston, 1853), Calcareous Manures (2d ed., 1835) and Report of the Commencement and Progress of the Agricultural Survey of South Carolina for 1843 (Columbia, 1843); Sawyer, Geo. S.: Southern Institutes (Philadelphia, 1858); Seabrook, Whitemarsh B.: A Memoir on the Origin, Cultivation and Uses of Cotton (Charleston, 1844); Simms, W. G.: Southward Ho! A Spell of Sunshine (New York, 1854); Taylor, John, of Caroline Arator, Being a Series of Agricultural Essays, Practical and Political, by a citizen of Virginia (anonymously published) (Georgetown, D. C., 1813), Construction Construed (1822), Inquiry Into the Principles and Policy of the Government of the United States (Fredericksburg, 1814), New Views of the Constitution (1823) and Tyranny Unmasked (Washington, 1822); Trescott, W. H.: The Position and Course of the South (Charleston, 1850); Tucker, George: Essays on Various Subjects of Taste, Morals and National Policy, by a citizen of Virginia (published anonymously) (Georgetown, D. C., 1822), and The Theory of Money and Banks Investigated (Boston, 1839); Tucker, St. George: Dissertation on Slavery, With a Proposal for Its Gradual Abolition in Virginia (Philadelphia, 1796, reprinted New York, 1861); Weeks, Stephen B.: Anti-Slavery Sentiment in the South (In the Southern History Association Publications, II., 87-130); Weston, George M.: The Progress of Slavery in the United States (Washington, 1857).

ULRICH B. PHILLIPS,
Professor of History, Tulane University.

CHAPTER IX.

THE SOUTH'S CONTRIBUTIONS TO MATHEMATICS AND ASTRONOMY.

N entering upon his task, the writer is somewhat appalled by the fact that, in his opinion, America has produced only one really great mathematician and that he lived many miles north of the Potomac River. It need hardly be said that he refers to Benjamin Peirce of Harvard. Simon Newcomb and G. W. Hill have labored mainly on the very banks of the Potomac, and these might rank next to Benjamin Peirce, but they should be classed as astronomers rather than mathematicians. In astronomy, America has been unusually fortunate, having produced a number of astronomers that have won a world-wide reputation. But though appalled, the writer is not altogether discouraged, and he hopes to bring out facts that will show that, considering drawbacks incident to the War of Secession the South has done her share—a share proportionate to her white population.

Harvard College, the first American college, was founded in 1636; William and Mary, the second in point of time, in 1688, and thirteen years later, in 1701, Yale began her career. Viewed from the year 1908, the mathematics taught in those early days seems very elementary, but then we must note the fact that when Harvard was beginning her career, it was only the chosen few abroad that possessed any special mathematical knowledge, and at Cambridge in England there was little mathematics taught. Before William and Mary was founded, the great Newton had naturally caused an immense awakening of mathematical interest at old Cambridge. Were we to follow the rise and growth of American colleges, we would see that love of mathematics for mathematics' sake was slow in coming. The brilliant success of the French and Swiss mathematicians during the last of the Eighteenth century and the beginning of the Nineteenth century was an obvious incentive to the study of mathematics in America, and accordingly there was what has been called an influx of French mathematics into America, which came partly direct from France and partly by way of England, which had been awakened through the scientific spirit of France. Pure English influence, which antedated the French, may be traced in some of the older colleges; but we are interested mainly in French influence, for the great advantage of French methods of presentation over the English was early recognized.

The United States Military Academy at West Point was virtually reorganized along French lines by Maj. Sylvanus Thayer, whose efficiency as superintendent from 1817 to 1823 raised the Academy to a high plane. During Thayer's administration, Professor Claude Crozet, the father of descriptive geometry in America, was brought to West Point. Crozet was a graduate of the Polytechnic School of Paris, and had been an artillery officer under Napoleon. In 1821 he wrote a treatise on Descriptive Geometry for use of his classes at West Point, where he also introduced that great adjunct to mathematical teaching—the blackboard. After leaving West Point, Crozet became state engineer of Virginia, in which capacity he did work of lasting importance in the construction of superb highways. Later he taught school in Richmond, Va. In 1858, Crozet published an "improved edition" of *An Arithmetic for Schools and Colleges*, which had been copyrighted in 1848.

Dr. Artemas Martin, in writing of this arithmetic, says: "This book is remarkable for its lucid statements of principles. * * * Crozet is the clearest writer on this subject I ever read." We quote from *Notes on the History of American Textbooks on Arithmetic,* in which is to be found what is doubtless the best bibliography of American arithmetics. This valuable paper was compiled by Artemas Martin and J. M. Greenwood, and is contained in the reports of the United States Commissioner of Education for 1897-8 and 1898-9. These "Notes" were reprinted in 1900 by the United States Bureau of Education. There are several interesting Southern arithmetics noticed in this publication. It would not be altogether foreign to our theme were we to give some extended account of the United States Military Academy, as so many Southern professors of mathematics owed their education to it, but we must confine our remarks more specifically to the South.

The first professor of mathematics in America whose name has come down to us was Rev. Hugh Jones of William and Mary College. He wrote for the use of his students a work (which existed only in manuscript) which he called an *Accidence to the Mathematick in all its Parts and Applications, Algebra, Geometry, Surveying of Land, and Navigation.* He established a course in mathematics at William and Mary fully equal to that given at Harvard and Yale in those early days. He was an Englishman of university education. As an historian his name is justly held in great esteem by the most competent modern authorities. One of Professor Jones's successors in the chair of mathematics was Joshua Fry, an Oxford man, who seems to have done some useful practical work in making with Peter Jefferson, the father of Thomas Jefferson, a map of Virginia. They also established a portion of the boundary line between Virginia and North Carolina.

Thomas Jefferson acknowledged his great indebtedness to Dr. William Small, professor of mathematics when Jefferson was a student at William and Mary. Jefferson was passionately fond of mathematics, and frequently in after life recommended its study to young men who came under his influence. The stimulus given to the study of mathematics by Dr. Small, who was evidently a teacher of marked ability, and especially his influence exerted through such a man as Jefferson, was no light contribution to the progress of mathematical learning and hence to the development of mathematics. We can see President Jefferson's mind and his keen appreciation of the mathematical sciences in the inauguration of the United States Coast Survey and in the development of the United States Military Academy. Neither can we forget right here that Jefferson was the ''Father of the University of Virginia,'' which institution he founded on such broad and sure foundations that its influence has even to this day continued paramount in the South. In passing we note the fact that Congress passed the bill authorizing the United States Coast Survey (now the United States Coast and Geodetic Survey) in 1807, during Jefferson's administration, and that a man of splendid ability, Ferdinand R. Hassler, was placed in charge of the work. Hassler had been for three years professor of mathematics at West Point, but his great work was the inception and prosecution of the Survey, in which for the first time in this country the method of triangulation was employed. At one time he lived in Richmond, Va., where he gave lessons in mathematics to the sons of prominent men. While there he published his *Elements of Geometry*. He had previously published the *Elements of Analytic Geometry*, and subsequently appeared an arithmetic, astronomy, and logarithmic and trigonometric tables, with introductions in five languages. He introduced in America the ratio definition of the trigonometric functions. In considering facts or persons connected with various colleges or universities, we shall now follow geographical situation rather than the age or reputation of the institutions; and just here we shall attempt to carry the subject down to the War of Secession, reserving more recent days for the latter part of this paper. The University of Virginia, founded by Jefferson in 1819, was the natural successor of time-honored William and Mary. The second professor of mathematics in the University of Virginia was Charles Bonnycastle, son of John Bonnycastle, of England, a prolific writer of textbooks. Charles Bonnycastle seems to have taught in a scientific way. He published a book on "Inductive Geometry," which included geometry, trigonometry, and analytic geometry. He uses the ratio definition of the trigonometric functions. There is ample evidence to show that Professor Bonnycastle's course of mathematics was far more advanced than that given in the ordinary college of that day. It is interesting to note that the brilliant J. J. Sylvester was elected professor of mathematics at the University of Virginia in 1841, and, though he did such signal service at Johns Hopkins many years later, it is to be regretted that in about six months he resigned to accept a professorship in England.

Edward H. Courtenay, a native of Baltimore, held the chair of mathematics from 1842 to 1853. He was a graduate of West Point, and was the first regular occupant of the chair educated in America. He had taught at West Point and at the University of Pennsylvania, and had had charge of important engineering work for the government. "Mr. Courtenay was a mathematician of noble gifts and a great teacher." He left the manuscript of an excellent work on the calculus, which was published soon after his death, and was used as a textbook in several institutions. Professor Courtenay was succeeded by another graduate of West Point, Albert Taylor Bledsoe, a native of Kentucky, a man gifted in several fields of learning. Before coming to the University of Virginia he had taught at Kenyon College, Miami University, and at the University of Mississippi as professor of mathematics and astronomy. He established a course in the history and philosophy of mathematics, perhaps the first course of its kind ever offered in America. His treatise on the philosophy of mathematics was widely known. His greatest work was in the field of metaphysical theology, constitutional law, and review articles. He resigned his chair in 1863, and became assistant secretary of war in the Southern Confederacy. After the war he was editor of the *Southern Review*. He died in 1877.

At the organization of the Virginia Military Institute in 1839, General Francis H. Smith, a graduate of West Point, was made its first superintendent, a position which he held for half a century. Professor Smith published a series of arithmetics and algebras, and a descriptive geometry. He also translated and published Biot's *Analytic Geometry,* Legendre's *Geometry,* Lefebure de Fourcy's *Trigonometry, with Tables,* some of which had a wide circulation. It is rather interesting that General Smith's latest successor, the present superintendent, E. W. Nichols, has published an Analytic Geometry and a Calculus.

A year after the University of North Carolina was opened, in 1796, Rev. Joseph Caldwell, a graduate of Princeton College, was elected professor of mathematics, which position he held till 1804 when he became president of the university. He was president until his death in 1835, except for four years from 1812 to 1816. In 1812 he voluntarily retired to the professorship of mathematics "to secure more time for the study of theology," but on the death of his successor he was recalled to the presidency. He arranged elaborate courses in mathematics, including conic sections and fluxions, but it does not appear that any student went beyond trigonometry. He published a textbook on geometry and one on trigonometry. Dr. Caldwell completed in 1831 an astronomical observatory, which Dr. Kemp P. Battle, in his *History of the University of North Carolina*, Vol. I., says was the first college observatory built in America, that of Professor Hopkins at Williams College being in 1836. It is possible that the honor of having the first observatory belongs to Yale, as about the year 1831 "the tower of the Athenæum was fitted up as an observatory" to receive a five-inch telescope that had just been given.

Caldwell's observatory was a brick structure about twenty feet square, and contained a transit, an altitude and azimuth instrument, a portable telescope, an astronomical clock, and some minor apparatus, all of which he bought in London from the best makers. Observations were made for longitude and latitude of various places, and on eclipses, comets, and so forth, but these observations were lost. Soon after President Caldwell's death the building, being constructed of bad material, fell rapidly to decay, and the instruments were removed. Later the building was destroyed by fire.

George Blackburn, a graduate of Trinity College, Dublin, was professor of mathematics in the University of South Carolina from 1811 to 1815. He taught mathematics "as a science, not as a matter of memory." After leaving the college, he made latitude and longitude observations for the state map.

James Wallace, professor of mathematics at the University of South Carolina from 1820 to 1834, contributed to the *Southern Review* articles on "Geometry and Calculus," and "Steam Engine and Railroad." He was also a contributor to Silliman's *Journal.* His treatise on the *Use of Globes and Practical Astronomy,* a work of 512 pages, was in advance of any American treatise on astronomy of its day.

James B. Dodd, a native of Virginia and a self-made mathematician, became professor of mathematics in Transylvania University (now Kentucky University) at Lexington, Ky., in 1846. He had a fine reputation, and wrote a series of textbooks on arithmetic, algebra, and geometry, some of which were very favorably received.

At the present time, when to the making of textbooks there seems no end, it is hard for the teacher to appreciate the great possible good that a textbook might do in the early days of the Republic and even down to the war. The making of a textbook fifty to a hundred years ago was a far more serious and important matter than in these latter days. There seems sufficient reason, then, for mentioning more of the ante-bellum books than those issued in the last fifty years, though the latter are in the main superior to the early ones.

Perhaps the most striking character that ever taught, wrote and wrought south of the Potomac, was Frederick A. P. Barnard. He was a scientist of the first rank. While a short sketch can not do him justice, the following facts may be noted. He was born in Sheffield, Mass., 1809, and died in the city of New York, 1889, twenty-four years of his long and useful life having been spent in the South. In 1828 he graduated at Yale. While teaching and pursuing his studies still farther at Yale, he wrote an arithmetic and edited an edition of Bridge's *Conic Sections.* In 1837 he became professor of mathematics, natural philosophy and astronomy in the University of Alabama, and in 1848 was transferred to the chair of chemistry and natural history, which position he resigned in 1854, to become professor of mathematics, physics and civil engineering in the University of Mississippi, where he remained till 1861, when the university suspended on account of the war. During the war he was for a while employed in the National Observatory and later in the Coast Survey. From 1864 to his death in 1889, he was president of Columbia College, New York, which institution was transformed during his administration from a mere college to a real university. Professor Barnard was a prolific writer on various subjects, some of them mathematical. He was a member of the government expedition sent to Labrador in 1860 to observe the eclipse of the sun. He was astronomer for the states of Alabama and Florida to settle a dispute concerning the boundary line between those states. In 1840, he induced the trustees of the University of Alabama to establish a small observatory, which was completed in 1844 and enlarged in 1858. Originally this building was fifty-four feet long and twenty-two wide in the centre. It contained a transit circle, by Simms of London. Under a revolving dome of eighteen feet internal diameter was an equatorial telescope, also by Simms. This telescope had a clear aperture of eight inches and a focal length of twelve feet. Besides clocks and other apparatus there were two portable telescopes, of four and three inches aperture respectively. This building was the only one of the public edifices that escaped destruction in 1865, when the university was set on fire by United States troops. It is quite remarkable and most commendable that in almost every Southern institution before the war much interest was taken in astronomy. The University of Mississippi, Barnard doubtless being the moving spirit, determined to purchase a telescope "that would put its observatory on a level with that of Cambridge or Ann Arbor, or any other in the country." Accordingly, Dr. Barnard, the president, contracted with Alvan Clark for a great telescope. This telescope, which has an aperture of eighteen inches, was completed in 1861, at which time the war prevented its delivery. Mississippi being unable to take it, it finally went to Dearborn Observatory at Chicago.

We have now brought our subject down to the beginning of the War of Secession. For four years, during which time Southern youths from sixteen years of age and upwards were with few exceptions enlisted in the army, nearly all colleges and universities in the South were closed. Some that managed to keep open a part of these four years were obliged to close their doors during the awful period of "reconstruction." This struggling period lasted in most cases for a decade or more after the war, and we may say that the rehabilitation of the colleges and universities south of Virginia was not well under way before 1875. The University of Mississippi was less affected, while the University of South Carolina, owing to political confusion, was not rehabilitated till 1882, at which time Dr. J. M. McBryde became president of that part of it located at Columbia and called the College of South Carolina.

Virginia colleges, with the University of Virginia in the lead, were practically the first to take up the work, so rudely interrupted by war. But in most of the states higher education was stagnant not only for the four years of strife but for eight or ten years afterwards.

In 1865 Charles S. Venable was appointed professor of mathematics at the University of Virginia, which position he held for more than a quarter of a century, resigning a few years before his death on account of failing health. Charles Scott Venable was born in Virginia in 1827. After graduation at Hampden-Sidney College he became a student at the University of Virginia where he soon distinguished himself. From 1846 to 1852 he was professor of mathematics in Hampden-Sidney, but got a furlough and spent the session of 1847-8 at the University of Virginia pursuing advanced work, and four years later he spent a year in Germany, studying astronomy under Encke and Argelander and attending lectures of Dirichlet and Borchardt. In 1856 he was elected to the chair of natural history and chemistry in the University of Georgia. but the following year accepted the chair of mathematics and astronomy in the College of South Carolina, which position he held till 1862. though he was on leave of absence the last two years of this period. In 1860 he was appointed one of five commissioners to go to Labrador to observe the total eclipse of the sun. His report is contained in the Coast Survey volume for 1861. During the war he served brilliantly in the Confederate army. While at the University of Virginia he published a series of textbooks on arithmetic, algebra and geometry. and also a brief work on solid analytic geometry. The best of his books was his *Elements of Geometry,* the later editions of which contained an admirable chapter on modern geometry. The publication of this geometry marked an epoch, as it and the somewhat similar work of the celebrated William Chauvenet of Washington University, St. Louis, did much to raise the standard of American textbooks, a special feature of both being the large selection of original *Exercises,* a practice now universally pursued. Colonel Venable was twice made chairman of the faculty, in which executive capacity he served the university with marked success. It was Colonel Venable who was mainly instrumental in raising an endowment for the astronomical observatory, thus fulfilling the condition that secured to the university the great McCormick telescope, to be referred to later. The superb personality of Colonel Venable was and is still felt all over the South, where many of his pupils are teachers of mathematics. He was a big-hearted, public spirited man and was too unselfish to refuse to serve in whatever way seemed best. Thus many routine duties left him no time for contributions to mathematical journals or other original work. Perhaps the brightest of Venable's older pupils is Professor William M. Thornton, head of the department of civil engineering at the University of Virginia. He was at one time associate editor of the *Annals of Mathematics,* to which he was a contributor. It is to be regretted that Thornton has not written more for publication. Here again, as is so often the case, multiple routine duties have caused apparent unproductiveness in original research. Another strong pupil of Venable's, and afterwards one of his most successful assistants, was R. D. Bohannon, a native of Virginia, and frequent contributor to the *Annals of Mathematics* in its early years. Since 1885, Bohannon has been head of the mathematical department in the Ohio State University, and has written a scholarly and at the same time a practical treatise on plane trigonometry. Professor Harris Hancock, a Virginian, now professor of

mathematics in the University of Cincinnati, has
been unusually prolific in contributions to mathematical journals. Hancock began his mathematical
studies under a pupil of Venable's, and he in turn
graduated in mathematics under Venable.

Mathematics at the University of Virginia is now
under the charge of Professors William H. Echols
and J. M. Page. Both have been contributors to
mathematical journals. Page has published an advanced work on differential equations, and Echols
has written a rigid treatise on calculus, a book in
advance of any previous American work on the calculus.

The Leander McCormick Observatory of the University of Virginia was founded by Leander J.
McCormick, of Chicago. The principal instrument
is the 26-inch refractor made by Alvan Clark & Sons,
and mounted in 1885. The present director, Professor Ormond Stone, has been in charge from the
beginning. The energies of the observatory have
been devoted principally to the observation of objects that could not be observed with smaller instruments. Several hundred new nebulæ have been discovered. Repeated examinations of the nebula of
Orion have been made. In conjunction with the
Harvard, Yerkes, and Lick Observatories photomet-
ric observations have been made for the determination of standards of stellar magnitudes. An expedition from the observatory observed the total eclipse
of the sun in 1900 at Winnsboro, S. C. The principal
work of the observatory at present is the observation
of double stars and long-period variables. The results of the activity of the institution have been
made known from time to time in the publications
of the observatory and in astronomical journals.
Among the astronomers trained by Professor Stone
at the University of Virginia, and who have con-

tributed to the work of the observatory, may be mentioned Professor F. P. Leavenworth of the University of Minnesota and Dr. E. O. Lovett, formerly professor of astronomy at Princeton, now president of the William M. Rice Institute, Houston, Texas. Others are making honorable record in various educational institutions in the South.

The *Annals of Mathematics* was founded in 1884 by Professor Ormond Stone. It was published at the University of Virginia until 1898, when the office of publication was transfered to Harvard University. Great credit is due Professor Stone and those who at different times acted with him as associate editors, who made it possible for the *Annals* to obtain recognition at home and abroad. The following necessarily incomplete quotation from a letter written in 1896 by no less an authority than Professor R. S. Woodward gives some idea of the scope and influence of this journal, which, owing to lack of endowment, was allowed to emigrate to Massachusetts two years after this letter was written. Among other things, Mr. Woodward said: ''It is matter of common remark at home and abroad that the *Annals of Mathematics* has taken a prominent place amongst journals devoted to the promotion and diffusion of mathematical science. Opening its columns to the domains of dynamical astronomy, mechanics, and mathematical physical, as well as to pure mathematics, it has enlisted the coöperation and inspired the efforts of a large number of investigators. Many of the contributions which have thus found their way to the public through the *Annals* are of unusual merit and have received the highest commendation from European mathematicians. It is worthy of remark that contributors and coadjutors have been aroused in all parts of the Union, and that the *Annals* has exerted through them a trulv national influence on mathematical thought.''

While on the subject of journals, we note the following: The *Mathematical Messenger*, at first called the *School Messenger*, was published for a number of years by G. H. Harvill, first at Ada, La., and later at Athens, Texas. It was devoted to the solution of problems in elementary mathematics. One of its ablest contributors was J. W. Nicholson of the Louisiana State University.

The *American Mathematical Monthly* was founded in 1894 by B. F. Finkel, now professor of mathematics and physics in Drury College, Missouri. At first J. M. Colaw, of Monterey, Va., was associated with him as co-editor. A few years ago an arrangement was made by which this journal is published under the auspices of the University of Chicago, and Dr. Finkel has since had associated with him one of the professors of the University of Chicago. It is published at Springfield, Mo. It contains original articles, usually of an elementary nature, and the solution of problems. Dr. Artemas Martin, of Washington, D. C., since 1885 connected with the United States Coast and Geodetic Survey, is an unique self-made mathematician. He has edited and published two magazines, *The Mathematical Visitor* and *The Mathematical Magazine,* both appearing at rather irregular intervals. The first number of the *Visitor* was issued in 1877. The *Magazine* first appeared in 1882. Several Southerners have contributed to these journals of Dr. Martin's, which have been devoted mainly to the solution of difficult or curious problems. Dr. Martin, though nearly seventy-five years old, is still an enthusiastic lover of mathematics. Some thirty or forty members of the American Mathematical Society reside in the South, and some of these are contributors to the *Bulletin* and some to the *Transactions* of the Society.

In 1877 Johns Hopkins University established the *American Journal of Mathematics,* with J. J. Sylvester as its first editor, which was designed to be a journal of high rank, in which might be published original research. It has kept up its high standard and has had for its contributors many foreign mathematicians and the ablest mathematicians in America. We do not give a more complete account of this, the greatest of our mathematical journals, because it can not be claimed as a product of the South. We mention it because it has had worthy contributors in the South, and its influence has been felt through the length and the breadth of the land. For a similar reason to that just mentioned it is hardly a digression to say a word or two about mathematics at Johns Hopkins University, while it would be entirely out of place to attempt to give anything like a comprehensive sketch of Johns Hopkins' contribution to mathematics. No better proof is needed of the astuteness of the late Dr. Daniel C. Gilman than the fact that when he was elected president of Johns Hopkins, he secured for the chair of mathematics James Joseph Sylvester. Sylvester came to this country at an opportune time, just at the close of the life of the great Harvard professor, Benjamin Peirce, the "Father of American Mathematics." In 1841 Sylvester, then only twenty-seven years old, but recognized as a brilliant mathematician, held the chair of mathematics for less than a year in the University of Virginia, as has been mentioned. It would be interesting to know whether his brief sojourn in Virginia had any influence on his acceptance of President Gilman's offer thirty-five years later. In the interim he held chairs in the University College, London, and in the Royal Military Academy,

Woolwich. He came to Baltimore in 1877, and resigned his position in 1883 to accept the Savilian Professorship of Geometry at Oxford, England. While he was at Johns Hopkins only seven years he not only stimulated to the highest degree the Hopkins students and established the reputation of the *American Journal of Mathematics,* but he with others drew the attention of the whole world to the Johns Hopkins University. We can not here give a sketch of his life nor any account of his great and multiple writings on mathematical subjects. The power of his genius will be felt in America for all time. Of his pupils, we shall have occasion to speak of two that labored in the South, G. B. Halsted and E. W. Davis. What Sylvester's successors have done in original research and in training men in mathematics, we must for lack of space pass by. Here and there in the South we find Hopkins graduates teaching mathematics in a true scientific spirit.

In the University of North Carolina, since the war, we note the names of Professors R. H. Graves, Archibald Henderson and William Cain as contributors to mathematical and scientific journals. For a few years, beginning in 1888, Dr. E. W. Davis, now head professor of mathematics in the University of Nebraska, held the chair of mathematics in South Carolina College. He was one of Sylvester's pupils, and his name appears as the author of articles of decided merit in various journals. William J. Vaughn, a native Alabamian, held the chair of mathematics in the University of Alabama for some years. Since 1882 Dr. Vaughn has been professor of mathematics at Vanderbilt University, and has sent forth well trained men in mathematics. A man with such a record does often advance the cause of mathematics more powerfully than some who are poor teachers but occasionally write an original article. To Van-

derbilt University belongs the credit of discovering
in a photographic gallery in Nashville about 1883 an
unknown but ambitious young man, the now famous
astronomer, E. E. Barnard. Vanderbilt gave Barnard a fellowship and thus assisted him in getting
a collegiate education. He had charge of the Vanderbilt Observatory from 1883 to 1888, during which
time he discovered several comets and nebulæ, and
gained for himself a national reputation as an observer. In 1888 he was called to the Lick Observatory where he more than sustained his reputation.
In 1892 he discovered the fifth satellite of Jupiter.
In 1895 he became astronomer at the Yerkes Observatory, a position which he still holds. His reputation as an observer is probably second to none in the
world.

Professor Florian Cajori, a native of Switzerland,
was in the mathematical faculty of Tulane University from 1885 to 1888, having previously been a
graduate student there. He is now professor of
mathematics in Colorado College. Professor Cajori
is the author of the following books, from the first of
which the writer has drawn copiously in preparing
this article: *The Teaching and History of Mathematics in the United States; The History of Mathematics; The History of Elementary Mathematics;
The History of Physics in its Elementary Branches;
An Introduction to the Theory of Equations;
Abschnitt XX. in M. Cantor's Vorlesungen uber
Geschichte der Mathematik, Band IV., Seiten* 37-198.
The preparation of Volume IV. of Cantor's history
was in the hands of nine collaborators, of which Professor Cajori was the American representative.
Cajori has published upwards of sixty papers in
scientific or educational journals. Many of these
papers were unusually good, perhaps three on series
being the most noteworthy. Professor William B.

Smith, a native of Kentucky, now professor of philosophy in Tulane University, was professor of mathematics in University of Missouri, 1888-93, professor of mathematics at Tulane 1893-1906. He has published a *Co-ordinate Geometry* and *Infinitesimal Analysis, Vol. I.* He contributed a 31-column article to *The Americana* on infinitesimal calculus, and his name appears as a contributor to one or two mathematical journals. The University of Texas was opened in 1882, and the following year Dr. George Bruce Halsted, a graduate of Sylvester at the Johns Hopkins, was made professor of mathematics, which position he held for twenty-one years. He is now professor of mathematics at the State Normal School of Colorado. Dr. Halsted has published the following books: *Metrical Geometry,* perhaps the best book of its kind in America; *Elements of Synthetic Geometry; Rational Geometry,* a textbook for the Science of Space, based on Hilbert's Foundations; *Pure Projective Geometry; Non-Euclidean Geometry,* for teachers. Professor Halsted did more than any one else to popularize non-euclidean notions, and for years he has been the authority in America on non-euclidean geometry. In 1891 he translated Bolyai's *Science Absolute of Space* and Lobatchewsky's *Geometrical Researches on the Theory of Parallels.* He also translated Seccheri's work. He has translated various other works and papers from foreign languages. His name is found as a frequent contributor to mathematical journals here and abroad.

In Missouri notable work has been done at Washington University and the University of Missouri. William Chauvenet, soon after his graduation at Yale in 1840, was made a professor in the United States Navy. It was largely through his efforts that the United States Naval Academy at Annapolis was established in 1845. Here he was professor of mathematics and later director of the observatory until he resigned in 1859 to accept the professorship of mathematics in Washington University, St. Louis. Here his great work, *A Treatise on Spherical and Practical Astronomy,* was published in 1863. While at Annapolis he had published an advanced trigonometry, and just before his death in 1870, his excellent *Geometry* appeared. William Chauvenet was a truly great man. He was one of the first American scientists to win recognition abroad.

The observatory of Washington University, from Chauvenet's time down, has stood for sound, scientific work. Henry S. Pritchett, now head of the Carnegie "Foundation," was director from 1881 to 1897. Professor Pritchett's principal investigations were on positions of fixed stars, double star systems and orbits of comets and satellites. At present the attention of the observatory is directed mainly to precise geodetic work. This observatory is equipped with a six-inch refractor and an eight-inch reflector and excellent minor apparatus.

At the University of Missouri the present head of the mathematical department, Professor E. R. Hedrick, not to mention his worthy colleagues, has been quite active, publishing a number of papers in various journals. He has also translated Goursat's *Course d'Analyse Mathematique.* Professor F. H. Seares is professor of astronomy and director of the Laws Observatory of the University of Missouri, where he has made contributions to various astronomical journals, besides editing the publications of the observatory.

The principal instruments of this observatory, founded in 1853, are two equatorial refractors of $7\frac{1}{2}$ and $4\frac{1}{2}$ inches respectively.

It would be interesting to trace more in detail the influence of individual universities or colleges, were it not necessary to condense this account. A bibliography of Southern textbooks and of original articles contributed to journals would be in itself a good index of what the South has done in mathematics and astronomy, but even if such a bibliography could be made fairly complete, space would forbid its insertion here.

BIBLIOGRAPHY.—Battle, Kemp P.: *History of the University of North Carolina;* Barnard's *Journal of Education;* Cajori, Florian: *The Teaching and History of Mathematics in the United States* (published by the Bureau of Education); The monographs published by the United States Bureau of Education on the history of education in Maryland, Virginia, North Carolina, Florida, Georgia, Alabama, Tennessee, Mississippi, Louisiana and Texas; Reports of the United States Commissioner of Education; various isolated articles and pamphlets.

SAMUEL MARX BARTON,
Professor of Mathematics, University of the South.

CHAPTER X.

THE SOUTH'S CONTRIBUTIONS TO PHYSICAL SCIENCE.

MERICA has produced no great masters in the physical sciences. There have been noted workers in physics and chemistry, men who have added to the world's store of knowledge, but none whose names can be placed along with such as Lavoisier, Dumas, Faraday, Clerk-Maxwell, Graham, Wöhler, Liebig, or Hofmann. Doubtless the sparse population, scattered over a great country, with few centres where scientific men could gather, formed an adverse condition for the development of any great scientific men. Then, too, our forefathers were busy with the development of a new country, involving the direct struggle with nature in the rough, and there was little encouragement for abstract scientific research. There were no old educational foundations such as Oxford and Cambridge, Paris, Leyden, Göttingen, and Heidelberg, affording a sheltered provision for the quiet scholar. There were no great Acadamies like those of Paris, London and Berlin where men could present their scientific contributions, compare notes, commend or amend, and thus feel the incitement which comes from friendly emulation. It is true that in the early days of the republic some such Academies were founded, as the American Philosophical Society at Philadelphia, and that they received the coöperation of such public men as Franklin and Jefferson, and certain early but short-lived chemical societies were formed but their influence was not great and their existence often a struggle.

These conditions are changed now. There are great centres, foundations, academies and a multiplicity of journals, but the change is too recent for the effect to be marked. There is splendid work being done, however, and great promise for the future. Yet, as one distinguished Southern man of science has written, ''We have been interpreters and not creators of knowledge.'' The peculiar genius of the American people also has been shown in that we have excelled in devising methods and improving instruments rather than in research by means of them. ''Rowland made the concave grating but Zeeman used it to discover the alteration of wavelength in a magnetic field.''

In the South, with its scattered plantations, a population almost entirely agricultural, and its weak and struggling educational institutions, the conditions were especially unfavorable to the pursuit of pure science or for any signal accomplishment in that sphere. There was but one city which drew men of learning to it or formed a centre for the cultivation of science. This was Charleston. The position taken by this Southern city was a notable one and impressed itself upon the country. It was the seat of a well-endowed college and an excellent museum was founded there. A flourishing Academy of Science for many years held its meetings and gathered its library and an influential *Journal,* devoted to the medical and physical sciences was published for a time. Wealth and an old-established society had brought ease and leisure. Practically all of these conditions were changed in the ruins of the War of Secession.

Contributions in Chemistry.

The first of the South's contributions to physical science were in chemistry. Schiff and Sentini*

---

*Anualen der Chemie, 228 p. 72.

mention, as the first work in pure chemistry done in America, a research upon the formation of a compound of arsenious acid with potassium iodide. This was described in the year 1830 by J. P. Emmet. He obtained the compound in the form of a white, crystalline powder by adding potassium iodide to a very dilute solution of arsenious acid, or potassium arsenite exactly neutralized with acetic acid. Emmet was professor of chemistry in the University of Virginia from its foundation in 1825 to 1842, one of the band of brilliant teachers gathered by Mr. Jefferson to aid in the upbuilding of his pet institution. With the exception of a few papers by Robert Hare and the elder Silliman, which pertained rather to analytical, technical and mineralogical subjects, the communication of Emmet belongs to the earliest period of chemistry in North America.

Emmet had a fine scientific mind and was a skilful investigator. He published articles on new methods of solidifying gysum, on a new method of magnetic galvanism, on the solvent and oxidizing powers of ammoniacal salts, on the cause of voltaic currents produced by the magnet, an essay upon caloric and a paper upon formic acid as a means of reducing metals. Many of his researches were not published as, for instance, upon air motors, the use of chemical agents for stimulating the growth of vegetables, upon kaolin and upon a new element which he believed he had discovered and named Virginium, also an ingenious series of experiments upon the Newtonian theory of refraction.

Gerard Froost, of the University of Nashville (1828-1850), contributed a number of papers, chiefly on mineralogical subjects. He established the alum works at Cape Sable, Maryland, one of the earliest chemical industries in this country.

Only a little of the scientific work of Denison Olm-

sted can be claimed for the South. He was professor of chemistry in the University of North Carolina from 1817 to 1825. His work in chemistry was
chiefly analytical and mineralogical. He established
in North Carolina the first state geological survey,
publishing the first report which was issued by such
a survey.

According to the elder Silliman, the first piece of
elaborate research ·work in organic chemistry by
an American was done by J. Lawrence Smith in
1842. His name stands out conspicuously among
American chemists not merely because of the pau-
city of the work done by others but because of the
sterling character of his own work and the number
of his important researches, which were extended
over a long period.

Born near Charleston, S. C., in 1818, he was a
pupil of Emmet's and afterwards studied under the
most famous teachers of Europe. A visit to Liebig's
laboratory at Giessen formed the turning point of
his life. His first organic research was entitled
*The Composition of the Products of Distillation of
Spermaceti.* In this he first made known the composition of such fats as spermaceti and refuted the
views which had been advanced by Chevreul. On
returning to America he founded at Charleston the
Medical and Surgical Journal of South Carolina, one
of the earliest and most influential scientific journals in the South.

He was selected by Secretary (afterwards President) Buchanan to meet a call for scientific aid by
the Sultan of Turkey, and for four years rendered
valuable service in developing certain of the natural
resources of that country. Several scientific researches were completed and published by him during this period. Later he became professor of chemistry at the University of New Orleans, then ac-

cepted a chair at the University of Virginia, and from there went to the University of Louisville. The later years of his life were spent in scientific work in his private laboratory and in travel. Between 1840 and 1873 he published in all seventy-eight scientific papers. The more important of these deal with analytical methods and mineralogical subjects. He devised important methods of analysis which have proved most useful to chemists and he was recognized as a leading authority upon the subject of meteorites. Only once or twice did he touch again upon organic chemistry, the subject of his first research. It is interesting to note that his graduation thesis, submitted at the age of twenty-one, was "a very ingenious thesis, entitled *The Compound Nature of Nitrogen.*"

In 1856, J. W. Mallet, then at the University of Alabama, completed his determination of the atomic weight of lithium from the chloride, and in 1859, the determination from the sulphate. This was the first of his long and brilliant series of investigations upon the atomic weights and the first atomic weight work done in America. The results then obtained, with very imperfect laboratory facilities, stand alongside with the best work of to-day. During the War of Secession Mallet devoted his scientific knowledge to the aid of the Confederate Ordnance Department. Afterwards he became professor of chemistry at the University of Virginia and a number of masterly investigations upon the atomic weights, notably those of aluminum and gold, have placed him by the side of Stas as a master in that field of work. During a long and singularly active life he has published a large number of papers, some of them worked out in conjunction with his pupils, covering a wide range of chemical subjects. His work for the National Board of Health upon the analysis of potable waters was very valuable in improving methods and contributed much toward the clearing up of problems connected with the processes then in use and devising new ones. This and his expert investigations of water supplies have made him an authority upon the subject. His published papers, including work done in connection with his pupils, considerably exceed one hundred.

The announcement of the Periodic System by Mendeléeff in 1869 has marked an epoch in the development of chemistry. Many chemists in various countries had been engaged upon the problems connected with this fundamental system of chemistry. One or two, as de Chancourtois in France and Newlands in England, had anticipated Mendeléeff in many of the features of the system. The law itself had been practically announced by Hinrichs of St. Louis. Little attention had been paid to these by the general body of chemists. Even the announcement of Mendeléeff received but scant notice for a year or so after it was made in St. Petersburg. It is of interest, therefore, to note that, quite independently, L. R. Gibbes of Charleston made use of his Synoptical Table, embodying much of the system. This was practically cotemporaneous with the work of Lothar Meyer in Germany. In this diagram, prepared for his classes in 1872 he made use of the spiral very much as was done by de Chancourtois, Meyer and Mendeléeff, anticipating, in a measure, the work of Spring, Reynolds and Crookes. Further, he anticipated some of the geometrical work of Haughton, observing that no linear equation can be constructed to give more than rude approximation of the atomic weights, and that to construct curves, two points of inflection or contrary curvature must be given. These are the serpentine cubics afterwards worked out by Haughton.

Robert E. Rogers was professor of chemistry at the University of Virginia. He was an active investigator during the period from 1842 to 1850. Much of his work was done in collaboration with his brother, William B. Rogers, who was professor of natural philosophy. The papers published by him, more than a dozen in number, were largely concerned with improved methods and apparatus. Analyses, determinations of solubility and problems of composition also engaged his attention.

While the contributions mentioned have been the most notable ones, a large number of investigations of lesser note have been carried out in Southern laboratories. Still, poverty of equipment and the pressure of duties in undermanned colleges have served to keep down the numbers of the workers. Aside from occasional scattered papers by a student here and there, however, the first institution in the country to send out annual reports of researches undertaken in its laboratory was the University of Virginia. These were regularly reported by Mallet in the *London Chemical News* beginning with the year 1872 and have continued for thirty-five years. In 1877 the Johns Hopkins University began its work and scientific research became an essential function of every true university. Lying on the border line this can scarcely be claimed as a Southern university and most of its workers have come from other sections.

In 1884 the University of North Carolina began the publication of a *Journal,* at first an annual and later a quarterly, containing chiefly the work done in the scientific laboratories. This is in its twenty-fourth year and reports several hundred chemical and physical as well as other scientific papers contributed by students and professors. Other institutions, as the University of Texas and Vanderbilt University, have reported important investigations.

Within the past quarter of a century a number of Southern investigators have contributed to the progress in chemistry. The following list is only partial but doubtless covers the more important work which has been done. The limited space prevents a fuller reference. The list is given alphabetically.

J. R. Bailey, of the University of Texas, has made a number of contributions in the field of organic chemistry. Among these are researches upon the hydrazin derivatives of propionic acid, derivatives of semicarbazino acids, of hydrazo acids and hydantoin tetrazones.

Charles Baskerville, of Mississippi, has published a number of papers upon the rare earths, especially zirconium, thorium and praseodymium, with a determination of the atomic weight of thorium.

Eugene C. Bingham, of Richmond College, has contributed a number of papers upon physical chemistry. These deal with conductivity, viscosity and fluidity, solubility, the relation of vapor pressure to chemical composition and the heat of vaporization.

A. W. Blair, of the University of Florida, has made contributions to the chemistry of fertilizers and soils as well as analytical chemistry.

R. N. Brackett, of Clemson College, S. C., has done a good deal of valuable chemical work in mineralogical and analytical lines.

W. G. Brown, of Virginia, while connected with the United States Department of Agriculture, made a study of the chemistry of wines. His remaining work has been chiefly mineralogical.

R. J. Davidson, of Virginia Polytechnic Institute, has made investigations in the chemistry of soils, foods and fertilizers.

F. P. Dunnington, of the University of Virginia, has published a number of papers covering his own work and that of his students. These contain improved analytical methods, analyses of minerals and rare substances besides a study of the distribution of titanium in soils.

William L. Dudley, of Vanderbilt University, has been busied with analytical and metallurgical problems. He has examined the action of fused sodium dioxide on metals, the solubility of platinum and the determination of fusel oil, besides contributing to the chemistry of iridium.

G. S. Fraps, of the Texas Agricultural and Mechanical College, in addition to several investigations in organic chemistry has made a special study of nitrification and the chemistry of foods, soils and fertilizers.

W. F. Hand, of the Agricultural and Mechanical College of Mississippi, has investigated the derivatives of amino benzoic acid and certain hydroquinazolines.

H. H. Harrington, of Mississippi, has taken part in the investigations carried on in the Experiment Stations upon foods and soils.

Charles H. Herty, of the University of North Carolina, has made important contributions to the chemistry of turpentine and the study of oils. Other researches of his bear upon double halides and the problem of the constitution of complex inorganic substances. He has published a number of papers upon inorganic and technical chemistry.

James Lewis Howe, of Washington and Lee University, has published a number of papers upon the salts of ruthenium, the chemistry of tellurium and certain complex malonates, succinates and tartrates. He has also done some work in physical chemistry.

J. H. Kastle, of Kentucky, while he has published

researches in organic chemistry, has especially devoted himself to physical and physiological chemistry making noteworthy studies in allotropism, the kinetics of oxidation, ferments, nitrification and certain changes in animal organisms.

R. K. Meade, of Virginia, has improved analytical methods and contributed to the study of hydraulic cements. He also founded and has edited the *Chemical Engineer*.

C. B. Pegram, of North Carolina, has made contributions to the study of the phenomena of radioactivity.

J. E. Mills, of the University of North Carolina, has published a series of important papers upon molecular attraction, deducing certain generalizations which promise to bear striking results. His chief work has been in the field of physical chemistry.

William B. Phillips, of North Carolina, has investigated the chemistry of and changes in chemical fertilizers besides making contributions to the study of Southern ores and ore deposits. He has made many contributions to engineering journals on mining and metallurgy.

B. R. Ross, of the Alabama Polytechnic Institute, has improved various analytical methods for sugars and fertilizers and made a study of the chemistry of sugars.

Atherton Seidell, of Georgia, associated with the Government Bureau of Chemistry, has done important work upon solubilities and other problems pertaining to physical chemistry. He has published an approved book on solubilities.

E. A. de Schweinitz, of North Carolina, for a number of years Chief of the Biochemic Division of the Department of Agriculture and Dean of the Medical Department of George Washington University, has been a pioneer in much of the work of biochemistry and has made valuable contributions to it.

Charles U. Shepard added to the wealth of his section by his discovery of the famous South Carolina phosphate deposits. He was professor of chemistry in the Medical College of Charleston from 1834 to 1861, continuing his work as a chemist from 1865 to 1880. He published about forty papers on analytical, mineralogical and meteorological subjects. His work on meteorites made him an authority upon that subject.

F. P. Venable, of the University of North Carolina, in addition to the publication of a *History of Chemistry*, the *Development of the Periodic Law* and the *Study of the Atom*, has contributed fifty or sixty papers upon various investigations, including derivatives of heptane, double salts, compounds of zirconium, with a determination of the atomic weight of this element. He has contributed also a study of valence and a modification of the Periodic System.

Charles E. Waite, of the University of Tennessee, has published a number of investigations in the chemistry of foods and nutrition, and has improved certain forms of apparatus and chemical processes.

A. S. Wheeler, of the University of North Carolina, has made a number of synthetic compounds by condensations with chloral and has also worked upon cellulose and other problems in organic chemistry.

Contributions in Physics.

When we consider the Southern contributions to physics we find the field more limited than in the case of chemistry. Few institutions could afford to have a distinct professorship of physics and very few had even the simpler appointments of a physical laboratory. Commonly, the study was made an adjunct to some such chair as that of chemistry or the professor in charge had to teach all or part of the so-called natural history studies. Under such circumstances little of original work, outside of the routine of teaching was to be expected.

The earliest original work in physics in the South seems to have been done by John William Draper while a professor at Hampden-Sidney College in Virginia. His most important work there was on the new science of photography. He began there the experimental researches which laid the foundation of his fame. Draper later moved to New York and there continued a long and brilliant career as an investigator.

Another noted name in physical science was that of Maury. While his work was chiefly that of a geographer and navigator, yet it also bore largely upon terrestrial physics. In pure physics and especially in his magnetic speculations and system of atmospheric circulation he met with some criticism at the time but his genius as an investigator of ocean currents and successful generalizer has been universally recognized and the world has accorded him the place of a leader in this field.

Matthew Fontaine Maury was born in Virginia in 1806. He entered the United States navy at the age of nineteen. After some years of active service, he was disabled by an accident and so was lead to devote his talents and energies to meteorological and hydrographical as well as other scientific studies. His earliest publication was a work on navigation. In a series of letters he laid bare a number of abuses in the navy, bringing about many reforms and largely determining the establishment of the United States Naval Academy at Annapolis. He was made chief of the Hydrographical Bureau, and later, upon the establishment of the National Observatory, was made superintendent of both. Many of the methods

MATTHEW F. MAURY.

at present in use in the Weather Bureau are due to him.

During this time he devoted much attention to the study of ocean currents and the direction of the winds. He wrote his most famous book, the *Physical Geography of the Sea,* which was translated into many languages and established his reputation among scientific men. Humboldt greeted him as one who had founded a new science.

By means of deep sea sounding he discovered the Atlantic Plateau. He suggested its use to Cyrus W. Field for the laying of a cable, thus establishing telegraphic communication between Europe and America. During the war he took the part of his native state, Virginia, and served as captain and commodore in the Confederate navy. He made improvements in the application of magnetic-electricity to torpedoes.

In 1868 he accepted the professorship of physics at the Virginia Military Institute and held this position until his death in 1873. While at Lexington he published a *Physical Survey of Virginia* and also textbooks on astronomy, and both a political and physical geography. His series of geographies have been very widely used and have retained their popularity through many editions for nearly forty years. He also had prepared *Wind and Current Charts,* and published two volumes of *Sailing Directions,* also a work on the *Relations between Magnetism and the Circulation of the Atmosphere* and *Laws for Steamers Crossing the Atlantic.*

John LeConte is another Southerner whose contributions to physics won for him a high reputation among the scientific men of the world. He was born in Georgia in 1818 and received his education at what is now the University of Georgia. After a few years of practice as a physician, he became professor

of natural philosophy in the University of South
Carolina, remaining there thirteen years. In 1869
the condition of political turmoil and the degrada-
tion of his institution led him to accept the chair
of physics and industrial mechanics in the University of California where the remaining years of his
active work were spent. He was acting president
of this now famous university and drew up its first
prospectus, giving a synopsis of the proposed
courses of instruction for the first year. A few years
later he was made president.

It was in 1857 that the discovery of the sensitive-
ness of flame to musical vibrations was made by him.
He had already won a respectful hearing among
scientific men by the publication of a number of
papers in this country and abroad, and his important
observations in this case "served as a starting-point
for Barrett, Tyndall and Koenig in the exquisite
applications that have since been worked out by
them, in the use of flame for the detection of sounds
too delicate for the ear to perceive and for the
optical analysis of compound tones." Tyndall in his
book on *Sound* makes graceful and appreciative
mention of LeConte's discovery. Lack of proper
laboratory equipment and facilities had prevented
LeConte from himself developing the application of
his discovery.

Again he attracted marked attention in Europe
by his paper *On the Adequacy of LaPlace's Explanation to Account for the Discrepancy between
the Completed and the Observed Velocity of Sound
in Air and Gases.* While his position was attacked
by a number of critics, especially among English
mathematicians, it met with the commendation of
Sir William Thompson and Tyndall and is generally
accepted to-day. The paper shows clear and exact
physical reasoning and contains an original investi-

gation upon the propagation of sound in air and the nature of the atmosphere, whether it is a mixture or a chemical compound.

His experiments upon the transmission of sound in water and what are called "sound shadows" were made in the Bay of San Francisco with the assistance of his son, Julian Le Conte. In explaining these observations, as well as the earlier ones of Colladon, he advanced certain theories which still appear the only tenable ones. This work was followed up by the investigation of sound shadows in air. In all he published something over one hundred papers in the scientific journals of this country and England.

William B. Rogers, whose chief work was in the field of geology, made some important investigations in physics while a professor at the University of Virginia. His father was a professor in William and Mary College at Williamsburg, Va. William B. Rogers received his education there and later succeeded his father in the chair of natural philosophy and mathematics. In 1835 he became professor of natural philosophy in the University of Virginia, remaining there until 1853. Later he established the Massachusetts Institute of Technology. The most noteworthy of his contributions to chemistry were a number of papers published in the *American Journal of Science* on improved methods of analysis and research. These appeared chiefly between the years 1840-1850 and the work was done in collaboration with his brother, Robert E. Rogers. He was the first to investigate the solvent action of water charged with carbon dioxide upon rocks and minerals. His chief work in physics was upon light, sensitive flames and vortex rings. Much also that he did in geology really pertained largely to physics. Among his more important books may be mentioned *Strength of Materials* (1838) and *Elements of Mechanical Philosophy* (1852).

One of his most distinguished pupils, and his successor in the chair of natural philosophy at the University of Virginia, is Francis H. Smith, who for fifty-four years has been a professor there. While he has not written a great deal he has made valuable observations upon Foucault's pendulum; sounding flames; the harmonic curves; latitude without astronomical observations; refractive index of gases and mixed liquids.

Among others who have made contributions to physics may be mentioned the following:

S. J. Barnett, of Tulane University, has worked successfully in the field of electrical displacement and unipolar induction.

John Daniels, of Vanderbilt University, has investigated voltameter polarization and the depilatory effect of Röntgen rays.

Edwin James Houston, who was born in Virginia, has won fame in connection with the Thomson-Houston system of electric lighting.

W. J. Humphreys, of Virginia, has done notable work in astro-physics, the pressure effect of arc spectra, solution and diffusion of metals in mercury, spark lengths, electric discharges, etc.

Charles A. Perkins, of the University of Tennessee, has investigated the magnetism of nickel, the vapor tension of sulphuric acid, etc.

H. B. Shaw, of North Carolina, professor in the University of Missouri, has done excellent work upon alternating current waves, energy losses in magnetic materials, and the regulation of alternating current generators.

James P. C. Southall, of Alabama, has worked chiefly in the field of geometrical optics. His most notable paper has been upon *Geometrical Theory of Optical Imagery*. This has led him to prepare a large and important treatise on the *Theory of Optical Instruments*.

W. LeConte Stevens, of Washington and Lee University, in addition to writing textbooks, has published a large number of articles in American and English journals covering a wide series of subjects in physics. The larger number of them deal with physiological optics, binocular perspective, the stereoscope, accoustics and radiation.

It is encouraging to note the increasingly large number of young physicists and chemists who are devoting themselves to research. Some of them have already done work under the direction of their laboratory chiefs which might place them in the above lists. As distinct contributors, however, their real work lies still in the future. Improved laboratory facilities and equipment, more leisure and the growing number of well-trained, enthusiastic young specialists give promise that Southern men will take a worthy share in the future progress of these and other sciences.

FRANCIS P. VENABLE,
President of the University of North Carolina.

CHAPTER XI.

SOUTHERN CONTRIBUTIONS TO NATURAL HISTORY.

N whatever field of activity the Anglo-Saxon has thought worth his endeavor he has placed his leaders.   The question is only whether he has always measured at its true value all lines of human effort.   There can be little doubt that in America too little estimate is to-day placed on the worth of scientific investigation in any field.   A similar plaint was uttered a few years ago by an English man of science on the occasion of the death of the immortal Pasteur.   He was convinced that the universal grief of the populace at the passing of a great man of science, demonstrating the devotion of the French people to their hero of peace, could not have had its counterpart in Great Britain.   The spirit of admiration for the man of executive ability has even invaded the field of science and scholarship in America.   Our naval heroes of the Spanish War are not the skillful and inventive engineers who by years of patient experiment made victory possible within a few weeks, but they are the commanders who directed the battles of a few hours.

There can be little doubt, therefore, that a greater popular appreciation of the real value of investigation in the field of natural history would attract much more attention to it on the part of our young men of superior endowment.   In this field, however, there have always been individuals who were ready like missionaries to sacrifice themselves if necessary for the sake of their ideals.   Thus we find even in

England that many of her greatest men of science have been amateurs rather than professionals, standing in this respect even to-day in striking contrast with Germany. While this insularity which has characterized the surroundings of men of science especially in this country has had its striking disadvantages, it also has one very important point in its favor: it encourages free and untrammeled thinking.

Within the narrow limits of this article one has only one of two alternatives in the discussion of this question. Either he must make his treatment of the subject a dry recital of facts or briefly stated annals for the sake of completeness, or he must choose from the great mass of details those most essential and typical or illustrative of the whole, and remain content to sacrifice completeness of detail. The writer has chosen the latter alternative, and much of paramount importance has of necessity been omitted.

When we attempt to divorce the exponents of natural history from those of other branches of physical science we are struck with the analogy of the developmental history of organisms themselves. We find that, just as the lines of descent of these organisms converge back to a common ancestry in the remote past, so were our early men of science "generalized types," and often included in the same individual the chemist, the physicist, the botanist, the zoölogist and the geologist. As knowledge advanced we find more and more specialization until the present time. Therefore, we are not surprised to find that many of the men more or less prominent in the early science of the South enjoy distinction in more than one field.

The Anglo-Saxon historian in America is prone to begin any branch of her history with the advent of his own race to this continent. The French and German elements of our population have played a promineut part in the natural history of the South. The early explorers from Spain touched mostly on the shores of the West Indies, Mexico and South America.

Naturalists of the Earlier and Later Periods.

The first English man of science to come to America was Thomas Harriott (1560-1621), Raleigh's mathematical tutor, who accompanied him on his voyage in 1585, and assisted in the establishment of the first English colony in this country. As was true of most scientific men of his time, Harriott was more of a mathematician and astronomer than naturalist. He published in 1590 a 33-page quarto volume, entitled, *Brief and True Report of the New Found Land of Virginia*. In this volume he listed twenty-eight species of mammals, eighty-six of birds, a number of fishes and crustaceans, besides various herbs, shrubs and trees wild and cultivated. John With, Harriott's companion, made drawings of many species which are still preserved in the British Museum. Harriott assigned for the most part the Indian names of his species. Many of his characters are easily recognized by the layman, as evideuced by the following: "Artamockes, the linguist; a bird that imitateth and useth the sounds and tones of almost all birds in the Countrie." American natural history thus began with Harriott, and was first planted on the shores of Virginia and North Carolina, if indeed we may dignify these early contributions as natural history.

The contribution next following Harriott's was by Captain John Smith, whose quaint descriptions were accurate and trustworthy. Goode gives some interesting quotations from his work: "An *opossum* hath a head like a swine and a taile like a rat, and is of the bignesse of a Cat. Under her belly she hath a bagge, wherein she lodgeth, carrieth, and suckleth her young." "Plums are of three sorts * * * that which they call *Putchamins* grow as high as a *Palmeta;* the fruit is like a Medler; it is first greene, then yellow, and red when it is ripe; if it be not ripe it will draw a man's mouth awry with much torment." Smith thus described about twenty mammals, some birds, fish and "shell fish."

Raphe Hamor, secretary of the Jamestown Colony, published in 1615 names of over sixty animals of Virginia. John Clayton visited Virginia in 1685 and published an important list of mammals, birds, and reptiles in the Philosophical Transactions of the Royal Society. About this time Thomas Glover in Virginia and Rev. Hugh Jones in Maryland made minor contributions. The latter collected plants and insects for Petiver.

Early in the Eighteenth century, Lawson, surveyor of the colony of North Carolina, published accurate lists and descriptions of North Carolina plants. About the same time Bohun and Lord (N. C.) and Vernon (Md.) also supplied specimens to Petiver in London.

During this period the collector's instinct was in the ascendency, and many curios illustrative of the fauna and flora of Virginia, Maryland and North Carolina found their way into the cabinets of curious monarchs and tavern-keepers of the mother country. James I. and Charles I. seem to have been especially active in this direction, and this doubtless contributed to a more widespread interest in such matters than exists even to-day.

Early in the Eighteenth century the French explorers began to penetrate "Louisiana" from the north. In 1672 Denyse published two works including discussions of the natural history of the coastal and interior of our territory. Père Laval and Le Page DuPratz may be mentioned as authors on various subjects relating to the natural history of Louisiana. Kalm (after whom our beautiful mountain laurel was named) and Swartz touched somewhat on the South.

In the latter part of the Seventeenth century an important group of naturalists of the "new school" appeared in Virginia, among whom were Bannister, Clayton, Mitchell and Garden.

John Bannister emigrated to Virginia before 1668, and was styled by John Ray, the great English naturalist, *"erudissimus vir et consummatissimus Botanicus."* He was the first to give serious attention to American mollusks and insects. He contributed in 1686 America's first systematic work on natural history to Ray's *Historia Plantarum, "Catalogus Plantarum in Virginia Observatarum."*

John Clayton, the naturalist (according to Thomas Jefferson, born in Virginia), published between 1739 and 1762 a work under the editorship of Gronovius, entitled, *Flora Virginica.* He was an acute botanist of his time, and left two volumes of manuscript and an herbarium, which were destroyed by fire during the Revolutionary War. His name is perpetuated in the delicate little spring flower popularly known as spring beauty, *Claytonia Virginica.*

Dr. John Mitchell (1680-1772) emigrated to Virginia from England early in the Eighteenth century, and spent nearly fifty years in the practice of his profession at Urbanna. He was a man of broad scientific tastes, and wrote on a number of different topics. He is known as a botanist and zoölogist as well as investigator of yellow fever. He was a correspondent of Linnæus, and the beautiful little trailer, partridge-berry, *Mitchella repens,* is dedicated to his memory. Tuckerman states, "Mitchell and Clayton together gave to the botany of Virginia a distinguished lustre."

Dr. John Tennent was a contemporary of Clayton and Mitchell, and introduced Seneca snakeroot to our materia medica. Dr. Alexander Garden (1728-1791), of Scottish birth, was a distinguished naturalist who spent about thirty years in Charlestown, S. C. He directed his attention to plants, fishes and reptiles. According to Goode, he was one of the most careful collectors of his day. He returned to England after the Revolutionary War, and was vice-president of the Royal Society in 1783. The well-known cape jessamine, *Gardenia Gardeni,* commemorates his name.

Mark Catesby (1679-1749) lived in Virginia and the Carolinas from 1712 to 1725, and also spent a year in the Bahamas. He wrote a valuable work on the natural history of Carolina, Florida and the Bahamas.

John Bartram, of Philadelphia, was an active collector of plants in the southern colonies, and supplied many specimens to Linnæus and his contemporaries. George III., in 1765, appointed him "Botanist to his Majesty for the Floridas," with a pension of £50 a year. Bartram is, however, to be classed as a collector and enthusiastic lover of nature rather than an investigator.

Moses Bartram, a nephew of John, was also a botanist, but William Bartram (1739-1823), son of Moses, is a more noted figure in American natural history. Coues attributes the beginning of an American school of ornithology to William Bartram's *Travels through North and South Carolina* (1791).

It is much to the credit of the American naturalists of colonial times that the revolutionary system of Linnæus found devotees at once, in marked contrast to the conservatism of English naturalists. The two distinguished Virginia botanists accepted the Linnean reforms, as shown in the following letter from Collinson to Linnæus in 1742: "Your system, I can tell you, obtains much in America. Mr. Clayton and Dr. Colden at Albany are complete professors, as is Dr. Mitchell, at Urbanna, in Virginia."

Thomas Jefferson was a scientist as well as a statesman. His *Notes on Virginia* was published in 1781. This work treated of the natural history, resources and topography of Virginia, and was the first publication of the kind brought out in the young republic. Goode says: "When Jefferson went to Philadelphia to be inaugurated Vice-President he carried with him a collection of fossil bones which he had obtained in Greenbrier county, Va., together with a paper, in which were formulated the results of his studies upon them. This was published in the 'Transactions of the American Philosophical Society,' and the species (a gigantic fossil sloth) is still known as *Megalonyx Jeffersoni.*" This is said to have been the first paper on paleontology presented in this country.

Jefferson maintained his interest in matters relating to natural history during his term as President. His dispatching of the Lewis and Clark Expedition, the precursor of the various scientific surveys and departments of the Federal government of to-day, is evidence of the part which he played in the development of science in this country. Goode says: "It is probable that no two men have done so much for science in America as Jefferson and Agassiz—not so much by their direct contributions to knowledge as by the immense weight which they gave to scientific interests by their advocacy." Jefferson's name is embalmed in the graceful little plant known as "twin-leaf," *Jeffersonia diphylla.*

It is a little singular that Jefferson's personal interest in natural history and his prominent part in the establishment of the University of Virginia did not result in a more general popular interest in the subject through the South. His service to science, however, was not so much as a propagandist as a political economist, resulting in giving science a wider opportunity for development in the entire country. He was thus an important factor in the building of the nation.

Dr. Hugh Williamson (1735-1819), of North Carolina, among important contributions in other fields of science, in 1775 published in the Philosophical Transactions a paper on the electric eel.

One of the most remarkable contributors to Southern natural history was Constantine S. Rafinesque (1784-1840), who was born of French parentage at Galeta near Constantinople, and came to Philadelphia in 1802. He was a pronounced, though erratic genius. It is hard to give an adequate estimate of his work. We find on the one hand that he held distinct views on evolution in advance of his time, while, on the other hand, we find him publishing in the regular binomial nomenclature of natural history twelve new species of thunder and lightning! Many amusing incidents are told by his contemporaries illustrating his eccentricities. While but little of his work in natural history has stood the test, he may be regarded as a genius who deserved better of the world than he received, and who might have left the world a much richer legacy had it received him more kindly. He was for seven years professor of natural sciences in Transylvania University, and during this period worked over much of Kentucky and adjoining states. Meehan says: "He endured rarely paralleled misfortunes, and sacrificed a large fortune for the sake of science * * * He died on a cot with hardly a rag to cover him, and without a solitary friend to stand by him in his last hours."

Shortly after the Revolutionary War there was a lull among the naturalists of the South, and the section was henceforth destined to play a secondary part in this field.   There were left Jefferson and Greenway in Virginia, Latrobe (ichthyologist) of Baltimore, and MacBride of South Carolina.   This retrogression has been attributed partly to the sparsely settled character of the region.

John Abbot contributed the materials for the first American volume on insects, entitled *The Natural History of the Rarer Lepidopterous Insects of Georgia* (1797).   The work was compiled by Sir James E. Smith.   Scudder calls Abbot "the most prominent student of the life histories of insects we have ever had."

Michaux, both father and son, visited America, and made important contributions to the botany of the South.   The elder Michaux founded in 1804 at Charleston the first botanical garden in this country, which, however, was destined to a brief span of life. Several other foreign collectors made similar excursions and published their work about this time, as Bosc in the Carolinas in 1800.

Dr. Lewis LeConte (1782-1838), father of Joseph and John L. LeConte, was an acute naturalist, and had a chemical laboratory and botanical garden on his plantation in Liberty county, Ga.   He refrained from publishing his own observations, which were entrusted to other contemporary naturalists.   His zoölogical manuscripts were destroyed by fire at Columbia near the close of the war.

Stephen Elliott (1771-1830) was born in Beaufort, S. C.   He graduated in the class of 1791 at Yale, and was prominent in the political affairs of his state. He founded the Literary and Philosophical Society of South Carolina in 1813. In 1829 he was chosen professor of natural history and botany in South Carolina Medical College. His chief work was his *Sketch of the Botany of South Carolina and Georgia* (1821-1827). In this work he was assisted by Dr. James MacBride, another South Carolina naturalist of note. Elliott's descriptions were all at first hand. The characters of each species were given in Linnean Latin and English in parallel. He exhibited great skill in his diagnoses of forms, and his work among the difficult family of grasses was especially well done. His herbarium is still in the custody of South Carolina College at Charleston, and is frequently consulted by botanists. The Elliott Society of Natural History, founded at Charleston in 1853, commemorated his labors. Ravenel says: "The versatility as well as the vigor of Mr. Elliott's mind may be seen in the variety of attainments in which he excelled. Beginning life as a legislator, in which capacity he served for many years, he took prominent and leading parts in many of the important measures of that time."

Gerard Troost (1776-1850) was born and educated in Holland, and came to Philadelphia in 1810. He helped to found the Philadelphia Academy and was its first president. In 1827 he was appointed professor of chemistry, mineralogy and geology in the University of Nashville. He was also state geologist of Tennessee from 1831 to 1849, and in this capacity brought out some of the first state geological reports published in this country. He made important studies of Tennessee and its geology, publishing papers on a variety of topics. He appears to have appreciated dimly the importance of fossils in the determination of the age of rocks. His extensive list of titles comprises matter on mineralogy, geology and paleontology. One of his im-

portant papers on crinoids found its way into the
hands of James Hall, state geologist of New York,
who kept it until the latter's death, after which, as
shown by Glenn, it appeared that Hall had described
from time to time many of Troost's species, thus
robbing Troost of the fruits of his labor.

John James Audubon (1780-1851) was born near
New Orleans, and had his first lessons in art under
the tuition of David, the French painter. While a
man of affairs in his younger days, he began his
monumental portraits of American birds, which
Cuvier, the great French anatomist, pronounced,
"Art's greatest Monument to Nature." Audubon
is to be classed as an artist rather than a man of
science, though his work must be considered one of
the world's great contributions to natural history.
When one reads of Audubon's enthusiastic devotion
to his work and of his privations in the forest, there
is a distinct touch of pity for the man of genius. In
order to atone for his lack of knowledge of zoölogy
he frequently associated with himself men of technical training, as Bachman and Baird.

Having now considered a few representatives
among the earlier Southern naturalists, a few types
will now be considered among the more recent ones.
In the choice of them one is at a loss to select. Many
must be omitted that ought to be included, such as
John Edwards Holbrook, of South Carolina, the
author of a monumental work on the reptiles of
North America (1842).

Southern science owes a great debt to New England and her older institutions of learning. Among
the men who came here from that section may be
mentioned Rev. Moses A. Curtis, who was born in
Berkshire county, Mass., in 1808. At the age of
twenty-two he went to Wilmington, N. C., as tutor
in the family of Governor Dudley. He was a very

JOHN J AUDUBON

active and energetic botanist. In 1834 he published an *Enumeration of the Plants Growing Spontaneously Around Wilmington, N. C.* Among the plants he especially investigated may be mentioned Venus's fly-trap (*Dionæa muscipula*), the most remarkable plant growing in this country. Curtis entered the ministry in 1835, and spent some time as an Episcopal missionary in western North Carolina. He carried his plant portfolio with him and collected specimens in the mountainous region. Asa Gray said of him, "No living botanist is so well acquainted with the vegetation of the Southern Alleghany Mountains." While Curtis published some papers on the flowering plants of North Carolina, he is best known as a student of the fungi. When one considers that in his day there was no descriptive manual of these remarkable and difficult plants, he is led to marvel at the skill and perseverance he displayed in working them out. He paid especial attention to the edible mushrooms and published several papers on this subject. In 1867 he published a *Catalogue of the Indigenous and Naturalized Plants of North Carolina,* enumerating 4,800 species. This was the first attempt made in the United States to list the lower as well as the higher forms of a local flora.

Henry William Ravenel (1814-1887) was born in the parish of St. John's, Berkeley, S. C. He graduated with distinction at South Carolina College in 1832. He formed early in life a passion for natural history, which soon centered on the field of botany. As a result of an attack of illness, resulting in serious impairment of his hearing, he was debarred from a career as a teacher in his chosen field. He devoted himself, like his friend Curtis of North Carolina, to a study of the fungi. Professor Farlow, his biographer, says: "It is doubtful whether any other American botanist has ever covered so

wide a range of plants. * * * He discovered a
surprisingly large number of new species. * * *
For a long time he and his friend, the late Rev. M.
A. Curtis, of North Carolina, were practically the
only Americans who knew specifically the fungi of
the United States." Between 1853 and 1860, he published *Fungi Caroliniani Exsiccati*, which was the
pioneer in this field in America. He also published
a number of minor papers, not, however, commensurate with his actual services to science. Professor
Farlow says: "Apart from the publications which
bear his name, if we would correctly estimate his
contributions to American botany, we must also include the very numerous notes and comments furnished by him to other writers, through whose pages
they are scattered, a monument to his liberality and
freedom from professional jealousy as well as to his
industry and acuteness." Ravenel's name is perpetuated in the very peculiar genus of rusts, *Rav-
enelia*.

The German revolution of 1848 sent to America a
number of worthy citizens, including prominent naturalists, of whom the South obtained a share.
Among these may be mentioned Gattinger, of Tennessee, and Mohr, of Alabama.

Charles Theodore Mohr was born in Esslingen on
the Neckar, Dec. 28, 1824. He brought with him to
America that enthusiastic devotion to science for
which his countrymen are so justly celebrated.
After a rather varied career in several sections of
the country, he finally settled in Mobile in 1857.
Here he engaged in a profitable drug business until
the period of the War of Secession, during which
time he was employed by the Confederate government in manufacturing and testing drugs. Dr. Mohr
subsequently came into touch with the prominent
botanists of the country and contributed a number

of papers, especially along economic lines. The greater part of Dr. Mohr's collections are the property of the Alabama Geological Survey, and are deposited with the University of Alabama. His name is perpetuated in the beautiful shrub, *Mohrodendron,* Silver Bells, which grows in his adopted state. Dr. Mohr was a careful, painstaking student, and kept fully abreast of the advancing thought in his field even to his ripe old age, as indicated by the fact that he spent his last days classifying and arranging the herbarium of the University of Alabama according to the latest advanced system of Engler and Prantl. Mohr's chief work was *Plant Life of Alabama,* published in 1900 by the United States Department of Agriculture from material furnished by the Alabama Geological Survey.

A name long to be honored in the annals of American botany is that of Dr. A. W. Chapman, the author of the *Flora of the Southern United States.* Chapman was born of English parents in Southampton, Mass., in 1809; died April 6, 1899, at Apalachicola, Fla., in his 90th year. After his graduation from Amherst College in 1830 he began life as a teacher near Savannah, Ga. He soon equipped himself as a medical practitioner, and finally made his home at Apalachicola, Fla., in 1847, where he spent the greater part of his long and useful life. Dr. Chapman became enthusiastically interested in the rich Southern flora, and an active collector in his adopted state. He was a constant correspondent of Drs. Torrey and Gray and contributed much material to their *Flora of North America.* Dr. M. A. Curtis, of North Carolina, and Dr. Chapman undertook to prepare a manual of the flowering plants of the Southern states east of the Mississippi River and south of Virginia and Kentucky, but on account of the latter's active interest in the fungi, Dr. Chapman undertook his task alone. He finally brought out his first edition in 1860, just at the opening of the war. He heard nothing of the results of his labors for four years, "when Dr. Gray," as he writes, "smuggled through the lines a budget of friendly notices of the work which appeared during those years in the periodicals of this country and Europe, and all at once I awoke to bigness." Dr. Chapman's work was for many years the leading authority on the plants of the South, and in the 88th year of his life he brought out a final edition of the work. Dr. Chapman was a man or rare physique, and in the quiet retirement of his Florida home enjoyed the high esteem of his neighbors and fellow townsmen. He was a hospitable gentleman of the old school and a delightful correspondent. His final collections went to the Biltmore Herbarium.

Dr. Chapman's loyalty to the scientific interests of the South is shown by statements to the writer in 1895. He was offering his collection for sale, and wrote: "I want it to remain in Southern hands." After disposing of the collection to the Biltmore estate, he wrote: "I have succeeded in keeping my herbarium at home. I have sold it to the Vanderbilt establishment at Biltmore, North Carolina." Dr. Chapman's biographer, Dr. Mohr, says of his critical work in systematic botany that it "evinces the scientific turn of mind and the method required for enduring work in phytography, which secured to the author a place in the ranks of the writers of authority."

As above stated, the bulk of the natural history work done in the South has been due to individual initiative. This is true even when we take account of the institutions and organizations such as the state geological surveys, for they were founded at the earnest solicitation of a few active individuals.

In this short sketch no full discussion can be given of institutions; they are treated elsewhere in this work. Yet, a general reference to their bearing on work in natural history must be made.

Geological Surveys.

Geological research in the South, though hardly to be considered "natural history," should perhaps be considered on account of its relation to the main subject; and with it a short sketch of the establishment and personnel of representative state geological surveys.

The earlier Southern state surveys were established—North Carolina in 1823; Tennessee in 1831; Virginia in 1835; South Carolina in 1844; Alabama in 1848; Missouri in 1853; Mississippi in 1854.

Denison Olmstead (1791-1859), "a Connecticut school-teacher," while professor of chemistry in the University of North Carolina, began a geological survey of that state in 1823. While this can scarcely be dignified with the title of survey, it nevertheless marks the first appropriation out of public funds made in this country for such a purpose ($250 for four years!) On Olmstead's call to Yale in 1825, he was succeeded by Elisha Mitchell (1793-1857). This survey suffered varied fortunes, but a notable point in passing is that Mitchell's geological map of North Carolina, published in 1842, was the first of its kind to be issued in this country. Mitchell made important contributions especially to the theories of the origin and distribution of gold deposits in North Carolina. He lost his life by accident while exploring the noble mountain peak which now bears his name. His name is also commemorated in the Elisha Mitchell scientific Society of the University of North Carolina, which is one of the most efficient organizations of its kind in the South.

L. Vanuxem (1792-1848), while professor at South Carolina College, was the first American to point out the probable absorption of atmospheric gases by the earth's crust, and consequent secular changes in the terrestrial atmosphere.

Michael Tuomey (1805-1857), a native of Ireland, was the first geologist of South Carolina, and went to Alabama in 1848. He deserves especial mention as one of the most active and earliest workers on Southern geology.

James M. Safford (1822-1907) was appointed state geologist of Tennessee in 1854. His *Geological Reconnoissance* was published in 1856. Merrill says: "From a strictly geological standpoint the matter given in * * * the closing chapters of the report was of greatest importance * * * This report shows on the part of Safford a thorough insight into the intricacies of the structure of the state and an ability to grasp the salient features and master the broader problems in a manner perhaps not realized by many of his contemporaries and successors."

Joseph LeConte (University of South Carolina) published his first geological paper on coral growth as exemplified on the peninsula and keys of Florida (1857). According to conclusions here reached—a fundamental contribution to the theory of the subject: "The peninsula and keys of Florida have been the result of the combined action of at least three agencies. First, the Gulf Stream laid the foundation; upon that corals built up to the water level; and, finally, the work was completed by the waves."

Joseph LeConte (1823-1901) was born on his father's plantation in Liberty county, Ga. His life reads almost like a romance, and cannot be even adequately glimpsed at in this brief sketch. His youth was spent on his father's plantation, and he attended college at Athens, Ga. He spent much time in travel through the North, and took his medical degree at the College of Physicians and Surgeons, New York. He later became dissatisfied with the field of medicine and spent some time at Harvard with Agassiz, where his surroundings served as an agreeable mental tonic.

LeConte's first professional charge was at Oglethorpe University, Midway, Ga., where he taught all the sciences. He next filled for four years the chair of botany and geology at the University of Georgia, to which he was called in 1852. Owing to administrative difficulties here he accepted the professorship of chemistry and geology in the College of South Carolina in 1857. In spite of his onerous duties here, he continued to write occasional important papers on various scientific and philosophical questions. During the period of the war the College disbanded, and LeConte served the Confederate government in several different ways, being in 1864 appointed chemist of the Niter and Mining Bureau with rank of major. In 1868, after the trying vicissitudes of the reconstruction period, Joseph LeConte, with his brother, received calls to the University of California, and the South thus lost the services of another of its men of genius.

In LeConte's estimate of his own life accomplishment, he says, among other things: 'In geology, I believe some real advance was made in my series of papers (1) on the structure and origin of mountain ranges; (2) on the genesis of metalliferous veins; (3) especially in that on critical periods in the history of the earth; (4) on the demonstration of the Ozarkian or, better, the Sierran epoch as one of great importance in the history of the earth."

The devotion of LeConte's students and friends in the University of California was sublime. He passed away in the embrace of his family and loving friends during a visit to the Yosemite Valley in 1901.

Among the especially effective geological surveys made or being made in the South may be mentioned the Arkansas Survey, under the directorship of Dr. J. C. Branner, himself a native of Tennessee, now of Leland Stanford Jr. University; the Alabama Survey, by Dr. Eugene A. Smith; the Texas Survey, by Dr. F. W. Simonds; the Mississippi Survey under Dr. E. W. Hilgard, now of the University of California, whose career in the South would make a fitting accompaniment to that of LeConte, his friend and colleague of many years.

It is to be regretted that in many states there has been a growing disposition to shift responsibility to the National Geological Survey. From the standpoint of purely scientific accomplishment, if not eventually from economic ends, there is no doubt that the cause may suffer in the hands of one immense bureau, dominated by one man or a few men, who are at least in danger of suppressing freedom of discussion.

Among the factors making for advancement in these fields in the South should be considered a number of institutions besides the state geological surveys. The educational institutions in the South are treated elsewhere in this work.

Especial attention should be called to two establishments that are active factors in the field of botany, viz., the Missouri Botanical Garden, at St. Louis, and the Biltmore Estate of Mr. George W. Vanderbilt, near Asheville, N. C. The former, established by Shaw, is one of the important scientific institutions of the entire country, and the latter has an important collection and library, and a corps of active workers in the field of forestry and systematic botany.

Much is, doubtless, in the future to be expected of the Agricultural Experiment Stations, which were founded by act of Congress in 1887. The bill establishing these institutions is known as the Hatch Act, Representative Hatch, of Missouri, having been a prominent advocate of the bill. The Experiment Stations were founded for the scientific investigation of problems related to agriculture, and some of the most important problems of biology are legitimate fields for exploitation under the terms of the Hatch Act. Unfortunately, in several Southern states the activities of the Experiment Stations have, in the hands of the demagogue, been diverted into improper channels, so that they have become rather bureaus of information exploited for political ends than really scientific institutions. Fortunately, these conditions are improving.

The field of natural history has now given way to the science of biology. Its problems have ramified into so many channels that no one man can now hope to compass it all. The great need of the South now in order to encourage real accomplishment in this and other fields so important to the industrial as well as cultural progress of the region, is adequate libraries and a healthy, enthusiastic public sentiment tending to attract amateurs to the study of the still incompletely explored region of the South.

In an attempt to trace out the factors that have produced the South's contributions to natural history, we find that the earliest devotees came with the first colonists from Great Britain, and brought some exponents of this field of culture among others to the shores of Virginia and North Carolina.

After the establishment of the United States as a nation, the encouragement given by Jefferson and others of Virginia was an exceedingly important factor to the whole country. During the Nineteenth century the South owes much of its accomplishment in this field to the influences of the older New England colleges, and especially to their alumni who emigrated southward. In Louisiana and other sections of the South much is due to scientific influences from France, as illustrated by Audubon and Langlois. Due consideration must also be given to the influx of Germans, as illustrated by Mohr, Hilgard and Gattinger. It is quite probable that up to the period of the war there was more local interest that might be considered indigenous in South Carolina than in any other Southern state. From the ethnical standpoint, judging from the leading lights among Southern naturalists, we are compelled to yield the palm to the French element of our composition, for considering their proportion they here certainly predominate, though much is due the Germans.

BIBLIOGRAPHY.—*Audubon, John James, Life of*, by his widow (New York and London, 1902); Call, Richard E.: *The Life and Writings of Rafinesque* (Filson Club Publications, No. 10, Louisville, 1895); Engelmann, George: *The Botanical Works of the Late George Engelmann*, ed. by Trealease and Gray (Cambridge, 1887); Gill, Theodore: *Biographical Memoir of John Edwards Holbrook* (Biographical Memoir, National Academy of Science, 5:49, 1903); Goode, G. B.: *The Beginnings of Natural History in America* (Proceedings of the Biological Society of Washington, Vol. III., 1884–86); Hilgard, E. W.: *Biographical Memoir of Joseph LeConte* (Biographical Memoir, National Academy of Science, 1907); Merrill, Geo. P.: *Contributions to the History of American Geology* (Annual Report Smithsonian Institution for 1904); Riley, F. L.: *Sir William Dunbar: the Pioneer Scientist of Mississippi* (Mississippi Historical Society Publications, 2: 85–112); Scribner, F. Lamson: *Southern Botanists* (Bulletin Torrey Botanical Club, 20: 315, 1893); Schweinitz, L. D. von: *A Sketch of the Life and Work of* (Journal Elisha Mitchell Scientific Society for 1885–6); Smith, E. A.: *Charles Theodore Mohr* (A biographical sketch in Mohr's *Plant Life of Alabama*); Trealease, W.: *The Academy of Science of St. Louis: A Biography* (*Popular Science Monthly*, 64:117, 1903) and *The Missouri Botanical Garden* (Ibid., 62:193–221).

SAMUEL McCUTCHEN BAIN,

Professor of Botany, University of Tennessee.

CHAPTER XII.

THE SOUTH'S CONTRIBUTIONS TO PHILOSOPHY.

IN his very unique and interesting *Autobiography*, Prof. Joseph LeConte relates, in expressions of grateful pleasure, the discussions upon scientific and philosophic subjects which he enjoyed in the summer of 1858 with Mr. Langdon Chevis, a South Carolina coast planter. He asserts that, in the course of their discussion of the famous *Vestiges of Creation* then exciting the world-wide interest of scientists and philosophers, Chevis expressed and amplified in considerable detail the identical thought regarding the "survival of the fit" as a prime factor in organic evolution that was subsequently enunciated and elaborated by Darwin in the *Origin of Species*. LeConte then says: "Why did he not publish his idea? No one well acquainted with the Southern people, and especially with the Southern planters, would ask such a question. Nothing could be more remarkable than the wide reading, the deep reflection, the refined culture and the originality of thought and observation characteristic of them; and yet the idea of publication never entered their minds. What right had anyone to publish, unless it was something of the greatest importance, something that would revolutionize thought?"

This, undoubtedly, expresses, with exactness, the mental attitude of the Southern scholar of former days. Deep thinkers were the men of the plantations; wide readers, keen observers and profound reasoners. And yet the dignified modesty and the

lofty ideals of intellectual culture which were the
outgrowth of their peculiar environment—the delicacy, refinement and seclusion of the family life
upon the large, slave-cultured plantations—led them
to shrink, instinctively, from obtruding the results
of their quiet reflections upon the notice of the world
at large, unless, indeed, it should be something so
important as to "revolutionize thought." Hence it
is that much of the best thought of the South has
been lost to permanent literature. This does not
mean, however, that it or its influence has been
lost necessarily to the world. The philosophic conceptions of the great thinkers were promulgated and
disseminated through oral discussion with friends
and neighbors and hospitably-received visitors from
abroad upon the great patriarchal estates, by voluminous correspondence, by family teaching and in
the schools and colleges which, for the most part,
were manned by instructors of the same modest and
retiring type.

No better illustration of this characteristic quality
of the Southern scholar is afforded than by the case
of LeConte himself. While a professor in Southern
colleges, before the war period, he observed and
reasoned and had reached practically all the great
scientific deductions which subsequently made him
famous, and yet he published no papers expository
of his work or ideas until his removal from the
South to California at the close of the war. The
influence of Southern thought upon philosophy, like
its influence, in the main, upon the literature and
upon the theories and practices of government, was
mainly in the development and the maintenance of
high ideals on the part of the individual and in the
immediate community, rather than in technical contribution to a general literature, and it was exerted
through actual living and in personal and oral teach-

ing rather than through the agency of the printed page. The libraries of the world therefore contain but few books or publications upon technical philosophic subjects furnished by writers of the South in the earlier periods of its history.

And yet, if the aim of the highest philosophy be the apprehension of the fundamental and eternal principles governing right living and determining the relations of man to God, his neighbor and Nature, the ideals of conduct exemplified by the men of the South in their individual lives and their social relations, born of their close observation and thoughtful reasoning and commended to their children and their immediate communities, must have had an influence upon current local thought and upon the development of the communal life even greater than that which would have been afforded by technical investigation and publication, no matter how profound. It is not contended, by any means, that exemplary living was universal throughout the South, nor is it denied that its peculiar social institutions involved something of evil to all concerned and something of injustice in the classification of its peoples consequent thereon. But all observers are agreed that, from its early settlement to the time when its intellectual energies were absorbed in the great political disputes which led to the War of Secession, the thought of the South and its communal spirit were directed and dominated by the quiet and profound thinkers of the great plantations and the superb examples of ethical living which they afforded. Perhaps, therefore, the noteworthy and the peculiar contribution of the South to philosophy in its earlier history was the creation and the fine effort at realization of high ideals of human conduct based upon the essential and immutable principles of truth, equity and justice. The great teachers of the schools and colleges of the South of the period, many of whom, after the fashion of the times, were clergymen as well, held to these ideals and exalted them in the estimation of their pupils and thus, although contributing but little to the literature of philosophy, they impressed upon the community at large a truly philosophic mode of thought which subsequently became creative and now bids fair to become highly and richly productive.

During the colonial period this lack of original contributions to philosophy on the part of Americans was undoubtedly due to the fact that the country was more imitative than creative, as became a political dependency. Foreign influences completely dominated and overshadowed whatever feeble attempts at philosophizing in the shape of printed books were made by the American colonists, and among the influences those of the British were, of course, predominant, through Locke, Berkeley and Reid; then followed the French naturalism of Montesquieu, the materialism of La Mettrie and the eclecticism of the positivists; and finally the German influence as known in the works of the Kantian and post-Kantian idealists. I. W. Riley, in his *American Philosophy—The Early Schools* (1907), says that though the study and writing of philosophical works was uncommon in the colonial period, still "not a few of the early planters were men of decided speculative tastes who were familiar with the abstract philosophy of their times; but their interest being chiefly practical, they fell back upon the fundamental principles of political and ethical science, because of their desire for political independence." The various philosophical movements in America became sectionalized in their broader aspects, the North standing for idealism, while the South stood

George Tucker

for materialism and the middle West for the philosophy of common sense.

Even so, the bibliography of the South's contributions to philosophy is not altogether a blank and barren page. Aside from the great political philosophers who were foremost in developing the genius and in shaping the governmental forms of the young American Republic, and who held it fast for many years to sound public policies, among the earlier writers of the South were some whose works are worthy to rank as original and valuable contributions to the technical literature of philosophy. The *Essays, Moral and Philosophical,* of the brilliant and versatile George Tucker (1775-1861), the biographer of Jefferson and for many years professor of philosophy at the University of Virginia, contain, among many other reflections which are valuable, a treatment of the Will which is strikingly original and suggestive.

Of the native materialists of the South probably the most original was Joseph Buchanan (1785-1812) of Kentucky, who, in his *Philosophy of Human Nature,* denied that the soul had an independent and immaterial existence and asserted that mind is merely an organic state of matter.

Another early materialist was Thomas Cooper (1758-1840) of South Carolina, who was offered the professorship of natural science and law in the University of Virginia. While Cooper was strongly condemned by many for his radicalism in philosophy, religion and politics, his influence throughout the South, and particularly in South Carolina, was powerful, chiefly because of his advocacy of the doctrines of extreme state's rights, nullification and free trade. He was therefore one of the political philosophers whose principal work consisted in shaping the policies of the country. His writings include *Political Essays* (1800); *Lectures on the Elements of Political Economy* (1826); and *A Treatise on the Law of Libel and the Liberty of the Press* (1830).

Thomas Jefferson, while he did not contribute much to original philosophy with his pen, greatly aided the study of philosophy by his broad-mindedness in planning for the University of Virginia and in the selection of works to be used. The influence of the foreign schools of philosophy is seen in his recommendation of Hutcheson's *Introduction to Moral Philosophy*, Locke's treatise on *The Conduct of the Mind in Search of Truth*, and works by Dugald Stewart, Lord Kames and others of their stamp. He then sought to instil into the minds of the students the principles of French rationalism through the use of Condorcet's works, and he also recommended Priestley's *Corruptions of Christianity*.

Another Southern philosopher was Frederick Beasley (1777-1845), who was born in North Carolina, entered Princeton in 1793, and after graduation was a tutor in the college. He subsequently became an Episcopal priest in Baltimore, a member of the Philosophical Society of Philadelphia and provost of the University of Pennsylvania. He wrote *Search of Truth* (1822); *Review of the Philosophy of the Human Mind by Thomas Brown;* and *Vindication of the Argument a Priori.*

The *Philosophy of the Animated Existence* of John Berry Gorman (1793-1864), of South Carolina, a semi-scientific, semi-philosophic explanation of the relations of mind and body is noteworthy as containing germ-ideas which have since been largely elaborated in our modern physiological psychology.

The *Follies of Positive Philosophy* of Thomas Lanier Clingman (1812-1897), of North Carolina, presents a trenchant, brilliant and very suggestive

T. L. Clingman

attack upon Comte and his followers as understood in his day.

Of later date the monographs on *Memory* by J. K. P. Sayler (1839), of Tennessee; on *The Law of Hypnotism* by R. Stewart Hyer (1860), of Georgia; and the more pretentious work on *Ethics, Descriptive and Explanatory* of S. E. Mayes (1863), of Texas, are admirable contributions to the topics indicated.

Another type of contribution of this period which should be taken into account in this connection is such as is furnished by writers of the character of Joseph LeConte and Nathaniel Southgate Shaler, some of whose works are more philosophic than scientific.

Joseph LeConte was born in Liberty County, Ga., Feb. 26, 1823, and died in the Yosemite Valley, Cal., July 6, 1901. In 1841 he was graduated from Franklin College, Georgia; studied medicine in the College of Physicians and Surgeons, New York; and later entered the Lawrence Scientific School at Harvard. He was professor of natural science in Oglethorpe University, Georgia, in 1852; of geology and natural history in Franklin College, 1852-56; of geology and chemistry in the University of South Carolina, 1856-69; and from 1869 until his death of geology and natural history in the University of California. His articles in philosophical journals created widespread comment because of the keen insight and originality and evidences of deep research. He contended that a true psychology must be reached through investigations in physiology. His *Religion and Science* (1873) was a series of Sunday evening lectures delivered in the Independent Church, Oakland, Cal., and gave what he called a rational view of the fundamental truths of religion from the scientific standpoint. His *Sight: An Exposition of the*

Principles of Monocular and Binocular Vision (1880) is an original contribution to science and is much used in psychological courses. In *Evolution: Its Nature, Its Evidences and Its Relation to Religious Thought* (1887) he strives to answer the three questions: What is evolution? Is it true? and If true, what then?

Nathaniel Southgate Shaler was born in Newport, Ky., Feb. 20, 1841, and died at Cambridge, Mass., April 10, 1906. After graduating from the Lawrence Scientific School, Harvard, in 1862, he served in the Union Army, then returned to Harvard as assistant and instructor in geology and zoölogy, in 1868 became professor of palæontology there, was transferred to the chair of geology in 1887 and from 1891 until his death was dean of the Lawrence School. From 1873-80 he was in charge of the Kentucky Geological Survey, was at various times commissioner of agriculture of Massachusetts, and from 1884 was in charge of the Atlantic division of the United States Geological Survey. As said above, many of his works were more philosophic than scientific, the chief of them being *The Nature of Intellectual Property; The Interpretation of Nature* (1893); *The Individual: Study of Life and Death* (1900); *The Neighbor* (1904); *The Citizen: A Study of the Individual and the Government* (1904). He also wrote *Kentucky: A Pioneer Commonwealth; The United States of America: A Study of the American Commonwealth* (1894); and many geological and scientific works.

Chief among what may be called the present-day philosophers of the South stand, of course, Noah K. Davis, late the distinguished professor of moral philosophy in the University of Virginia, whose prolific pen has contributed numerous standard texts to the literature of philosophy, and James

NOAH K. DAVIS.

Mark Baldwin, of the Johns Hopkins University, whose frequent and brilliant papers rank him among the most acute and profound of modern psychologists.

Noah Knowles Davis was born at Philadelphia, May 15, 1830, and when he was six years of age his parents moved to Tuscaloosa, Ala. In 1849 he was graduated from Mercer University, Penfield, Ga., and then spent several years in the study of chemistry, also during these years editing *The Model Architect* and *The Carpenter's Guide*. In 1852 he was appointed to the chair of natural science in Howard College, Marion, Ala.; in 1859 became principal of the Judson Female Institute at the same place; in 1868 was elected president of Bethel College, Russellville, Ky.; and in 1873 was appointed to the professorship of moral philosophy at the University of Virginia, which he held until 1906, when he became professor emeritus. He has given much thought and attention to metaphysical studies and many philosophical treatises written by him have been published. The first of these was an extensive work on deductive logic entitled *The Theory of Thought* (1880), a work which, based on the writings of Aristotle, is one of the most acute, comprehensive and satisfactory treatises on logic written in English. He also published *Elements of Deductive Logic* (1890) a work intended as a text-book for students; *Elements of Psychology* (1892); *Elements of Inductive Logic* (1895); *Elements of Ethics* (1900); and *Elementary Ethics* (1900).

James Mark Baldwin was born at Columbia, S. C., June 12, 1861. His early education was obtained at Thompson's Military Academy, Columbia, S. C., and at Salem Collegiate Institute, Salem, N. J.; he then entered Princeton University from which he graduated in 1884, during the years of 1884-86 further pursued his studies at Berlin, Leipzig and Tübingen, and in 1886-87 studied at Princeton Theological Seminary. During the latter years he was instructor in French and German at Princeton; from 1887-89 was professor of philosophy at Lake Forest University (Ill.); and in 1889 became professor of philosophy at Toronto University, Canada. While at Toronto, Dr. Baldwin established the first laboratory of experimental psychology in the British Empire. In 1893 he was called to the chair of psychology at Princeton and while at that university established a similar laboratory. After ten years of service at Princeton, he became professor of philosophy and psychology at Johns Hopkins University, Baltimore, Md., where he now is.

Dr. Baldwin is a strong believer in experimental psychology and a weighty exponent of evolution as applied to consciousness; and has made a special study of illusions, social heredity, organic selection, and genetic psychology. Among his contributions to philosophy and psychology are the following works: *German Psychology of To-day* (translation, 1886); *Handbook of Psychology* (1890); *Elements of Psychology* (1893); *Mental Development in the Child and the Race* (1896); *Social and Ethical Interpretations in Mental Development* (1898); *Story of the Mind* (1898); *Fragments in Philosophy and Science* (1902); *Development and Evolution* (1902); *Genetic Logic* (Vol. I, 1906). He was also editor-in-chief of the *Dictionary of Philosophy and Psychology* (1901-6); and edited the *Psychological Review, Princeton Contributions to Psychology,* and the *Library of Historical Psychology.*

HENRY C. WHITE,
University of Georgia, Athens, Ga.

CHAPTER XIII.

CONTRIBUTIONS OF THE SOUTH TO THE CHARACTER AND CULTURE OF THE NORTH.

NEW Englanders at all stages in the history of the country have busied themselves so actively with advertising in print their part in the making of America; the compact circle of New England authors before the war managed so effectively to enhance each other's reputations by piling criticism on authorship and authorship on criticism again; that most foreigners and many busy Americans have absorbed the notion that American character is a New England product, and "culture" a plant nourished solely in that region. This idea has been reinforced by the assiduity of New Englanders since the war, in working over their material, in composing voluminous biographies, appreciations, memoirs, poems, critiques, histories about every New Englander who ever wrote a book, or, indeed, did anything out of the ordinary.

This assiduity reflects, of course, no discredit upon New England. Quite the contrary. But it must be taken into account in reducing to its actual value New England's real part in the making of the country. Especially it must be taken into account in any attempt to get at what the South has contributed to the character and culture not only of the nation at large, but of that part of it which New England is currently reported, on her own authority, to have moulded—the Northern half. As a matter of fact, what is called the Puritan influence, what is fathered on the New England conscience, is not essentially

Puritan at all; it is British seriousness, aggravated by a hand-to-hand conflict with a new country, and the responsibility for it is shared about equally by Massachusetts and Virginia.

The New England conscience flourishes vigorously even to-day in the inhabitants of the Old Dominion, and while the expression is sometimes different, the variation may be charged chiefly to the effect of climate and soil. The truth is, that so long as America was distinctly a nation of transplanted Britons, the New England conscience, so-called, was a common heritage of all. It is only since the flood of alien blood has swamped the country and diluted the original strain that this conscience has ceased to be the common standard, however modified as to particular judgments by differences in the conditions to be faced. In New England proper at one time, for instance, it approved capital punishment for witches, promoted piracy and drew sustenance from the slave traffic. In the South, at another period, it sanctioned the duel and the holding of the involuntary black man in bondage. At the present time, because the white population of the South is still of preponderantly British decent, because the alien has not swarmed over the land and diluted the original stock, the last stronghold of the New England conscience is actually below Mason and Dixon's line, with its citadel at Richmond, Va. The thing survives, in spots, in New England also, but only in little pools and back waters not yet reached by the tide. Even the presence of the negro, with his stone-age morals, has not sufficed to destroy it in the South —though it has, of course, modified it—for the negro stands outside the stream.

So much in general, in order to clear the air for the consideration of the effect of the South proper upon the North proper; that is, the influence of the characteristics acquired by the Britons transplanted to the country south of Philadelphia by contact with their new environment upon the Britons, and others transplanted to the country north of Philadelphia as modified by their new environment.

In the first place, then, the Briton in the South, even if he were not descended from the landed gentry, a special breed of masters of other men in the old country, presently developed for himself a special breed of masters of men by reason of his training on a plantation where he ruled over many. At the same time he gained a boldness, an initiative, an adaptability quite foreign to the stay-at-home Briton. For he had to rule over an alien and barbaric people in a new and unformed country strange to him and to them.

In the second place this Briton in the South did not develop technical skill—having no use for it; did not develop parsimony, because with so rough an instrument as the negro to do his work cheese-paring methods were impossible. Also, living mostly out of doors, having few long winter nights to kill, he was not tempted to read and write over much.

The Briton settled in New England (for we must exclude New York, New Jersey and Pennsylvania from this classification; indeed, all three up to the time of the War of Secession had more affinity with the South than with New England) was forced by his environment into a narrowed life. He lived in villages, in small towns, and his kingdom was his house and garden, not a thousand acres; he bred citizens, not rulers; he worked in a country not physically lavish and he learned parsimony. For the same reason he acquired technical skill; he built ships. In the long winter nights he read and wrote. His library had been selected and brought over from England at the very height of the Calvinistic mad-ness which possessed that country for a while, did its work and then receded as all such movements normally do. Upon these books thus selected, the New Englander fed—he had few others—and from them he drew inspiration. Hence in New England the theological taint grew and stamped permanently upon the people certain marks of the religious fanatic and the doctrinaire which linger to this day.

Beginning of Southern Influence upon Northern Culture.

The influence of the South upon the character and culture of the North begins with the Revolution, when the colonies, which up to that time had pursued their separate evolutionary paths, joined together to march in company upon a broader way. It is a commonplace of history that, in the movement which divorced the colonies from the mother country, the South, concentrated for the moment in Virginia, instinctively took command; that New England not without resentments (for her training was no more in taking orders than in giving them) accepted Virginia's leadership and continued to accept it in the national government until the West, grown to manhood, snatched the sceptre which it was to hold till the great corporate interests of the present decade, and the one just before it, laid hands on it. These brought it for a season to Wall Street—a Northern habitat, geographically, but representing actually the collected masterfulness of all the sections, with the West preponderant in the list of masters.

Thus the first influence of the South upon the character of the North was in furnishing a type of statesman—a type which modified profoundly New England's native idea, the glorified selectman. That selectman, in the person of John Adams, demonstrated very early that the qualities which made the ruler of a pent-up Utica were not the qualities which made a President of the United States. The larger qualities, dormant in the New Englander because of disuse, were promptly developed with the hint the Southern statesman gave. That section furnished presently a Webster, at the same time that the theological ferment working in her was busy manufacturing John Brown and William Lloyd Garrison and Horace Greeley to carry on her influence in another and later stage of the country's development.

Just here it is well to note that the influence of Thomas Jefferson is one the nation is constantly acknowledging without anything like an adequate comprehension of what it is or how it is applied. Everybody knows that in the last resort every professor of democracy appeals to Mr. Jefferson, and labels as "Jeffersonian" any brand of heresy which he is desirous of palming off upon the plain people, North, South, East or West. The truth is that the influence of Jefferson in these later generations has been largely maintained and applied by the institution which he founded with the loyal assistance of Joseph Carrington Cabell under the shadow of his home at Monticello—the University of Virginia. That foundation, the first educational establishment on the continent the inspiration of which was not at all religious but purely civic—indeed, it remains in a certain very real sense the only educational institution in any English-speaking country which is of purely civic inspiration; which retains no taint of the original monastic ideal of the college—has been the interpreter to the whole country of the civic spirit of the Revolution, best embodied in Mr. Jefferson's person ever since it opened its doors in 1825. In a manner the whole South is alumnus of it—for it has been the meeting place of the selected youth of the ruling families of that section from the beginning, the point from which, after imbibing that civic spirit, they streamed out over the land.

The cumulative influence has been enormous—for if you are a Southern man, whether your point of origin is Maryland or Texas, whether your residence is Mobile or Bangor or San Francisco, either you are yourself an alumnus of the University, or your father was—or, at the remotest, your grandfather. Thus the University has become the nurse of a whole political school, an entire attitude toward law and authority, the formative power behind the party—by whatever name it has been called from time to time —which has insisted on the strict limitation of the centralizing tendency in our government, which has upheld the rights of the states as against the federal power, and been, by and large, the apostle of local self-government.

All this again is no more really "Jeffersonian" than the New England conscience is Puritan. It is the British instinct of local independence and personal privacy, and is stronger in the South to-day for exactly the same reason that the New England conscience is stronger there; because the original British stock is least dilute there and holds still to its instincts, though the manifestations are, as in the other case, widely determined by the local conditions. The influence, in question, concentrated in the South, and absolute master there, has permeated the West and served in the North to put a drag upon the drift, constantly increasing in that section, to wipe out local independence—a drift which is due to the same pervasive alien who has destroyed the New Englander's own New England conscience. How powerful the drag has been it would, of course, be rash to attempt to estimate, but it has at least served to keep the conservative minorities alive.

The model of statesmanship continued to be the

Southern planter-aristocrat type until the advent of Andrew Jackson, who represents the effect of a rude backwoods environment of more than one generation's duration upon material not very different from that which furnished Washington on the one hand and Adams on the other. He made possible the appearance in public life of what has since come to be considered the typical Yankee—by no means a New Englander, but a product of the ragged edges of British civilization. Such a product, also, was Abraham Lincoln, possessing no more of the theological taint, which is New England's hall mark, than Jackson himself; being, in fact, the direct descendant of the transplanted Englishman placed in circumstances where he had to civilize himself, without a model, with hardly any guide but the strong grain of the stock from which he sprang, however irregularly and uncanonically.

Lincoln furnished the next type, and it is a Southern, not a Northern type. The like might be found all along the edges of the Southern wave of population as it pushed westward into the wilderness. It could not be found along the edge of the wave which had its origin in New England, because, among other things, the creation of the type demands the skipping of at least one generation of literacy and thrift. The man must start from the very bottom.

The uncouth Westerner who gave the tone to American statesmanship and the cachet of Americanism abroad from Jackson's time, almost to our own, is thus an offspring of the South rather than the North, though the South is apt to disown him and the North to claim and glorify him. Actual geneological back-tracks in the case of any one of the notable examples of the type in our history, whether it be Lincoln or Jackson or Davy Crockett, or more florid specimens like Thomas H. Benton and Sam

Houston, usually lead to a Southern origin, and anybody who chooses to survey the field may easily convince himself from statistics that the Yankee grew up in the Southwest. He made Missouri and Texas, and Missouri and Texas made him. He did not make the Lake States nor was he made there. That region is of the foreigners' building.

Having begun thus iconoclastically and robbed New England of the fatherhood—nay, even the grand-fatherhood—of the American type which was sired along the Mississippi and came by descent of blood from all the states east of the Father of Waters, but more especially from those South of the Ohio, the contribution of the South to the national character and its influence upon the North is made moderately clear.

Influence of Environment.

We have said, however, that the characteristics of the American as he now is—not as he will become after he has assimilated the multitudinous Latin, Slav and Jew, are essentially British characteristics modified variously by various environments. We have indicated that the main differences between the type of American found in the South and the type of American found in the North are products pure and simple of such differences of environment. To clinch that proposition it may be well to take account of the population of that part of the original South which lies west of the Tide-water country in the foot hills and in the mountains.

The primary and original governing type in the South was evolved in the Tide-water belt. This was the type of Washington and the elder statesmen almost to a man. The population of the inland section was formed partly of those who had passed through the Tide-water and acquired the Tide-water characteristics, but it was made up largely of newcomers—many of whom were Scots and came down by way of Pennsylvania. This type, except that it did not tend to group itself into towns (because it was settled for the most part in a magnificent farming country with ideal conditions for stock-raising), became very much more closely assimilated to the New England type than did that of the Tide-water. The belt of this composite population extending South as far as northern Alabama and sending out colonies and individuals in every direction in every generation was always more or less closely affiliated with New England—the bonds being more especially those of religion and the result being the importation of a great number of teachers and preachers from that section. This tendency was increased by the fact that institutions of classical culture were few in the South (the scattered population conspiring to make them so), and by the further fact that the Southern young man classically educated preferred, if he were not a planter who had acquired his education for its own sake, to pursue the law or politics as a career rather than the Christian ministry or the art of the pedagogue.

The net result was an enormous number of New Englanders employed as teachers in the South, and the selection of many of them as presidents of colledges, like Hampden-Sidney in Virginia, which were under the Scottish-Presbyterian influence. Either, however, these good men soon returned to their own people or they were utterly absorbed into the Southern community which had employed them. Their descendants teem in the South now and are in no way differentiated from other Southerners—in fact, whatever peculiar coloring a stay of a couple of generations in New England had given their original English or Scots substance was in the very nature of things wiped out by a stay of a like extent in the new environment. The Piedmont type of Southerner was, in fact, entirely congenial to the New Englander, except in minor details—and in these minor details it was the newcomer who adapted himself.

The process has continued steadily, and is still going on with immigrants from the states north of the Potomac and Ohio. For, except in rare cases, these immigrants came, and still come, singly or in small groups, and the mass influence promptly reduces them to type. A Southern community has a very exceptionally powerful assimilating influence— a much greater one than a Northern urban community because of its homogeneity and solidarity— qualities due in their turn to the fact that these communities have developed as organic wholes through generations of the same families in the same relative positions and have not been required to absorb new people in bulk.

Southern Influence in the North Since the War.

Since the war the influence of the South on the Northern population has changed its working method. Before the war it was indirect; it worked by example in high places by reflex from the type developed, first on the Southern plantation, and second by Southern emigration to the West. Since the war it has been direct. The Southerner has come North to live. Wherever he has come he has brought with him, naturally, a certain number of characteristics acquired by his English stock during its generations of existence in the Southern states. These characteristics may be seen at work in the new environment producing results very different from those produced in the old, and strangely modified by their applications. A Southerner practices poli-

tics by instinct. He may be found in all the Northern
cities, therefore, holding office. In New York he
joins with those other instinctive politicians, the
Irish, and his inbred specialty being the handling
of men in masses, he is apter, even among the Irish,
to lead than to follow.

Further, the Southern white man is apt to grow
up in his native community unaware of the existence
of any social stratum above that in which he moves—
the sky is the limit that way. He forms the habit
of looking level at other men, or down, never up.
Consequently he comes into the more complex Northern urban community as free as is the Westerner of
any obsession of a barrier behind which fortune's
favorites move in their orbits. He walks with assured feet where the native (who is more often than
not of quite un-American parentage) would hesitate
to enter, and wins his way rapidly in liberal professions and in business by virtue, in part, of that assurance. The number of men of Southern birth and
breeding who are high up in their professions, as
doctors, lawyers, clergymen, teachers, in New York,
for instance, is quite out of proportion to the total
number of Southerners in the city. Only the West
has anything like a corresponding number, if we
exclude, as we must for the purpose of this article,
those furnished by the immense alien element in the
city, chiefly Jewish.

There is not a great newspaper in the city in the
year 1909, the editorial staff of which does not contain in responsible position several young men who
have come within a few years from small Southern
towns. There is hardly a publishing house or a
magazine where they are not to be found exercising
similar responsible functions. There is none of
these establishments in which the number of Southerners is not steadily increasing. One New York

newspaper, and that not the smallest, draws almost half its editorial staff from the South. On many of the others the number is almost as large, while the West, England and Canada furnish a great part of the remainder. In fact, nearly all the new blood is drawn from these three sources.

The distinguishing characteristic of the majority of these young men from the South is a certain cool alertness, an untiring energy—those very qualities which are popularly supposed to be Yankee specialties. They are workers. Their watchword is efficiency. They are utterly destroying the traditional Northern notion of the easy-going, impulsive Southern character. They are actually emphasizing and strengthening in the all-American urban character, those qualities of which the Northener has been apt to suppose he had a monopoly. Further, they are doing what the Northerner, who visits the South as a tourist merely, would never have done. They are, by transforming his preconceived erroneous idea about them, by showing him that an American in a New York environment will show pretty much the same whether he was born in South Carolina or Maine, doing more to promote the solidarity of the country than all the abolitionists and secessionists put together ever did to divide it. At the same time also, because they have smoother edges in certain ways, by reason of their inheritance of qualities acquired in a more generous climate, they are promoting a taste for similar smooth edges. For one thing, they have tended steadily to reduce the frigidity of social intercourse in the upper circles and to increase the amenities in circles less high. For all of these young men have had time in their youth to learn what the Southern darky calls "behavior."

The Southern woman has, of course, exercised the greatest influence in this particular direction, and it is an influence which was not interrupted even during the war. Long before that time Southern families had been continuously residing in New York, and the tone of its society had been strongly influenced by the women of these families. For women are great conservers, and those who have been brought up in a leisurely civilization and taught from the cradle to expect certain observances, having once grown to maturity in the midst of them, will insist ever after on the continuance of these same observances even though conditions have radically changed.

Since the war the Southern woman, thanks largely to Mr. Thomas Nelson Page, has been surrounded with a special atmosphere of what is known as Southern "chivalry" and crowned with a nimbus of romance. Aided by this nimbus, her influence personally exercised in the town—whether as wife and daughter of Southern colonists, the humble boarding housekeeper (she has been an institution for a long time in that capacity, a sort of social centre around which the errant bachelor population of the city has revolved), or lately as the student, school teacher, or social worker—has been continuous and powerful. Especially in the last three capacities in the last decade, and with the West as ally, she has affected profoundly the tone of middle-class life in New York, and in a lesser degree that of other great cities in the North. It is enough in all these cases to show the effect in New York, however, because New York is the clearing-house of the country—the place where all influences focus and work upon each other, and whence these same influences flow out in every direction so that each geographical extreme of the land feels, less or more, the effect of the life of the other extreme.

The process may be indicated as follows:

Immediately after the surrender at Appomattox there was a sudden exodus of Southerners—usually comparatively young men who had entered the Confederate army at the beginning of the struggle, remained in it throughout and returned to their homes to find there no means of making a living. These exiles flowed into all the larger cities of the North, but especially into New York. In each of these cities, and again especially in New York, they founded solid businesses, and were the nucleus of the Southern colony which up to a few years ago was a characteristic feature of all the larger Northern cities. This colony grew up socially as an *urbs in urbe,* sufficient to itself, but its influence permeated by degrees the whole life of even the greatest of these towns, working generally in the direction of probity in business and sanity and simplicity of life.

For the exiles were selected men, and had been tried in a furnace exceeding fiery. And besides, the Southerner is, necessarily, a conservative force wherever he settles in America. As a member of the original stock which established our institutions, social and political, he clings to these institutions though they be now shaken and submerged by the invasion of the continental European and his rapid increase.

A review of the list of merchants and bankers in New York city from 1870 to 1900 reveals a surprising number of Southerners among them doing a business, remarkable rather for solidity than expansiveness, yet rather large than small. A similar review of the list of merchants and bankers to-day reveals, though in lesser degree, since New York now draws its foremen from all the world and not from the country merely, a number still disproportionately large. All of which does not exclude the contributions from the South to the sphere of high finance proper as in the person, say, of Thomas F. Ryan. What we are getting at, however, are contributions to Northern character distinctly Southern. The high financier, it may be admitted, is an American type not indigenous to that section. Types which are indigenous and upon which the country at large, and the North in particular, has founded its ideal in each case, are the statesmen of the old school and of the middle century, the soldier, the pioneer and woman on her more gracious side. The newest type of statesman, the man of business, is the offspring of no section. He has his origin in the complex commercial organization of the country at large, and the raw material comes from wherever it may be most conveniently got at.

Special Contributions to Literature and Science.

Consider next the matter of culture, which, of course, is inextricably entangled with that other of character and many of the phases of which have already been presented incidentally. While the New Englander was writing sermons and histories and voting as one of many in his town meeting, the Southerner was ruling his plantation autocratically and administering his province as one of few. When the War of Independence was over, then, the one continued to write sermons or histories or what not, and the other wrote state papers, reports and orations. He wrote these with a practical purpose. Nevertheless, they were the expression of his culture, which was the culture not so much of books as of life. Thus he actually formed American oratory and American political style upon the most approved English models at the very time that New England was attempting to found American literature upon models good and bad borrowed from the same source.

No American literature was then founded or has yet been founded upon any models. American literature is still merely English literature, and the contributions to it which are significant come from all parts of the country about equally, and borrow from each part some particular flavor. Washington Irving wrote English literature with a New York flavor, meaning by that a hint of broad Dutch. Nathaniel Hawthorne wrote English literature with a New England flavor—the theological taint. Edgar Allan Poe wrote English literature with a flavor of his own, belonging not distinctly to any section—though the South has left its mark there—yet having a wider appeal than either. Joel Chandler Harris and George W. Cable, since the war, have written literature with the Southern flavor strong. Mark Twain has written it with the tang of the Southwest and Bret Harte with the salt sting of the Farther West which stretches over the Rockies to the Golden Gate. Finally, the man who calls himself O. Henry is writing English literature here and now with the bitter-sweet taste of the New York mixing machine of hetrogenious populations in the very ink of them. This is a hasty survey which, nevertheless, sweeps the whole field and catches all the most upstanding peaks of original achievement.

But to take the South's contribution chronologically, the influence of George Washington's writings—not his state papers only, but his painstaking reports and letters on a thousand homely subjects—of Jefferson's, of Madison's, of Marshall's and of the rest of the founders of the nation, have been acknowledged perfunctorily and then overlooked. It would be just as intelligent to overlook the influence upon American culture of the public press of to-day. Political writings were the chief reading in the post-Revolutionary period for the plain people as news-

papers are now. For one who read Cooper's novels
or Irving's *Sketch Book,* there were a thousand who
read the Farewell Address, a hundred who read
after Mr. Jefferson, fifty who perused the *Federalist.*
Witness the larger public taste of the country (including the North), only latterly conducted to romance and poetry and clinging even to this day to
the political page of the newspaper—lineal successor
of the *Federalist* and the admired orations of
Webster, Clay, Calhoun, Benton, John Randolph, of
Roanoke, Stephen A. Douglas and Abraham Lincoln.

It is customary to leave out of account what the
South did in pure letters before the war, and it is
fair enough to do so. It is customary, also, to write
expansively of what New England did for pure letters in the same time. As a matter of cold fact,
though the early flower of New England studiousness
and midnight lucubration bloomed luxuriantly in
print, the most of what was written was very distinctly second-hand and second-rate, and resulted in
the setting up of many false gods of culture. Much
that was second-rate was printed in the South also
—though not so much. In other words, the difference is that one section, having a population concentrated in narrow geographical limits, became a
reading circle sufficient to itself and developed a
school of minor poets and other minor writers which
this reading circle studied, adulated and celebrated;
the South could not develop such a circle—since its
population was scattered sparsely over a vast territory—it did not, therefore, develop a school of
writers. The writers were there, they wrote, and
their writings were printed, but they were scattered
like the population; they could not build a composite
reputation as bees build honeycomb in a hive, and as
New England built her literary reputation. In short,
New England's culture was concentrate and cumu-

lative, the South's was dissipated. Thus the second was spread, not by books but by individuals. The South talked. The North talked and took notes. We have the record of one; of the other we have no record. But all the while the South visited the North; the North has only lately got the habit of visiting the South.

We may set the work of Poe over against that of Hawthorne as choice literary flowers of the culture of the North and South, respectively—both, by the way, in a certain fashion noxious flowers, born of the taint rather than the wholesomeness of each section —and say that the influence of each on the section of the other is about equal. In both cases this influence is less than it should have been from a standpoint of pure literary merit. For the moral flaw on one side and theological flaw on the other held, and still hold, many aloof. Poe is not yet admitted to Chancellor MacCracken's Hall of Fame. To be sure there are those who would make the point that the flaw in one case was in Poe and in the other in the subject matter—but that does not change the fact that the flaws in each case narrow the audience.

However, culture is not all literature. It includes science as well—as a basis, as a stimulus. And the two most considerable scientists of the country, in the ante-bellum period, the only American contributors to the world's sum of knowledge, after Benjamin Franklin, were Maury and Audubon.

John James Audubon (born in 1780 at Mandeville, near New Orleans, La.), died in New York in 1851. His *Birds of North America* (1830-1839) called by Cuvier the "most magnificent monument which art has yet raised to ornithology," may be consid. ered, outside of any mere scientific value, to have furnished the impetus of a very favorite branch of culture in New England nowadays, a fad in the schools, and to be the *fons et origo* of the whole nature study business considered as a cult. New England has erected it into a cult with Thoreau for its prophet; New England makes cults of everything, and every cult must have a prophet. But Audubon was the real ornithologist. It was Matthew Fontaine Maury (born in 1806, near Fredricksburg, Va., officer in the United States and Confederate navies, died in 1873), who, after circumnavigating the globe in the *Vincennes* and getting a hurt which crippled him, mapped out the ocean currents and discovered the circulation of the sea—a piece of knowledge to which modern science and modern navigation owes an incalculable debt. Everybody who has enhanced his own personal store of culture by acquiring a smattering of physical geography owes something to Commodore Maury.

While we are upon this point we might mention the fact that the South has furnished also the greatest classicist of the country. Basil Lanneau Gildersleeve (born at Charleston, S. C., of Princeton, Berlin and Bonn, and of Göttingen, Ph.D., with degrees also from Harvard and Yale), long at the University of Virginia and now professor of Greek at Johns Hopkins in Baltimore, is that great classicist. He has written a Latin grammar which sparkles with wit between the paradigms and a work on Greek syntax which breathes life into the dryest part of what many persons choose to consider the dry bones of the language of Homer, Herodotus, Aristophanes and Plato. Most persons North and South with a modicum of classical education are in debt to Dr. Gildersleeve for glimpses of what culture really is.

Following after the first tide of Southerners who came to New York to seek their fortunes when the war had made that quest obligatory—the tide which took up business with a will—came another wave, made up, usually, this time of younger men who had managed, somehow, to go to college for a few years just after fighting was done and who, in the absence of paying occupations at home, had been forced upon literary ambitions. These came to New York as the market-place of letters. Wave after wave of like young men has flowed into the great city steadily since, pushed on by the poverty and lack of opportunity of the native environment, part of it from the beginning being diverted into those newspaper channels where literary ambitions are subtly transformed into something of which the city has greater need. Reënforcing these emigrants have come, one by one, attracted also toward the market-place, those Southerners who have done their earlier writing at home and won recognition at long range.

The result has been that the literary colony in New York, shading on one side into the cool and capable company of newspaper men and publishers already mentioned, and on the other into the main commercial stream, has lost every trace of a New England complexion and acquired one which takes its color largely from the South with a strong dash of the Pacific Coast, and, of course, not insignificant traces of other regions, as of Indiana. Some of its Southern-born members live in town, some appear periodically in the haunts which fringe Broadway, and their influence flows out steadily into the community and beyond into the nation both by what they write and by what they do. The roll of them is the roll of all the contemporary writers of Southern origin. You will find their names in the tables of contents of the magazines and in the publishers' lists. The catalogue is too long for inclusion here.

The direct influences of the South since the war proceed chiefly, however, in two streams. Samuel

Langhorne Clemens, called Mark Twain (born in 1835 at Florida, Mo., the son of John Marshall Clemens—sign of the Southern statesman's pervasive influence, already mentioned, in that name), printer-errant, Mississippi pilot, and in these times the acknowledged and acclaimed great American humorist, is the channel of one of them. Mark Twain stands in the whole world's eye as the embodiment of American—Yankee—humor. He stands for it in the North's eye. He is proof of what was said before that the Yankee is a product of the Southwest—not of New England. His influence upon both culture and character in the cities of the East has been too considerable to admit of estimate, and both the culture and the character are of the South, by origin and by quality.

The other stream comes from east of the Mississippi and is racy of that soil. Joel Chandler Harris (born in 1848 at Eatonton, Ga.), a member of the staff of the *Atlanta Constitution* for many years, in his "Uncle Remus" stories has taken a phase of life, a picture of a mental state, where the child's mind meets the negro's on a sort of level, a state through which every Southern-born white has passed, and fixed it as Mark Twain has fixed the mental state which was a phase and a product of the rapid growth of the West.

Harris has given to the Northern reader something which he takes in as naturally and absorbs as avidly as a fastidious scholar the uncouth verses of Walt Whitman—because the thing is fresh, strange, yet shot through with something which is felt by instinct to be real. The same sort of effect upon the Northern reader—an opening of the mind to a new actuality—has been produced by the Creole stories of George W. Cable, and the pictures of the starved life of the Tennessee mountaineers which have made the name of Charles Egbert Craddock (Mary Noailles Murfree, born in 1850 at Murfreesboro, Tenn.).

In all of these the element of unfamiliarity in the dialect has piqued curiosity and contrived a vogue (like that of broad Scots stories), which has carried the influence much farther into the Northern community than it would have gone had the authors used plain English.

The most influential of all the writers of the South east of the Mississippi, so far as the North at large is concerned, is, however, Thomas Nelson Page (born in 1853 at Oakland, Va.), at one time a lawyer in Richmond. His *Marse Chan,* published in a New York magazine in 1884, practically created for the generation in the North then growing up the three or four Southern types which, to their dying day, will represent to them what the South is. Mr. Page has enlarged on the same types since. He set a fashion which has been much followed by linking the Blue and Gray in *Meh Lady,* and he is responsible largely for the picture which appears before the Northern eye when the word South is mentioned.

It is a very charming picture, full of figures romantic, picturesque, pathetic, touched with a very lovely sentiment. It is even, to a Southerner who can make allowances for the indulgence of the loving hand that wrote, a very true picture, but as the average Northener takes it it is deplorably false and misleading in many particulars. The influence on Northern culture is not less on that account, and Mr. David Belasco and other wise managers of playhouses have recognized the hold the phantasy has taken upon the imagination of New York and made melodramas in which the romance and pathos is still more emphasized, the sentiment extra sugared. By which means the influence has grown—and grown awry. Also Mr. George Cary Eggleston has worked the same vein without Mr. Page's skill and feeling, and filled New England with notions of a romantic, chivalrous, flightly and somewhat childish-minded South, which does the hard-working common-sense population on the warmer side of the Potomac great injustice, although it has, no doubt, an excellent softening influence on the New England reader for whose delectation it is primarily composed.

Then there is Francis Hopkinson Smith (born in 1838 in Baltimore, Md.), lighthouse builder, constructor of the foundations for the Statue of Liberty in New York Harbor and of the seawall of Governor's Island, charming painter in water colors. He began by creating Colonel Carter of Cartersville, who stands in the Northern eye for the Southern gentleman as Page's women stand for the Southern gentlewoman. Colonel Carter has much to answer for—delightful as he is. But Mr. Smith has long lived in New York diffusing in his own person the real quality of the Southern gentleman, he has written books which breathed his genial spirit, almost one a year for many years. His influence among a smaller and selecter audience than Mr. Page's has done much to show the North what Southern culture is in fact. Mr. Smith's writings produce upon the reader much of the effect which might be gained by visiting (properly introduced) the best families of Baltimore, Richmond and Charleston.

The influence of Sidney Lanier (born in 1842 at Macon, Ga., died in 1881) has grown since his death, but is like Poe's influence; it does not focus upon the North. Amélie Rives, however (born in 1863 in Richmond, Va.), guilty very early in her life of shocking the country with her *The Quick or the Dead,* has been a forerunner of much. Whether it has been her example or whether she was merely a symptom of a movement, it is certain that the subjects she selected when she was a young authoress, and the side of those subjects which she elected to emphasize, are those upon which the authors of twenty years later in New England and New York are centering much attention. Miss Rives, now Princess Troubetzkoy, was the beginning of woman insurgent against the conception of herself (in literature at least) as the demure child of the proprieties.

Mrs. Burton Harrison (born in 1846 in Fairfax county, Va.), who, as Constance Cary, of a famous Virginia family and married to Jefferson Davis's private secretary, was a figure in her youth distinctly Southern, has in her later years grown up with New York, as it were, and written very modernly—quite putting out of countenance Mr. Page's lay figure of the Southern woman which refined melodrama has made its own.

A distinct influence in magazine literature may be traced to James Lane Allen (born in Kentucky in 1849). The sentimental mood which Mr. Allen cultivates is distinctly decadent, but it appealed, nevertheless, and *The Kentucky Cardinal* and *The Choir Invisible* have had many readers and many imitators. And one might go through the list of Southern contributors to current fiction and cite name after name —as Miss Mary Johnson, Miss Ellen Glasgow, Mr. James Branch Cabell, whose influence as a cumulative force is quite as considerable as that of any similar group of minor writers.

On the more serious side especial account must be taken of the work of men like Walter Hines Page (born at Cary, N. C., in 1855, and educated at Randolph Macon College in Virginia and Johns Hopkins in Maryland). Mr. Page, in a riper stage, is the very type of the cool, capable, tirelessly ener-getic Southerner already mentioned, as having such

a strong and direct influence on New York and the
country at large. The record of what he has accomplished from editing the *St. Louis Daily Gazette* and
the *Raleigh State Chronicle,* through his service on
the *Evening Post* of New York city, on the *Forum,*
as manager from 1887 to 1890, as editor from 1890
to 1895, on the *Atlantic Monthly* in Boston, again as
editor, up to the founding of the publishing house
of Doubleday, Page & Company well indicates
exactly the kind of work the Southerner is now doing in the North and the kind of influence he exercises. Something of the same sort of influence is
exercised by Adolph S. Ochs, chief owner and publisher of *The New York Times.* For though Mr.
Ochs is the son of Jewish parents of German nativity
and was born in Cincinnati, the influences which surrounded his upbringing were those of East Tennessee, and the tendency of his newspaper has been to
collect and focus upon the field in New York a large
number of Southern men whose influence is the more
effective because it is concentrated.

In lines academic and scholastic the South is
strongly represented in most of the larger institutions of the country outside of New England. It is
not hard to see that Woodrow Wilson, President of
Princeton (born in 1856 at Staunton, Va., educated
at Princeton and at the University of Virginia), is
in a position to make the influence of the South felt
upon a large number of sons of the North in a most
impressionable stage, both directly, as head of the
great university which has always been a sort of
link between North and South, and indirectly
through his voluminous historical writings.

At Columbia, as Professor of English, William
Peterfield Trent (born in 1862 at Richmond, Va.,
educated at the University of Virginia and at Johns
Hopkins, editor of the *Sewanee Review,* 1892-1900,

extensive writer on literary subjects and with the late Dr. John Bell Henneman, his successor as editor of the *Sewanee Review,* editor of Thackeray), exercises a similar moulding influence which, by the way, from the nature of the attendance at the New York institution, is spent largely upon the youth of what we have called the alien flood. It touches directly the sons of recent emigrants from the continent of Europe—chiefly Jews—who, in receiving our civil‑ ization, are subtly modifying it. The South, curiously, has shown itself better able to absorb these people than the North, and though the difference is largely due to the fact that the South has never been called upon to digest large masses of them at once, it is also true that the edges of contact are less sharp.

The peculiar culture of the South, then, the peculiar character of the South, is very busy in New York working on that composite city and assisting steadily and effectively in the creation of the composite American which it is the business of New York to evolve, perhaps. From New York a composite influence streams out, a composite upon which the South has put its mark indelibly. In other cities, not quite dissimilarly composite, the same influence works, in some more, in some less. The cumulative effect on the northern half of the country from Maine to Oregon is very great—is greater even than the effect of the northern half upon the southern. For the North has not yet been able to go to the South to live without utterly losing its identity, perhaps because it comes in such small numbers, perhaps because it is constitutionally less British in blood, less conservative, less clannish.

H. I. BROCK,
New York City.

CHAPTER XIV.

CONTRIBUTIONS OF NEW ENGLAND TO THE SOUTH'S CULTURE.

THEODORE ROOSEVELT, in his *Life of Thomas H. Benton,* speaking of the fact that Benton was prepared for the University of North Carolina by a New Englander of "good ability," says: "Indeed, school teachers and peddlers were, on the whole, the chief contributions made by the Northeast to the Southwest." This is the statement of a partial fact in a characteristic way. Mr. Roosevelt overlooks hundreds of men and women, in other fields, who, born in New England, gave honor and service to their adopted section, and imparted a reflected glory to that of their birth.

The statement of President Roosevelt gives a very inadequate idea of the work and influence of New Englanders in the South. The truth is, from the beginnings of the republic up to the time of Lincoln's election, when the South's voice was dominant in the councils of the nation, when its political principles and policies controlled largely the trend of public affairs, the permanent value of the New Englander's contributions to its development and welfare is almost altogether ignored in estimating the formative and guiding influences of this brilliant and thrilling period of national history. It is safe to say that in the forces that stood for moral culture, intellectual development, high civic ideals and political purity, no leaven worked in the mass of Southern life and thought with more potent and salutary effects.

Early Influences.

Before the cleavage between abolitionism and slavery became sharply defined, the Southern states presented an attractive field to New Englanders from every point of view. Not by the scores and hundreds they migrated thither, but by the thousands. There were few settlements attempted, composed exclusively of New Englanders. Two of these will illustrate their achievements. The colony of Dorchester, S. C., that in 1695 settled about twenty miles inland from Charleston, found itself much hampered after a fifty years' existence. Not to speak of an unfavorable location in the swamps, families had grown and intermarried until the lands became too narrow for further expansion.

Finding that they could not hold their young people and desiring to continue their compact existence, the Dorchester community determined to seek a habitation elsewhere. Between 1752 and 1754 the Dorchester of South Carolina became the Medway of Georgia. Between the Altamaha and Ogeechee rivers a grant of nearly 30,000 acres of land had been obtained, whereon settlement was made. In the Georgia abode the New Englanders prospered and exercised a large influence in colonial affairs. Religion flourished. Education was in the hands of skilful schoolmasters. Just and wise officials were selected. The part played by this settlement deserves to be emphasized. In Georgia it took the initiative in espousing the cause of independence.

The leader of the Revolutionary forces in Georgia was Dr. Lyman Hall, a native of Connecticut and a graduate of Yale College. He was one of the signers of the Declaration of Independence, was made governor of the state immediately after peace was declared, and a charter member of the board of trustees of the University of Georgia. Another New Englander of the Medway settlement, almost equally conspicuous in the public and educational life of the state, was Nathan Brownson, graduate of Yale, governor of the state and charter trustee of the university. An original member of the same board was Rev. Abiel Holmes, father of Oliver Wendell Holmes, who was pastor of the Medway congregation.

Another New England colony that entered significantly into the cultural life of the South was one that settled in Mason county, Ky. Just after the admission of the state many families from Connecticut settled therein. At once their influence in favor of good schools became pronounced. Mason long enjoyed the reputation of being the best-schooled county in Kentucky. From it went forth a noticeably large number of teachers, preachers and editors. Some of the families became distinguished, particularly the Johnstons and Wadsworths. Dr. John Johnston, who moved to the state from Salisbury, Conn., was a favorite physician, noted for scholarly tastes and activities. His eldest son, Josiah Stoddard, became a United States senator. Another son, Albert Sidney, became the eminent Confederate general.

However, it was not in settlements that the New Englander influenced most the higher life of the South. Either singly or in groups, as merchants, lawyers, doctors, ministers, educators, inventors, manufacturers and editors, they exerted a powerful influence in the moral and intellectual uplift of the section. Before the construction of railroads, the approach almost invariably followed three definite lines of travel. These were by way of the Atlantic Ocean and the Gulf of Mexico; or through the Middle states to some point on the Ohio River, thence down that stream and the Mississippi River; or by way of the Valley of Virginia. Following their movements, one will find them gathering in cities, counties or regions in little pockets, as it were. This was true, in a marked degree, of the graduates of New England colleges. In Charleston, S. C., could be found a cluster of Harvard men; in Savannah, Ga., of Brown men; in Mobile, Ala., of Yale men; in East and West Feliciana Parishes, La., of Wesleyan men; in Middle Georgia, of Middlebury men; in East Tennessee, of Amherst men, and in Natchez, Miss., of Bowdoin men.

Wherever the New Englander settled permanently, when neither teacher nor pastor, he became a factor in intellectual and social life. It was as trustee of schools, as the founder of public libraries and of historical societies, as the builder of churches and as the orator of public occasions. Their homes were centres of cultural influence. To illustrate, in Natchez, their mansions, libraries and works of art bespoke the best that was in American civilization. Winthrop Sargent, a Harvard alumnus, was the first governor of Mississippi territory. His home, "Gloucester," commemorating his birthplace in Massachusetts, was a refined abode. "Arlington" was the home of S. S. Boyd, a classmate of Seargent S. Prentiss at Bowdoin College and his fellow-citizen at Natchez. The private library at "Arlington" contained 8,000 volumes, while among the paintings that adorned its parlors were Raphael's "Galatea," a copy by Cecconari; Vernet's "A Marine Piece"; Schweinfurt's "Convoy of Prisoners"; Barrocio's "An Annunciation," and a "Magdalen" of Carlo Dolci.

In the Educational Field.

While in business and professional life the New Englander affected potently the life of the South from the cultural viewpoint, it was in the educational field that this influence was most evident. For purposes of demonstration, let it suffice to follow with some detail the work of the New England college president in the South.

Georgia was the leader in the introduction of the New England college president. Abram Baldwin may be justly designated the father of the University of Georgia. A native of Connecticut and graduate of Yale College, he was at one time a tutor in his *alma mater*. As soon as the Revolutionary War ended he went South and settled in Georgia. At once his talents were recognized. He was elected to the legislature, where he began to advocate the establishment of a state university. Securing the passage of an act for its charter, at the first meeting of the board of trustees, among whom sat five New Englanders, he was elected president, to serve until the institution should go into operation. In 1800 the trustees determined to elect a professor of mathematics. Next to an unavailable endowment, all that the university had was a name, without even a local habitation.

Baldwin had known in Yale Josiah Meigs as a graduate, tutor and scholar of approved standing, and recommended him for the position. The salary tendered was $1,500, with $400 additional for the expense of removal to Georgia. Upon his arrival Baldwin vacated the nominal presidency and Meigs was chosen his successor. He was instructed by the trustees to erect "one or more log buildings for the college," and was requested to teach all studies and classes until students enough to justify the employment of a tutor should be in attendance. Accordingly, in the woods of north central Georgia, he laid the modest foundations of the young institution, laid off a town, in prophecy called it Athens, and devoted himself resolutely to the tasks assigned. After two years of toil and hardship he congratulated the board of trustees upon an attendance of "between thirty and thirty-five students."

Differences with trustees in regard to the management of the lands belonging to the university brought about rupture. After a service of eight years he was removed from the presidency and made professor at a reduced salary. Because of criticisms upon the action of the trustees, he soon lost his professorship. He labored untiringly and unceasingly for the success of the infant institution. Established in a frontier state, far removed from the population most disposed to patronize a higher institution, with no buildings, no equipment and a faculty of one or two tutors, the university achieved a moderate success.

After trying several administrations, only one of which was successful, the trustees, again, in 1829, elected a New Englander, Alonzo Church. In the meantime the office had been offered to another New Englander, N. S. S. Beman, an alumnus of Middlebury College, who had enjoyed marvelous success as principal of Mount Zion Academy in middle Georgia. President Church was a native of Vermont and a graduate of Middlebury College. Soon after graduation he went South and taught in a Georgia academy at Eatonton. Ten years preceding his election he had been professor of mathematics in the university. His success as a professor and his zeal in all college affairs had commended him. The confidence was not misplaced, as thirty years of fruitful administration testified. During his entire administration he held the institution in a firm grasp. He was a man of fine address and cultured tastes, accurate in scholarship and eloquent in speech, just and rigid as a disciplinarian. After giving forty years to the institution, Dr. Church resigned and betook himself to the quietude of a farm near Athens, where he died in 1862.

In providing other Georgia colleges with presidents, New England was further called upon. The first president of Oglethorpe University, the Presbyterian college of the state, was Charles P. Beman; the second president of Mercer University, the Baptist institution of Georgia, was Otis Smith. Both of these men were Vermonters and graduates of Middlebury College.

In point of time, the College of South Carolina was the next institution which called a New Englander to start it upon a career of usefulness and prosperity. Determined by the representative character of its alumni and by the influence they exerted, South Carolina's college ranked as a leading institution of the South up to the War of Secession. It is certain that in molding and crystallizing the peculiar doctrines and distinctive policy of the South, it had more to do than any other institution of the section. The first president who shaped the policy of this hotbed of slavery protection and tariff opposition, and placed it at the outset upon high ground, was Jonathan Maxcy, a native of Massachusetts and graduate of Brown University. It is not asserted or implied that he had part in shaping or discussing the momentous issues which threatened the life of the republic, for he died in 1820, just as they appeared above the political horizon; but he had much to do with training some of the minds most prominently identified with their agitation.

Taking charge in 1804, Dr. Maxcy directed its affairs until his death. Within this period of sixteen years he made for himself a fame as deservedly imperishable as any in the list of early American college presidents. In a peculiar significance he suited the traditions and conditions of the people with whom his lot was cast. A trained logician and rhetorician, by his arguments and eloquence he captivated his

audiences.   It is little wonder that under him were
trained three men, William C. Preston, George
McDuffie and Hugh S. Legaré, who, living in the
same state and at the same time, yielded superiority
to no other three men of the same period in natural
endowments and oratorical power, or who stood
more distinctively representative of the culture and
sentiments of their section.   Add to this fact that
under his régime were educated eight governors of
Southern states, four lieutenant-governors of South
Carolina, eight United States senators, twenty-five
representatives in Congress, sixteen judges and
chancellors, seven college presidents, not to speak of
college professors, ministers, lawyers, members of
state and national governments, and journalists, and
one may judge somewhat of the fruitfulness of his
work and administration.   Wherever opportunities
offered he was in every part of the state making
public addresses, by his eloquence stirring up the
people to the importance of their institution and to
the need of higher education.

Another New Englander who wrought effectively
for college education in South Carolina was Rev.
Jasper Adams, born in Massachusetts and graduated
at Brown University.   He presided ten years over
the College of Charleston.   In 1824, attracted by a
salary of $2,500, he took charge.   For two years he
labored assiduously to elevate it from a grammar
school rank to the dignity of a college in fact as it
was in name.   The trustees gave feeble support to
his efforts, sympathizing more with the state institution, South Carolina College.   Despite the broadening of the work, increased attendance, the raising of
funds for new buildings and outfit, the trustees so
hampered his administration that, in disgust, he resigned, to accept the presidency of Hobart College
in New York state.   The trustees, after attempting

in vain to put their own ideas in force, recalled him and gave him unrestricted control. For eight years the growth and expansion of the college was unprecedented, and it registered the high-water mark in its history. With his acceptance of a professorship in West Point Military Academy, the institution declined in numbers and efficiency.

Other New Englanders who presided over South Carolina colleges were Rev. George Howe, born in Massachusetts and graduated at Middlebury, for fifty-two years a professor in Columbia Theological Seminary and at the time of his death president, and Abiel Bolles, from Connecticut and a Brown alumnus, who for a brief period was the head of the College of Charleston.

The first New Englander to become president of a Tennessee college was Rev. Charles Coffin, a Massachusetts man and Harvard graduate. In early manhood he went to East Tennessee to aid in the moral and intellectual elevation of the mountaineers. This was in 1800. For ten years he was professor in Greeneville College, of which he became president in 1810. He continued in this position until 1826, when he was called to the presidency of East Tennessee College at Knoxville. This position he vacated in 1832, and spent the remainder of his life in pastoral work and on his farm near Greeneville. He trained many men who became distinguished on the bench, in Congress and in journalism.

Dr. Coffin was followed into Tennessee by Rev. D. A. Sherman, from Yale and Connecticut, who from 1820 to 1825 was president of East Tennessee College. His work was not effective, and he went thence to Middle Tennessee where he was engaged twenty years longer in educational work. Joseph Estabrook, born in Massachusetts and graduated at Dartmouth, was the most noted New Englander in the college work of Tennessee. Through the Valley of Virginia he found his way into the state, and in 1828 became principal of Knoxville Female Academy. His success in this field was so great as to point to him as the man best fitted to restore the waning fortunes of East Tennessee College, in 1834, at the lowest ebb in its checkered career. Taking charge, the institution at once felt the quickening touch of his masterly hand and entered upon a course of unexampled prosperity. Making Amherst, in which he had formerly been professor, the model and bringing in the main his professors thence, he felicitated the state upon having a second Amherst within its bounds. Horace Maynard, a native of Massachusetts and a graduate of Amherst, who became congressman, minister to Turkey and post-master-general, was one of the young men persuaded to cast his fortunes with the college, thus becoming permanently a citizen of Tennessee. George Cooke was another New Englander and Dartmouth man who presided over East Tennessee University, as it came to be called by legislative enactment under Estabrook's administration.

Among other New Englanders who made enduring records in the Southwest was Rev. Franceway R. Cossitt, representing New Hampshire and Middlebury. Soon after graduation he migrated westward and became a Cumberland Presbyterian minister. The first college organized under the auspices of this offshoot from the Old School Presbyterian Church was at Princeton, Ky. Of this Dr. Cossitt became president at the outset of the enterprise, in 1826. When, in 1843, the institution was moved to Lebanon, Tenn., and became Cumberland University, he accompanied the college to its new home.

The most unique and remarkable career of any president of a Southern college was that of Rev.

Horace Holley, nine years president of Transylvania University in Kentucky. He was born in Connecticut and graduated at Yale. In 1817, while pastor of Hollis Street Unitarian Church in Cambridge, Mass., he received an urgent call to Transylvania at a salary of $2,250. For years the institution had been the battleground of sectarians and politicians, who well-nigh wrecked its fortunes. Dr. Holley, after visiting the university and weighing long and carefully the field and its possibilities, determined to throw himself unreservedly into the work, hoping to rival the foremost Eastern colleges. His energy, enthusiasm and magnetism excited unbounded confidence and elicited active support from all quarters. Henry Clay was added to the board of trustees and gave cordial coöperation. The legislature was induced to make liberal appropriations. Students came in annually increasing numbers from the South and Southwest, the attendance mounting from about 100 to over 400. Distinguished travelers, if Transylvania was not in the immediate line of their travels, went out of their way to visit it and were entertained by the honored, brilliant president. Lexington became best known as the seat of Transylvania University, and was called the "Athens of the South."

Despite the success, there were disintegrating influences at work from the outset of Dr. Holley's administration. His religious views and affiliations were distasteful, especially to the Presbyterian Church which had hitherto controlled the institution. Other denominations were gradually alienated, and established rival colleges. Dr. Holley finally succumbed to the storms of opposition that he had aroused by his liberal theological views and free speech. Attendance upon theatres, horse races and other places of popular amusement was another occasion for condemning his conduct, impugning his motives and reflecting upon his private life and character. On the eve of engaging in educational work in Louisiana, while on a sea-voyage from New Orleans to the North, he was attacked by a more deadly enemy than hostile theologians, and died at sea from yellow fever.

Northern scholars of reputation and experience were induced by liberal salaries to undertake the revival of interest in Transylvania, but after a few years gave up the task as hopeless. Rev. Alva Woods, a native of Massachusetts and graduate of Harvard, was Dr. Holley's successor. While professor in Columbian University at Washington, Henry Clay had learned his worth, and influenced him to leave the professorship of mathematics and natural philosophy at Brown University and to accept the Transylvania presidency. For three years he vainly endeavored to revive interest. After an interval Rev. T. W. Hoit, from Connecticut and Yale, was inducted into the presidency. Two years sufficed to show that he could make no headway in buffeting the counter-currents that had set in during the Holley administration. When the various denominations in Kentucky began their college enterprises, they invited New Englanders to organize them. In 1827 Dr. Martin Ruter, Massachusetts-born but a non-college man, was made president of the Methodist College, Augusta, retaining the position five years. In 1826, as mentioned, the Cumberland Presbyterians opened their new college under Dr. Cossitt. In 1830, after two unsuccessful attempts to induce New Englanders to accept the presidency of their new college at Georgetown, the Baptists succeeded in getting from Newton Theological Seminary Rev. Joel S. Bacon, a native New Yorker. His term of office was brief, when Rev. B. F. Farnsworth, from Maine and Dartmouth, was chosen president and held the position only a few months. Not dismayed by frequent changes, the Baptists secured Rev. Rockwood Giddings, a native of New Hampshire and graduate of Colby University, as president. He died during his first year in office, but had filled the position long enough to have it said that his administration was most successful. He put the college upon a sound basis and, for the times, secured a good endowment fund. As the result of his unceasing labors and ardent enthusiasm he fell the victim of overtaxed energy and consecrated zeal.

The forces controlling the higher education in North Carolina were almost wholly from Princeton, in New Jersey. In the second decade of the Nineteenth century Yale furnished to the University of North Carolina a distinguished trio of professors in Denison Olmsted, Ethan A. Andrews and Elisha Mitchell. The University never had a New Englander as its president. It barely escaped, inasmuch as its most distinguished and efficient president was Gov. David L. Swain, the son of a New Englander. The founder and first president of Wake Forest College, the leading Baptist institution of the state, was Samuel Wait, a New Yorker and the first honorary alumnus of Colby University in Maine. Rev. J. B. White, born in New Hampshire and graduated at Brown, was connected sixteen years with Wake Forest, and was its president four years.

In Virginia the presence and influence of New England in college administration was marked. There were four men who left their impress upon Virginia colleges. These were Jonathan P. Cushing, Stephen Olin, Charles Collins and Ephraim E. Wiley. Cushing, born in New Hampshire and graduated at Dartmouth, was called, immediately upon graduation, to Hampden Sidney College, serving as tutor and professor. In 1821 he became its president, a

position he filled and adorned to the time of his
death in 1835. Previous to his administration the
affairs of the college had been in a disordered state.
Financial troubles had hampered its usefulness and
threatened its suspension. Out of its difficulties he
brought it triumphantly.

Dr. Olin was a native of Vermont and a graduate
of Middlebury. After graduation he went South and
taught in South Carolina. Then he was chosen professor in the University of Georgia. From this position, in 1833, he was called to the presidency of Randolph Macon College, the leading Methodist college
of Virginia. For five years he filled the office with
great acceptability, when he resigned to take the
presidency of Wesleyan University in Connecticut.

When the Methodist Church in Southwest Virginia
determined to establish Emory and Henry college,
they applied to Wilbur Fisk, president of Wesleyan
University, for a president. Fisk wrote frankly that
Southern colleges had suffered most from the offi-
cious interference of trustees, but he thought an entirely satisfactory man could be had, provided he
had a controlling voice in administration. The con-
cessions were readily made. Dr. Fisk recommended
Rev. Charles Collins, born in Maine and a Wesleyan
graduate. Dr. Collins brought with him his faculty
of New England men. For fourteen years he directed the affairs with conspicuous fidelity and eminent success. Resigning, he was succeeded by Dr.
E. E. Wiley, a native of Massachusetts and an alumnus of Wesleyan, who belonged to his predecessor's
first faculty. How successful his administration was
may be judged by the fact that he presided over the
institution twenty-nine years and educated some of
the most prominent Southern men in church and
state.

When the University of Alabama was established,

Alva Woods, already mentioned in connection with Transylvania University, became its first president. His success as an administrative officer and as a disciplinarian was not altogether satisfactory. He was not suited to a pioneer condition of society. After six years of unremitting toil, not without some fruitful results, he resigned and returned to Rhode Island. When the Baptists of Alabama founded their leading institution, Howard College, S. S. Sherman, a New Englander and graduate of Middlebury, was called to its head. He had been tutor in the University of Alabama. He taught some years in the state, and at one time was president of Judson Institute, the Baptist school of Alabama for young women.

The most distinguished president in the college annals of Mississippi was F. A. P. Barnard, whose fame was increased by his twenty years' presidency of Columbia College in New York. A native of Massachusetts and a graduate of Yale, after varied experiences as teacher and editor in the North, he was called, in 1837, to a chair in the University of Alabama. His seventeen years as professor in this institution contributed greatly to the intellectual development of the institution and the state. In 1854 he was elected professor of mathematics and astronomy in the University of Mississippi, then in the sixth year of its existence. Two years afterwards the presidency became vacant. It was a time of growing political excitement, and of strong opposition to Northern men who were not pronouncedly in sympathy with the South upon the slavery issue.

However, considering Dr. Barnard's wide knowledge of educational systems and his successful experience, the judgment of the trustees commended him as eminently qualified for the presidency, and the office was entrusted to him. With energy and prudence the task was undertaken. Despite the cavillings of envy and the prophecies of failure, under him the university moved forward, increasing in attendance and public confidence until the outbreak of the war. During the five years of his incumbency vital reforms were instituted, the standard of scholarship was elevated, patronage from surrounding states was attracted, progressive methods prevailed and the university was lifted to a dignified rank among similar institutions. When the students withdrew almost in a body to become enrolled in the Confederate army, he resigned the office and went North to his own people.

There were other New Englanders who presided over a Mississippi College. Consider Parish, a graduate of Williams, and Walter Hillman, Massachusetts-born and a Brown alumnus, were presidents of the Baptist college of the state, Mississippi College. They were widely useful and representative men.

In Louisiana colleges were started on an elaborate foundation, only to succumb to adverse fortunes after a skyrocket experience and a spasmodic existence. A few New Englanders were engaged to preside over these, but their administrations were short, uneventful and unproductive. Alexander H. Everett, from Massachusetts and Harvard, after some experience as diplomatist and writer, was president of Jefferson College, but after one year returned to the North. D. O. Shattuck, born in Connecticut and honorary alumnus of Wesleyan University, presided over Centenary College, the Methodist college of Louisiana, but abandoned it after four years. Beginning as a peddler he attained to a position of eminence at the bar and in politics. In 1853 the Baptists of Louisiana organized a higher institution of learning, whose first president was Rev. Jesse Hartwell, a native of Massachusetts and graduate of Brown. The institution, with the high-sounding title, Mount Lebanon University, he conducted with wisdom until death cut short his administration in 1857.

In Texas, in 1837, not so long after a fellow New Englander, Moses Austin, had received from Mexico a large grant of land for colonization purposes, Martin Ruter, who appeared in Kentucky's educational life, was appointed by the authorities of the Methodist church to superintend the establishment of colleges. After beginning the work, overcome by fatigue and exposures, health soon gave way and death ensued. His work was undertaken, in large measure, by Chauncy Richardson and William Halsey, graduates of Wesleyan University in Connecticut. In a desultory field and under primitive conditions these men worked faithfully and planted ideals that have borne some good fruit. Named for the son of Moses Austin was Austin College, the Presbyterian college of Texas. One of its first presidents was Rev. R. W. Bailey, a native of Maine and graduate of Dartmouth, who, in 1863, died in office.

For the most part, efforts in behalf of the higher education in Arkansas and Florida belong to the post-bellum era. Under the reconstruction régime, in some states college presidents from New England were sought. Among those elected who declined was Cyrus Northup, now the president of the University of Minnesota, who was invited to the presidency of the University of Alabama. Instead of arousing any enthusiasm, such executives, as a rule, were classed among carpet-baggers and were, therefore, odious to the intelligent population of the section.

Having followed the New England college president into the states where his ability was recognized and where his services were utilized, it is seen that he was a most efficient cultural force. In a new environment and under new conditions, with little to encourage and much to dishearten, with few precedents to guide and with pathways to cut, he seized the reins with masterly hand, pushed on with unfailing courage, and reached a lofty eminence whence he could look back over the devious ways passed and the divers difficulties overcome. Such was the representative type of the presidents coming from New England who administered the affairs of the colleges of the Old South. They are seen to have organized the leading colleges of church and state; to have infused new life into institutions threatened with extinction; to have appealed successfully to legislative bodies and church assemblies for larger endowments and better equipments; to have been great factors individually in popularizing education and broad culture, and to have given themselves unwaveringly and unceasingly to the cause advocated and to the duties imposed. Some failures are attributed to them, but the largeness of their achievement in the aggregate, the honesty of their efforts and the value of their labors far overbalance the account on the debit side of these devoted servants of state and church. In practical sagacity and conservative management, one will find with difficulty their wisdom excelled; for fruitful results in behalf of intellectual awakening and spiritual uplift, one will have to go far to find their labors surpassed.

For every New England college president who labored in the South, there were at least five college professors and a hundred schoolmasters who exemplified New England culture and set up New England school methods in the Southern states. It may be safely maintained that among the wholesome currents of influence that permeated the ante-bellum South and gave an uplift to its civilization, that emanating from the New England educator was the most effective and lasting. Scant memorials, otherwise than in the lives of those taught, exist of many of these men of cultured brain and heart. They poured forth from Harvard, Yale, Dartmouth, Amherst, Williams, Brown, Bowdoin and other colleges of the East, and from almost every New England community not like the stream irrigating the parched desert, but adding its beneficent waters to the forces that sweetened and enriched the life of the Old South. Many like Horace Maynard in Tennessee, Sergeant S. Prentiss in Mississippi, Hiram Warner in Georgia, Amos Kendall in Kentucky, Albert Pike in Arkansas, rose to distinction in political life; but the great majority, with the passing away of those who were under their tuition, passed into oblivion, leaving no inheritance where they labored save the impulses to the higher intellectual and spiritual life they sought unceasingly to cultivate and to perpetuate.

BIBLIOGRAPHY.—Adams, Herbert B.: *Thomas Jefferson and the University of Virginia;* Clarke, Alvin LaFayette: *History of Higher Education in Kentucky;* Clarke, Willis G.: *History of Higher Education in Alabama;* Collins, Richard H.: *History of Kentucky;* Elton, Romeo: *President Jonathan Maxcy's Remains;* Jones, Charles Edgworth: *History of Higher Education in Georgia;* Meriwether, Colyer: *History of Higher Education in South Carolina;* Merriam, Lucius S.: *History of Higher Education in Tennessee;* McDonnold, B. W.: *History of the Cumberland Presbyterian Church;* Mayes, Edward: *History of Higher Education in Mississippi;* Peter, Robert: *History of Transylvania University;* Smith, William R.: *Reminiscences of a Long Life;* Stevens, William Bacon: *History of Georgia* (2 vols.); Tyler, William S.: *History of Amherst College;* White, George: *Historical Collections of Georgia;* White, Moses: *Early History of the University of Tennessee;* General Catalogues and Necrologies of Harvard, Yale, Dartmouth, Middlebury, Brown, Amherst, Williams, Vermont and Wesleyan.

GEORGE FREDERICK MELLEN,

Formerly Professor of Greek and History, University of Tennessee.

CHAPTER XV.

LOUISIANA'S CONTRIBUTION TO THE LITERATURE OF THE UNITED STATES.

LOUISIANA occupies a unique position in the literary history of the United States, inasmuch as it possesses a literature written in two languages, in French and in English. The establishment in New Orleans by the Ursuline nuns, as early as 1727, of a school for girls gave to the women of Louisiana a culture which produced a refined and polite society in colonial times. Many boys belonging to wealthy families were sent to France to be educated, and brought back to New Orleans a French culture, which, added to that acquired by the girls at the convent of the Ursulines, maintained in Louisiana a French atmosphere, even during the Spanish Domination.

Indeed, while Louisiana formed part of the colonial empire of Charles III. and of Charles IV. of Spain, the French language was as much the mother tongue of the Louisianians as when the colony was under the rule of Louis XIV. and of Louis XV., of France. Most of the Spanish officials married wives of French origin, and the language of the mother became that of the family. The best proof that French was the language generally used in Louisiana during the Spanish Domination is the fact that the first work in the literature of Louisiana was written in French in 1779, seventeen years after the colony had been ceded to Charles III. by Louis XV.

Having become Spaniards, in spite of their love for France, the Louisianians had endeavored, in 1768, to throw off the Spanish yoke and to establish an independent government. They had failed in their heroic efforts, and the chiefs of the Revolution against Spain had been ruthlessly put to death by General O'Reilly. Governor Unzaga had ruled mildly and wisely, and the colonists had become somewhat reconciled to the rule of Spain in 1779. In that year Bernardo de Galvez was Governor of Louisiana. He was young and wished to acquire military glory, and this opportunity was given him when Spain joined France in her alliance with the United States and declared war against Great Britain. The latter power had obtained Mobile, Baton Rouge and Pensacola by the Treaty of Paris of 1763. Galvez resolved to expel the British from their possessions adjoining New Orleans, and succeeded in doing so in campaigns which took place from 1779 to 1781.

Baton Rouge was captured by Galvez, in 1779, with an army composed almost entirely of Louisianians of French origin. This exploit was related in an epic poem published in New Orleans in 1779, *La Prise du Morne du Bâton Rouge par Monseigneur de Galvez*. The author of this work was Julien Poydras, a native of Brittany in France, who had arrived in Louisiana in the beginning of the Spanish Domination and had succeeded in amassing a fortune by his intelligence, his energy and his perseverance. He had begun his life in the colony as a peddler, going with his bundle on his back from house to house along the coast of the Missisipppi River, received with boundless hospitality and selling all his wares. When Louisiana became American, Julien Poydras occupied important political positions in the territory of Orleans and in the state of Louisiana, and, at his death in 1824, he left large sums of money for charitable purposes. Among his bequests we may mention $30,000 to the parish of Pointe Coupée, and

the same amount to the parish of West Baton Rouge.
Each year the interest of the money bequeathed was
to be given to the young girls without fortune who
had married during the year.

Poydras's poem is not a work of great literary
merit, but it is interesting as being the first product
of the literature of Louisiana. It was evidently inspired by Boileau's epistle on the crossing of the
Rhine by the cavalry of Louis XIV. Like the Rhine,
the Mississippi was sleeping when he was awakened
by a noise like thunder. He sends Scæsaris, one of
his nymphs, to find out what is happening, and on her
return she relates the exploits of Galvez and his
army. The Spanish governor is described by Poydras with as much splendor as Louis XIV., by Boileau, and the Mississippi is delighted with the prow-
ess of Galvez. The epic poem is followed by a short
song which ends as follows:

"He is a magnanimous hero,
Let us vie with one another in singing,
And with a unanimous voice,
Let us raise him to the skies.
In the beautiful temple of memory
Let us erect altars to him.
Galvez merits the glory
Of becoming immortal."

The second work of the literature of Louisiana is a
tragedy, *Poucha Houmma,* by Le Blanc de Ville-
neufve. It is a drama of the classic school and was
published in 1814. The subject is the sacrifice of an
Indian who gives up his life to save that of his son.
The tragedy begins with a dream, as in Racine's
Athalie, but seems to imitate Corneille more than
Racine, inasmuch as there is in the whole play the aspiration towards the sublime and the superhuman to
be found so often in Corneille's great works.

Of the romantic school is A. Lussan's *Martyrs de
la Louisiane* (1839), and L. Placide Canonge's
France et Espagne and *Qui Perd Gagne.* The latter

is a witty comedy, dedicated to Alfred de Musset and deserves to be compared with some of Musset's best proverbs. The other two works are of the *genre* of *Hernani* and *Ruy Blas*. Among our dramatists may be mentioned Oscar Dugué, Dr. Charles Deléry, and Dr. Alfred Mercier who published in 1888, *Fortunia*, an interesting drama in five acts.

As it is not our purpose to give a complete history of the French literature of Louisiana we shall name, in regard to history, only Charles Gayarré, whose *Essai Historique sur la Louisiane* (1830), and his *Histoire de la Louisiane* (two volumes, 1846 and 1847) preceded the author's excellent work published in English in four volumes.

French Poetry in Louisiana.

It is in poetry that the French literature of Louisiana is the richest. Indeed, many poems of great merit have been published in New Orleans, and the works of our authors deserve to be better known. Adrien and Dominique Rouquette, Alexandre Latil, Dr. Charles Testut, Mrs. Emilie Evershed, and Dr. Alfred Mercier were our best poets. The following translation from *Les Soleils* ("The Suns"), by Dr. Mercier, is given as an example of sublime thought and beautiful language:

THE SUNS.

"We are the suns, the victors of Night,
Before us she flees and dies. To us space!
To us eternity, to us whose flame encircles
The profound immensity and shines everywhere.

Glory to us, powerful Kings, whose look gives birth
To the spheres describing the orbit around us!
Our warm light rejoices each world;
Life is a benefaction of our pure and sweet fires.

To us alone belongs the infinite space;
Immortal, we float and always advance.
Born of our movements, rivers of harmony
Circulate in the ether everywhere we pass.

NIGHT.

You lie, O Suns, to me alone belong
Space without limits and immortality.
Beyond the distances which your beams reach,
My dark abyss extends its gloomy immensity.

Scattered here and there on my cloak of ebony,
You adorn for a time my severe beauty;
It is allowed only to me, me your sovereign,
To say aloud:—I have always existed.

Numberless suns before your birth,
Were sparkling already on the bottomless abyss;
Where are they to-day? Who bemoans their absence?
Who looks for their splendor which disappeared from my forehead?

Cease, then, conceited ones, to sing your praises!
Give light, give warmth to the inhabited worlds.
I shall absorb you, fleeting phalanxes,
When by time which flies your days will be counted."

Dr. Alfred Mercier was also the author of the novel *l'Habitation St. Ybars* (1881), which gives the best idea of life on a large sugar plantation in Louisiana before the great war between the states. We may not agree with the ideas of Dr. Mercier on social questions, but we admire the accuracy with which he has described customs of by-gone days. He gives local color to his book by an occasional use of the Creole patois, which is very pleasing. The following page is really charming:

"Démon, the little son of the planter, has caught two birds and has put them in a cage. He goes to the kitchen to show them to his nurse, Mamrie, who says:

"'Sit here and tell me how you caught those bullfinches.'

"Démon did not need to be urged; he related his expedition in all its details. He expressed himself with an animation which delighted Mamrie. Seated on the floor in front of him, with a smile on her lips, she followed with increasing admiration, all the phases of his story. Her face, mobile and expressive, reflected everything that passed on that of the little boy, as if he had spoken before a mirror.

"Démon ended his epic, accompanying his words with great gestures which frightened the birds; the male renewed his efforts to pass through the bars of the prison; his head was covered with blood. Démon pushed him back, saying with impatience:

"'Stay quiet, fool!'

"'You take it easy,' said Mamrie to him, 'You took away his freedom and you want him to be pleased. I should like to hear what you would say, if you were put into a cage like this.'

"'Put me into a cage,' exclaimed Démon with a tone of wounded pride. 'I should break everything. I would get out and take vengeance on the persons who had imprisoned me.'

"'Bah! That is only idle talk,' replied Mamrie: 'If you were put into a good cage with good iron bars you would not break anything; you would cover yourself with blood, and as you would see your efforts amounted to nothing, you would bend your head and stay quiet as the bullfinch will do in a day or two.'

"'No!' answered Démon, 'I would not eat anything and I would die.'

"'That is a fine reply,' said Mamrie: 'You are very proud, you are indeed a St. Ybars."

"The unfortunate bullfinch, exhausted, was lying down; his breast swelled painfully; his black eyes sparkled with anger. The female, which had taken refuge in a corner, uttered low plaintive cries. After a moment of silence Démon said,   .

"'Mamrie, see how the female is sad.'

"'It is not astonishing,' answered the good negress, 'She is thinking of her little ones! They are hungry, they are calling their mother; but the mother will never come again; it is a screech owl or a snake that will come to eat them.'

"Démon was pensive. While his nurse attended to one thing and to another, he was looking at his prisoners. He got up and went out without saying anything. After a few minutes Mamrie saw him reenter; his bird trap was empty.

"'Well,' said she, astonished, 'Where are your birds?' False pride prevented Démon from saying what he had done; he answered with embarrassment:

"'They escaped.'

"'They escaped,' said Mamrie, shaking her head, 'You are lying. I am sure that you freed them.'

"'Well! It is true,' acknowledged Démon, 'It is your fault; what you told me about the female and her little ones pained me.'

"The eyes of Mamrie filled with tears; she stretched her arms towards Démon, showing him all her teeth and saying:

"'Come here, rascal, let me eat you alive.'"

French Literary Societies.

Dr. Alfred Mercier rendered a great service to the French literature of Louisiana, not only by his writings, but principally by founding, in January, 1876, the Athénée Louisianais, a literary society which has greatly contributed to the preservation of the French language in Louisiana. The Athénée is affiliated with the Federation of l'Alliance Française in the United States and Canada. It publishes a quarterly magazine which contains interesting articles and poems in French, and which is the oldest of its kind in the United States. The presidents of the Athénée since 1876, have been Dr. Armand Mercier, Gen. G. T. Beauregard, and Professor Alcée Fortier, and the perpetual secretaries have been Dr. Alfred Mercier and Mr. Bussière Rouen.

A great many people speak French in New Orleans as a mother tongue, and a visit to the old French quarter of the city is very interesting. In the "Vieux Carré" one sees a curious mixture of the architecture of France and of Spain, and one enjoys the charm of what is left in Rue de Chartres and Rue Royale of the Latin civilization, of which the influence is felt to a lesser degree, in every part of the Crescent City. To that civilization is due, to a great extent, the artistic taste of the people in New Orleans, their talent for music and the beautiful pageants during carnival time, which come to a climax at Mardi Gras.

Besides the Athénée Louisianais, a society has lately been organized in New Orleans to introduce again the study of French into the primary and grammar grades of the public schools. The knowledge of French in Louisiana not only gives culture, but is of great practical use. In southwestern Louisiana there are still many persons who speak but little English, and merchants, lawyers and physicians who deal with them must know French; and no one can be very successful in the legal profession in Louisiana if he does not at least read French well. Our civil code is based principally on the Code Napoleon, and decisions of the *Cour de Cassation* of France are often accepted as authoritative by the Supreme Court of Louisiana, for our law, like that of France, is derived, to a great extent from the *Corpus Juris Civilis* of Justinian.

The importance of French in Louisiana is considered so great by the lawmakers of the state, that the laws enacted by the legislative assembly must be promulgated in French as well as in English, and in some parts of Louisiana, in New Orleans, for instance, judicial advertisements must be published in French and in English.

English Literature in Louisiana.

The French literature of Louisiana is interesting and characteristic, but there is also in the state an important English literature which has felt somewhat the influence of the French literature and of Latin civilization. We shall give a brief account of it and shall quote as an introduction to the subject the following lines from our *Louisiana Studies:*

"For several years after the cession to the United States the conditions were not favorable to English literature. The settlers from other states were not very numerous, and they were too much absorbed by their material interests to attend to literary pursuits. As the prosperity of the state increased, more attention was paid to education, but the culture of the people, as in other Southern states, was directed principally to statesmanship, and we had great orators, distinguished journalists, but comparatively few authors of note. It is proper to state, however, that the celebrated *DeBow's Review* exerted a great influence upon literature for many years. Its pages contain papers of value on all kinds of subjects, and it is a complete encyclopedia of the Old South.

"The institution of slavery is said by many to have been detrimental to literary activity. It was not, perhaps, so much slavery itself as the material prosperity accompanying it which was a drawback to literature. The Southern people were content with attending to their mercantile and agricultural interests and with governing the nation, to a great extent, and although many were highly educated, few wrote works generally included in the term 'literature.' Too many, however, spent their energy and their talents in defending, with their pens, the cause of slavery, a cause which was naturally considered by them legal and just. Slavery, in that way, injured literature."

The learned jurist François Xavier Martin, was our earliest historian. His *History of Louisiana,* published in 1827, is written with French clearness and conciseness. The battle of New Orleans, Jan. 8, 1815, is related in detail, as well as the events leading to the imposition of the fine upon General Jackson. Judge Martin justifies the action of Judge Hall, and the opinion of this great jurist is very valuable.

Charles Gayarré's *History of Louisiana* and his *History of Philip II.*, are important works. The author, born in 1805, died in 1895, and was the best known literary man in the state. He was an admirable example of the highest culture brought about by the French and Spanish Dominations in Louisiana. Besides his histories he published two historical novels, *Fernando de Lemos* and *Aubert-Dubayet,* and many magazine articles dealing with life in Louisiana.

Miss Grace King's *New Orleans, the Place and the People,* is an interesting work, and her *Balcony Stories* are charming. Miss King gives a far better idea of the customs of the people of New Orleans than Mr. George W. Cable. His *Old Creole Days* have some artistic merit, but in most of his work he gives a totally false picture of the Creoles of Louisiana.

Two books dealing with the War of Secession are of great value, Col. William Preston Johnston's Life *of Albert Sidney Johnston,* and Col. Alfred Roman's *Military Operations of General Beauregard.* Colonel Johnston was president of the Tulane University from 1884 to 1899, and was a master of English prose. He wrote also excellent poetry and was an accurate student of Shakespeare. Col. Alfred Roman gives a correct history of the Confederate general who fought so well at Manassas, at Shiloh, at Petersburgh, at Drury's Bluff, and whose defense of Charleston was a marvel of the art of the military engineer. Another important work relating to the war is Gen. Richard Taylor's *Destruction and Reconstruction*. The son of Zachary Taylor played an enviable part in the war, and has related his campaigns in an interesting manner.

One of the best biographies published in this country is Professor Pierce Butler's *Life of Judah P. Benjamin*. The author has succeeded admirably in his picture of ante-bellum days, as well as of the terrible war times. The *Life of Bienville*, by Miss Grace King, is a scholarly history of the colonization of Louisiana.

Our dramatists are Judge T. Wharton Collens, whose *Martyr Patriots* represent on the stage the tragic story of the Revolution of 1768 against Spain; Charles Gayarré, whose *School for Politics* is a sharp and amusing criticism of American politicians; Espy Williams and E. C. Wharton.

We have already mentioned as novelists Charles Gayarré, George W. Cable and Miss Grace King. Other writers of fiction have distinguished themselves in Louisiana. Charles Dimitry wrote *The House on Balfour Street*, which has been compared with *Dombey and Son* and with *Vanity Fair*. Dr. W. H. Holcombe wrote *A Mystery of New Orleans*, in which he makes a curious use of hypnotic influence; Lafcadio Hearn produced in New Orleans his remarkable *Chita*, which is as poetic in its descriptions as Pierre Loti's *Pêcheurs d'Islande;* Mrs. Ruth McEnery Stuart began her literary career while living in Louisiana, of which she is a native, and wrote her initimable stories of negro life; Mrs. C. V. Jamison published in 1891 her delightful *Lady Jane,* and Mrs. Mary Evelyn Moore Davis contributed to the English literature of Louisiana many interesting novels and stories, among which are, *At War Times at La Rose Blanche, Under the Man-Fig, An Elephant's Track,* and *The Wire Cutters.*

Mrs. Davis was a distinguished poet as well as a novelist. Her *Père Dagobert,* and *Throwing the Wanga* have been greatly admired and *My Love Went Sailing O'er the Sea* is graceful and tender:

"My Love went Sailing o'er The Sea,
And gold and gems he promised me,
But one white shell he had for me.

A sailor lad my love was he,
But 'Captain yet, my lass, I'll be,'
He cried with that last kiss to me.

I watched the ships sail in from sea,
With white sails spreading wide and free,
And sailors chanting merrily.
And captains tall and fair to see
Stood on their decks; but none to me
Held out the hand or bent the knee.

At last a ship crawled in from sea,
Crippled, and stained and old was she,
And over her side my Love stepped he,
And down at my feet he bent his knee;
'A sailor still, my girl!' cried he,
And one white shell I bring to thee."

Mrs. Davis was a charming woman and had, for a long time in Royal Street, in the "Vieux Carré," a *salon,* where men and women of letters and musicians met most pleasantly.

Mrs. Mary Ashley Townsend, (Xariffa), was one of our best known poets. Her *Creed* is celebrated, and *Lake Pontchartrain* is beautiful:

"Into thy sapphire wave, fair Pontchartrain,
Slow sinks the setting sun; the distant sail,
On far horizon's edge, glides hushed and pale,
Like some escaping spirit o'er the main.
The sea-gull soars, then tastes thy wave again;
The bearded forests on thy sandy shore
In silence stand, e'en as they stood of yore,
While yet the red man held his savage reign,
And daring Iberville's adventurous prow
As yet had never cut thy purple wave,
Nor swung the shadow of his shining sail,
Across the bank of the Biloxi brave.
Ah, placid lake! Where are thy warriors now?
Where their abiding places — where their grave?"

James R. Randall wrote *My Maryland* while he was a school teacher in Louisiana and Richard Henry Wilde, author of the charming poem, *Lament of the Captive,* better known as *My Life Is Like a Summer Rose,* was a professor of law for several years in the University of Louisiana at New Orleans. Adrien Rouquette wrote English poetry as well as French, and so did John Augustin, author of *War Flowers.* Mrs. Eliza J. Nicholson (Pearl Rivers), was also a graceful poet, and so is Mrs. Julia K. Wetherill Baker.

Louisiana is proud of having given birth to John J. Audubon, the great naturalist and artist, whose descriptions of the birds of America are masterpieces of clearness and accuracy. Gottschalk, the renowned musician, was also a native of Louisiana, and so was Richardson, the great architect. Henry Vignaud, the distinguished Columbian scholar, is a native of New Orleans.

Louisiana's contribution to literature and art has been noteworthy. Her French literature is unique, and her English literature is interesting and important.

BIBLIOGRAPHY.—Fortier, Alcée: *Louisiana Studies* (New Orleans, 1894); McCaleb, Thomas: *The Louisiana Book* (New Orleans, 1894).

ALCEÉ FORTIER,

Professor of Romance Languages, Tulane University of Louisiana.

CHAPTER XVI.

THE LAW WRITERS OF THE SOUTH.

HE five men distinguished above all others, according to John Fiske, in the work of constructing our national government and putting it into operation, were George Washington, James Madison, Alexander Hamilton, Thomas Jefferson and John Marshall. Of these "five founders of the American Union," as Fiske terms them, three might in a broad sense be regarded as Southern law writers, namely, Madison, Jefferson and Marshall. *The Writings of John Marshall, Chief Justice of the United States, Upon the Federal Constitution* is the title of a small volume published in 1839. No law book has yet been given to the public to which one wishing to acquire a thorough comprehension of the spirit of the Federal constitution could be more safely referred; for it contains the greatest decisions of the greatest American chief justice, who has been aptly described by James Bryce as "a second maker of the constitution." Marshall's law writings, however, are confined to his judicial opinions, and in a paper like the present any treatment of the written decisions of the Southern courts of last resort would be altogether impracticable. Nor can Thomas Jefferson, in the strictest sense, be classed as a law writer, for while his published writings not infrequently deal at some length with various questions of law, there is not among them a treatise or essay entirely devoted to any legal topic. Of the trio above named, therefore, James Madison is the only one who, for the purposes of this article, can be deemed a law writer.

Distinguished Southern Law Writers.

James Madison was born in Port Conway, Va., March 16, 1751, and died at Montpelier, Va., June 28, 1836. He must be ranked as one of the two or three greatest writers on constitutional law that America has produced. "To him and to Hamilton," said Judge Story, "I think we are mainly indebted for the constitution of the United States." His papers in the *Federalist*—being about one-third of the entire number—and his *Reports of the Debates of the Convention Which Framed the Constitution of the United States,* are invaluable to the student of constitutional law. Certainly no one had a larger share in the framing and the adoption of the Federal constitution than Madison. His services in the Convention of 1787 entitled him to be called the "Father of the Constitution." John Fiske declares that "he was the constructive thinker who played the foremost part among the men who made the constitution." He acted as chairman of the committee which reported the constitution. Among his contemporaries, his knowledge of constitutional law was regarded as unequaled. His affection for the constitution and for the Union that it accomplished found utterance in these words: "The advice nearest to my heart and deepest in my convictions is, that the Union of the states be cherished and perpetuated."

St. George Tucker was born on the Island of Bermuda, July 10, 1752, and died in Nelson county, Va., Nov. 10, 1828. Coming to Virginia in 1771 to complete his education he was graduated at the College of William and Mary in 1772, finished a course of law, and began practice in the colonial courts. After a distinguished career at the bar and on the bench, he was, in 1789, made professor of law at William and Mary, succeeding Chancellor George Wythe. His best known legal work is his annotated edition of *Blackstone's Commentaries,* published in 1803. Tucker's Blackstone was for years a valued textbook in Virginia and other states. The appendix to the first book contains a disquisition upon the origin and nature of the Federal constitution. It has been said that it is a tribute to the originality as well as to the ability of the author that all subsequent controversial disquisitions on the subjects treated in this work "have appealed to him as authority, or have attempted to overthrow his doctrines." He also published an essay on the question, "How Far the Common Law of England is the Common Law of the United States."

Henry St. George Tucker, eldest son of St. George Tucker, was born in Williamsburg, Va., Dec. 29, 1780, and died in Winchester, Va., Aug. 28, 1848. After graduating at the College of William and Mary he became a lawyer and settled at Winchester, Va. He was appointed chancellor of the state in 1824 and served until 1831, when he was made president-judge of the Virginia Court of Appeals. This last named position he resigned in 1841 on being elected professor of law at the University of Virginia. He published *Commentaries on the Law of Virginia* (2 vols., Winchester, 1836-7); *Lectures on Constitutional Law* (Richmond, 1843); and *Lectures on Natural Law and Government* (Charlottesville, 1844).

Nathaniel Beverley Tucker, the second son of St. George Tucker, was born at Williamsburg, Va., Sept. 6, 1784, and died at Winchester, Va., Aug. 26, 1851. He was elected professor of law at William and Mary in 1834. Though known chiefly as the author of *The Partisan Leader* and *George Balcombe,* he is

Edw Livingston

also known as the author of the following law books:
*Lectures Intended to Prepare the Student for the
Study of the Constitution of the United States* (Philadelphia, 1845); and *Principles of Pleading* (Boston,
1846).

Edward Livingston was born in Clermont, N. Y.,
May 26, 1764, and died in Rhinebeck, N. Y., May 23,
1836. As the works by which this great jurist made
such a deep impression on his own age and on posterity were all written during the portion of his
life that he was a citizen of Louisiana, it seems not
improper that his name should be included in a
list of Southern law writers. He became a member
of the New Orleans bar in 1804, just after Louisiana
had been acquired by the United States. In 1820,
having been elected a member of the Louisiana legislature, he, with two other members, was commis-
sioned to prepare a civil code for the state. Having
made a close study of the legal systems of Rome,
France and Spain, as well as that of Great Britain,
he was especially fitted for this undertaking. The
draft of the code, which was chiefly his work, was
adopted by the legislature in large part in 1825.
Livingston's most notable work, however, is *A System of Penal Law*. This was divided into a Code of
Crimes and Punishments; a Code of Procedure; a
Code of Evidence; and a Code of Reform and Prison
Discipline. It also included a Book of Definitions.
The merits of this work were acknowledged by the
most advanced thinkers of every civilized nation,
and entitled the name of its author to be "arranged," in the language of Jefferson, with those of
the sages of antiquity. It was in recognition of the
value of his *System of Penal Law* that Livingston
was chosen an Associate of the French Academy of
Moral and Political Science. In 1831 President
Jackson appointed him secretary of state, and in

1833 sent him as minister plenipotentiary to France. His works on criminal jurisprudence were published in New York in 1873.

Hugh Swinton Legaré was born in Charleston, S. C., Jan. 2, 1797, and died in Boston while on a visit to his friend George Ticknor, June 20, 1841. In 1832 he accepted the position of charge d'affaires at Brussels, where he remained until the close of 1836. After his return he was elected to Congress from South Carolina. In 1841 he was appointed by President Tyler attorney-general of the United States and after the withdrawal of Webster from the cabinet, discharged for some months the duties of secretary of state. Among the articles in the two volumes of his "writings," edited by his sister, the only contributions to legal literature are: *The Constitutional History of Greece* (Vol. I., p. 367); *The Origin, History and Influence of Roman Legislation* (Vol. I., p. 502); *Kent's Commentaries* (Vol. II., p. 102); *Codification* (Vol. II., p. 482); and *Chancellor D'Aguessau* (Vol. II., p. 559). With regard to Legaré's paper on *The Origin, History and Influence of Roman Legislation,* Judge Story, in an address to the students of Dane Law School, said: "Whoever reads that essay, and I hope you all will read it, will perceive his vast attainments in the civil law." These essays are characterized by a brilliancy and breadth of scholarship that are hardly paralleled by the writings of any other American jurist. So highly did Judge Story esteem Legaré's judgment that in the lecture to his students above mentioned he declares: "To me, had my own career closed before his, a single word of praise from his lips, could I have looked back to know it, would have been as valuable a tribute as from any other human being." One of the chief objects of the latter part of Mr. Legaré's life was to expand the common law

of this country by infusing into it the more liberal principles of the civil law. His studies had brought him to the conclusion, also reached by Edward Livingston, that it "was practicable and desirable to infuse a larger portion of the spirit and philosophy of the civil law and even of its forms and process into our system of jurisprudence." His untimely death interrupted this work, and no American since, perhaps, has been so well qualified to continue it.

John Caldwell Calhoun was born in Abbeville district, S. C., March 18, 1782, and died in Washington, D. C., March 29, 1850. Though he was actively engaged in the practice of law only a few years after his admission to the bar of South Carolina in 1807, his writings have caused him to be regarded by competent and impartial critics as one of the greatest masters of constitutional law who has appeared during the history of the American people. The two treatises written towards the close of his life, entitled *A Disquisition on Government,* and *A Discourse on the Constitution and Government of the United States,* were published after his death and are contained in one volume of 400 pages. John Stuart Mill, in commenting on the great ability of this posthumous work speaks of its author as "a man who has displayed powers as a speculative political thinker superior to any who has appeared in American politics since the authors of *The Federalist.*"

James M. Walker was born in Charleston, S. C., Jan. 10, 1813, and died in the city of his birth Sept. 18, 1854. Upon graduating at the South Carolina College in 1830 he devoted himself to the study of law and was admitted to the bar in 1834. In 1850 he published a pamphlet entitled *An Inquiry Into the Use and Authority of Roman Jurisprudence in the Law Concerning Real Estate.* In 1852 his *Theory of Common Law* appeared. Professor Greenleaf, in a letter written on Aug. 24, 1852, says of this essay: "I have mentioned it to Professor Mittermaier, of Heidelburg, as the only philosophical treatise which our profession has of late produced."

Conway Robinson was born in Richmond, Va., Sept. 15, 1805, and died in Philadelphia, Pa., Jan. 30, 1884. His *Law and Equity Practice,* in three volumes, was published during the years 1832-1839. He spent some time abroad in gathering the materials for his *Principles and Practice of Courts of Justice in England and the United States,* which was published in two volumes in 1860. The value of this work, as alike comprehensive and profound, has been recognized by high authorities both in England and America. The closing years of the author's life were devoted to his *History of the High Court of Chancery and Other Institutions of England From the Time of Julius Cæsar Until the Accession of William and Mary.* The first volume of this work was published in Richmond in 1882.

Alexander H. Stephens was born near Crawfordsville, Ga., Feb. 11, 1812, and died in Atlanta, Ga., March 4, 1883. He was elected to Congress in 1843 and remained there until 1858, when he retired for the time from public life. In 1861 he became vice-president of the Confederacy. After the war he was twice United States senator, and at the time of his death was governor of Georgia. His *Constitutional View of the War Between the States* shows him to be one of the closest and most logical thinkers who has dealt with the great questions at issue. His remarkable gift of clear statement and his general vigor of intellect, which caused Abraham Lincoln, after listening to one of Stephen's speeches, to pronounce it "the very best speech of one hour's length" he had ever heard, are everywhere evident in this masterly treatise.

Judah P. Benjamin was born in St. Croix, West Indies, Aug. 11, 1811, and died in Paris, France, May 6, 1884. He removed to Wilmington, N. C., in 1815. After spending three years at Yale, he studied law and in 1832 was admitted to the bar of New Orleans. Two years after entering upon the practice of the law in New Orleans he published a work entitled *Digest of Reported Decisions of the Supreme Court of the Late Territory of Orleans and of the Supreme Court of Louisiana.* This work proved of great value to the members of the New Orleans bar and to students of the rather unique legal system which at that time prevailed in Louisiana. In 1852 and again in 1857 he was elected United States senator for Louisiana. During the War of Secession he served as attorney-general and secretary of state for the Confederacy. After the war he escaped by way of Florida and the Bahamas to the West Indies, and thence to England. He entered as a student of Lincoln's Inn in January, 1866, and the following June was called to the English bar at the age of fifty-five. After one year of practice he published *A Treatise on the Law of Sale of Personal Property,* which passed quickly through several editions, and is now recognized as a legal classic throughout the English-speaking world. Baron Pollock says: "Few works in English law have been so readily accepted and so universally used as Benjamin on *Sales.*" Of Benjamin's remarkable career in England, Senator Hoar, in an address to the Virginia Bar Association in 1898, declared: "I suppose there is no American, certainly no American lawyer, who did not feel a thrill of pride when the famous Southern statesman, Judah P. Benjamin, after the war, made his way over every barrier and

easily took his place as leader and head of the bar
of Great Britain.''

John Barbee Minor was born in Louisiana county,
Va., June 2, 1813, and died in Charlottesville, Va.,
July 29, 1895. He was professor of common and
statute law at the University of Virginia from 1845
to 1895. In 1873 appeared the first and second volumes of *Minor's Institutes of Common and Statute
Law.* The fourth edition of these volumes appeared
in 1891 and in 1892. In 1878 the fourth volume was
published—the third edition of which in 1893 appeared in two parts. The whole work as published
in 1895 covers nearly 5,000 pages; yet Senator Daniels, author of the well-known work on *Negotiable
Instruments,* has declared: ''Minor's *Institutes*
contain more law in fewer words than any work with
which I am acquainted.'' This monumental work
has been very generally cited as authority by the
courts of last resort throughout the United States,
and is regarded as indispensable by a great many
Southern lawyers.

John Randolph Tucker was born in Winchester,
Va., Dec. 24, 1823, and died in Lexington, Va., Feb.
13, 1897. He was admitted to the bar in 1845. He
was elected in 1870 professor of equity and public
law in Washington and Lee University. He was a
member of Congress from 1874 to 1887, and served
as chairman of the ways and means committee, and
again as chairman of the judiciary committee. He
was president of the American Bar Association
1892-93. His treatise on *The Constitution of the
United States,* in two volumes, edited by Henry St.
George Tucker, was published in 1899. This work
amply sustained his reputation as one of the ablest
constitutional lawyers of the country and is regarded by those who have made a close study of it

as one of the most valuable contributions yet made to this branch of the law.

Augustus Hill Garland was born in Tipton county, Tenn., June 11, 1832, and died in Washington, D. C., Jan. 26, 1899. He was admitted to the bar in Washington, Ark., in 1853. Served in the United States Senate as senator from Arkansas from March 5, 1877, to March 5, 1885, when he took his seat in the cabinet, having been appointed by President Cleveland attorney-general of the United States. Senator Davis states that Garland was regarded by his fellow-senators as "one of the ablest constitutional lawyers which this country has produced in a generation." His work on *Federal Practice* met with a favorable reception immediately on its appearance, and continues to hold its place as one of the leading treatises on the subject.

John Warwick Daniel was born at Lynchburg, Va., Sept. 5, 1842. In 1887 he was elected to the United States Senate from Virginia. His well-known work on *Negotiable Instruments,* published in 1876, has proved of great value to the profession. It has passed through several editions, and has probably been more frequently cited as authority by the appellate courts of the United States than any other American work on the subject. He is also the author of the work on *Attachment,* published in 1869.

William Wirt Howe was born in Ontario county, N. Y., Nov. 24, 1833. He graduated at Hamilton College in 1853, and subsequently studied law in St. Louis and in New York City. Shortly after the close of the War of Secession he became a member of the New Orleans bar, and from 1868 to 1873 was one of the judges of the Supreme Court of Louisiana. In August, 1897, he was elected president of the American Bar Association. In 1885 he published *Municipal History of New Orleans.* The value of his scholarly treatise entitled *Studies in Civil Law,* published in 1896, is distinctly enhanced by its charm of style.

Hannis Taylor was born in New Bern, N. C., Sept. 12, 1851. In 1870 he was admitted to the bar at Mobile, Ala. He rose rapidly to prominence in the state and Federal courts, and is recognized as one of the leading living authorities on questions of constitutional law. The first volume of *The Origin and Growth of the English Constitution* was published in 1892, and has since gone through several editions. This work has met with an enthusiastic reception from many of the foremost scholars and jurists of the day, and in recognition of its merits the degree of LL.D. has been conferred upon the author by the universities of Edinburgh and Dublin. In 1893 Mr. Taylor was appointed by President Cleveland minister plenipotentiary to the court of Spain. The second part of *The Origin and Growth of the English Constitution* was published in 1900. This part is entitled *The Aftergrowth of the Constitution.* Mr. Taylor is also known as the author of *International Public Law, Jurisdiction and Procedure of the Supreme Court of the United States* and *The Science of Jurisprudence.*

Christopher G. Tiedeman was born in Charleston, S. C., July 16, 1857, and died in New York City, Aug. 25, 1903. After graduating from the Charleston College, he attended lectures at the Universities of Goettingen and Leipsic. On his return to this country he entered the Columbia Law School and graduated therefrom in 1879. He began the practice of law in his native city, but in 1881 accepted the offer of a chair in the law faculty of the University of Missouri, which he held for ten years, resigning then to accept a similar chair in the New York University Law School. In 1883 he published his *Law of Real*

Property, which has since been largely used as a textbook in law schools of the country. His *Limitations of Police Power,* published in 1886, met with a particularly favorable reception, some prominent critics declaring that it was one of the most important and most interesting of the law books which had been published in the United States during the preceding quarter of a century. Other books published by Dr. Tiedeman are *Law of Commercial Paper, Law of Sales, Municipal Corporations,* and *Unwritten Constitution of the United States.*

Contributions of Southern Law Writers.

The law writers of the South above named constitute a comparatively small portion of the total number. During the past two or three decades there has been a marked increase in the output of law books by Southern lawyers. Some of these treatises are of great merit, and deserve extended notices, but the limits of this paper permit merely a bare enumeration. The following is a partial list of the works of Southern law writers not heretofore mentioned:

New Views of the Constitution of the United States (1823), by John Taylor, Caroline, Va.; *A Treatise on Criminal Law* (1838), by J. A. G. Davis, of the University of Virginia; *Treatise on the Law of Executors and Administrators* (2 vols., 1st ed. 1841; 2d ed. 1857), and *Digest of the Laws Representing Real Property* (3 vols., 1st ed. 1839; 2d. ed. 1855), by John Taylor Lomax; *An Essay on Limitations* (1844), by William T. Joynes, of Petersburg, Va.; *History of a Suit in Equity, as Prosecuted and Defended in the Virginia State Courts and in the United States Circuit Courts* (1st ed. 1854; 2d ed. 1882), by Alexander H. Sands of Virginia; *The Practice of the Courts of Law in Civil Cases*

Founded on Robinson's Practice of 1832 (1st ed. 1877; 2d ed. 1891-92), and *Pleading and Practice in the Courts of Chancery* (2 vols., 1st ed. 1882-83; 2d ed. 1889), by R. T. Barton, of Winchester, Va.; *Notes to Vol. I. of Minor's Institutes on Corporations* (1894), by William M. Lile, of the University of Virginia; *The Law of Tax Titles in Virginia* (1898), and *Conflict of Laws* (1901), by Raleigh C. Minor, of the University of Virginia; *Hughes on Admiralty* (1901), and *Hughes on Federal Procedure* (1904), by Robert M. Hughes, of Norfolk, Va.; *A Treatise on the Law of Domestic Relations* (1905), by Joseph R. Long, of Washington and Lee University, Lexington, Va.; *The Fourteenth Amendment,* by Hon. Henry Brannon, of West Virginia; *Equity Procedure* (2 vols.), and *Equity Principles* (1 vol.), by Charles E. Hogg, of the University of West Virginia; *Procedure in the Courts, Law and Equity,* by W. P. Willey, of the University of West Virginia; *Pleading and Practice,* by John Prentiss Poe, of Baltimore, Md.; *Juridical Equity,* by Hon. Charles E. Phelps, of Maryland; *Sylabus of the Law of Real Property,* by Richard M. Venable, of Maryland; *Principles of the Law of Personal Property,* and *Digest of Criminal Law,* by William T. Brantley, of the University of Maryland; *Equity Procedure,* by Edgar G. Miller, Jr., of Maryland; *Elements of Corporation Law,* by Joseph C. France, of Maryland; *Domestic Relations,* by Hon. Henry D. Harland, of Baltimore, Md.; *Marriage and Divorce* (1884), *Husband and Wife* (1888), by David Stewart, of Maryland; *Criminal Law* (3d ed. 1904), *Custody of Infants* (3d ed. 1899), by Lewis Hockheimer, of Maryland; *Testamentary Law* (1878), by Ed. Otis Hinkley; *Criminal Law* (1886), by William H. Malone, of Maryland; *History of a Law Suit* (6 eds., 1st ed. 1852), by Abraham Caruthers, of Lebanon, Tenn.; *Suits in Chancery* (5 eds.), by Henry R. Gibson, of Knoxville, Tenn.; *Studies in the Constitutional History of Tennessee,* by Hon. J. W. Caldwell, of Knoxville, Tenn.; *Wills and Administrations* (1894), by Robert Pritchard, of Chattanooga, Tenn.; *Foundations of Legal Liability* (3 vols.), by T. A. Street, of Nashville, Tenn.; *Hand-Book of the Law of Public Corporations,* by Henry H. Ingersoll; *Due Process of Law Under the Federal Constitution* (1906), by Lucius Polk McGhee, of the University of North Carolina; *Regulation of Commerce Under the Federal Constitution* (1907), by Thomas H. Calvert, of Raleigh, N. C.; *The History of a Suit at Law* (1st ed. 1856; 2d ed. 1860), by James Connor, of Charleston, S. C.; *The Federal Courts* (1st ed. 1896; 2d ed. 1898), by Hon. Charles H. Simonton, of Charleston, S. C.; *The Law of Personal Injuries* (2d ed. 1902), by Hon. John L. Hopkins; *Domestic Relations* (1899), by W. C. Rogers, of Nashville, Ark.; *Telegraph and Telephone Companies* (1906), and *Modern Law of Failing and Insolvent Corporations* (1908), by S. Walter Jones, of the University of Mississippi; *A Treatise on Land Titles* (1895), by Lewis N. Dembitz, of Louisville, Ky.

M. HERNDON MOORE,
Professor of Law, University of South Carolina.

CHAPTER XVII.

THE INFLUENCE OF THE BENCH AND BAR UPON SOUTHERN LIFE AND CULTURE.

"IN America there are no nobles or literary men, and the people is apt to mistrust the wealthy; lawyers consequently form the highest political class and the most cultivated circle of society."

These words are taken from *DeTocqueville's Democracy in America,* a book of weight and authority in its time, but now almost forgotten. It is still true that we have no nobles and that we are apt to mistrust the wealthy. But it is no longer true that we have no literary men. We have them in abundance, nor do we lack literary women. The declaration in regard to lawyers is now to be considered, more especially as applied to the South. When the sentence quoted was written it was, perhaps, as nearly true as the average generalization, a comprehensive qualification in view of the extent to which this country, and especially the South, has suffered from the generalization of philosophic, philanthropic and corrective commentators. The statement was not unqualifiedly true when it was written, because from the days of Capt. John Smith we have never been entirely without literary men. It was incorrect, also, in that it failed to take into account as "cultivated" the clergymen, all more or less "literary," who, from the first, were conspicuous and influential in America and who frequently combined teaching with preaching. In so far as the particular matters with which the French philosopher dealt in his book were concerned, his statement was fairly correct, because the preachers and teachers, usually, did not take part, actively, in politics.

Influence of Southern Lawyers.

The position of the lawyers in the South was in no respect different from their position in the North, their influence arising from the same causes and having the same limitations in both sections. That is to say as education, intelligence and competency in public affairs, have advanced among men of other occupations, the influence of the lawyers has in some measure decreased.

Not proportionately, because the lawyer deals with a subject of great importance which requires special knowledge, and constantly and to an unusual degree, attracts the public attention, and therefore his prominence is greater than his intellectual superiority to men of other callings alone could produce. This last fact is illustrated by the continuing consequence of lawyers in England and in those parts of the United States where the masses of the people are best educated and most attentive to public concerns. At this time, in our country, the persons of greatest prominence and greatest influence are the very rich; the very learned in all branches of knowledge; the greater educators, such as college presidents; the writers and the lawyers. The clergy, even more than the lawyers, have suffered, temporarily at least, a distinct loss of position in recent years, but this is less true, perhaps, in the South than in any other part of the country. There are fewer very rich men, fewer authors, fewer great institutions of learning in the South than in some other sections of the country, and, to the extent that this is true, the lawyers continue to be relatively more prominent and more influential.

The first century of the life of our country was a

period of political development and adjustment, and
that fact alone would have made the legal profession
of especial prominence even if the diffusion of culture had been more general. Whatever the causes
may have been, the fact is indisputable that, down
to the War of Secession the attention and the intelligence of the South were directed mainly to public
questions, and that condition has continued, though
in steadily lessening degree, until the present time.
For the last thirty years the legal profession has
been losing its monopoly of public attention and of
public affairs. It is very common to hear the speak-
ers in the campaign of education, which is now going
on in the South, say that formerly the centre of life
in every community was the courthouse, but now
it is the schoolhouse, and the statement contains
much truth. The change is precisely such as has
occurred in other parts of the country.

We must not conclude, however, that the lawyer
is in the way of losing position entirely, for, obviously, that can never occur in the South or in any
other part of the country. In every law-making
body the lawyer is still dominant except, perhaps,
in matters of economic legislation, despite all that
is said of the invasion of such bodies by men of
wealth, and to a large extent this must continue to
be true of necessity, because the time will never come
when the lawyer will not be needed in making, as
well as in administering, the laws. While it is true
that the prominence of the legal profession in the
South is attributable to the same general causes that
gave it influence elsewhere in America, in the early
days, it is also a fact that these causes were more
persistent in the South than in the North.

The rolls of the Continental Congresses contain
the names of many learned and capable lawyers,
but the distinctively American lawyer was the prod-

uct of conditions succeeding the Revolution. The great crisis did not make demands exclusively upon any one class of men.

Washington, Franklin and Hancock were not lawyers, and Jefferson's renown and influence were never dependent in any degree upon his proficiency at the bar, or upon his attainments as a student of the municipal law. Independence, changed conditions, new institutions, made the opportunities and created the necessity for the American lawyer. The peculiar genius of Marshall would have had but little chance for development in an English colony, for his gift was in the line of what we may call constructive jurisprudence. And this same capacity to apply the principles of English law to new conditions, to adapt them to the requirements of new institutions, to reject the common law and the Westminter decisions when necessary, and, sometimes, to make new law without the aid of legislation, was the distinguishing characteristic of nearly all our great lawyers for half a century after the Revolution. This process of legal and institutional evolution and innovation was less obstructed in the younger than in the older communities. The freer life of the new West and Southwest encouraged progress and change. Therefore, in the younger communities the lawyer found his best opportunities and was most in demand. The most important, or, certainly the most radical, legal and institutional changes have, as a rule, had their origins in the younger states. These states led the way in abolishing the property qualifications for voting and holding office, which were to be found in all the early constitutions; they have made the most important modifications of the township system; some have extended the suffrage to women; some have adopted the referendum and the initiative, while the very latest Western state

constitution has startled the conservatives by its
many daring innovations. A century ago Tennessee
and Kentucky were the West, and when Tennessee
adopted her first constitution in 1796, Mr. Jefferson
declared that it was the most democratic of the sixteen state constitutions then in existence.

In building new institutions the lawyers were indispensable, and many men eminent in the profession followed the frontier southward or westward
and were makers of laws and institutions successively for the new communities as they reached the
point where civil organization became necessary.
John Haywood, probably the most learned lawyer
and one of the most scholarly men in the Southwest
at the beginning of the Nineteenth century, was a
judge first in North Carolina and then in Tennessee.
W. C. C. Claiborne was a leader in Tennessee and
then in Louisiana. William Cocke went from Virginia to the Watauga country, then in North Carolina but now in Tennessee, in the last quarter of the
Eighteenth century, served in the legislatures of
Virginia and North Carolina, aided in founding the
republic, so called, of Transylvania, was a leader in
the short-lived state of Franklin, a judge and United
States senator in Tennessee, and at last one of the
foremost men in the Mississippi territory. Probably no other American has participated in the
making of so many constitutions or represented so
many constituencies.

Just so soon as a community became sufficiently
settled and secure, for civil rights to become matters
of concern, the lawyers came and took charge.

In the Southwest the Indian wars were succeeded
quickly by strife, sometimes hardly less sanguinary,
over land titles, and the lawyers reaped rich har-
vests of fees and of political preferments. In the
midst of the first period of exceptional progress, in

the "flush times" of the Southwest, came the panic of 1837, and everybody and everything got into court. But this was only an additional and temporary source of influence for the lawyers. No sooner had the Federal constitution been adopted than grave questions of construction arose, demanding knowledge of the law for their determination. The combative spirit of the frontier delighted in politics, and as there were very few newspapers, the orator became a mighty power. Never was public speech so much in demand, never was the public speaker so much admired, or so influential, and nearly always he was a lawyer. It was also to the great benefit of the lawyers that the combativeness of the frontiersman made him a ready and persistent litigant, while his want of training in business was a prolific source of contention.

It is to the credit of the Southern people that they esteemed not only the speaking lawyers, but also the learned lawyers, for it happened frequently that the oratorical advocate was not a profound jurist and the people were quick to see the fact. No one ever put Patrick Henry and John Marshall, as lawyers, in the same class. The law was, as it is yet, essentially an esoteric science, and substantial acquirements in it unaccompanied by the gift of speech were sure guarantees of public admiration. The Old South, until the war, was rural, and population was dispersed far more than in the least populous parts of the North. The Virginia, Carolina or Alabama planter lived isolated in the midst of his spreading plantation, and came in contact with his fellows, mainly, at the remote church on occasional Sunday mornings, and at the remoter courthouse on Saturdays and court days. Conditions were unfavorable to the creation of a literature, and nearly all the books were written in the North. Southern men universally regarded public service as the most honorable of pursuits, and the bar as the avenue to such service. Sons of the rich and prominent families frequently turned to the law, and there were few members of the profession who did not expect and seek office. There were public men who were not lawyers, as, for instance, Andrew Johnson and W. G. Brownlow, of Tennessee, but a list of the prominent men of the South down to 1861 would be, mainly, a roll of attorneys. In 1860 the Southern leaders were in Virginia such men as Hunter, Mason, Wise and John Tyler; in North Carolina, Vance and Clingman; in Georgia, Toombs, Stephens and Cobb; in South Carolina, Rhett, Chesnutt and Barnwell; in Alabama, Yancey, Walker and Clay; in Tennessee, Nicholson, Bell, Harris, Johnson; in Mississippi, Davis, Lamar and Barksdale; in Arkansas Pike, Garland and Rector; in Texas, Sam Houston, Reagan and Wigfall; in Florida Yulee, Mallory and Morton; in Louisiana, Slidell, Benjamin and John A. Campbell. These were nearly all lawyers and they are not a tithe of the members of the profession in the South who were of national reputation and large influence at the time referred to.

The final attitude of the South upon the great constitutional question which divided the sections was determined in large measure by Jefferson and Madison, and in much larger measure by Mr. Calhoun. Of the active and efficient advocates of states-rights just before the war, the most conspicuous were Rhett, of South Carolina, and Yancey, of Alabama. The lawyers of the South led in the secession movement, as they had led for seventy-five years in all public affairs. If we look as far back as the second quarter of the Nineteenth century the great names are: Jackson, Polk, Houston, Pinckney, John

Marshall, Calhoun, Hayne, Grundy, King, Crawford. Always it is the lawyers.

The Lawyers in Literature.

The literature of the South before the war was produced in large part by the lawyers. Mr. Calhoun was an author of no little merit, and Jefferson and Madison are among the foremost writers of the country on political science. John Marshall wrote a life of Washington, and there were many contributions by lawyers to the literature of political controversy. Jere Clemens, of Alabama, wrote novels which were read fifty years ago, and Judge Longstreet was the author of *Georgia Scenes,* of which he was much ashamed, not dreaming that it was to become a classic. Albert Pike was a poet of international reputation.

The Lawyers and the Aristocracy.

A fact of the greatest importance is that the profession corrected certain inevitable tendencies toward aristocracy in the South. The bar was attainable by every aspiring young man, and success waited upon intelligence, probity and industry. The young man of the humblest origin came to the bar and succeeded if he had the capacity, and it happened not infrequently that the sons of poor and obscure men rose to the highest positions. There can be no better illustrations of this than Andrew Jackson and Henry Clay.

It was due thus very largely to the influence of the bar, that while the South indisputably presented certain features of aristocracy, it was essentially democratic. Nowhere in the country was merit more certain of reward or ability more promptly recognized, without regard to considerations of birth or fortune, and the dominant sentiment in the

South, notwithstanding the institution of slavery and imperfect local institutions, was not only genuinely but intensely democratic. Mr. Lincoln's birth was not more obscure, or his early life harder, than that of Andrew Jackson, not much more than that of Henry Clay. The legal profession attracted and encouraged talent very much as the church did in the Middle Ages, and with very much the same result. It was the bulwark of thorough Americanism and pure democracy.

It is not true, as so often asserted, that there were only two classes of whites in the South—the aristocrats and the "trash." The aristocrats, so named, the old families of large, landed estates, were comparatively few in number, and the "poor white trash" less numerous than is generally believed. The great body of Southern whites did not belong to either class, but were plain average, middle-class people, intelligent, of sound morals, independent and patriotic. There was, probably, no part of the South where this good element of population was not in the majority. It furnished many of the more prominent lawyers, and, by its numerical strength, enforced a regard for itself which sometimes degenerated into demagogy.

Nothing could be more absurd than the conception of the South as the home of a domineering, haughty, slave-holding aristocracy, without any other white population than the "crackers" and the mountaineers, to whom recent fiction has assigned so many and such impossible varieties of uncouth speech. That the rich slaveholders had an influence disproportionate to their numbers, such as wealth always gives, is true, of course, but the middle class of respectable and intelligent whites, often slaveholders to a limited extent but in no degree aristocratic, in fact or in pretense, was everywhere in the majority, and it was from this class that the bar was most largely recruited. Moreover, the aristocratic element owed its indisputable prominence not more to wealth and family standing than to the ability and personal worth of the men whom it put forward as its representatives. That the Southern aristocracy was composed, as a rule, of men of high character and of honorable pride is true, but it is also true that it was not only limited in influence and restrained from excesses, but spurred to greater exertions by competition with the more numerous plain people; and the principal, or, at least, the most conspicuous field of endeavor and of honorable rivalry was the bar. It is only just to add that the aristocracy, in turn, by its intelligence, moral worth and high standards of conduct, exercised a strong and valuable influence upon all other elements of population. Let us examine the antecedents of a few of the great Southern lawyers and political leaders. If we leave out Washington, the most conspicuous names in the Old South are Jefferson, Clay, Jackson and Calhoun. Not one of these was of Cavalier blood or, strictly speaking, of the aristocratic class. Jefferson was, in part, Scotch-Irish, in part Welsh, without pride of lineage and intolerant of aristocracy. Jackson's birth was so obscure that there is dispute as to where he was born. Clay was popularly known as "the mill boy of the slashes." Calhoun was of plain, good, Scotch-Irish descent. His mother's family came to America not more than forty years before the Revolution, a part of the Covenanter migration in search of civil and religious liberty.

William H. Crawford, of Georgia, the rival of Jackson and John Quincy Adams, was a poor boy and began his career as a school-teacher. William R. King, Vice-President of the United States, was

of a plain but good North Carolina family. William
Wirt, of Virginia, was born of a Swiss father and
a German mother, and was too poor to obtain a college education. Sam Houston was of a frontier
Scotch-Irish family. These are sufficient illustrations of the fact that the bar of the South contained,
from the first, many eminent men who were not in
any sense aristocratic by descent or in sentiment.
On the other hand it must be acknowledged that it
was benefited both in morals and in manners by
those of its members who were of high social standing and culture.

The opposition of the South to liberal constructions of the constitution was inherited from the
great Virginia statesmen of the first period of our
history, but it was kept alive and strengthened not
only by sectional differences, but also by the strong
democratic opinions and the conservative attitude
of its lawyer leaders. It is not necessary to my
present purpose that I should demonstrate, or even
assert that this attitude of the profession was due
to the influence of the plain people in its ranks.
Neither is it within my province to consider whether
the tendency was right or wrong. I am concerned
directly only to show the influence of the bar on
Southern thought and life, and the conservatism of
the bar is a fact of the first importance because it
accounts in large measure for the course of the
South, in politics from the adoption of the constitution to 1861, and has had not a little to do with the
direction of events since the war.

Another fact worthy of special attention is the
record of the Southern statesmen of the old régime.
I make no comparison between them and the public
men of other sections. It is enough to say that without exception, so far as I know, the great statesmen
of the South before the war were men of unques-

tioned integrity and of sincere patriotism. By force of intellect and of character they long exerted a controlling influence in affairs and almost, without exception, deserved and received public respect and confidence. They were always positively, sometimes unduly, insistent upon their rights and those of their constituency, but they were strong, fearless, capable, honorable men, strenuously and genuinely patriotic, and their long ascendancy in affairs of state was marked by efficiency, honesty, economy and fidelity to duty.

The South has a right to be proud of these statesmen of the old time, and so has the legal profession, for the great majority of them were lawyers.

The tone of the profession must have been high when it produced the long line of great and good men and strong lawyers that began with Peyton Randolph, Madison, Monroe, Marshall, Wirt, Pinckney, and contains the names of Clay, Calhoun, Crawford, King, Berrien, Hayne, Jackson, Overton, Hugh L. White, Polk, Grundy, Cobb, Stephens, John Bell, Toombs, Rhett, Yancey, Davis, Wise, Breckenridge, Benjamin and Catron, to say nothing of such lawyers of the border Southern states as Luther Martin, Pinkney, Menton, Reverdy Johnson and Taney.

Long ago a representative of one of the old and aristocratic families of the South, a genuine "fire-eater," consulted me with regard to the choice of a profession for his son. I said to him that in my opinion the law did not offer so many advantages as formerly. He replied that the law was, and always would be, "the ruling profession of the world," and repelled with warmth my suggestion of the opportunities for success in commercial life. His scorn of the "shopkeeper" was outspoken and emphatic. His estimation of the law was characteristic of his generation, and I have tried to show how much there was to support it. I am very sure that, on account of the conditions prevailing from 1789 to 1861, lawyers commanded more respect and wielded more influence in the Southern states than ever before, or afterwards, in any part of the world. The intellect of the entire section went almost exclusively into the profession, and the result was a long line of lawyers, judges and statesmen, whose names reflect honor upon our country.

They were learned lawyers, eloquent advocates, just and wise judges, capable and incorruptible statesmen. No single man so profoundly affected the politics of the country as Thomas Jefferson; none has exerted so powerful an influence on its jurisprudence as Marshall; Webster's arguments were not so effectual in determining the real nature and effect of the constitution as Jackson's uncompromising attitude toward nullification; no statesman has had such a personal following as Clay, unless it was Jackson; and, until 1861, Hamilton had not attracted or convinced so many minds as Jefferson or Calhoun.

When we consider the facts here briefly outlined, it is no wonder that to the people of the Old South the law appeared as "the ruling profession of the world."

Influence upon Culture.

As to the influence of the bar upon the culture of the South there can be but one opinion. The logical inference is supported, abundantly, by the facts. The lawyers being, usually, men of education were examples to others, and were also the active supporters of every movement for the advancement of learning. Mr. Jefferson founded and fixed the policy of the most notable Southern university. As a rule, the early Southern colleges were corporations created by the legislatures and controlled by self-perpetuating boards of trustees, and an examination of the records of these institutions will show not only the numerical preponderance of the lawyers, but also their controlling influence in these corporations. It would be interesting, if.it were possible, to ascertain how many prominent Southern lawyers were school-teachers. Sometimes they became presidents of colleges and universities. Frequently they were editors. Judge Nicholson, who was twice senator from Tennessee, Yancey, of Alabama, and Rhett, of South Carolina, were engaged, actively, at times, in newspaper work. Every calling that required intellectual training, every movement for the advancement of education and the improvement of morals were supported actively by the lawyers. In all respects their influence upon culture in the South was wholly good and strikingly effective.

In their general social relations their conduct and their influence were excellent. The prominence of their position and the almost universal desire and expectation of public service made them exceptionally responsive to the ethical requirements of the communities in which they lived. But beyond this negative virtue, which might be attributed to an intelligent self-interest, there were a genuine and positive desire and purpose to serve their fellow men and their country. No body or class of men ever had higher ideals or exhibited greater excellence in private or public life than the old-time Southern lawyers, with whom, mainly, I am now concerned. They were not free from the infirmities and faults of their time and of their environment, but impartially judged they are entitled to all the commendation I have given them, and their honorable example is an inspiration to their successors. At the bar the Southern lawyer was zealous but honest; on the bench fearless, impartial and incorruptible; in politics his record, known to all his countrymen, is clear and altogether admirable; in private life he was guided by the strictest standards of conduct, and by a constant regard for the courtesies of life and the rights of his fellowmen. It is not my purpose to idealize him. That he had his share of the weaknesses common to men is admitted, of course, but my present business is to depict him as he appeared in the large to his fellow citizens, and thereby show what his influence must have been on Southern life and culture.

The Lawyers and Religion.

This account would be incomplete without reference to the connection of the lawyers with the religious life of the South, and here again I may be suspected of indiscriminate praise and of a desire to arrogate to my profession all the virtues. The assertions which I am about to make do not admit of positive proof. Nevertheless, they are well founded.

The profession did not escape in early times the Eighteenth century French influences, but it was not seriously infected, and it is affirmed confidently that in proportion to numbers, the lawyers of the South have been very much more largely represented in the churches than any other class of men. To an extent wholly exceptional, the lay activities and leadership in churches of all denominations have been in the hands of lawyers. It has been so in the past, and it is so now. The assertion is made without qualification, and an examination of the facts, past and present, would confirm it.

JOSHUA W. CALDWELL,

Author of The Bench and Bar of Tennessee.

CHAPTER XVIII.

THE SOUTH'S CONTRIBUTION TO THE PROGRESS OF MEDICINE AND SURGERY.

THE first century of the colonial era produced no contributions to science. Existing conditions demanded few physicians, and those not of the highest type. The colonies were infested with quacks and charlatans. "They abounded," says an old writer, "as the locusts of Egypt." That the practitioners of the day were chiefly noted for their extortionate charges is evident from the fact that masters permitted their sick servants to die without calling in a physician, rather than pay the fees demanded. This led to the passage of an act by the House of Burgesses in 1639 to correct the evil.

The House of Burgesses, in 1736, enacted a law regulating the fees to be charged by physicians. This is the earliest fee-bill on record in this country, and it is interesting to note that it encouraged higher medical education in that it allowed physiciaus who had taken a degree to charge nearly one-half more than it did those who were educated by serving an apprenticeship.

The Eighteenth century found the colonies so increased in population and wealth, the latter bringing increased education and refinement, that a field was opened for more and better equipped physicians. During the first half of the century the best practitioners were, chiefly, Englishmen or Scotchmen, well educated men, some of whom were investigators and writers, and made important contributions to medicine or natural science.

After 1750 a number of Americans went abroad to study medicine, and after the establishment of the medical school in Philadelphia in 1765, a still larger number of young men from the Southern colonies sought degrees there. The University of Edinburgh attracted the larger number of those who went abroad, and at the time of the Revolution nearly all our best educated physicians were graduates of that school. The Southern colonies were better supplied with educated physicians than were those of the North.

Contributions to Medical Science and Literature.

The first physicians of the Southern colonies to make contributions to medical literature were John Mitchell, M. D., F. R. S., and Dr. John Tennant, of Virginia. Dr. Mitchell was an Englishman who came to Virginia about 1700, and resided there nearly fifty years. He was an eminent botanist and physician, and wrote on medicine, botany and history, and was a man of genius, originality and accuracy of observation. He made a study of yellow fever and prepared a paper on the subject, which, through Dr. Benjamin Franklin, fell into the hands of Dr. Benjamin Rush during the terrible epidemic of that disease in Philadelphia in 1793, when he and the physicians of that city were at their wit's end as to some treatment by which to check its ravages. Adopting the treatment suggested and making it known to his confreres, by a combined effort they were able thereby to check the terrible mortality.

Dr. John Tennant is said to have been a native Virginian. His most important writings are a description of the climate and epidemic diseases of the colony, and several articles on the therapeutic value of the plant *Polygala Senega,* which he was the first to make known.

John Clayton, of Virginia, was a noted botanist, a correspondent of Linnaeus, and the author of a much quoted work entitled *Flora Virginiaca.* He discovered many new plants and wrote on the several species of tobacco and their cultivation.

During the first half of the century Virginia had not a few men who were eminent both as citizens and physicians. Among these were Dr. Thomas Walker (of Albemarle), who is accredited with having been one of the first to trephine bone for abscess, which he did in 1757; Dr. Thomas Walker (of Caroline); Dr. William Cabell, the founder of the family in Virginia; Dr. Walter McClurg and Dr. John Baynham. Dr. Cabell maintained a private hospital in Nelson county for his patients from a distance, and performed many operations.

The Carolinas, from a comparatively early period, furnished numerous contributions to medical literature, and for some years led all the colonies in the study of the natural sciences.

Dr. William Bull, of South Carolina, was the first native American to graduate in medicine. He took his degree at Leyden in 1734. Ten natives of South Carolina graduated from Edinburgh between 1768 and 1778. This colony had several very eminent physicians, who were Scotchmen and graduates of Edinburgh, and who contributed to the literature of medicine and natural history, prior to the Revolution. Of these, Dr. Lionel Chambers contributed, among other articles, *An Account of the Weather and Diseases of Charleston;* Dr. John Lining, *A Description of Yellow Fever,* a work which to-day stands unrivaled for accuracy; and Dr. Alexander Garden, numerous communications to the Royal Society on natural history. Drs. James Moultrie,

Alexander Barron, David Ramsay and Samuel Wilson were prominent physicians of the same period. The names of these men, says the late Dr. N. S. Davis, "will always make the early history of medicine in that State illustrious."

In that stormy period leading to and including the Revolution, the medical profession contributed its contingent to that brilliant galaxy of statesmen, patriots and soldiers furnished by the Southern colonies, and who had so large a part in the founding of the nation.

The profession in Virginia contributed Arthur Lee, Theodoric Bland, Hugh Mercer, Walter Jones and Adam Stephen (also sometimes spelled Steven) to the service of the state, or to the army; while some score gave their services in the medical corps. It is of interest to note that two of the first six regiments raised by the state were commanded by physicians, viz.: Hugh Mercer and Adam Stephen.

North Carolina furnished, too, her quota in the persons of Drs. Ephraim Brevart, Nathaniel Alexander, Hugh Williamson, the author of a *History of North Carolina,* and Robert Williams. Dr. Brevart was the author of the *Mecklenburg Declaration of Independence.*

Drs. David Ramsay and David Oliphant were among those given by South Carolina to the cause. Dr. Ramsay was the author of *The History of the Revolutionary War.*

Dr. Lyman Hall, of Georgia, was a signer of the Declaration of Independence, and later governor of his state. Drs. Noble W. Jones and Nathaniel Brownson, also of Georgia, lent the cause their aid.

The credit of having established the first institution for the care of the insane, exclusively, is Virginia's. This institution was also the first in which provision was made for the colored insane, and its founding marked the beginning of the rational treatment of insanity in this country. This hospital, established in 1769, still exists as the Eastern State Hospital at Williamsburg.

The earliest known quarantine act was that passed by the General Assembly of Virginia in 1722, and was for the prime purpose of keeping yellow fever out of the ports of the province.

In the latter half of the century, inoculation for the prevention of smallpox was extensively resorted to in the colonies, having been introduced into Charleston, S. C., as early as 1738. Many hospitals for the purpose were opened throughout the country, the first in Virginia, being that of Dr. Walter McClurg, at Williamsburg. Mrs. George Washington was inoculated while in Philadelphia, as was Thomas Jefferson, who went there for the purpose in 1776. It is said that General Washington seriously contemplated having the whole army inoculated, as smallpox was more fatal to the troops than the weapons of the enemy, but the project was never carried out. The practice of the use of calomel in the after treatment of inoculation, as originated by Huxham, was introduced into this country by a Dr. Thomas, of Virginia, and is said to have reduced the mortality from one in one hundred to one in one thousand.

When the Nineteenth century dawned upon the infant, but rapidly developing nation, the standard of the medical profession was advancing along with the other lines of progress. A review of the contributions of the South to medical progress and literature shows that a constantly increasing number of physicians, who were, practically, all native-born and well-educated, were contributors. In the literature of the period (1790 to 1860) may be found

descriptions of the numerous epidemics which occurred; other articles treat of the indigenous fevers
and other diseases, and many describe surgical cases
and operations. While it is unfortunately the fact
that many of our ablest physicians wrote little or
nothing, and failed to give the world the benefit of
their knowledge, many of the articles published are
of great interest, and are valuable contributions to
medical and surgical literature.

The names of a few of the contributors, with a
mention of their contributions, will be made in the
following pages, as examples of the highest type of
the Southern physician and surgeon and their work.
Many others, not a few of whom are equally as de-
serving as those mentioned, are worthy of their
names, deeds and writings being here recorded, did
only the length of this article permit. Convenience
only has been consulted in the selection of the names
used.

An excessive use of the lancet was one of the chief
therapeutic errors of the period, Dr. Benjamin Rush
being the foremost advocate of the practice. Pro-
tests against these excessive bleedings were beginning to be heard, and among the first to inveigh
against the error were some Southern physicians,
notably Dr. B. W. Dudley, of Kentucky, Dr. William
Hubbard, of Virginia, and Dr. Elisha C. Dick, of
Alexandria, one of the consultants in the last illness
of Washington, in whose case he strenuously opposed further resort to the lancet, advocating, instead, tracheotomy, but was overruled.

Not until the early decades of the last century was
typhoid fever recognized as a distinct disease, having been confounded with typhus, and in malarial
districts, with remittent fever, and here again we
find Southern physicians at the front in helping to
bring order out of chaos. Dr. J. P. Mettauer and

Dr. Alexander Somervail, of Virginia, and others of the Southern states wrote valuable articles showing that they recognized a variety of continued fever which was neither typhus nor remittent fever.

In 1785 a Virginian had the honor and renown of receiving the Harveian prize for that year. The prize was awarded to John Lee, of Virginia, for his essay, *An Inquiry Into the Properties of Opium.*

In the period of years between 1785 and 1875, two native-born surgeons lived and practiced surgery in Virginia, and deservedly acquired more than national fame. The older and first of these was William Baynham (1749-1814), of Essex county, a profound anatomist and skillful surgeon, of whom it was said that, with the single exception of Dr. P. S. Physick, of Philadelphia, he was the only surgeon in the country up to that time who had done anything for the improvement of his calling. He made, while studying in London, some original discoveries in human anatomy, and there was scarcely any known operation in surgery that he did not successfully perform. His operations for extra-uterine gestation alone made for him an enduring name in the annals of surgery.

The second of these, Dr. John Peter Mettauer (1787-1875), of Prince Edward county, was probably the most remarkable man the profession of this country has produced. He deserves to rank at the head of the list of the surgeons of this country up to his time, while, as a matter of fact, surgical history gives him mere mention. So great did his reputation become in a very few years after his graduation that patients flocked to him from all the surrounding country, and even from other and distant states. The number of young men desiring to study under him was so large that he established, and maintained for a number of years, a medical school, and graduated quite a number of physicians. He used these young men as assistants and nurses. In the fifty years of his most active work he performed an enormous number of operations of every variety, in the last week of his life performing three operations, one of which was for cataract. He was the first in Virginia and one of the very first in America to operate for cleft palate, which he did in 1827. However, the work for which he is entitled to the greatest renown was his successful operation for vesico-vaginal fistula, a terrible affliction that had never before been cured. He did his first successful operation for this condition in August, 1838, antedating Sims, who has received all the credit, by a number of years. He was, too, a most voluminous author, and published an enormous number of articles dealing with almost every subject in surgery and medicine, for he was a very able physician as well. A man of great versatility, he could invent and devise, and when he needed some new instrument or appliance he devised and made it. Truly, he was in deed and word a contributor to medicine and surgery.

Another benefactor of his race was Dr. Ephraim McDowell (1771-1830), a native of Virginia, but later of Kentucky. He acquired fame as a surgeon, and has the enviable credit of being the first surgeon to successfully do an ovariotomy at a time when the operation was universally considered impossible. He did this in 1809, when it required the highest degree of moral and physical courage to make the attempt, so unjustifiable was the operation held to be. Had he failed, his life would have been in danger. The published report of his two first operations, both successful, excited much comment at home and abroad, their authenticity being doubted and the author's veracity questioned. ''A back set-

tlement in America—Kentucky—has beaten the
mother country, nay, Europe itself, with all the
boasted surgeons thereof, in the fearful operation of
gastronomy with the extraction of diseased ova-
ries." The writer, the editor of an English medical
journal, here speaks the truth, but in a bitter spirit
of sarcasm, as is shown by another sentence: "Our
skepticism, and we must confess it, is not yet removed." This operation, now one of the best established and most successful, has proved a Godsend
to innumerable women in saving immeasurable suffering and many thousand lives.

Dr. William C. Daniel, of Georgia, has the credit
of priority in the employment of extension in the
treatment of fractures of the thigh. Dr. Charles
McCreary, of Kentucky, in 1811, performed the
operation of excision of the entire clavicle. In 1816
Dr. John King, of South Carolina, did one of the
most remarkable operations on record. In a case of
abdominal pregnancy, in which the head of the fœtus
presented in the pelvis outside the vagina, he in-
cised the walls of the latter, and while pressure
was exerted on the abdomen above, applied the
forceps, and had the rare good fortune to save both
mother and child.

Dr. J. L. E. W. Shecut, of South Carolina, was a
contributor of some valuable observations on medical subjects. His most important articles may be
found in his *Medical and Philosophical Essays*
(Charleston, 1819), one of which is an account of the
yellow fever epidemic of 1817.

*An Account of a Pestilential Fever As It Pre-
vailed In Wilmington, N. C.,* was published by Dr.
A. J. DeRossett, of North Carolina, in 1790 (*Medical
Repository*), and is an early paper of interest. Dr.
Mathias Lengue and Dr. John Newman, of North

Carolina, published some valuable articles in the last decade of the Eighteenth century.

Dr. Benjamin W. Dudley, a native of Virginia, but a citizen of Kentucky, was a surgeon and teacher of extended reputation. He was noted for his successful operations for vesical calculus, an operation which he performed 225 times, and was probably only surpassed by J. P. Mettauer with his 400 similar operations. Dudley was declared in England to be the foremost lithotomist of the Nineteenth century. He was a pronounced opponent of bleeding, and never failed to inveigh against the practice. He taught anatomy and surgery in the Transylvanian University. Prior to 1828 he trephined for epilepsy in several cases, with 60 per cent. of recoveries.

Dr. William McDowell, of Virginia, published, in 1828, an essay *On the Pathology of Bone,* in which he advanced views far ahead of his time, and advocated the principles of treatment of the present day in diseases of bone.

Dr. Paul F. Eve, a native of Georgia, who in his early career was a volunteer surgeon in the Polish Rebellion, was a noted surgeon and teacher. During his career he was professor of surgery in several Southern medical schools, and published over 600 articles on professional subjects, of which mention may be made of the following: *Remarkable Cases in Surgery; What the South and West Have Done for American Surgery;* and a *Report of Twenty Amputations and Thirteen Resections of the Hip-Joint By Confederate Surgeons.* He is believed to have been the first American surgeon to have done an hysterectomy, and he performed many of the most difficult operations in surgery.

Dr. Daniel Drake, born in Kentucky in 1788, was a very noted physician of the West. He was at one time professor of medicine in the Transylvanian

University. He published numerous works and papers, notably, *The Climate and Diseases of Cincinnati* (1810); *Diseases of the Interior Valley of North America, etc.* (1850); and *Practical Essays on Medical Education and the Medical Profession in the United States* (1832), a book well worth reading to-day.

Dr. Henry Miller, of Kentucky, introduced the method of applying caustics in solution to the cavity of the uterus by means of applicators wrapped in cotton. He was the first in the West to use anæsthetics in midwifery.

Dr. J. C. Nott, of Alabama, a prominent surgeon, excised a diseased coccyx for coccygeal neuralgia to the entire relief of his patient. He was the first to describe the disease and its remedy, which he did in 1844.

An abdominal surgeon of note and a teacher of obstetrics was Dr. Robert Battey, of Georgia, who did many difficult operations, of which some were original. He was also the author of numerous papers.

An History of Medicine and Surgery in Georgia has been written and published by Dr. L. B. Grandy of that state.

Vaccine virus was first brought to the United States in 1799, when Dr. Jenner sent Dr. Waterhouse, of Boston, a small quantity, and from the latter Thomas Jefferson obtained some, from which he supplied his own and other states. Vaccination was received with much favor in the South, the opposite being the case in the North, and immediately took the place of inoculation, many Southern physicians writing articles setting forth its efficacy and advantages.

In the earliest decades of the Nineteenth century Louisiana, in Champ Manuoir, Trabue, Randolph,

Davidson, Marshall, P. G. Thomas, E. H. Barton, J. A. Riviere and M. M. Halphen, furnished contributors of valuable papers on yellow and other fevers and diseases.

In later years the Louisiana profession has had some markedly able men, as examples of whom we may mention Drs. S. E. Chaillé and Joseph Jones, physicians, and Rudolph Matas and Edmond Souchon, surgeons.

It is now acknowledged that the priority in the use of a general anæsthetic in the performance of an operation belongs to Dr. Crawford Long, of Georgia, he having first used ether for this purpose in 1842 (March).

Dr. Eli Geddings, of North Carolina, was the first operator to pare the edges in operating for lacerations of the cervix uteri.

In 1852 Dr. Marion Sims, a native of South Carolina, but then a resident of Alabama, published his essay on vesico-vaginal fistula, and introduced a speculum which developed a new principle of examination. Mettauer, of Virginia, had successfully operated for this condition for years prior to this, and had described his operation in the journals, but the profession did not seem to appreciate the value of the operation until Sims introduced his simple method. It is probable that the ease with which the operation could be done with Sims' speculum, and the fact that he went to New York and demonstrated it, had much to do with this. To Dr. Sims and his coadjutor, Dr. T. A. Emmet, who was a native of Virginia, the world owes much for their work in the advancement of gynæcology, and in establishing and disseminating an exact and systematic method of studying the diseases of women, much facility in so doing being afforded by the use of the Sims speculum. His fame, most deservedly, became world-wide. Every physician in the land, and in the South particularly, should read Sims' *Autobiography.*

Dr. Norwood, of South Carolina, was the first to call attention to the value of preparations of the plant, *veratrum viride,* as a vascular sedative, now regarded as of great value in the treatment of puerperal eclampsia.

The first amputation of the hip-joint done in the United States was by Dr. Brashear, of Kentucky, early in the Nineteenth century.

Drs. Thomas Penniston, E. D. Fenner, E. S. Chaillé and W. Stone, of Louisiana, were noted experts in yellow fever, and Dr. Joseph Holt in quarantine and disinfection.

One of the greatest discoveries of recent years, that of the true means of the transmission of yellow fever through the medium of the mosquito, was made by a Southerner, a native of Virginia, Dr. Walter Reed, of the United States army.

Dr. Greenville, a native of Virginia, who became a prominent surgeon of Texas, and was professor of surgery in the Texas Medical College at Galveston, was the deviser of several valuable inventions applicable to surgery. He was also a yellow fever expert, and the author of a work on *Yellow Fever and Malarial Diseases, Embracing An History of Yellow Fever in Texas.*

The devotion to duty and the heroism of the profession was never better illustrated than in the time of that terrible epidemic of yellow fever in Norfolk and Portsmouth, Va., in 1855. While this epidemic was only one of many that have visited Southern cities, it serves well to illustrate the fact that when duty called the profession has not been found wanting. Beginning about July 7 and lasting more than three months, it depopulated the two cities, causing 2,000 deaths in Norfolk alone, a mortality of one in three of the white inhabitants, and was equally fatal in Portsmouth. During this terrible visitation, not only did the local physicians remain steadfastly at the post of duty, but from North and South, and from the latter particularly, came heroic men, physicians and others, "who for naught but the love of their race, flew into the jaws of death." No less than forty-five physicians are known to have filled martyr's graves, giving their lives to the cause of stricken humanity. Did space permit, their names should be here recorded.

In the War of Secession.

We come now to the War of Secession, with all the suffering and horrors entailed by it upon the Southern people. Like their brothers of the rank and file, the medical corps of the army answered well and truly their country's call. Coming from civil life and practice, for there were comparatively few who had had experience in the United States army, how rapidly and well did they adapt themselves to the requirements of army life and practice. Says Dr. Hunter McGuire, and no one was better qualified to judge than he:

"I can say with truth that, before the war ended some of the best military surgeons in the world could be found in the Confederate Army. His scant supply of medicines and hospital stores made him fertile in expedients of every kind. I have seen him search field and forest for plants and flowers whose medicinal virtues he understood and could use. The pliant bark of a tree made him a good tourniquet; the juice of a green persimmon, a styptic; a knitting-needle, with its point sharply bent, a teanculum; and a penknife, in his hand, a scalpel and bistoury. I have seen him break off one prong of a common table fork, bend the point of the other prong, and with it elevate the bone in depressed fracture of the skull, and save life. * * * Years before we were formally told of Nelaton's method of inverting the body in chloroform narcosis, I have seen it practised by the Confederate surgeon. * * * Many of the medical officers of this corps were killed or wounded on the field. * * * During the terrible six days which followed the retreat from Richmond, the medical men, by their unswerving devotion to duty and cheerful support, contributed no little to inspire the heroism which turned our defeat into honor, and made Appomattox one of the proudest memories of the war."

Many remarkable operations were done and valuable contributions to the literature of military surgery were made by Confederate surgeons, some of which are to be found in the *Confederate States' Medical and Surgical Journal,* which was published in Richmond, Va., from January, 1864, to January, 1865, and in other publications.

Two interesting historical facts may be related in connection with the Medical College of Virginia. It was the first medical school established south of the Potomac that attracted Southern students from the Northern colleges in any considerable number. Again, during the War of Secession, it was the only medical school in the Confederacy to continue its work, except the University of Virginia, which only graduated five men during the period. Two sessions annually were held, and a supply of surgeons for the army thus kept up.

Since the War.

In the period of nearly half a century which has elapsed since the war, the South has not fallen behind in her contribution of able men to the profession, men who have made and are making their mark in all departments of medical science, and who are doing their full share in its advancement. Space does not permit the mention of names or contributions, but post-bellum literature teems with both.

No more important subject has engaged the attention of the profession of late years than that of higher medical education, and it is gratifying to observe that the Southern profession is doing its part to bring about a standard to which it may point with pride. It may be here observed that the University of Georgia, as early as 1835, advocated an association for the purpose of bringing about an elevation of the standard of medical education, and the first object in view in the organization of the American Medical Association was a similar one. (See article on MEDICAL EDUCATION, Volume X.)

No one means to the end has done half so much towards accomplishing the purpose as the establishment by the various states of boards of examiners, for by this means the inferior colleges have been forced to elevate their standard of requirements in order to graduate men of sufficient education to pass the examinations of these boards.

At present the great object to be attained is the elevation of the preliminary requirements for entrance upon the study of medicine, or, in other words, that the applicant should possess a liberal academic education in order to enter a college of medicine. This object is gradually being attained and, ultimately, the end will be accomplished.

No account, however brief, of the contributions of the South to medicine and surgery would be complete were no mention made of the professional men she has given to other parts of the country. Let us name, in conclusion, just a few of these physicians. Such men, for instance, as Nathaniel Chapman, William E. Horner, John K. Mitchell, Thomas D. Mutter, Joseph Hartshorne and Joseph Price, of Philadelphia; T. A. Emmet, R. C. M. Page, S. D. Powell, L. C. Gray, W. G. Wilie and J. A. Wyeth, of New York, and a host of others who have migrated to various cities of the country and have "acted well their part wherever they were." The army, navy and marine hospital service, too, have had in their Southern members some of their very best officers.

BIBLIOGRAPHY.—Beck, J. B.: *Historical Sketch of American Medicine before the Revolution;* Billings, J. S.: and others: *A Century of American*

Medicine, 1776 *to* 1876; Davis, N. S.: *Contributions to the History of Medical Education and Medical Institutions in the United States;* Da Costa, J. M.: *Physicians of the Last Century;* Dennis, F. S.: *A System of Surgery* (Chapter on the *History of Surgery* by J. S. Billings); Forest: *Great Pestilence in Virginia;* Gross: S. D.: *American Medical Biography;* Hening: *Statutes at Large* (Vols. I. and IV.); Johnston, George Ben: *A Sketch of Dr. John Peter Mettauer of Virginia;* Slaughter, R. M.: *History of Medicine and Surgery in Virginia* (Unpublished); Tennent: *Epistles to Richard Mead;* Thacher, James: *Medical Biography with History of Medical Science in the United States;* Toner, J. M.: *Medical Men of the American Revolution;* Watson, I. A.: *Physicians and Surgeons of America; Medical Repository* (1817, Vol. III., containing report of case operated upon by John King of Edisto Island, S. C.); Various articles in medical journals and the transactions of state societies.

ROBERT MADISON SLAUGHTER,
Member Virginia Board of Medical Examiners; Author of History of Medicine and Surgery in Virginia.

CHAPTER XIX.

THE SOUTH'S CONTRIBUTIONS TO MUSIC.

1732-1800.

THE story of Southern music, as a part of the general history of American art, has never been adequately told. The making of the books has been left to Northern and New England investigators, and they have naturally laid stress on the sources of the sections with which they were most familiar. Elson and Ritter, the two great compilers of the musical data of American history, failing to collect the facts of early concerts and opera life in the Southern colonies, have filled their pages with the minutest references to happenings in New York, Philadelphia and New England, and in neglecting to collate the Southern statistics have lost all perspective in their induced generalizations. It is undoubtedly true that the cavaliers of Virginia and the English Huguenot settlers of Carolina made no attempt to absorb into their music any local color from the new world. It remained a more or less foreign thing in a strange land, yet it is also undoubtedly true that the taste of the early Southerners was more refined and their performance more artistic than were the narrowly limited and strictly pious utterances of the *Bay Psalm Book* and its grace-giving predecessors.

But although no indigenous music phase evolved, concerts were given in the Southern colonies which would have pleased the modern educated ear far more than the tuneless and timeless praises to the Almighty in New England, where secular music was anathematized as frivolous and sacrilegious. In

Carolina, Virginia and Maryland there were no such
religious and musical prejudices, so that the trans-
planting of English musical culture to the new world
was not thwarted here by prohibiting Scriptural
quotations.

In thus shifting the stress of our early musical
life to the South, it will be necessary to cite some
facts in order to win conviction for so unorthodox
a conclusion. From the several dates of colonial
settlement until about 1725 there was practically no
music, save such as new settlers in a savage country
can find time, heart, and throat for. These men, although in a barbarous land, were not barbarians
themselves. Many were educated and refined—no
doubt some were musically cultivated—and as soon
as room was found on the small vessels that bound
them to the mother country, it is not surprising to
find mention made in inventories of imported organs, violins and harpsichords.

The culture of the South was more refined, but it
must be admitted that the seriousness of New England was more creative. If a typical American
school of composition can be alleged even to-day—
which is a very open question—there is little doubt
but that its roots will be found in the ear-splitting,
but—to them—soul-satisfying hymns of the Puritans. The music of the Southern cavaliers and
royalists was a luxury and an adornment of society,
while the singing of the Puritans and Pilgrims was
an intimate expression of their deeply protesting religion. Therefore, it is only natural that the latter
should have taken root and become truly American.
For, until music is regarded seriously and is used
to express some vital process, it is unlikely that a
really national school of art can arise.

There is record of an organ imported into Carolina in 1723, and it is probable that this was not the

first instrument of the kind in the South. An old
colonial inventory of 1740 includes, among other
articles of luxury, "eighteen pieces of painting, five
hundred pounds worth of books, and a violin." A
study of the files of Eighteenth century newspapers[*]
shows clearly that the first large musical activity
of artistic significance on these shores was developed in Charleston, S. C. This city, before the end
of the Eighteenth century, had over 20,000 inhabitants,[†] who bore a wide reputation for culture and
good taste due to the close contact with aristocratic
life in England and the wealth of the traders and
planters. In the *South Carolina Gazette* for Satur-
day, April 8-15, 1732, appears this notice: "On
Wednesday next will be a *consort of musick* at the
Council Chamber for the benefit of Mr. Salter."
The publication of the *Gazette* was only begun in
January of this year, and, in all probability, concerts had taken place considerably before this date,
for that they were then well established is evidenced
by the fact that in the summer and fall of 1732 three
more "consorts" were advertised. The programmes of this early date were never published—
nor were they in Europe—but since the colonials
were ambitious to do all things as London did, it is
probable that Corelli, Purcell, Handel and Gemini-
ani were among the favorite composers. It is by no
means certain that the concerts advertised were the
only concerts that took place. Indeed, it is far from
likely that this was the case, for chance after-men-
tion now and then reveals instances in which there
was no antecedent notice. Two concerts are advertised for 1733, one each for 1735, 1737, 1738—all
"for the benefit of Mr. Salter," which merely means

---

[*]See the invaluable source-book of O. G. Sonneck, *Early Concert-Life in America* (Leipzig. 1907).
[†]Statistics of population in this article are from estimates published in Seventh Census, 1850.

that this gentleman was the business manager and promoter of the enterprise. The first song recital of America—"none but English and Scotch songs" were sung—took place in Charleston on Feb. 26, 1733. Other concerts are noticed in frequent succession, as many as four in 1734. There are many lacunæ from this time up to 1751, probably due to a failure to advertise for some reason, since many musicians are mentioned as coming to Charleston and settling there during this period. Sacred music was taught, and "Psalmody according to the exact rule." Concerts are fashionable, and if "accompanied by obliging behavior they may bring in three or four hundred guineas per annum." An English surgeon, Dr. Milligan, after a visit to the provinces, published in London that the ladies "are fond of dancing, sing well, and play upon harpsichord and guitar."

A decade later occurred an event of first importance in American musical history. Historians of music are accustomed to cite the "Stoughton Musical Society of Massachusetts," founded in 1786, as our pioneer musical society, but the "St. Cœcilia Society" of Charleston has that honor, coming into the world in 1762 as a serious musical organization, provided with an elaborate set of rules and regulations.* It had a competent orchestra of gentlemen performers who had sufficient skill, and professionals who were engaged by the season. Its managers went far afield to secure the best talent in the market. This advertisement appears in the *Boston Evening Post* for June 17, 1771:

"CHARLESTOWN, South Carolina, April 11, 1771.
"The St. Cœcilia Society give notice that they will engage with, and give suitable encouragement to musicians properly qualified to

---

*See *South Carolina Historical and Genealogical Magazine*, 1900, pp. 223-227.

perform at their concert, provided they apply on or before the first day of October. The performers they are in want of are: a first and second violin, two hautboys and a bassoon, whom they are willing to agree with for one, two or three years.

"JOHN GORDON, President.

"THOMAS LN. SMITH, Vice-President."

This society's concerts were rarely noticed in the local papers, since they were not open to the general public. Until 1822, with an interruption during the Revolutionary War, concerts were given regularly every fortnight during the season, and music was its first and only love. After that date it became a purely social organization such as the Philadelphia Assembly. Josiah Quincy, of Boston, writing of a Southern journey in 1773, describes the music of one of these concerts as "grand, especially the bass viol and French horns." A Frenchman, whose salary was 500 guineas, was the best violin soloist he had ever heard, and many of the performers were amateurs like Gen. C. C. Pinckney, who played the cello, and Ralph Izard. That he thought the respect and attention paid to music were more sincere in Charleston than in his own Boston is evidenced by his observation that the ladies are "in taciturnity during the performance greatly before our ladies; in noise and flirtation after the music is over pretty much on a par."* In 1792 Maj. Thomas Pinckney, then Minister to England, was requested by the managers to send out "one grand pianoforte and twenty pounds worth of the best modern concert music." President Washington, speaking in his journal of his visit to Charleston in 1791, wrote that he went to a concert. His soul seems to have been more impressionable to feminine inspiration than to musical enkindlement, for he commented: "There were

---

*Quoted by Mrs. St. Julien Ravenel in *Charleston, the Place and the People.*

400 ladies, the number and appearance of wch. exceeded anything I had ever seen.''

The young men of the day were often educated in England, the Southern tide-water strip was in close relationship with the mother country, and music and instruments were now a precious portion of many a shipload.

''Vauxhall Gardens,'' in the usual imitation of London fashion, were opened in 1767, ''with concerts of vocal and instrumental music.'' An Orphæus Society is mentioned in 1772. ''Benefit'' concerts are advertised more or less frequently by Peter Valton, Franceschini, P. A. von Hagen, Junr., and others.

After the war musical activity revived with an increased interest. Theatrical companies visited Carolina and the local and itinerant musicians of the older concerts found competitors in the members of these troupes, who improved the shining hours of their stay by organizing benefits for themselves, assisted by local talent and by other members of the troupe.

From 1793 to the end of the century music flourished like a green bay tree. In 1794 the Harmonic Society appears. English opera was introduced. French and Italian opera was sung by a French company which had escaped the Revolutionists in San Domingo. These companies joined forces with the local musicians, and ''full pieces'' were performed with well-balanced orchestras of thirty instruments. At this period in opera were heard the works of the English Arne, Atwood, Shield, and the French and the Italian Rousseau, Grétry, Cimarosa, Paisiello. In concert the compositions of Stamitz, Gossec, Haydn, Gyrowetz, Pleyel, Mozart, Gluck. London herself could offer no more. On

Dec. 17, 1795, the following typical programme was given:

ACT 1st

SYMPHONIE..Hayden
SONG, by Mrs. Pownall
CONCERTO ON THE BASSO, by Mr. Le Roy................... . ...Pleyel
DUETT, by Mrs. Pownall and Mr. Bergman
LA CHASSE................................... ....Stamitz

ACT 2D

SYMPHONIE..Pleyel
CONCERTO, PIANOFORTE, Mr. De Villers.....................Kotzeluch
FRENCH SONG, by Mr. Pownall
CONCERTO VIOLIN, by Mrs. Pownall
OVERTURE, THE BATTLE OF IVRY...............................Martini
    N. B.—Between the acts Mr. Le Roy will perform several pieces on the Spanish guitar. Silence is requested during the performance.

The French Revolution had driven many good musicians to seek exile in America, and this remarkable programme is an index of the good taste of the period. In 1773 a Grand Musical Festival, consisting of "the celebrated Stabat Mater of Doctor Haydn," was perhaps the first use of the term "Musical Festival," which has become so important a movement in our day.

These are a few of the facts gleaned from the precious records of the Charleston Library. They could doubtless be paralleled for the last quarter of the century in the case of other Southern cities, if only their newspaper files were in such excellent preservation. Music in Charleston was earlier cultivated than in other Southern cities, and had, down to the Nineteenth century, a more vigorous life, but Maryland and Virginia also enjoyed concert and opera towards the end of the century. The *Maryland Gazette* for Jan. 24, 1793, announces a "musical performance" at Annapolis. Baltimore, outgrowing Annapolis, from 1784 on enjoyed sporadic concerts and regular seasons of subscriptions after 1788. Symphonies, overtures and various forms of chamber and vocal music appear on the programmes. Alexander Reinagle, the harpsichordist and conductor, Mrs. Oldmixon and Miss Broadhurst, the singers, J. H. Schmidt, the organist, contributed to the entertainment. Gallic influences after the French Revolution was marked until 1798, when, for political reasons, the whole of America suffered a reaction against that country. German, Italian and English musicians were also here in numbers and worked together harmoniously. Our music then, as now, was distinguished for its cosmopolitan character: all of Europe was drawn upon. In Virginia, Williamsburg, Richmond, Fredericksburg, Alexandria, Norfolk and Petersburg all had music at an early date. George Washington in his ledger noted his expense for concerts at Williamsburg in 1765 and 1767. Fredericksburg has a concert advertised in the *Virginia Gazette* for Jan. 10, 1784, a concert by the "Harmonic Society," which proves a well-established and organized activity. Petersburg is first noticed in 1795, Richmond in the same year, Alexandria in 1793, Norfolk in 1796.

Savannah, Ga., had a remarkable musical life for her size. In 1766 the *Georgia Gazette* mentions the usual "benefit concert of musick," and in 1796 a "grand concert" is heralded with all the trappings of symphony, song and concerto. New Orleans probably had concerts in the last decade of the century. In 1791 a company of French comedians, refugees from San Domingo, began a series of operatic performances there. The Louisianians have found opera necessary to their happiness ever since.

These dusty facts have been thus itemized in order to lay carefully the foundations for the novel and unpopular contention that the South had a comparatively rich and ripe musical experience before New England had found it in her conscience to open a very ready ear to the seductions of secular music. This conclusion is reinforced by contemporary letters and by all tradition, besides by the survival of a considerable quantity of printed copies of music of an early date. The music is such as the cultivated taste of England approved in the Eighteenth century.

Although the population of the Southern colonies was more heterogeneous than is superficially supposed, in general the English element absorbed the others, and so the service of the Established Church of England stamped its characteristic on Southern church music. The Low Church tendencies of Southern churchmanship were, in part, Anglophobic results of the Revolution. Yet, until 1807, there were choirs of surpliced boys in the South, and at times bands supported the organ, a performance which afterwards, and even nowadays, would be good cause for a parochial secession.

1800-1861.

All attempts at composition were nothing but English transferences, and there was little of that. The first American composer, rough, ungrammatical, but vigorous and native, was William Billings, of Boston. One of his contemporaries, Andrew Law (1748-1821), himself a composer of hymn-tunes, did some pioneer work in the South as a teacher of singing. He seems to have been the first connecting link between the Southern colonies with their cultured exotic music, and the stammerings of American composition in the Billings School of Boston. Law, with the hopeful desire of providing an easy means for teaching his refractory pupils how to read, invented an odd system of notation which abandoned the use of the conventional staff with its five lines. He was one of the first to give the air or tune to the soprano part. The usual habit had been to give the contralto and melody parts to male voices

and the tenor to women. The school thus brought
into connection with the South produced a regiment
of psalm-tune composers. It was but a pulling infant, but, at least, it was alive.

Music—and good music—was the ordinary enjoyment of the plantation household. Many planters
brought teachers from abroad, some English, some
German, Swiss or French. The harpsichord, piano,
violin, cello, flute and guitar were domesticated on
rice and cotton plantations. Voices were intelligently trained by these foreign teachers. The
memoirs and 'letters of the period almost invariably
depict home scenes to the accompaniment of music.
Perhaps nowhere in America during pre-Revolutionary days was there so vivid an enjoyment of the
best that music had to offer. And this love of music
continued, in varying mood, up to the War of
Secession.

Why then did not a school of native composition
arise? A general answer would be, Why has America never, to this day, developed a really national
musical expression? The more specific answer is,
of course, to be found in the aristocratic construction of Southern Patriarchal Society. To write
worthy music requires, first, a long and studious
application to the laws of its grammar, and second,
an impulse of genius which is usually attended by
a profound personal or social crisis. The rich
Southerner could acquire the first in England. His
condition of life was not apt to make him suffer
the second. The poorer man of the middle class
might have suffered the second, but had no opportunity to acquire the first. When the wars of Revolution and Secession came and the stimulus of
national tragedy was at hand, the cultured men who
could have made the music were shouldering the
muskets. There were no men to spare; none to

permit of a body of inactive spectators, with feelings wrought to a high pitch and with leisure to express themselves artistically.

In the first two decades of the Nineteenth century a new movement is inaugurated in Massachusetts, fostered by the Stoughton (1786) and Handel and Haydn (1815) Societies. Oratorios are published and collections of music which far surpass any previous American attempts. The South furnished the man who made the best of these collections and whose achievements swung American composition from the Billings and Law psalmody to the broader ambitions of the last century. "The father of American church music" was Dr. Lowell Mason, born at Medfield, Mass., Jan. 8, 1792, who spent his youth and young manhood (until 1826) in Savannah, Ga. He was, at first, only an amateur musician and studied composition with F. L. Abel. Some of his sacred music came to the attention of Dr. G. K. Jackson, "the severest critic in Boston" (Elson). Jackson wrote: "It is much the best book I have seen published in this country, and I do not hesitate to give it my most decided approbation." It found a publisher in Boston, becoming "The Handel and Haydn Society Collection of Church Music, harmonized for Three or Four Voices, with figured Bass, for Organ and Pianoforte." Mason's name is absent from the title page at his own request. He explained: "I was then a bank officer in Savannah and did not wish to be known as a musical man, as I had not the least thought of ever making music a profession." He realized in five years over $4,000 from his copyright, and then determined to make music his profession.

He went to Boston on a guarantee of $2,000 a year and soon became president of the Handel and Haydn Society. The contrapuntist, Hauptmann, said that the "harmonies of his tunes were dignified and church-like, and that the counterpoint was good, plain, singable and melodious." Charles C. Perkins, in the *History of the Handel and Haydn Society*, asserts his peculiar fitness to lead American music in these words: "First and foremost he was not so very much superior to the members as to be unreasonably impatient at their shortcomings. Second, he was a born teacher who, by hard work, had fitted himself to give instruction in singing. Third, he was one of themselves, a plain, self-made man who could understand them and be understood of them." This third reason is an interesting commentary on his Savannah environment.

He published as many as fifty manuals, instruction books and musical collections. Even after he had gone to Boston to live, his influence was felt in the South through his "Teachers' Conventions," which assembled representatives from many states and returned them missionaries. His adoption of the Pestalozzian system over the old psalm tune method of singing brought about the "Boston Academy of Music," an institution for teaching vocal music. Its propaganda influenced teaching in the South, for the third annual report (1835) of the Academy states, "Letters have been received from persons in Georgia, South Carolina, Virginia * * * Missouri, Tennessee * * * Maryland * * * asking for information relative to measures which they ought to adopt in order to introduce music as a branch of education into the communities where they live." It is interesting to note that the programmes of the St. Cecilia Society in Charleston contained many names of the "first families" of the state and province. The list of Billings's class in Boston is no such Debrett of Massachusetts.

Popular taste in instrumental music in the early

years of the Nineteenth century was generally bad—
but popular taste in America still is.   There seems
to have been a revival of those noisy and unmusical
"battle pieces" and marches that must have made
the days—and nights—of the early Eighteenth century in England hideous.   In proportion to the increased tone of the hammer of the pianoforte over
the goosequill of the spinet, this last period must
have been even more hideous.   *The Battle of New
Orleans* was a prime favorite.   *Yankee Doodle* and
Washington's March gave frequent delight to the
patriot who was so fortunate as not to be an artist
also.

The South has a passing connection with, though
no real claim on, Gottlieb Graupner, who could honestly be called the "Father of American orchestral
music."   He was a Hanoverian oboe player; he
spent some time in Charleston in orchestral work,
and in 1797 married a singer in that city.   He went
on to Boston and became the founder of the Boston
Philharmonic.   In the South musical taste seems to
have risen with the passing decades until the war
swept everything away.   Great artists like Ole Bull,
Grisi, Mario, Brignoli, the young Patti, were heard
in the larger cities.   In 1850 broke out what was
called the "Jenny Lind fever."   She toured the
country extensively, carrying everything before her.
Phenomenal prices and enormous crowds were her
generous portion, and enthusiasm such as even Patti
in her prime could not inspire greeted her in every
place.   Besides the New Orleans opera (of which
more later), Charleston and Baltimore from early
in the Nineteenth century shared with New York
several operatic troupes.   Even Boston, the cultured,
was passed by, for she was still obsessed with the
frivolous evil of secular music.   Only Handel and
Haydn and staid psalmody were safe.   Henry C.

Timm, born in Hamburg, Germany, in 1811, came to the United States in 1835. Writing for *Musical America,* he gives this account of his activities in the South:

" * * * I became musical director of a dramatic company; the orchestra consisted of fourteen musicians only. We went to Charleston, S. C., and played during the season of six months such operas as Mozart's *Marriage of Figaro* (Henry Bishop's version), Rossini's *La Gazza Ladra* and *Cinderella* (R. Lacy's version), *La Sonnambula,* and even *Freischütz,* and with the players in the orchestra! I had to write additional notes in both the wind and stringed instrumental parts, in order to cover the deficiencies caused by the missing parts. Yellow fever during the summer months was, at that time, a regular visitor at Charlestown and I went, therefore, with the company to Buffalo; and after another season in Charleston we went to Baltimore, where I played, during the six months we were there, the organ at the Episcopal Church. But before leaving for Charleston again a complimentary concert was given me at Baltimore, when I played Mendelssohn's Capriccio in B-minor, with a fairly complete orchestral accompaniment.

"A few days before the close of our third season in Charleston the theatre burned down. * * * On leaving Charleston I joined Signora Velane, an excellent singer, and Signor De Begnis, the original 'Figaro' in Rossini's *Il Barbiere.* We gave concerts in Norfolk and some other places in North Carolina (sic), but made little more than our expenses."

The musical taste of these days was formed more or less directly on New York, which had now established opera. A glance into the bound volumes of sheet music for piano of the before-the-war Southern home will soon reveal their musical gods. Rossini, Donizetti, Gluck, Beethoven, Mendelssohn, had displaced Handel and Haydn. *La Sonnambula, Norma, Orpheus and Eurydice, The Barber of Seville, Fidelio, Robert le Diable,* were among the operas whose selections were much played and admired. Beethoven was exalted to his rightful place at the summit of the musical Olympus, which is always a touchstone of sound appreciation. The Italian school was on the crest of the wave, although the English light opera had had seventy-five years of popularity. The musical experience of the South and of the whole country was distinctly broader and taste more catholic. By the thirties and forties troupes and single artists came from the continent of Europe to make money in the new world, and English supremacy was displaced.

Opera in New Orleans.

Long before anything more than occasional operettas were given in the North, New Orleans was sustaining a regular company in light musical farces and operatic pieces. It was the first American city to establish opera permanently. The French opera of New Orleans, although not of the same high standing as the New York opera of to-day or the national operas of Europe, has certainly been of the greatest importance in the musical life of the nation, and is the South's greatest institutional contribution towards it.

As early as 1791 the record begins. Just what pieces were performed in the first years is not ascertainable. At a theatre on St. Peter's Street in July, 1810, the *Barber of Seville* was sung by a French company, and in the next month a *Romeo and Juliet* was put on. In the usual careless habit of Southerners about preserving documents, the castes of none of the operas remain to us. In St. Philip's Street stood the Théâtre St. Philippe. In 1808 operas and ballets were given there. Entirely independent of New York taste and New York money, foreign artists were sought abroad and most of the operas sung in France were heard in this Paris of America. The theatre was unusually large and handsome, having "two circles and a parterre accommodating 700 persons with seats." In 1813 a grand opera house was completed. It was called the Théâtre d'Orléans, and soon attracted to itself the patronage of the other theatres. Four years of success ended with a fire that destroyed it. The splendid phœnix that arose from its ashes cost nearly $200,000, and was the finest theatre in America. In 1818-19 John Davis, from San Domingo, began there a triumphal career as impresario. For twenty-five years he presented the best French and Italian opera in a manner not unworthy of the highest praise. Scenery, costumes, mise-en-scène, were the best that could be secured abroad. The artists came from Paris in the fall and stayed through the season. Stars were not the main attraction; the companies were of a high general average and the musical scores were given complete—not cut, arranged and doctored—as they usually were in New York, to suit the limited capacities of singers and orchestra. Rossini, Mozart, Méhul, Boieldieu, Spontini, Auber, Meyerbeer, received entirely capable treatment. New York had an occasional taste of good opera from these French troupes as they went to and fro between seasons.

The opera was the focus of social life in the picturesque city, crowded with the belles and the gallants who filled New Orleans in "the season" from the plantations of Louisiana and Mississippi. Memoirs of that day never fail to mention the brilliant scene—the jewels and the beauty of the women, the dashing chivalry of the men, the perfection of the music.

In 1859 Mr. Boudouisqué was the moving spirit in the erection of a new opera house, still in existence, and in arrangement still the most beautiful in America. In 1866 the Théâtre d'Orléans burned down after an honorable life of fifty years of sincere and artistic endeavor and splendid achievement. The new opera of Mr. Boudouisqué took its place, and the two most brilliant seasons New Orleans had ever known were the two years before the knell of civil war.

Since the war the opera has changed hands frequently, and has never again been established on so sound a basis. The brothers Alhaiza made desperate efforts against odds of death and shipwreck to furnish opera in 1866-67, and one of them, Paul, did succeed in giving some Italian opera that year with Madame Patti-Strakosch (sister of Adelina Patti) as the star. Struggling against debt, the Opera House Association has at times emerged victorious for art, notably in '68, '72, '80. In recent years our standards of achievement in opera have advanced considerably with such performances as the Metropolitan Opera House Company, and later Mr. Hammerstein's company, have offered in New York. The relative importance of the New Orleans opera has therefore diminished. And yet, although in constantly precarious uncertainty as to box office success, it is still the great rendezvous of New Orleans society. Its chorus and orchestral work are not up to the highest modern standards, but the novelties of the French and Italian school have several times been heard in New Orleans before the New York managers have dared to present them—for instance, Puccini's *La Bohème*—and more than one singer has been introduced to fame in New Orleans and thence been introduced to fortune in New York. In light opera, Offenbach was an old friend to New Orleans long before New York cultivated him so zealously. Among the artists who have sung in New Orleans opera are Patti-Strakosch, Michat, Castelmary, Duonestre, Ambré, Pellini, Jourdan, Bouxmann.

On the whole, New Orleans can be justly proud of her record. She led America in giving opera a permanent home. During the luxurious years before the war, she was unstinted in her money and uncalculating in her demand for the best art. Only a few years ago it was possible for Ritter to write, "The Opera Comique, the refined unique form of lyrical comedy, as originally developed by French musical genius, is, with the exception of New Orleans, not much known, neither is it cultivated in the United States." The late reaction to French and Italian opera in New York nullifies that statement to-day, but the New Orleans opera was the pioneer. For instance, *La Fille du Regiment, Lucia di Lammermoor, Norma, Gemma di Vergy*, were, in 1843, introduced to New York by a French company from New Orleans. At present many of the favorites of the Opéra Comique in Paris, and of the new Italian school (Puccini, Leoncavallo, etc.), are creditably sung in the Crescent City; and with the rapid growth of wealth we may hope for even better things to come.

Two Great Composers.

The first American to win European notice in composition and performance was Louis Moreau Gottschalk, born in New Orleans of English-Creole parentage, May 8, 1829. With Dr. William Mason, son of Dr. Lowell Mason mentioned above, he marks the budding recognition of America in cosmopolitan music. His childhood boasts of all the prodigious feats usually ascribed to musical genius, for he played the organ in church at the precocious age of six! At thirteen he studied pianoforte under Stamaty in Paris. The Gallic capital was presently stirred into a furore over the young American. Chopin predicted the highest things for him; Berlioz called him a "consummate pianist." He toured France, Switzerland and Spain. It is related that in Spain a bull-fighter presented him with his sword and that the Infanta made a cake for him with her own hands. Orders and decorations without number were showered upon his Bohemian head. In 1853 he returned to America and began traveling as the great native virtuoso, playing his own compositions almost to the exclusion of other and more virile music. His technique was equal to all demands, his touch exceedingly lovely, and his rendition poetic, although, like Chopin, he sometimes fell as he inclined and became too sentimental. He appeared more than a thousand times in this country, and it is alleged gave eighty concerts in New York in one season—an astonishing number for those days certainly. His life was overcharged with the feverish atmosphere of footlights and green-room, and on Nov. 26, 1869, at forty years of age, he fell senseless while playing in Rio Janeiro, dying three weeks later.

Gottschalk was eminently a composer for piano. The larger forms did not suit his genius, although he wrote two operas (which were never performed), two symphonies and some marches scored for orchestra. In piano composition he is passionate, poetic, with Southern grace and tropical languor.

The Last Hope, of boarding-school popularity, is not typical of his highest reach. *Ossian* is worthy of him, and *Bamboula, Banjo, Le Bananier* are considered to have foremost rank. They are elaborations on negro and creole themes. A pseudo-school of young imitators sprang up after him, but soon withered away. In the first place, Gottschalk was too original for successful emulation. In the second place, his tongue, his education and half his birth were foreign. His compositions are distinct echoes of France and Spain, with too little Americanism in them to become foundations for a cis-atlantic type.

John Henry Wilcox, born in Savannah, Ga., in

L. M. Gottschalk

1827, may be mentioned here as an organist of some repute.

The South has given to music one of the greatest post-bellum composers of America in Frank Van der Stucken, born in Fredericksburg, Gillespie county, Tex., Oct. 15, 1858. His father, of Belgian descent, fought as a captain of cavalry in the Confederate army, and after the war removed to Antwerp. The boy studied music under good teachers and acquired considerable reputation as a composer. Grieg and Liszt admired him exceedingly. In 1884 he returned to America and has lived here ever since. He has been very active in directing choral societies and symphonic concerts, first in New York and then in Cincinnati, where he is now the most important musical figure. Twice he has played the part of missionary to Europe, taking the Arion Male Chorus on a tour in 1884 and directing a series of exclusively American programmes in Paris (at the Exposition) and other cities in 1889. As conductor of the Cincinnati Orchestra and dean of the Cincinnati College of Music (1897-03), he has done for the musical culture of Cincinnati what Thomas did for Chicago.

In composition he has created important works in the largest orchestral forms with all the novel devices and elaborate scoring of the most modern masters like Strauss and De Bussy. All the resources of the orchestra are taxed for effects of tone color and contrast. A symphonic prologue, *William Ratcliffe,* interpretative of Heine's poem, is of the ultramodern school. Explanatory motives, unaccustomed combinations, violent contrasts, freedom in form, dissonance and cacophony are employed to accompany a printed programme story. An early and beautiful composition in a less iconoclastic style, is his music for Shakespeare's *Tempest.* His

songs are much admired, though they are entirely
and sometimes too insistently "up to date," losing
charm in the strenuous intensity of the emotional
delineation.   There is probably no other man in the
West of his rank as a composer—and there are only
two or three in America.

Negro Music.

The plantation song of the Southern negro is the
only real development of folk-music that America
has known.   The Indian melody can hardly be included.   It belongs to a race that has come into no
contact with American civilized life, and need not
be considered in a sketch of Southern music.   But
the quaint melodies and fascinating rhythms of the
old-fashioned "befo'-de-war" darky of the rice and
cotton fields are not negligible.   They constitute a
rich field of melodic material for future composers,
and have already furnished themes for some important American compositions—Chadwick, in the
Scherzo of his Second Symphony, has used this
material; Dvorâk has constructed his *New World
Symphony* out of it; Gottschalk employs it in some
of his piano morceaux; Schoenfeld's Suite, op. 15,
has a plantation movement.

It is not at all likely that any considerable part of
this negro music was brought from Africa.   Fétis
(*Histoire Génerale de la Musique*) recognizes no
musical sense among the African tribes.   Captain
Burton (*The Lake Region of Central Africa*) describes their primitive monotonous cadences and
strongly nasalized recitatives.   He asserts that,
though they are "admirable timists and no mean
tunists," they have no creative originality and rest
satisfied with the ceaseless reiteration of a few
favorite forms.   They display a good deal of emo_
tion and often use the modes of mourning and dis_

tress. This primitiveness under the new conditions of American slave life developed into the plantation song which every Southerner familiar with the cotton field knows so well. The early barbaric but keen sense for rhythm and emotional voice-expression evolved into the odd religious syncopated laments. A great deal of nonsense has been written by various misunderstanding gentlemen of the North concerning the tragedy of soul which the Southern slave experienced and which he sang out to find comfort and refreshment from the sting of the lash. These writers read into the minor phrases of the melodies the bleeding heart of a persecuted race. It is time for such superficial statements to be corrected. The advance in artistry from the primitive African recitative to *Swing Low, Sweet Chariot,* or *Motherless Child,* is not accounted for by a stimulus of suffering in the lives of these people, but is the direct result of that marvelous imitative faculty which the race has always shown. The negro is a born copyist. He absorbed manners, customs, language, ideas of his new white neighbors with a facility that to every observant Southerner was perfectly obvious. This racial trait is still evident in a hundred ways. Where then did he get the pattern to copy? The stuff out of which his songs are composed was the imported raw material of Scotch, Irish and English songs which came to the South with the early colonists and have disappeared, except in this form. In addition, many of his songs are transformed Protestant and Congregational hymn tunes. In Louisiana the French influence is perceptible. In the Mississippi Delta the life of the river-boat leaves its traces. Occasionally a song is heard which, with its intervals and slurs that defy transcription, is probably, in part, indigenous to Africa. Even in this class it is practically impossible to determine how much is African and how much is simply the result of primitive uncertainty of tonality (vid. Parry, *Evolution of Music*, chapter on "Folk Music") in using the later material. That the negro had a latent musical gift cannot be denied, for the plantation songs have charming melodic character and irresistible rhythmical attractiveness. The potential musical capacity of the race seized on the material offered with avidity— under the favorable conditions of a temperately warm climate and in contact with a generally friendly civilized race—and has produced the only body of folk-song certainly American, one which is not so far inferior to those of many of the European nations. The melodic phrase is often artistically wrought, the contrasts are well set off, and the rhythm is varied, yet sufficiently law-abiding. Harmony is very rarely employed—it is never used in genuine folk-song. The songs are sung to successive physical motions in executing some task, or else "shouted," *i. e.*, with dancing and patting of the hands.

The ante-bellum negro, speaking broadly, was a happy individual, well fed and contented. A pathos similar to that in the negro melodies is found in folk-song the world over—being due to the employment of certain repeated cadences and intervals unusual in the more self-conscious music of ballads and patriotic airs. From its appeal one cannot draw a soul-tragedy.

The words are often highly imaginative, as in figures like the "bleeding of the moon." The negro is intensely superstitious and emotional. His imagination, in larger share than his reason, working on fragments of the Bible stories, which were the only human documents he knew, inspired the words of many of his songs. They are sometimes striking, often anachronistic incantations to various Scriptural characters and twisted historical allusions; not seldom the source was completely misunderstood and sheer absurdity results—meaningless combinations of letters doing semi-phonetic service for the original intent.

Both major and minor modes are used with a frequent tendency to the pentatonic scale, although the diatonic is found also. Common-time is usual; but to give the real effect, one has to hear them sung to the swing of the oar or "shouted" in ecstatic worship. Grace-notes, slurs, quaint postponements of accent, gliding attacks abound. And all gain strong character from the sweet voices, the out-of-door verve and emotional gesture of the singers.

It is necessary to state that the vulgar "ragtime coon-songs" of the concert hall and minstrel show are decadent types and bear little relation to genuine negro melody.

Stephens Collins Foster modeled his folk-songs on the plantation type, as his *Old Uncle Ned* and *Oh, Susannah.* From a study of negro camp meetings he composed songs that have gone true to the heart of the nation—*My Old Kentucky Home, Old Folks at Home* or *Suwanee River,* and *Massa's in the Cold, Cold Ground.* Of some of these songs a million copies were sold. Foster was a Pittsburger, and, therefore, the story of his pathetic life lies outside the limits of this article. Poe—the great Southern poet—was his favorite author, and surely his folk-songs, caught from the lips of the darkies and moulded into ballad form, are as intimately Southern as any musical tradition the South could have.

Patriotic Songs.

For the Revolution and the War of 1812 no songs were composed by American authors. There were no native composers to supply the demand. Such tunes as were sung, *Yankee Doodle, America, Star Spangled Banner,* were boldly appropriated from the enemy or from other foreign sources.

In the War of Secession, *Dixie,* the Southern song par excellence, was composed for a minstrel show by an Ohio man, and the Southern soldiers, simply because they liked it, sang it into the heart of the Confederacy; and nowadays it seems to be thoroughly nationalized, arousing almost as much enthusiasm on one side of the Potomac as on the other. Southern ownership in *Maryland, My Maryland,* is vested only in the words, which are by James Ryder Randall. Another Baltimorean, Miss Hattie Cary, wedded the words to the splendid German folk-song, *O Tannenbaum.* This immortal wedding was made in Heaven and it gave wings to the words, so that they flew to every camp-fire in the Southern armies. The *Bonnie Blue Flag* is of Southern origin in words and music.

If the North was levied upon for *Dixie,* the South gracefully paid her debt by providing the music for the most popular song of the Union soldiers, *Glory Hallelujah,* alias *John Brown's Body.* The air cannot be positively traced back of 1859, when it was heard at a colored church in Charleston. William Steffe, who wrote Sunday-school tunes, claims it. It became popular among the negro congregations, worked its way north and appeared in Methodist hymnals there. The words began, "Say, brothers, will you meet us?" The tune was drafted into the martial cause in Boston to the present familiar words. It inspired Julia Ward Howe to write for it the splendid *Battle Hymn of the Republic,* beginning, "Mine eyes have seen the glory of the coming of the Lord"; but the Northern soldiers preferred

to continue the requiem of John Brown and the execution of Jeff Davis.

When upon the Field of Glory, by J. H. Hewitt, was one of the Southern battle songs effectively set to music by H. L. Schreiner. A. E. Blackmar also wrote spiritedly for the Southern soldiers.

The real national anthem of the South, as well as the North, has not yet been written. *Dixie* is not dignified enough to hold the content of a nation's ideal, and *America* is not American.

The Present.

When the war broke out the foreign artists lost no time in departing these shores. After the war the South was, of course, too utterly impoverished to support the fine arts. There was little music of any kind. The decade and a half of "carpet-bag rule" was a time of suffering and struggle, and there was no leisure and no money for music. Taste naturally declined under these conditions, and when traveling companies found their way South again, Offenbach was in great demand. *La Belle Hélène* and *La Grande Duchesse* were the watery gems that shone to most applause. Gilbert and Sullivan's sparkling superficialities were received with even keener delight, and for a time the South, in common with the rest of the country, went mad over them.

New Orleans usually had seasons of French opera, but recently the rest of the South has been accustoming itself in these days of rapid transportation to go to New York for its grand opera.

Emma Abbott and others have toured the South. Grau and Savage have brought companies through —even *Parsifal* with the Metropolitan orchestra visited the larger cities. Damrosch has brought his orchestra to many Southern cities. It is the custom **for** musical societies to bring great artists like

Schumann-Heink and Sembrich to give recitals. Paderewski and Rosenthal have played almost everywhere, but the list would soon grow out of all bounds. In general, the great artists cover the whole country, radiating from New York. This is becoming more and more the artistic, as well as the financial, centre. There will not be a provincially Southern school of American music, because the country is daily becoming more thoroughly nationalized. There is not yet an American school, and philosophers are contending that true art must, in the future, be international and not sectional. But in this great art work of the world America will play an increasingly important part, and the South, as musical culture is more and more widely diffused, will contribute much to America.

The most hopeful sign is the spread of musical intelligence through the agency of choral societies, organizations for ensemble playing and institutions of music. Cities like Louisville, Baltimore, Charleston, have their orchestras or choruses which give experience to their members and inculcate higher ideals among the public. The Peabody Institute of Baltimore—the best conservatory in the South—has sustained an orchestra of excellent quality for years. The Baltimore Symphony orchestra* has done some good work. These institutions have made Baltimore the most important musical city of the South to-day. Nashville, Tenn., a live educational centre, has much music in connection with her colleges and schools. There is no permanent orchestra or choral society, but good programmes of the small forms of ensemble-playing are given from time to time. In connection with Converse College for Women at Spartanburg, S. C.—one of the most roundly devel-

---

*Sidney Lanier, the poet-musician, should be mentioned as a flutist in this orchestra.

oped musical departments in the South—a festival is held every spring. Local chorus and orchestra combine with great artists to make a festival of high rank. Louisville has organized her music and has done choral work of the first class. In Atlanta, Constantin von Sternburg (the well-known Russian) did much for the ideals of one of the new cities of the South, which have no traditions. Charleston has the famous old Wagnerian singer, Anton Schott. He gives recitals every season. A Philharmonic helps to keep alive the local spark that once gave light to lighten musical America. New Orleans, outside of her opera, is still in very close touch with the new French school of composition, and there one can hear Gallic novelties before New York knows them.

St. Louis has a flourishing musical life. Ever since 1838 it has had a Philharmonic society, at first under the auspices of St. Louis University. The Liederkranz, the Musical Union, the St. Louis Choral Society, the Mendelssohn Club, and several German male choruses cultivate the forms of chamber music, symphony, chorus, etc. Alfred G. Robyn, born in St. Louis in 1860, is widely known for his artistic songs. Homer Moore is engaged upon an elaborate operatic trilogy, intended to embody in musical form the drama of American social evolution. The titles are *The New World, The Pilgrims* and *The Puritans.*

The special gift that America has made to the musical world is in her array of prima donnas. Of these the South has produced Clara Louise Kellogg, of South Carolina, Minnie Hauk, of New Orleans, Alice Nielsen, of Tennessee, Carrie Bridewell, of Alabama.

Institutional Work.

There is an incalculable amount of work done by private teachers of varying quality in practical instruction for violin, voice and piano. But it is gradually being recognized that the art of music is not consummated in the ability to play or sing a few "pieces" acceptably. A serious study of the forms, history and technique of composition are necessary to effect that artistic comprehension which must be more generally possessed before a musical atmosphere and a consequent fertility of invention can exist among us. To this end the growth of the musical college and the department of music in other institutions is tending. In the bulletin of the United States Bureau of Education, 1908, No. 4, an attempt has been made to collate statistics of these centres of education. Although the figures are not entirely complete the result is striking. This recent organization of what was before more or less aimless endeavor is only just begun, and is the best of all auguries for future musical vitality. Based on this report the figures for the South follow:

	NO. OF INSTITUTIONS.	NO. OF PUPILS.
Independent Schools of Music........	7	1,797
Musical Departments of Universities and Colleges	38	3,106
Musical Departments in Colleges for Women	39	4,786
Normal Schools......................	33	5,898
Secondary Schools...................	72	3,912
Grand Total......................	189	19,499

This report includes only the institutional work being done. The number of free lances teaching music it is impossible to determine accurately. It is very large and is being constantly recruited from the graduates of the above institutions. To-day, when the South is financially prosperous again, an appreciable percentage go to New York, Boston, Baltimore, Cincinnati and Chicago to study; and not a few to Berlin, Paris, Vienna, Munich, Dresden, Brussels and London. The whole movement, in most of its phases, is little more than fifteen years old, and the cumulative effect of so many lines of serious interest steadily converging towards a riper musical culture is an important item in Southern life to-day.

Teachers' conventions are regularly established; festivals are increasing each year. The secondary school awakening is one of the most encouraging signs (see table p. 400). Sight-singing and the elements of musical grammar are being grafted into the high school curriculum, not with the intention of discovering prima donnas and virtuosos, but on account of the inherent right of music to a place in the educational programme. This sound point of view, if faithfully adhered to, will, of itself, do much in laying solid the foundations of a worthy music-temple for a country whose climate, traditions, manner of life and increasing wealth ought some day to predispose towards art.

BIBLIOGRAPHY.—Sonneck, O. G. T.: *Early Concert-life in America* (1731-1800), Leipzig, Breitkopf & Härtel, an invaluable source-book for this period; Ritter, Frédéric Louis: *Music in America*, new ed., New York, Scribner's, 1890; Elson, Louis Charles: *The History of American Music*, Macmillan, New York, 1904; *Immortal Songs of Camp and Field*, by L. A. Banks, Cleveland, The Burrows Brothers Company, 1899; Baker: *Biographical Dictionary of Musicians*, N. Y., 1900; Mathews: *One Hundred Years of Music in America*, Chicago, 1889.

From all these books it is necessary to pick the material bearing on Southern Music from a mass of facts developing the general story of American music. There is no book devoted exclusively to Southern music. In working up the Southern history in detail, main dependence must be placed on the early newspaper files and unpublished records of individuals and of societies.

HUGER W. JERVEY,
Professor of Greek, University of the South.

CHAPTER XX.

THE SOUTHERN PRESS.

Characteristics.

THE Southern press, as it exists to-day, is the creation of the last twenty or twenty-five years and of men, most of whom are still living. This is true of the newspapers of the country as a whole, for at no previous period has there been such rapid change, such marvelous development; but that journalistic development has, for obvious reasons, been most marked in the South, for its press until lately was backward, suffering from many restrictions and limitations, with the most serious obstacles to overcome and arduous duties and obligations to perform. These conditions and difficulties have made the Southern press characteristic of the South and its people, for it has been closely identified with them, called on not only to furnish the news but to lead and encourage all popular movements, to act as educator and adviser. As a consequence, it has been, far more so than any other press, the patron and developer of home literature and of industrial and material activity. The South lacking magazine and publishing houses, those who sought fame or distinction in the field of letters have found the only encouragement, the only sympathetic opening for them, in the newspapers, which became, as it were, the ante-room to the Temple of the Muses. In an altogether different line, but for similar reasons, the Southern press has played a far more important part in the industrial development of its section. That development was naturally from without rather than of internal origin and growth; and it called for education and encouragement. The papers were expected to find the needed capital, to attract immigrants, to arouse enthusiasm. During the period 1885-1900, no journals in the country gave more space or showed more interest in industrial development, in manufactures, mining, agriculture and every branch of production than those South of "Mason and Dixon's line;" and it is mainly to their efforts that the great progress of that period was due. These efforts are still echoed in their columns.

In proportion to the amount of matter they publish, a much larger share is given to industry in the South than elsewhere; and an equally larger proportion to local literature, to home poets, novelists and essayists. The Southern press has thus become the nursery of home talent in the same way that it has sought to build up new industries, to develop natural resources, to establish factories and to promote education. These efforts are responsible for the trend of Southern journalism and give it those characteristics which make it sui-generis and distinctive.

There is a natural similarity in the papers of all countries and yet a marked difference. All are supposed to cover the same field, to give the news of the world with timely comments thereon, and explanations when necessary; but nevertheless, no one will ever mistake a French journal for an English one, even if written in the same language; and the antithesis between English and American newspapers is nearly as great. While the papers North and South are written on somewhat similar lines and have the same American characteristics, they are different both in the matter they contain and in their attitude toward their subscribers and readers and on most public questions. In this first particular, a writer of a statistical turn of mind, in a recent pub-

lication of the University of Pennsylvania, giving
the class of news furnished by the leading papers of
our several cities, showed by the unquestioned evidence of statistics that the Southern press gave proportionately, a much larger amount of industrial
and religious matter, more local literature, poetry,
etc., but less gossip, theatrical and dramatic news;
in fine that the Southern press was more serious,
assuming more the attitude of guide, counselor and
educator, than of simple news gatherer and amuser.
Thus, the editorial page of the Southern paper plays,
in proportion to its size and circulation, a more
important part than in the North and West, where
there is a disposition to minimize it or drop it altogether, on the theory perhaps that the people have
outgrown the necessity of editorial advice; whereas
in the South, it is still the form and practice for a
paper to advise its readers on all questions of local
moment, and not on politics alone. It naturally follows that the Southern journals usually exercise
more influence than their confreres "across the
line,"—an influence probably largely gained during
the period succeeding the War of Secession, when
the people had to turn somewhere for advice and
generally turned to their papers.

While it is true that the character of the Southern press of to-day has been largely formed during
the last twenty or twenty-five years, it must not be
imagined that the South was deficient in journals
before that time. On the contrary, its press has a
long and honorable record, and many of the papers
of to-day are continuances or successors of those
having their origin in the Eighteenth century. In
this respect, there was very little difference in the
history of the two sections. Journalism started in
both under similar conditions, but the character of
the people and of the country, the vicissitudes of

fortune, the mode of life, the ideas current, soon
brought about "a parting of the ways," a difference
in methods and ideals which grew greater in time as
is the case in all lands. The Frenchman finds an
English paper dull and heavy; the Englishman denounces the American journal as flippant and un-
trustworthy—each has a press which meets its
ideals and its tastes; and this is equally true of all
sections of the country and especially so of the
South.

Early Journalism.

The source of early American journalism was, of
course, the mother country. There were no printers
and consequently no publishers in America until
Englishmen, or more generally Scotchmen, came
over and set up their presses among us. In "the
art preservative of arts," Philadelphia is entitled
to the leadership and held that position for many
years, although Boston issued the first newspaper.

It was William Bradford, of London, who establishing himself in Philadelphia became a publisher
there, both of books—generally acts of the council—
and of newspapers; and whose sons and grandsons
spread journalism through Maryland and Virginia
and into the wilds of Kentucky and "the territory
northwest of the Ohio," leaving honorable names
and reputations as publishers. They were printers
rather than editors and their gazettes would scarcely
be classed as newspapers to-day, as they lacked
news and were mere official "papers" giving the
proclamations of governors and the proceedings of
the councils. These publishers were generally practical printers hired in England by the colonial
agents and paid in produce. They printed the laws,
and having the type handy, added to their official
salaries by issuing "gazettes," as newspapers were
then almost universally called. Being officials of

the government it was natural that they should avoid criticism; and editorial comment on their part was practically unknown. Some of the early royal governors viewed printing and the newspapers with great suspicion. The famous boast of Governor Berkeley of Virginia that, "thank God there is no printing press in the colony," is well known. On a par with him was Governor Nicholson of South Carolina who opposed the bringing of a printer to the colony, and wanted to know what bond of assurance would be given that if the printer came, he would publish nothing objectionable or which might cause any bad blood.

Such were the humble beginnings of that journalism, without which the South would never have reached its present freedom or prosperity. In later years, at the time of the American Revolution, the gazettes had made some little progress. They gradually dropped the colonial title "gazette" and showed a tendency to long and magnificent names. It was a period of flamboyancy, of exaggerated expressions and the ordinary newspaper would have thought it was belittling itself if it used so simple a title as the "News" or the "Times." They called themselves "The Rights of Man," "The Children of Pallas," "The Eagle of Liberty," "The Banner of the People," and even Ben Franklin modestly gave his paper the grandiose title of "Universal Instructor in all the Arts and Sciences." Next to the name, the most important feature was the motto, for each paper bore next its title a long and bombastic motto, Latin the favorite, then English and French, indicative of its devotion to the people, its patriotism, its independence and its courage.

There were only thirty-seven newspapers in the country in 1775 when the Revolutionary struggle began, publishing in all less in a week than the ordinary Sunday edition of a first-class paper to-day. McMaster, who is not always free from prejudice, notes that only eight of these papers were published in the South, Maryland not being included; but, as a matter of fact, in proportion to white population, this was a fair showing. Nor did the number of papers after all indicate circulation, influence, popularity or their character. Virginia and North Carolina had two each, Georgia one and South Carolina three. After the revolution (in 1784), the total had grown to fifty-three, of which eleven were published in the South, or fifteen including Maryland.

There were, however, both North and South, sorry excuses for papers, as we know them to-day, although even then the sections were moving on different lines in the matter of journalism. News was as yet unknown, an undiscovered item. There were no means of getting it; no system of collecting or exchanging it. There were no correspondents and few of the papers thought of getting news from any point fifty miles away. Circulation outside of the town in which they were printed was not looked for, and no attempt was made to secure it. Papers were denied the use of the mails; they were not received at the post office, and the only way in which they could be sent to subscribers outside the town of publication was by bribing the post carrier to put a few copies in the portemanteau or valise in which he carried the letters. It is needless to say that under these unfavorable circumstances, it was impossible to send out more than a dozen papers although they were small affairs, never over four pages, with each page about a quarter of the present standard size. Later, a Maryland paper ran a post system of its own to supply those subscribers who lived in the suburbs or in the neighboring districts and towns, this being the first appearance of the modern newspaper carrier and delivery wagon. Another Maryland paper showed still more enterprise for it operated a post line from New York and thus supplied itself with the Eastern and English papers from which it could occasionally get items.

But with few exceptions, there was very little news published. The average paper was a weekly or bi-weekly of four small pages, printed on the shabbiest kind of paper. There was no editorial page, its place being supplied by vigorous editorial appeals to subscribers who seemed to be in a chronic state of delinquency, to pay up in money or produce. There were a few advertisements, of which runaway slaves and stray horses were the most numerous and the most conspicuous. The news was obtained almost wholly from private letters which were solicited from every quarter, introduced with the remark that ''a letter received by Mr. Brown from a friend in New York,'' conveyed the intelligence that half that city had been destroyed by fire a month or two previous. When no letters were received by subscribers, the paper had no news and found it no easy matter to fill up. In such case, the printer took any copy he could lay his hands on. The result was absurd, for papers, having little space and no news, published merely as ''space fillers'' ponderous volumes, theological and historical; for instance (one of them republished in its columns Robertson's *History of America,* a book altogether out of date, although it took three years to complete the task.

There were, of course, differences between the early papers, some being much better than others. As a general rule, the South Carolina and Maryland papers ranked highest in the South, containing the most news and spoke out most earnestly and strong_ ly on public questions. On the other hand, the Vir_ ginia, North Carolina and Georgia papers were weak in news and in editorial utterances.

Colonial Press Conservative.

The colonial press presents generally the same characteristics whether the papers were published in the Northern or Southern colonies; but after the Revolution, the difference between them became more marked, and the divergence steadily grew greater. The Southern journals as a class, were more conservative and less abusive and vituperative. The extravagant language used in denunciation at that time is well known, and has confused not a few historians for it has required some effort to rescue the reputation of Washington from the abuse poured on him by the scurrilous writers of his day. The language used was never quite as abusive in the South as in other sections, either because public sentiment did not approve of it or because of the prevailing belief than a person thus abused enjoyed the right of calling to personal account the editor who assailed him. In still later day, the duello, although responsible for many disgraceful rencontres between editors, and the loss of many valued lives, generally checked the tendency to abuse and scurrility.

Journalism in the Southern Colonies and States.

The experience and vicissitudes of papers and editors varied considerably in the several colonies and states. Maryland led the South in journalism. It brought out the first Southern newspaper, yielded a much larger crop of "gazettes" than its neighbors to the South, and its press showed great journalistic zeal, vigor and force. A printing press had been set up as early as 1689 by William Nuthead at St. Mary's, then the capital of the colony, but the publications, both at St. Mary's and Annapolis, were almost wholly of a religious character.

In 1727, John Parks began at Annapolis the publication of the first newspaper in the South, *The Maryland Gazette*. He was the printer to the colony of Maryland, and the *Gazette* was merely the side issue, usual at that time, when every colonial public printer issued a journal for the publication of certain official papers.

The *Maryland Gazette,* the humble beginning of the powerful and influential Southern press of to-day, was printed on a sheet a little larger than foolscap, four pages, two columns to a page. The everlasting motto in this instance was from Cicero, "Cuius vis est hominis errare; nullius nisi insipientis, persevare in errare,"—an unusually modest declaration for the time.

Parks was a practical printer, educated in his trade in England. He came to Maryland at the invitation of the colony which had grown tired of having all its printing done in Philadelphia. His success brought him the business of the neighboring colony of Virginia, and in 1729 he became official printer for the latter as well as for Maryland, each colony paying him for his services a salary of £200 per annum "in country produce." Finding Virginia the more populous and richer province, Parks left Annapolis for Williamsburg, then the capital of Virginia, in 1732, and made the latter his permanent abode. This left Maryland wholly without a printer, and it had again to send to Philadelphia for all its printing, even for handbills.

The *Maryland Gazette* was revived at Annapolis in 1745 by Jonas Green, but died again in 1765 from the Stamp Act, which closed out so many of the early American papers. Green published the last edition in mourning rules, declared that the "times were dismal, doleful, dolorous and dollarless''; and announced his purpose to cease the publication of his newspaper rather than submit to "the intolerable and burdensome taxes imposed on the newspapers by the Stamp Act." The *Gazette*, however, was revived after the Stamp Act was repealed, and proved one of the strongest supporters of the colonies during the Revolutionary War. Because of the stress of the times, and the high price of provisions, it was compelled during the war to reduce its size to that of a half sheet and to raise its price to £5 per annum. It survived until 1839.

The first Baltimore paper was *The Maryland Journal and Baltimore Advertiser,* published in 1773 by William Goddard. Typographically, it was probably the best paper in the country at the time, the type being new and very beautiful elzevir instead of the second-hand type which most of the other papers used; the paper was heavy book paper, and the presswork was admirably done. The *Journal and Advertiser* showed enterprise in other lines than in its typographical and mechanical make-up for it established a rider from Philadelphia to Baltimore so that it could get the earliest papers from Philadelphia, New York and other cities to the North and East of Baltimore, as well as the British and French papers and thus keep abreast of the news.

Goddard seems the prototype of the journalist of the day. He announced himself as independent, that his paper would "be free and of no party," that its purpose was not to indulge in acrimonious debate but to publish the news. He took practical and intelligent action to that end; and the mails being uncertain and neglected, he announced in his paper as early as 1774, a plan for an American postal service, which within a year, was well under way from Maine to Georgia. His sister was appointed

postmistress at Baltimore and held that position for
fifteen years. Goddard retired in 1792, the paper
subsequently passing through many hands and finally ceasing publication in 1797.

The Maryland Gazette and Advertiser, was established at Baltimore by John Dunlap in 1775 to ex-
pire in 1779; another paper of the same name started
in 1786 to fail in 1791. Thus, papers sprang up and
faded away, year after year, with such a similarity
of names as to confuse the modern student of journalistic history. This is well shown in the flood of
newspapers which struck Frederick and Hagerstown, Maryland, in the last years of the Eighteenth
century when the politics of the young republic,
which had just thrown off the British yoke, was becoming partisan and bitter if not abusive and vituperative. In the short space of ten years, Frederick
saw five new newspapers, *The Federal Gazette and
Advertiser, The Maryland Gazette, The Rights of
Man, The Herald* and *The Key;* while the small town
of Elizabeth (now Hagerstown), had three, *The
Washington Spy, The German Washington Correspondent,* and *The Centinel of Liberty,* each paper
abusing all the others and all persons who were not
members of its party.

Among the Baltimore papers of which there were
three established during the last years of the Eighteenth century, the most important was *The Baltimore American and Daily Advertiser,* founded in
1799 by Alexander Martin, and which survives to-
day in the *Baltimore American,* after passing
through several hands and a number of variations
in its name.

The press of the District of Columbia naturally
saw its birth at Georgetown, for Washington was
unbuilt or inchoate until about the beginning of the
Nineteenth century, whereas Georgetown was a

prosperous town with great social attractions and advantages. It is not to be wondered, therefore, that of the nine first papers established in the District of Columbia, six should be at Georgetown and only three at Washington. *The Times and Potommack Packet* was established by Charles Frerer and Thomas N. Fosdick in 1789, struggling under the stupendous motto borne on its first page "Let it be impressed upon your minds, let it be instilled into your Children that the Liberty of the Press is the Palladium of all the civil, political and religious Rights of Freemen." *The Packet* seems to have been a progressive paper for its day, as it pledged itself to deliver its papers in the homes of subscribers, and "to serve those at a distance at the quickest convenience," and it guaranteed to furnish them "articles of intelligence, original essays, etc."

The George-Town Weekly Ledger, published by Day and Hancock, followed in 1790; and *The Columbian Chronicle* in 1793, published by Samuel Hanson. The latter carried the motto from Junius, "For a people to be Free, it is sufficient that they will it." *The Ledger* was swallowed up by *The George-Town Centinel of Liberty and Advertiser,* which went still further in the motto line, starting out with the quotation from Montesquieu: "Liberty is the right of doing whatever the laws permit; and if a citizen could do what they forbid, he would no longer be possessed of liberty because all his fellow-citizens would have the same power." This evidently did not please the editor, those days when the fortunes of a paper were supposed to be bound up, in some way, with the force or appropriateness of its motto; and Montesquieu was dropped for Washington in 1798 with the declaration "Every portion of our country finds the most commanding motives for carefully guarding and preserving the Union as a whole."

Thus in the short space of five years the *Chronicle, Centinel and Advertiser* (all one paper), had gone through Junius, Lafayette, Montesquieu and Washington in the search for an appealing motto.

The first Washington paper, *The Impartial Observer and Washington Advertiser,* was begun in 1795 by T. Wilson; *The Washington,* printed by Benjamin More, followed in 1796. More was candid with his subscribers, frankly acknowledging that *The Washington* was started not "to fill a long felt want," but primarily to make a living for himself and secondarily to amuse and inform his readers. Whether he succeeded in his second prosposition is unknown, but he certainly did not in his first, for the paper survived but little over a year.

The National Intelligencer and Washington Advertiser, established by Samuel Hanson Smith of Philadelphia in 1800, was one of the first great papers of the country. It was originally a tri-weekly but became a daily in 1813, publishing a weekly called *The United States Gazette.* In 1812 William Seaton and Joseph Gales, Jr., secured control of *The National Intelligencer,* dropping the extra title "Advertiser." These two men were the only congressional reporters for many years, and we depend to-day on the columns of *The National Intelligencer* for some of the most important debates in the earlier days of the republic.

Virginia does not show as well in the matter of early newspapers as Maryland, this being probably due to the early internal troubles of the colony. A prejudice had grown up against the printing press and printing was, for a while, prohibited by the House of Burgesses; but this prohibition was ultimately withdrawn.

The first newspaper did not arrive until 1732 when John Parks who had done the public printing for both Maryland and Virginia moved down to Williamsburg from Annapolis and started *The Virginia Gazette.* It prospered under him, although never more than an official paper issued by the colonial printer; but when he died in 1750, the *Gazette* died also.

Three other papers followed in pre-revolutionary times, all "Gazettes." One year after Parks died, another printer, William Hunter, turned up at Williamsburg and started *The Gazette,* which may be considered as a continuation of Parks' paper. It was a better edited journal, however, than its predecessor and contained, during the tempestuous times just before the Revolution, a number of valuable political articles signed "Virginia Centinel," evidently written by one of the statesmen who were leading the popular cause—but who the writer was has never been made known. Hunter died in 1801 and *The Gazette* was enlarged and improved by his successor, Joseph Royle, and still further improved by Purdie and Dixon.

From 1766 to 1773, another *Virginia Gazette* was published at Williamsburg by William Rind and continued by his wife Clementina after Rind's death, finally falling into the hands of John Pinckney.

The fourth of the Williamsburg "Gazettes" was started in 1775 by John Clarkson and Augustine Davis and afterwards removed to Norfolk where the British captured the press and carried it off with them when they evacuated that town.

The first North Carolina paper was *The North Carolina Magazine of Universal Intelligence,* started at New Berne in 1755, a vapid paper containing no news and little of public interest, given up mainly to extracts from theological writers and British magazines. Andrew Stewart, the provincial printer started the same year (1755) *The North Carolina*

Gazette and Weekly Post-Boy at Wilmington, fairly
good, containing some news and a most decided improvement on *The Universal Intelligencer.* In 1767,
The Wilmington Advertiser was established, and in
1769 *The Cape Fear Mercury* by A. Boyd, a badly
printed paper, destitute of all system in its arrangement and contents.

Of all the Southern colonies, South Carolina
ranked first in the number and standing of its newspapers. It came a little behind Maryland and Virginia in the date of the establishment of its first
journal. As early as 1712, South Carolina had
sought to get a printer to establish himself in the
colony if only for the printing of the laws which
had to be sent to London to be ''set up.'' When
Francis Yonge went to London as the colony's
agent in 1722 he was instructed ''to procure by the
first opportunity a printer with his tools'' and he
was authorized to advance any printer who would
come £1,000. Governor Nicholson and his successor
Middleton did not like this idea, regarding the proposal to print the laws ''unreasonable'' and expressing fear lest the printer might publish something
objectionable and without license. In 1730, Eleazer
Phillips of Boston was persuaded to come to Charleston as the first printer to the colony of South Carolina, but died soon after of yellow fever. A second
printer, Thomas Whitemarsh, arrived the same year
and started *The South Carolina Gazette,* but he also
fell a victim to the yellow fever. *The Gazette* was
revived a few months afterwards by Louis Timothée,
a Huguenot, who subsequently anglicized his name
to Lewis Timothy. The paper thus established was
one of the best and most influential in America and
played a prominent part in the revolutionary politics of South Carolina. Timothy was a violent whig,
a man of great force and always on the side of free-

dom and liberty. He bitterly opposed the Stamp Act, and was one of the most ardent supporters of the non-importation agreement. His paper suspended in 1775, on account of his politics, was revived in 1777 and published until the fall of Charleston in 1780 when he was captured and sent as a British prisoner to Philadelphia. He was lost at sea while returning to Charleston. The paper was carried on for some years by his widow and her son Benjamin Timothy. His great-grandson, Peter Timothy Marchant, was one of the members of the house of Marchant, Willington & Co., publishers of *The Charleston Courier,* founded in 1803, thus forming a connecting link between *The Charleston News and Courier* of to-day and *The South Carolina Gazette* of 1732.

At the time of the Revolutionary War, South Carolina led all the Southern colonies in the matter of newspapers, boasting of three as against two each in Virginia and North Carolina and one in Georgia. These were *The South Carolina Gazette* (founded in 1732), *The South Carolina General American Gazette* (1766) and *The South Carolina Country Journal* (1766). In proportion to its white population, it had more newspapers than any of the American colonies. The papers, too, were of a rather higher grade than those of the other colonies, containing an unusual amount of news, the doings of the court in London and the proceedings in parliament, a page or two of advertisements, the shipping lists, a good deal of local news including marriages, births and deaths, moral and social essays after the model and style of those in the *Spectator,* all in the most approved Johnsonian periods.

Among the unfortunate South Carolina editors of these days was John Wells. Although educated in the trade at Edinburgh, and although his father,

like him, a printer, was a stout royalist, Wells took
a prominent part in the work of the patriots, and
fought and issued newspapers in the cause until he
was captured by the British in 1780. Although he
had served with courage and distinction in the Revolutionary War at the siege of Savannah, when ordered after his capture by the British to sign a paper to the British government acknowledging his
rebellion and error, he did so to save his property
in Charleston, it is said. This act, he followed up
by the publication of *The Royal Gazette* at Charleston. He was prosecuted, in consequence, by the
state government and left with the British army
when the town was evacuated, going with a large
number of other South Carolina loyalists to the
Bahamas where he established at Nassau, *The Royal
Bahama Gazette.* He had always hoped to return
to his native country and was arranging his affairs
to enable him to do so when he died.

The first Georgia newspaper *The Savannah Gazette,* like most of the other originals, was established
simply for the purpose of publishing the official matters of the councils. The publisher, James Johnston, was a Scotchman, a printer by trade, who received a handsome pecuniary consideration for coming to America and becoming the printer of the
colony. He published an edition of the laws, and, in
1763, established *The Gazette.* It was issued twenty-
seven years by Johnston and suffered the usual vicissitudes of a newspaper in those days. It was compelled to suspend by the British Stamp Act which
put an almost prohibitive price on newspapers and
which was the subsequent cause of the rising of the
colonists against the mother country. The Revolution later caused a suspension of *The Gazette* for
several years especially as Johnston had put the
royal arms on his paper; but, after the struggle was

over, it became ardent in support of the patriotic cause.

The Augusta Chronicle and Gazette of the State, founded in 1785, was the second newspaper established in Georgia and is one of the few survivors of that period. It bore, as its motto, the quotation from the constitution of Georgia "The Freedom of the Press and trial by Jury shall remain inviolate." It was printed by John E. Smith, at that time state printer, Augusta being then the capital of Georgia. *The Chronicle* has been a great absorber of other papers. In 1793, it swallowed *The Southern Centinel and Universal Gazette,* and in 1877, *The Constitutionalist,* becoming then known as *The Chronicle aad Constitutionalist.* In 1885, it issued a centennial edition, giving the history of the paper for the previous hundred years.

Alabama was late in getting out in journalism, and its first paper was not established until 1812 when *The Madison Gazette* was printed at Huntsville. At that time St. Stephens was the capital of the territory, and the official journal and acts of the territorial legislature were printed there.

Florida was also late in the matter of newspapers, its oldest being *The Weekly Floridan,* established at Tallahasse in 1828.

Early Mississippi journalism centres altogether around Natchez, where lived all the white population of the territory, the northern and eastern portions being still in the hands of the Indians. In 1800, *The Mississippi Gazette* was established at Natchez by Benjamin M. Stokes. It passed, within a year, into the hands of Sackett and Wallace who showed considerable more enterprise than its founder, and made arrangements to send the paper to subscribers throughout the settled portion of the territory.

In 1801, *The Intelligencer* was established by D.

Moffett and James Ferrell at Natchez; and in 1802 *The Mississippi Herald,* by Andrew Marschalk, also at Natchez. The latter was by far the best paper published in Mississippi up to that time, containing an excellent variety of reading matter, and six columns of advertising, a prodigious amount for the time and the territory. Perhaps the most striking feature of that journal and wholly out of accord with the journalistic practices of the time was a column of friendly notice of a rival paper soon to be established in Natchez, *The Mississippi Republican and Advertiser.* The *Herald* was decidedly in advance of the time in speaking in this amiable manner of a rival, instead of denouncing it, and this may explain its early collapse. Four other papers followed in the next five years, all at Natchez; *The Constitutional Conservator* by John Wade (1802), *The Republican and Advertiser* (1802), *The Mississippi Messenger* by John Shaw and Timothy Terrell (1804), and *The Chronicle* by John A. Winn & Co. (1808), making seven papers established in that little town in as many years.

The first newspapers in Louisiana were naturally published in French as that was the language of a large majority of the population, before and at the time of the Louisiana Purchase. *Le Courier du Vendredi* (*Friday Courier*), is said to have been published as early as 1785 when Louisiana was under Spanish control, but not a copy of that paper has survived and little is known about it, and, indeed, there are grave doubts as to its existence.

Le Moniteur de la Louisiane (*The Louisiana Monitor*), started in 1794 and was of much the same character as the American papers of the day, although giving more news, particularly European news, than they did.

With the establishment of the American Dominion

in 1803, *The Telegraphe,* published at New Orleans, as indeed all the other early Louisiana papers were, started life, having a motto in French from Bailly "Publicity is the Safe-Guard of the People." *Le Telegraphe,*—the name was used by many papers of those days, forty years before the magnetic telegraph was invented,—was issued by Beleurgey and Renard, and published originally, wholly in French; but in 1810, part in French and part in English.

In 1804, a year after the purchase of Louisiana, the first English paper in Louisiana, and the first in that language in the Mississippi Valley, was issued at New Orleans by John Mowery. It started with only nineteen subscribers, but as the subscription was $10 it lingered for some years.

In 1810, Louisiana possessed eight newspapers, all in New Orleans, of which one was wholly in English, one in French, four in French and English and two in Spanish.

The first newspaper published in Kentucky was *The Kentucky Gazette* at Lexington in 1787, by James Bradford of the same Bradford family which, coming from London to Philadelphia, had established a chain of newspapers through Pennsylvania, Maryland and Virginia. The people of Kentucky were so desirous of having a newspaper in their territory that the Board of Trustees of Lexington gave Bradford all the land he needed for an office. The press was brought overland from Philadelphia, and took nearly a year to reach Lexington. The office of *The Gazette* was a one-story log cabin covered with clapboards. Under every possible disadvantage, the paper became a success from the start. As a matter of fact, it was the only paper in all the west and without a rival within a radius of 500 miles. A copy was too precious for personal use, and Perrin describes how *The Gazette* was sent, far and wide, through Kentucky, Ohio, Tennessee and neighboring territories by post riders. When it reached a settlement, the best reader among the inhabitants was called on to mount a stump or chair and read to "the assembled multitude" every word in *The Gazette,* advertisements included—which incident is presented in the well-known American picture, "Reading the News." Bradford subsequently became printer to the state of Kentucky in 1792 and left the paper to his sons at his death. It survived until 1848.

Stewart's *Kentucky Herald* was established by Thomas H. Stewart at Lexington in 1795; *The Kentucky Journal* by Benjamin J. Bradford at Frankfort in 1795; *The Rights of Man or Kentucky Mercury* by Darius Moffett at Paris in 1797; *The Mirror* by Hunter and Beaumont at Washington, the same year, and *The Guardian of Freedom* by John Bradford at Frankfort in 1798. The Bradfords, John, Daniel and Benjamin, thus controlled four papers in Kentucky at that time, constituting a majority of the territorial press. The first daily paper was published at Louisville, *The Public Advertiser* by Shadrach Penn in 1826.

Conditions were very similar in Tennessee, where the first paper, *The Knoxville Gazette,* was established in 1793 by a printer from Massachusetts, R. Roulstone, during the exciting period when the people living in what is now East Tennessee were endeavoring to secede from North Carolina, of which state they then formed a part, and to set up a state government of their own. From the very beginning, *The Gazette,* which was a paper of considerable force and ability, exercised great influence among the mountaineers who constituted its chief subscribers.

MEXICAN NEWS

The Texas press was the outgrowth of the war of
independence against Mexico, and the newspapers,
first established there, might almost be called a part
of the Texas army. A printing press had been set
up by Baker and Borden at San Felipe (now Austin), with the coming of the Austin colony and a
paper was issued therefrom, *The Weekly Telegraph,*
publishing extras without number, whenever news
came in by the early mail from the United States, via
Fort Jessup. At nearly the same time, 1835, the
people of eastern Texas established at Nacogdoches,
The Emigrant Guide—mainly, however, for circulation in the states, to induce emigrants to come to
Texas and cast their fortunes with that young republic. *The Telegraph* was an army paper, moving
from point to point as the Mexicans advanced. When
they reached Austin, *The Telegraph* retreated with
the Texan forces to Harrisburg where it was printed
for a while. But the Mexicans advancing further,
the press and type were captured by them and destroyed. The indefatigable and patriotic editor,
however, did not abandon the field but bought a new
press and type, made his headquarters at Columbia
and there continued to publish his paper which
proved one of the most useful and valuable friends
of the republic during the period of its war with
Mexico. The growth of the Texas press was rapid
from that time, and five years afterwards the single
weekly, *The Telegraph,* had grown to twelve, two of
them bi-weeklies.

Arkansas, being among the Southern states last
settled and organized, naturally did not develop an
early press. The original settlements were along
the Mississippi or the Arkansas near its junction
with the mother river and the first paper was established there, *The Arkansas Gazette.* The founder
was one William E. Woodruff, a printer who moved

there from Long Island and settled at Arkansas
Post. Woodruff was probably invited to Arkansas
for he was at once made "printer to the territory."
He printed the laws and edited *The Gazette* which
was merely an official publication of proclamations,
acts and official notices, without news and with no
comments on the events of the day. Woodruff, as
a matter of fact, was a printer rather than an editor
and attending to the former duties properly, there
were no causes of complaint. The territorial government moved from "the post of Arkansas" on the
Arkansas River to Little Rock in 1820 and *The Gazette* moved with it. It is one of the few of the first
papers in a state to survive in *The Little Rock Gazette* of to-day.

Such was the early record of Southern journalism. It is impossible to follow the history through
all the phases of the next sixty years. It is sufficient
to say, that during that period, hundreds of papers
rose and fell in the South. There was a disposition
to spread rather than to centralize, and each leader
and faction wanted an organ as mouthpiece. The
result was an immense number of papers which were
necessarily weak because of this excess. New Orleans, which supports only two English morning
dailies to-day, boasted in its earlier days of twelve;
and Raleigh, N. C., at a period when it was only
one-third its present population, had no less than
ten, a majority of which are now represented by
The News and Observer.

Many of the Southern papers rose to national importance. *The Richmond Enquirer,* for instance, became the organ of Jefferson, Madison and Monroe,
and attracted the attention of the whole country by
its utterances. It was *The Enquirer* which, in laying down the proposition, that Mr. Jefferson must
not and would not become a presidential candidate

for a third term, established that great doctrine of our unwritten law on that point. It was another Virginia paper, published in Alexandria, which when summoned before Congress for publishing the news of the capital, established the principle and right of the press to publish all the news.

Weakened by division, the Southern papers during the greater part of the period from the revolutionary days to the War of Secession, devoted themselves excessively to political discussion and ignored far too much the news of the day. During the War of Secession their condition was miserable, and they necessarily exercised little influence. It was considered in the South more patriotic to fight than to write. In the heat of battle, there was naturally little opportunity for discussion and the bad news service that existed and the difficulty of getting any news whatever reduced the Southern press to its lowest and weakest stage. The Richmond, Va., papers, *The Enquirer, Examiner, Sentinel* and *Whig,* alone showed any great activity; while the *Louisville Courier-Journal,* under George Prentice, has been credited with having prevented Kentucky from seceding. Elsewhere, in the South, the papers were not only without news but frequently without paper, sometimes printing their editions on packing or wall paper. Of one North Carolina editor, it is said that, for lack of paper, he wrote the editorials on a shingle, scraping the writing off after the article was "set up" and being then ready for another. It is significant of the press of the two sections during that period that no paper in the South was ever "suspended" by the Confederate government, the fullest latitude being allowed in the discussion of all questions; whereas in the North, there were scores of papers suspended or mobbed. Only occasionally were the Southern papers requested not to publish any information about military movements, lest the news might reach and inform the enemy; and such requests were in all instances complied with.

Date of Establishment of Leading Southern Newspapers.

The following table gives the date of establishment or consolidation of some of the leading Southern papers of to-day:

1785 Augusta Chronicle,
1799 Baltimore American,
1803 Charleston News and Courier,
1816 Knoxville Tribune,
1819 Little Rock Gazette,
1821 Mobile Register,
1827 New Orleans Bee,
1828 Montgomery Advertiser,
1828 Columbus (Ga.) Enquirer-Sun,
1832 Louisville Courier-Journal (Courier),
1835 Nashville American,
1837 New Orleans Picayune,
1837 Baltimore Sun,
1840 Memphis Appeal (Avalanche 1857, Commercial 1889),
1842 Galveston News,
1849 Louisville Anzeiger (German),
1850 Richmond Times-Despatch,
1850 Savannah News,
1863 New Orleans Times (Democrat 1876, Times-Democrat 1881),
1865 Jacksonville (Fla.) Times-Union.

1865 San Antonio Express,
1868 Atlanta Constitution,
1869 Louisville Herald,
1869 Chattanooga Times,
1871 Austin (Tex.) Statesman,
1872 Baltimore News,
1872 Raleigh News and Observer,
1876 Nashville Banner,
1876 Norfolk Ledger-Despatch,
1877 New Orleans Item,
1880 New Orleans States,
1880 Chattanooga News,
1881 Louisville Times,
1881 Memphis News-Scimitar,
1884 Birmingham News,
1885 Houston Post,
1885 Dallas News,
1886 Charlotte Observer,
1886 Knoxville Sentinel,
1891 Houston Chronicle,
1891 Columbia (S. C.) State,
1898 Atlanta Journal,
1906 Atlanta Georgian,

Seven Southern papers have passed the century mark, *The Annapolis Gazette* (1745), *Baltimore American* (1773 or 1799), *Annapolis Republican* (1809), *Alexandria Gazette* (1800), *Lexington, Va., Gazette* (1804), *Charleston News and Courier* (1803), and *The Augusta Chronicle* (1785).

It will be noticed that a large proportion of the papers in the table given above are hyphenated consolidations. These forty-four thus represent over 150 journals, established at various times, and purchased or combined with the more successful ventures.

There are two characteristic features of the Southern newspapers which illustrate the distinction and difference between them and the Northern journals, resulting from conditions prevailing in the South—their literary tendencies, both before and since the War of Secession, and their editorial work in developing the national resources and in building up the industries of their several states. This latter work became especially necessary after the four years of war, and the ten years of even more destructive political strife that followed under reconstruction.

The absence of magazines in the South (for the few established, with possibly the exception of *The Southern Literary Messenger* were short lived and far from inviting or prosperous), and the absence of publishing houses of note, forced the young Southern writer into the columns of the press. For this reason, the Southern papers were naturally led into the fields of literature and nearly all of them gave special encouragement to local talent. Moreover, newspaper work seemed then the only opening for those who had literary ambition or a taste for writing, to show what they could do.

The result was to give a distinctly literary flavor or tone to the Southern press, which has turned out a much larger proportion of writers of the first class than that of the North; the latter devoting their attention more to the collection of news.

Journalism and Literature.

It will thus be found that nearly all the Southern writers won their spurs in journalism and that the newspaper was the stepping-stone to literature. Scarcely a first-class paper in the South but has graduated one or more writers who rank high in the world of books.

A glance over the journalistic field will show how nearly identical it is with the field of literature.

In New Orleans, for instance, *The Crescent* had

428 HISTORY OF THE INTELLECTUAL LIFE.

Walt Whitman as its editor for some years. The staff of the *Delta* included Henry Linden Flash, the poet, Alexander Walker, the author of *Jackson and New Orleans.* Brennan, the Irish poet and patriot, Richard Henry Wilde, author of numerous poems, and especially "My Love is like a Summer Rose," while among the many other contributors to its colums was Mary Ashley Townsend (Xariffa) author of *On the Bayou* and other poems.

The Times gave the first opening to Irwin Russell, that American Chatterton, father of negro dialect poetry, and author of *Christmas in the Quarters,* and other charming poems, not fully appreciated until after his sad death; and it numbered as one of its editors Bishop Hugh Miller Thompson, author of many lay as well as religious works.

When consolidated with the *Democrat,* it blazed with literary glow. Among the editors were Lafcadio Hearn, who published, while in that position, several promising books and who was afterwards to obtain world-wide reputation as a writer of unexcelled brilliant style, and as the only foreigner to thoroughly read Japanese character and to see behind the Japanese screen; and Henry Guy Carleton, the playwright ,author of *Memnon, the Egyptian, The Pembertons, Paul Durand* and other plays, while among the staff writers were Miss Bessie Bisland (now Mrs. Wetmore), author of *Alas the Poor Widower,* a *Life of Hearn* and other books; Miss Jeannette Duncan, author of a dozen novels and books of travel, Charles Gayarré, the Louisiana historian, Charles Patton Dimitry, Samuel Minturn Peck, Julie Wetherill Baker, and others.

The Picayune contributed through two of its editors, Lumsden and Kendall, the best history of the Mexican War, while George W. Cable, the novelist got his literary start in life as a reporter on that paper with his *Drop Shot Sketches,* and John Dimitry also worked on its staff. The *Yazoo Sketches* with their inimitable "bar" stories, the rules of the Crescent City, which has contributed more slang to the American language than any other book, *Down Among the Dead Men,* and a hundred other productions that have since been received into American literature, all saw the light through the medium of the press of a single city, New Orleans.

The list might be extended a thousandfold, if all the papers were included, and if this article dealt with Southern literature instead of with Southern journalism; and it might thus be shown how much the press of the South did for the literature of the whole country, how it trained and disciplined the younger writers. And this large invasion of "literary fellers," into journalism as opposed to news gatherers is probably responsible, in part, for the careful, elevated and classical style which characterizes the writings of leading Southern newspapers.

What is said of New Orleans could be said with equal truth of nearly the entire South. The *Atlanta Constitution* has given the country "Uncle Remus" (Joel C. Harris), Henry Grady, the Southern orator, Frank Stanton, and a host of others.

Among others who took an active part in journalism or made their first appearance in literature in the columns of the Southern newspapers may be mentioned Richard Malcolm Davis, T. C. De Leon, Opie Read, Thomas O'Hara, Simon Chaudron, Henry Timrod, James Barron Hope, Alexander Beaufort Melke, George D. Prentice, George Henry Calvert, William J. Thompson, A. B. Longstreet, Edward A. Pollard, E. L. Didier, and many others.

The union between journalism and literature is perhaps best illustrated in the case of Thompson and Longstreet who together started *The Augusta States,* and who are respectively the authors of these popular classics, *Major Jones' Courtship* and *Georgia Sketches.*

Chaudron was editor of the *New Orleans Bee;* Timrod was war correspondent of the *Charleston Mercury.* Father Ryan whose *Banner of the South, The Sword of Robert Lee* were among the best literary products of the War of Secession, was editor of several religious journals; O'Hara of *The Bivouac of the Dead* edited *The Mobile Register, Louisville Times* and *Franklin* (Ky.) *Yeoman.* Randall, whose *My Maryland* was probably the most stirring of all the war poems, edited *The Augusta Chronicle* and afterwards the *New Orleans Morning Star.* Hope was editor of *The Norfolk Landmark,* Opie Read of *The Arkansas Gazette.* The list could be made pages longer, but enough has been given to show the close relationship between literature and journalism in the South.

The Press and Industrial Development.

Even greater in importance to the South and the Union were the services rendered by the Southern press in the upbuilding of the country. Without this assistance the losses and injuries of the War of Secession and Reconstruction would not have been overcome. When Judge Kelly of Pennsylvania, "Pig John" Kelly as he is generally called, the apostle of protection and industry, said, in the gloomy days succeeding the War of Secession, "The development of the South means the enrichment of the nation," he laid down a proposition the truth of which we can fully appreciate to-day. But for the active work of the Southern press, the attention it gave to industrial development, the many manufacturing, commercial and industrial editions its papers issued, the space they devoted to natural resources, etc., the new growth of the South would have been delayed many years, its agricultural and manufacturing wealth would have remained undiscovered or undeveloped, and the country as a whole, would have been much poorer to-day.

The same idea had occurred to many Southern leaders before; but they failed to secure the popular support necessary for success, and except here and there, the march of industrial development in the South had been slow. The explanation probably lay in two conditions—the fact that slavery tended to magnify agriculture, for which the slaves were best fitted, and to minimize manufacturing; and the lack of interest shown by most of the Southern newspapers of ante-bellum times in industries in the restricted sense of manufactures.

During the period just previous to the War of Secession, a period of apparently great prosperity to the South, when it was playing the leading part in the affairs of the nation and when its sons were administering, in large part, and administering well, cleanly and efficiently, the government of the country, it was natural that politics should assume an exaggerated importance in the eye of the people and of the press. The latter devoted itself mainly and in many cases, almost exclusively, to the discussion of political and constitutional questions. The discussion was on a broad and high plane, national rather than local, and as many and as able articles were published during this period of partisan and sectional debate as saw the light of day during the formative period of the republic, when Hamilton, Madison, Adams, Monroe and Jefferson contributed their papers to *The Federalist* and other journals of the times.

A few editors took a different view of the situation and saw in the development of resources, the building up of manufactures and wealth of all kinds, the influences that would, in the end, settle the issues of constitutionalism, states' rights, secession, etc. Among these stands out most conspicuous in his services and far in advance of his time and his section, Daniel D. B. DeBow, who for so many years, edited DeBow's *Review* in New Orleans and who, insisting that the future of the South lay in industrial development, in the use of all its manifold resources, preached these lessons for years and, through the columns of his magazine, did all he could to awaken the South to its opportunities and its needs.

When the great Southern convention over which John C. Calhoun presided, met at Memphis in 1845, it sent a thrill of inspiration through the South; by showing that it was not doing, in certain lines of industrial activity and in internal improvements, as much as the other sections. Among the delegates to that convention was DeBow. He was inspired by the speeches made and by the general tone of the convention for, establishing himself at New Orleans, he began the publication of his magazine, devoted to commerce, manufactures and every other line of industry. Its success was instantaneous and great and had the other Southern press followed the path he blazed, the South would have reached the highest point of development many decades before it did. Unfortunate, there were few men as enthusiastic as he on the subject and few as capable in this particular line. DeBow was only twenty-five years of age when he established his magazine but he showed himself far in advance of his time, and a genius in his able treatment of all matters bearing upon the material progress of the South. He was only thirty years old when he was appointed professor of political economy in the University of Louisiana, one of the first if not the first professorship of the kind in the United States, and only thirty-five when he was appointed superintendent of the United States census, and performed that work so admirably. The thirty odd volumes of his magazine tell the industrial and material development of the South during the period preceding the War of Secession, and his earnest efforts to awaken and arouse the South to its neglect of its opportunities. It was treated by the politicians as a hobby of his; we can now realize that he was a statesman of the highest order, a prophet, seeing far in advance of his day. DeBow worked at his task during all the long years when the political and constitutional struggle between the sections was growing more and more bitter. He kept it up even after actual war was under way; and not until New Orleans surrendered to Farragut, did he abandon his mazagine and his efforts to develop and strengthen the South through commerce and manufactures. Six months after Appomattox, he took up his work again and determined to revive his publication and wrote: "The restoration of the South can, it is hoped, be effected upon the basis proposed by the President [Johnson] and no greater field could be opened for the investment of capital, from every quarter." DeBow's *Review* was revived, "devoted," as its editor expressed it, "to the restoration of the Southern states and the development of the wealth and resources of the country."

He never realized his hopes but died soon afterwards in 1867, during the gloomiest period in the history of the South; and we can realize now that he, even with all his enthusiasm and energy could not have triumphed over the unfavorable conditions that then existed. No industrial revolution was possible during the unsettled and demoralized period from 1865 to 1872. A great deal of political agitation, of preliminary work and of constructive statesmanship was necessary before the South would be in a position to take up the work of industrial development.

The history of the Southern press during that period of reconstruction was honorable in the highest degree. It was a period which tried men's souls. The Southern newspapers which had barely survived the War of Secession, were poor and disabled when peace came. A number of new journals sprang into the field to plead and fight for the restoration of civil government. None in the South suffered more during this second warfare, no less destructive than the actual battles in the field, than the editors who aroused and organized the Southern people to free themselves. Many papers perished in the struggle; many editors were arrested and imprisoned; but the fight was kept up until complete victory was won. As Governor Chamberlain has pointed out in his account of his administration in South Carolina, the fall of the reconstruction governments was sealed when the press of the South took the lead in the movement against them.

Mr. DeBow was therefore premature by fifteen or more years; it was not possible to build up any industries under the conditions and government that then prevailed. It was necessary to change conditions first before the task of rebuilding could begin with any hope of success. This was accomplished through the efforts of the press; and in the early eighties all the friction and demoralization that had formerly existed being removed, the work of industrial regeneration was inaugurated.

To-day when the development is proceeding satisfactorily it is difficult to realize how much hard work was necessary to start the ball a-rolling. Little was known about the South at the time; some prejudice still existed against it, the outgrowth of sectional and political prejudice. And it was not regarded as a good field for investment as its resources were, as yet, hidden from view and unknown.

Nearly all the work of genuine reconstruction— the reconstruction of industry—was done by the Southern press; and it had in this a task unknown to the papers of the North or West, but one which brought it closer.to the people; and in the end, by the greater wealth thus produced it tended to benefit the papers themselves. The Atlanta Exposition of 1881, was mainly the work of the newspapers of that city and, although on a small scale, it succeeded in attracting a great deal of attention to the South and in giving the rest of the world a beter knowledge of what it had to offer. The World's Cotton Centennial at New Orleans, in 1884 and continued in 1885, was distinctly a newspaper enterprise with the editor of the *Times-Democrat* as its originator and director-general. It made the North acquainted with the wealth of the Southern press, with the iron and coal of the Birmingham district, with the possibilities of rice-growing in Louisiana and Texas, and the lumber, iron and rice industries of the South of to-day may almost be said to have had their birth there.

It is impossible, for lack of space, to tell the whole story of Southern material development since then and the close and intimate part of the press the newspapers as well as trade papers like the *Baltimore Manufacturers Record* has had in it; but it can be said, in a general way, that in the quarter of a century since the New Orleans Cotton Exposition, the Southern press has given more attention and more space to industrial questions,—manufactures, immigration, education, etc.—than any papers in the world; and that it is to their active, intelligent and persistent work that the South owes so much of its present prosperity.

From this short sketch, it is possible to see how much the Southern press is the outgrowth of the last few decades and what wonders it has accomplished for the South during that period. The work it has had to do, the difficulties it has encountered, have naturally given it characteristics not shared by the newspapers of other parts of the country, has brought it closer to the people, and has made it distinctly representative of the South, preserving the best traditions of the past, at the same time that it is in line with the activity and spirit of progress of the present day, and, instead of a few papers, as it had a short time ago, it now boasts of 5,550 to lead and aid the people to still greater and better things.

NORMAN WALKER,
Associate Editor New Orleans Times-Democrat.

CHAPTER XXI.

SOUTHERN MAGAZINES.

INCE 1828, when the *Southern Review* was established in Charleston, the South has not been without a magazine. The history of these magazines is an interesting, if not inspiring, one. Projected by some ambitious publisher, or by some man of letters desiring an organ through which he might communicate to the world as well as give opportunity to other writers, they have risen and fallen with the successive years. Not one of the ante-bellum magazines continues to be published to-day; the oldest of those that survive is but sixteen years old. And yet the story of their careers is one of the significant chapters in the intellectual development of the Southern people.

Although not first in point of time, the *Southern Literary Messenger* is the most significant in point of duration and importance of all these magazines. The first number appeared in August, 1834, and the last in June, 1864, Richmond being all the while the place of publication. The man who conceived the project was Thomas W. White, a practical printer of Richmond, who had spent some of his early life in Boston. Although he was not a man of the highest culture, he had the practical knowledge necessary for the publishing of a magazine. He knew how "to write a very good and coaxing letter," and thus secured as contributors some of the most prominent men of letters in the country. His liberal views on national questions conciliated Northerners, and his being a native of Virginia strengthened him in the South. While his professed object was to "call forth the slumbering and undeveloped talent of the Southern people,'' at the same time he sought to command the best talent in all sections of the country.

In the first nine numbers of the *Messenger* White was aided in his editorial duties by James E. Heath, auditor of Virginia.   Furthermore, he immediately secured contributions from Richard Henry Wilde, Mrs. Sigourney and Alexander B. Meek.   Wilde, besides contributing prose and poetry, obtained nearly one hundred subscribers in Augusta, Ga.   Such Virginians as Thomas R. Dew of William and Mary College, Beverley Tucker of the law department of the same institution, and Lucian Minor rendered him valuable assistance by contributing thoughtful articles on current subjects.   College commencement addresses form a large part of the contents.   As early as 1835 Judge Tucker published an argument in favor of slavery based on Blackstone.   He was answered, however, by more than one contributor, and by the editor, who said:

"Whilst we entirely concur with him that slavery, as a political or social institution is a matter exclusively of our own concern, as much as the laws which govern the distribution of property, we must be permitted to dissent from the opinion that it is either a moral or a political benefit.   We regard it, on the contrary, as a great evil which society, sooner or later, will find it not only to its interest to remove or mitigate, but will seek its gradual abolition, or amelioration, under the influence of those higher obligations imposed by an enlightened Christian morality."

These words are a notable expression of the best sentiment of Virginians before the South became fixed in its advocacy of slavery as an economic and political necessity.

Still more noteworthy was a series of articles, which began in the third number of the first volume, written by Lucian Minor, giving his observations and impressions of life in New England in 1834.

They had appeared first in the Fredericksburg *Arena,* but had been revised by the author for the *Messenger.* In 1871, James Russell Lowell published in the *Atlantic Monthly* some extracts from Minor's Journal from which the articles were written, commenting on his "Boswellian genius for observation," "his constant reasonableness and good taste, the fine breeding of letters," and above all on his catholicity of spirit in serving to show the feeling of the better type of Southerners. As these articles are read now in the files of the *Southern Literary Messenger,* they strike one as among the most discriminating and balanced studies ever made of New England life. The author describes the social customs and the educational development of that section, trying always to find those points which would be most beneficial to the people of Virginia.

"No other six weeks of my life have had compressed into them half so much excitement, or half so much interest. * * * Those Northern states have very far the start of us Virginians in almost all the constituents of civilization; yes, further than my state pride will even now let me own without a struggle. They are more public spirited than we. They are more charitable. They possess better organized social and civil institutions. * * * In their thorough practical understanding of the word *comfort,* they are as far before us, as we are before the Hottentots."

At the conclusion, he appeals to Virginians and New Englanders to understand one another better, anticipating by half a century the well-known words of L. Q. C. Lamar: "My countrymen, know one another and you will love one another."

The greatest impetus was given to the newly formed journal, however, by the fact that in March, 1835, Edgar Allan Poe began to contribute to its columns. White had written to John P. Kennedy for contributions, and Kennedy, who had recently had an opportunity to judge of the artistic work of Poe, commended him to the editor. Poe began

by sending his short stories *Berenice* and *Morella,*
and then book reviews. In June he was invited by
White to come to Richmond and assist him in the
editing of the magazine. He went in August and
in December he was made editor-in-chief at a salary
of approximately $800. Poe remained as editor
through January, 1837. During the eighteen months
in which he was connected with the magazine he published fourteen stories, nearly all of his early poems
—either in their original or revised form,—and more
than one hundred book reviews and editorials, his
contributions to each number varying from ten to
thirty pages. In the last number which he edited
he contributed more than one-third of the entire
contents. The number of titles in the Poe bibliography for 1836 is larger than in any other year of
his life. There is no question that a later editor
was right in claiming that "no magazine ever published so many shining articles from the same pen"
in the same length of time. *The Atlantic Monthly,*
twenty years later published the writings of men
most of whom had become famous; but Poe was
as yet unknown. In every number he was making
a reputation for himself and the magazine. In his
contributions to the *Messenger* he anticipated all
his later work. The general type of his tales, the
particularly haunting quality of his poetry, the
penetration and fearlessness of his criticism, even
his "anthography" and marginalia are all to be
found here; later years only served to develop powers and characteristics already evident to the reader
of the *Messenger.*

He seems at one time to have been interested in
his work. In a most enthusiastic letter to Kennedy,
he says:

"My health is better than for years past, my mind is fully occupied,
my pecuniary difficulties have vanished, I have a fair prospect of future

J. P. Kennedy

success — in a word, all is right. * * * Mr. White is very liberal. Next year, that is at the commencement of the second volume, I am to get $1,000. Besides this, I receive from publishers nearly all new publications. My friends in Richmond have received me with open arms, and my reputation is extending, especially in the South. Contrasting all this with those circumstances of absolute despair in which you found me, and you will see how great reasons I have to be grateful to God, and to yourself."

For a while he worked at his task with zest as well as energy, and at one time planned a number of the magazine to which all the leading writers in the country would contribute; we have his letters to them, glowing with hopes of the future. We are justified in concluding that he was a most industrious and indefatigable editor, author and critic during this period, and that if he had continued as he began in Richmond, he would have led a far different life.

That which contributed most to the success of the magazine and to his fame was the criticism written by Poe of contemporary American literature. He was, as Lowell said, "almost the only fearless critic in the country" at that time. In one of his reviews of two popular poets of the day, he set forth his view of the state of contemporary literature and his ideals of criticism. Following the period in which American criticism had simply reflected contemporary English views, there had come a time when American critics indulged in an excessive laudation of native writers.

"We are becoming boisterous and arrogant, in the pride of a too speedily assumed literary freedom. * * * We get up a hue and cry about the necessity of encouraging native writers of merit; we blindly fancy that we can accomplish this by indiscriminate puffing of good, bad, and indifferent, without taking the trouble to consider that what we choose to denominate encouragement is thus, by its general application, rendered precisely the reverse. * * * Deeply lamenting this unjustifiable state of public feeling, it has been our constant endeavor, since assuming the editorial duties of this journal, to stem, with what little ability we possess, a current so disastrously undermining the health and prosperity of our literature."

He was true to his ideals, too.

From the time when he created a sensation by his caustic review of *Norman Leslie,* a novel by one of the most popular men in New York City, he insisted on high standards of literary work; "No true, we mean sensible, American, will like a bad book the better for being American," was one of his theses. He had the word "damn" in his critical vocabulary. In Simms' *Partisan* he found "instances of bad taste, villainously bad taste." He characterized another book as "utter folly, bombast, and inanity." Of G. P. R. James, he said, "He has fallen apparently upon that unlucky mediocrity permitted neither by gods nor columns." While such criticism sounded harsh, it was the honorable course to be pursued where low standards of art prevailed.

Such criticism, coupled with superior creative writing, caused Paulding to write to White in January, 1836: "Your periodical is decidedly superior to any periodical in the United States, and Mr. Poe is decidedly the best of our young editors."

Poe strongly resented the charge made by a Richmond paper that his reviews were of a slashing kind, and altogether destructive, claiming that of the ninety-four reviews published in six months, the overwhelming proportion was favorable. Perhaps a modern critic would complain of Poe's favorable criticism more than of his unfavorable. But at the time his great service was in letting the public know that an editor would adopt a conscientious attitude towards all books that came before him. Along with much work that is necessarily temporary in its character, there were some reviews that anticipated the philosophical breadth of his later works, the *Rationale of Verse* and the *Philosophy of Composition.* Such papers as those on Bryant's poetry, on Coleridge, on Longstreet's *Georgia Scenes,* and on

KNOW ALL MEN BY THESE PRESENTS, That we *Edgar A. Poe* (and) *Thomas W. Cleland* *and acting as governor* are held and firmly bound unto *Wyndham Robertson, Lieutenant* Governor of the Commonwealth of Virginia, in the just and full sum of ONE HUNDRED AND FIFTY DOLLARS, to the payment whereof, well and truly to be made to the said *acting* Governor, or his successors, for the use of the said Commonwealth, we bind ourselves and each of us, our and each of our heirs, executors and administrators, jointly and severally, firmly by these presents. Sealed with our seals, and dated this *16th* day of *May* — 183*6*.

THE CONDITION OF THE ABOVE OBLIGATION IS SUCH, That whereas a marriage is shortly intended to be had and solemnized between the above bound *Edgar A Poe* and *Virginia E. Clemm* of the City of Richmond. Now if there is no lawful cause to obstruct said marriage, then the above obligation to be void, else to remain in full force and virtue.

Signed, sealed and delivered }
in the presence of }

Cho. Howard

Edgar A Poe   SEAL.

Tho. W. Cleland   SEAL.

CITY OF RICHMOND, To wit :

This day *Thomas W Cleland* above named, made oath before me, as *Deputy* Clerk of the Court of Hustings for the said City, that *Virginia E. Clemm* is of the full age of twenty-one years, and a resident of the said City. Given under my hand, this *16* day of *May* 183*6*

Cho. Howard

MARRIAGE AGREEMENT BETWEEN EDGAR A. POE AND
THOMAS W. CLELAND.

Halleck and Drake, are worthy of Poe at his best. They are not simply quotations from, and summaries of, books, as are the reviews so often found in the quarterlies of the time; they are genuinely critical, telling why the forms are fair or foul, and furnishing a basis for a sound critical judgment of other books.

It must not be thought, however, that Poe's work completely monopolized the *Messenger*. During his editorship, Paulding, Simms and P. P. Cooke were regular contributors. He also secured an unpublished lecture by Benjamin Franklin and some letters from Randolph, and obtained the right to publish extracts, in advance of their publication, in book form, of Bulwer's *Cromwell* and Chorley's *Memoirs of Mrs. Hemans*. When he retired from the editorship in January, 1837, probably on account of his irregular habits which grew more and more distasteful to White and also on account of his inability to work within the limitations demanded by a steady job, White became editor as well as proprietor. He was aided in his editorial work by some of the Virginians already mentioned and especially by Matthew Fontaine Maury, who for a number of years was considered by many to be the editor. Through Maury, who was just at the beginning of his brilliant career, the magazine became a special factor in calling attention to needed reforms in the army and navy. Maury was always an enthusiastic and aggressive writer, a man of ideas, who stirred up more than one controversy.

The magazine had as contributors a good many Northern writers also, especially James Ticknor Fields, Henry Theodore Tuckerman and Park Benjamin. In 1839 and 1840 it was made notable by some of the early poems of Longfellow and Lowell. In fact, Lowell published twelve poems in the year 1840 under the pseudonym "Hugh Perceval"—all the poems he wrote that year. His biographer, Mr. Scudder, says: "The *Southern Literary Messenger* was one of those impecunious, but ambitious journals, and the editor teased Lowell constantly for contributions. Lowell gave them freely, for writing was his delight." Soon, however, Lowell refused to write, because he did not receive recompense therefor. When White asked him to translate a long poem of Victor Hugo's, he wrote to a friend:

"When I do I shall tell him that reading and writing come by nature, but to be a translator is the gift of fortune, so that if he chooses to pay me he shall have a translation. I do not think I shall write any more for him. 'Tis a bad habit to get into for a poor man, this writing for nothing. * * * Perhaps if I hang off, he may offer me somewhat."

This last quotation suggests that the *Messenger*, even in its seemingly successful days, was not in the habit of paying for contributions, and this, notwithstanding the fact that Poe claimed that he increased the subscription list from 700 to 5,500 and that White made $10,000—a statement that must be accepted with caution, however. Still White wrote in 1841 that within the last year his subscription list had increased largely. He added:

"If the *Messenger* has been good in times past, it shall be better in times to come. It has never had such a list of correspondents as those whose pens are now engaged to adorn its pages. * * * With the growing popularity of the *Messenger*, such has been the increase of contributors, that it would now keep one person constantly employed to overhaul MSS. and do nothing else."

In 1843 White died and the *Messenger* was continued by Benjamin Blake Minor, a brother of Lucian Minor. During his editorship he offered prizes for stories and poems, at one time as much as $190. He was especially interested in furthering the interests of the University of Virginia, of which he was a graduate, in the preservation of colonial records and in the promotion of a real historical spirit through the medium of the Virginian Historical

Society, of which the *Messenger* was for sometime the organ. Campbell's *History of Virginia* appeared serially during his editorship. In 1845, on his way to the commercial convention of Southern and Western states, at Memphis, Minor visited William Gilmore Simms at "Woodlands" and purchased from him his recently established magazine *The Southern and Western Review*. Accordingly, the *Messenger* appeared in 1846 with the cumbersome title *The Southern and Western Literary Messenger and Review*.

The old title was restored however in 1848 by John R. Thompson, who became editor in October, 1847. Thompson was probably the best editor the *Messenger* ever had. He wrote poems which appear in all American anthologies; he was master of a delightful prose style which was in evidence in personal essays written for the *Messenger;* and he was a critic of insight and balance. He also had the power to attract literary people to his magazine, the same quality that charmed Thackeray on his visit to Richmond, and won the sympathy of Carlyle in London, and caused him after the war to be appointed by William Cullen Bryant as literary editor of the New York *Evening Post*. He tried for thirty years to establish a magazine worthy of the support of Southern as well as Northern people on its intrinsic merits. He secured the work of such promising Northern writers as Ik Marvel, whose *Reveries of a Bachelor* began to appear in the *Messenger* September, 1849, Stoddard and Aldrich, whose poetic merit the editor was one of the first to recognize. Furthermore, he did all he could to encourage Southern writers. Besides holding Simms, he added to his list of contributors Margaret Junkin (afterwards Mrs. Preston), Paul Hamilton Hayne, Henry Timrod, Moncure D. Conway, Joseph G. Baldwin, Barron Hope and John Esten Cooke. Perhaps the

best way to form an idea of the magazine at its best
is to notice the contents for March, 1849.   The leading article is entitled *Glimpses of Europe During
1848*, with a special study of the German parliament.
Then follow: *Jonathan Swift*, by H. T. Tuckerman;
The Castle by the Sea, a translation from Uhland;
a chapter in a serial by Philip P. Cooke; *Sketches of
Southern Life; Letters From Paris and New York*,
by Park Benjamin; *Boccaccio and His Writings;* and
a review of Lowell's *Fable for Critics*, by Edgar
Allan Poe.

Poe's review suggests that in 1848-49, just before
his death, he spent several months in Richmond.
The *Messenger* office was his headquarters; and
Thompson was quick to seize the opportunity to
secure him as a contributor once more.   In five successive numbers he contributed *Marginalia*—short
quotations and chance impressions.   His *Rationale
of Verse*, revised and expanded from an earlier form
was published October and November, 1848.   It is
noteworthy that in his critical work at this time
Poe was distinctly Southern in his prejudices against
the writers of New England and especially against
Lowell and the *North American Review*.   Some of
his most sarcastic remarks are to be found in such
comments as: "Pinckney was born too far South";
"Had the *George Balcombe* of Beverley Tucker been
the work of anyone born north of Mason and Dixon's
Line, it would have been long ago recognized as one
of the very noblest fictions ever written by an American"; "It is high time that the literary South took
its own interest into its own charge."

Thompson, however, reduced the spirit of sectionalism to a minimum.   It is recorded that when he
visited Simms in 1855 Simms urged him to make
the magazine "a proper vehicle for the true political
opinion of Virginia."   But Thompson could not rise

to the necessity of the case. He felt, as he, or one of his contributors, afterwards wrote in the magazine: "Slavery may be pushed in the defense of it to absurd extremes. It is a wholesome and a beneficial relation * * * But it does not make poems, nor carve statues, nor evolve the harmonies of music. We want other culture in the South besides the cotton culture; we want the influence of literature and art."

In 1860, Thompson, who had moved to Augusta, Ga., to become editor of the *Field and Fireside,* was succeeded as editor of the *Messenger* by Dr. George W. Bagby, who immediately made it the organ of the secession movement in Virginia. In striking contrast with much of its earlier history, the *Messenger* allied itself aggressively with the forces that were making for the breaking up of the Union. The editor pleads for "home-made, purely Southern articles." Under the pseudonym "Mozis Addums," he himself wrote of the progress of the war, in the homely dialect of the mountaineer. For three years he continued to edit the magazine, which became, however, more and more eclectic in its character. On Jan. 1, 1864, there was an announcement that the future editor would be Frank H. Alfriend, afterwards the biographer of Jefferson Davis. He and his business manager announced themselves as "young gentlemen, brim full of energy and ambition, with abundant means, and above all with correct opinions in regard to the proper mode of developing a literary journal." They intended to make the *Messenger,* both externally and internally, "far more inviting than it had hitherto been; to pay for contributions, to advertise liberally; to secure agencies in all the principal cities and towns in the Confederacy; to enlist the best and brightest talent in the land—in a word, to enlighten and invigorate the old magazine." But their hopes were not to be realized. The light was but flickering, before total darkness.

Four years before the *Messenger* succumbed to its fate, *Russell's Magazine,* in Charleston, had come to its end. It was the last of some eight or ten magazines that had been published in that city since 1828. It was but natural that Charleston should have been the first of Southern cities to establish a magazine. In the early years of the Nineteenth century the city was equaled only by Boston for its culture and scholarship. If to a modern novelist like Mr. Owen Wister, it should seem, in contrast with the reign of modern democracy and industrialism, "the most wistful, the most lovely and the most appealing town in America," a Charlestonian of the period indicated might be pardoned for his pride in the architectural beauty of the city and in the culture of the people. With characteristic self-complacency, one of the writers in the *Southern Review* said, in speaking of the aristocracy of Charleston: "There can be no doubt that their attainments in polite literature are very far superior to those of their contemporaries at the North, and the standard of scholarship in Charleston was, consequently much higher than in any other city on the continent." There was a well-defined tradition that her best young men should be educated in the colleges and universities of the old world. It is not surprising therefore that we find in the year 1828 a group of able and cultured public men, such as Robert Y. Hayne, James L. Petigru, William J. Grayson, Thomas S. Grimké, and above all Hugh Swinton Legaré. Legaré had spent two years on the Continent, most of the time studying civil law in Edinburgh, but also traveling in the most interesting places of Europe. He was a man of the same general type as Edward Everett, uniting a keen appreciation of classical literature with the highest ideals of public service.

It was but natural that one, who had lived at Edinburgh when the *Edinburgh Review* and *Blackwood's Magazine* were in the full glory of their early triumphs, should conceive the idea of establishing a quarterly review in Charleston. He would be all the more inclined to do so by reason of the establishment of the *North American Review* in Boston in 1815. His idea met with hearty response in Stephen G. Elliott, first professor of natural history and botany in the Charleston Medical College, and founder of the Literary and Philosophical Society of Charleston. As joint editors they brought out the first number of the *Southern Review,* February, 1828. In spite of almost immediate discouragement, due to the lack of response on the part of the people, the *Review* continued to exist until the end of 1832. The articles, when read now, seem heavy and somewhat pedantic, but compare most favorably with articles in other quarterly journals of the time. There was necessarily much padding. While the editors were aided by the group of Charlestonians already mentioned and by professors in the College of South Carolina, notably Cooper and Nott, the main contributions were made by the editors themselves, Legaré contributing as many as four articles to one number. It was very characteristic of the *Review* and of the ideals of the community that the first article should have been a plea for training in the classics, a fine statement of the claims of the old ideals of higher education as opposed to the increasing demand for instruction in modern literature and in science. There was scarcely a number in which there was not some article on Greek or Roman literature, generally written by the scholarly chief editor. Another characteristic point of view is seen

in the disparagement of so-called American literature, as illustrating the indifference of most Southerners to the encouragement of native talent, the
writer maintaining that in proportion to an American's knowledge of classic literature the less inclined
was he to engage in literature of his own creation.
Standard English literature was good enough for
Americans at present, and might actually continue
good enough for perhaps a century to come. "Even
if we did need a separate literature, we have nothing
wherewith to make it." Characteristic also are
articles on contemporary English literature, notably
the well-known critical estimate of Byron and the
reviews of Scott's works as they appeared from time
to time. Gradually, however, political articles increased in number, especially as South Carolina was
in those years much taken up with the nullification
discussion. There was still difference of opinion
enough to cause debate between Unionists and the
advocates of nullification. As an illustration of the
fairness of the editors, we quote the following editorial:

"The two last articles in this number have been furnished us by two
of our immortal statesmen. If they differ somewhat in their views, if
they differ sometimes from the opinions we ourselves have advanced, we
yet publish them with great pleasure, from a wish that at a moment like
the present, subjects of paramount importance may be fairly and under
different aspects placed before our readers."

Legaré became more and more involved in political life, and the people less and less inclined to
support the magazine. But Charleston was destined,
as a brilliant American critic has recently said, to
be the graveyard of more than one magazine. The
very same year in which the *Southern Review* was
started, William Gilmore Simms, then a young man
just beginning his career, united with James W. Sim-
mons in the establishment of the *Southern Literary*

Gazette, which was to be a monthly magazine of sixty-four pages.

"The experiment was continued through two half-yearly volumes," says Professor Trent; "but as each number fell dead from the press, and as the pockets of both partners began to suffer, it was considered that enough had been done for the glory of Southern literature, and publication was soon discontinued."

Simms, however, did not let this failure or many others diminish his desire to establish a worthy periodical. Either as chief contributor or as editor he was connected with eight periodicals in Charleston. He is the hero of ante-bellum magazines. During his lifetime he contributed 250 stories, poems, and miscellaneous articles to magazines and annuals, most of them to the Charleston periodicals. With indefatigable energy and amazing resourcefulness and unusual self-sacrifice he wrought valiantly if not always wisely for the maintenance of a high standard of periodical literature in the South. His biographer summarizes his work in the years 1842 to 1850 in the following suggestive sentence:

"Simms edits two magazines, begins to edit a third, is his own chief contributor, and favors his New York, Philadelphia, and Richmond confrères with a perennial supply of manuscript."

Some of the less important and short-lived magazines were the *Cosmopolitan,* an annual after the order of Irving's *Salmagundi;* the *Southern Literary Journal,* which with Daniel K. Whitaker, a New Englander by birth, as editor, and Simms as chief contributor, lasted from September, 1835, to the spring of 1839; the *Magnolia,* which was an imitation of *Godey's Lady's Book,* and lasted for one year, June, 1842, to June, 1843; *The Orion,* edited by William C. Richards and afterwards by Simms, in 1844.

Simms was more vitally interested, however, in the *Southern and Western Monthly Magazine and Review,* generally known as *Simms's Magazine,* of which he was sole proprietor and editor. During the time that he edited it (January, 1845-1846) he wrote twenty-five long articles and tales, and secured as contributors Duychkinck, Meek, Albert Pike, J. M. Legaré, and Caroline Lee Hentz. The magazine was sold in 1846 to the editor of the *Southern Literary Messenger*, which enlarged its title to include its Charleston contemporary.

Meanwhile the *Southern Quarterly Review*, first established in 1842 at New Orleans by Whitaker, had been moved to Charleston in 1844. Although it had had some success, especially when the young J. D. B. DeBow was associate editor, it had by 1849 reached "a condition of worthlessness not even to be conceived." Simms was then elected its editor-in-chief at the salary of $1,000, and with the right to offer his best contributors a dollar a page. It is with this Review that the fame of Simms as an editor largely rests. While he maintained a healthy interest in literature, his main emphasis was laid on the secession controversy, which was then at its height in South Carolina. No Southerner was at this time a more enthusiastic advocate of slavery and secession than Simms. In the year 1850 alone he wrote ten articles, few of them under forty pages, and four departments of critical notices in which upwards of one hundred and fifty books were reveiwed. He received valuable assistance from such contributors as Hammond, Poinsett, Lieber, Grayson, DeBow and other South Carolinians; from Meek of Alabama, H. R. Jackson of Georgia, Professor Holmes of the University of Virginia, Maury and the aged Beverley Tucker of Virginia. Although he did not contribute articles, Calhoun was deeply interested in the success of the magazine and helped Simms to procure contributors. The magazine finally went down in 1855. Six of the articles in the January number of the last volume were on slavery, or on subjects closely related thereto. Nowhere can one better see the very form and pressure of the secession movement in South Carolina than in the volumes of the *Southern Quarterly Review.*

This was Simms's last effort to establish a magazine of his own. But he was to play an important part in the projection and maintenance of *Russell's Magazine,* of which Paul Hamilton Hayne was editor from its first number in April, 1857, to its last, June, 1860. This magazine was the result not so much of one man's idea as of the plan of a most interesting group of men who then lived in Charleston. Perhaps there has never been so near an approach to what may be considered a literary atmosphere in the South as there was in Charleston in the few years just before the war. Five years before the establishment of the magazine we learn from *DeBow's Review* that there was an effort made to establish a publishing house which should vie in interest and power with some of the most successful of the North and that this house should maintain a quarterly and a monthly magazine, besides publishing the works of the native writers. But like so many other schemes, this one fell through, to be succeeded however by *Russell's Magazine.*

Hayne and Timrod were just in the dawn of most promising careers, having published volumes of poetry that were indicative of real poetic excellence. Besides these there were survivors of the generation of men already suggested in connection with Legaré, cultivated professional men, like Dr. Bruns and Dr. Michel, young scholars like Samuel Lord, David Ramsay and Basil L. Gildersleeve, all three having just returned from German universities, and John Russell, the owner of a book store that must have rivaled in interest the "Old Corner Book Store" in

Boston. It was the habit of these men to meet often
at one another's homes, and especially at Simms's,
and in the afternoons at Russell's book store. Hayne,
in after years wrote his reminiscences of these
golden days:

> "Many and jovial were the "little suppers" of which we partook at his
> pleasant town residence.   It was here that the idea originated of start-
> ing a monthly magazine in Charleston, which might serve as an exponent
> of Southern talent and culture.   The idea speedily assumed a definite
> business form.   An enterprising, intelligent, and popular bookseller then
> doing business in the city, Mr. John Russell, was induced to take the
> practical management of the work, which, in honor of its founder, was
> named *Russell's Magazine.*

In the first number the object of the magazine is
indicated in the following words:

> "It is established and designed to meet a commonly felt want, and to
> give utterance and circulation to the opinions, doctrines, and arguments
> of the educated mind of the South especially, and to promote in its
> sphere and measure the progress of a sound American literature, free
> from party shackles or individual prejudices."

It was to be "another depository for Southern
genius and an incentive for its exercise." The magazine was noted for its political articles by William
J. Grayson, its steadfast championship of Simms
against all Northern critics, the publication of many
of the best poems of Hayne and Timrod, the excellent
papers of Timrod on the theory of poetry and the
sonnet. The most noteworthy article was one which
appeared in June, 1858, presumably written by
Simms, on the *Literary Prospects of the South.* This
last article, it may be safely said, is the best discussion that we have of literary conditions in the
South before the war; a kind of summary of Simms's
entire experience as a creative writer and as an editor of magazines. It is brilliantly written, and is a
manly, straightforward discussion of the place of
literature in the life of a people and of the defects
of the Southern people. Indeed, the final effect of the

reading of the volumes of this magazine is to cause one to feel the necessity of creative work in the Southern states. One cannot but compare, however, its feeble success with the pronounced success of the *Atlantic Monthly* which was started the same year, and which has but recently celebrated its fiftieth anniversary.

Meanwhile another Charlestonian had established a far more successful magazine in New Orleans.

In 1845, J. D. B. DeBow, a young lawyer, attended a convention of Southern and Western states held in Memphis. As the result of this enthusiastic meeting, he became tremendously impressed with the possibilities of the South in industry. That he might be of some assistance in promoting the great cause of Southern progress, he resolved to establish a Review which should have as its main object the setting forth of the commercial life of the South. Accordingly in January, 1846, there appeared in New Orleans the first number of *DeBow's Commercial Review*—a "Monthly Journal of Trade, Commerce, Commercial Polity, Agriculture, Manufactures, Internal Improvements, and General Literature." On the outside cover was a quotation from Carlyle: "Commerce is king"—an expression indicative of the spirit of the editor and of the purpose of the magazine. One cannot but think of the immense difference between this review and the *Southern Review,* started by Legaré. It was fortunate that DeBow, who had been born in Charleston, and who had spent his literary apprenticeship there, should have established his review in the commercial metropolis of the great Southwest. Years afterward in speaking of his foolhardiness in undertaking such a project he said:

"Without experience, without pecuniary means, without friends or influence, scarcely attained to the age of majority, I issued a prospectus of a monthly periodical. * * * It was a new field, in which there were no guiding lights. * * * The odds were one hundred to one against success. * * * I have triumphed. * * * When has the *Review*, or its editor, been lukewarm upon such matters, and in what period of doubt or difficulty were they silent?"

DeBow might well rejoice in his triumph. Although the magazine all but failed two years after it began, its continuance was made possible by the public spirit of Maunsel White, a captain of industry of New Orleans, who had also made possible the chair of political economy which DeBow held at the University of Louisiana. In spite of the failure of many subscribers to pay their dues, the *Review* was from that time an assured fact. Its policy was approved by the leading chambers of commerce of the South, and it became a more and more vital factor in that industrial awakening which was such a pronounced feature of Southern life between 1850 and 1860. Such historians as Gayarré and Dr. Monette, and such publicists as Judah P. Benjamin and Joel R. Poinsett, contributed to the success of the magazine. But in the main it was the work of one man, the editor. DeBow wrote in one volume sixteen, in another twenty-one articles. These writings were full of statistics as to the actual conditions of various Southern states. But there was more than that; DeBow had a sort of imperial imagination, comparable to Daniel Webster's. He saw, as few men saw, the romance of the Southwest, and the expansion of the country towards the great unexplored West. If he had seen with the same imagination the evils of slavery, he might be reckoned as one of the wisest men who ever lived in the South. As it was, he must be credited with editing and largely writing a review which is the most important firsthand material for the study of ante-bellum conditions, for the *Review* was more than a commercial journal. The editor was constantly adding new features. From 1850 on, literary and political subjects began to occupy a prominent place. In 1855 there was added a department of education in which one may see that efforts were being made in the years just before the war for the creation of a public school system in Georgia and other Southern states. It is no wonder that the *Review* has been of such excellent service to such recent historians as Mr. Rhodes and writers of Southern monographs. In his *Southern Sidelights,* a particularly illuminating discussion of the ante-bellum South, Mr. Edward Ingle has relied almost altogether upon *DeBow's Review* and the *Southern Literary Messenger* for his study and interpretation of Southern life of the time.

Not the least significant of the services done by the editor of the *Review* was his criticism of certain aspects of Southern life:

"The true secret of our difficulties lies in the want of energy on the part of our capitalists, and ignorance on the part of those who ought to labor. * * * The fashion of the South has been to consider the production of cotton and sugar and rice the only rational pursuits for gentlemen, except the professions, and like the haughty Greeks and Romans to class the trading and manufacturing spirit as essentially servile. The truth is, it is impossible to rouse the Southern people on any subject whatever of enterprise, and the sooner we admit it and ground our arms, the better."

Like the *Messenger,* the *Review* lived well on into the war, not suspending publication till the Northern fleet entered New Orleans in 1862.

Scarcely had the war ended when magazines sprang up in all parts of the South. Partly on account of poverty which some thought could be relieved by writing and publishing, partly because Southerners now felt more than ever that they needed to be represented in a proper way at the bar of public opinion, and partly to revive old magazines, there was a perfect avalanche of magazine writing in the devastated Southern states. Charleston was to the front again with the *Nineteenth Century,* which lived only a few months. At New Orleans in April, 1866, the *Crescent Monthly,* devoted to literature, art, science and society, was established with William Evelyn as publisher. In the announcement of the first number the editor says:

"We now enter the field, the youngest adventurer among the monthlies, confidently expecting to occupy a prominent place in the literature of our country. * * * The influence of all who have the best interests of Southern literature at heart is respectfully solicited."

The publisher thought that the circulation would soon reach 15,000 copies. "This number can soon be reached," he adds naïvely, "if one friend of literature in each town and village will secure a few names." He makes the whole survey of the failures of magazines of the past, but is confident that he will succeed. About all that is noteworthy about this magazine, however, is the fact that Joel Chandler Harris served an apprenticeship as secretary to its editor. About the same time there appeared *Scott's Monthly* in Atlanta, the *Field and Fireside* in Raleigh, *The Land We Love* in Charlotte, and *DeBow's Review* in Nashville.*

Of these we need notice in detail only two. *The Land We Love* was edited by Gen. D. H. Hill, who issued the first number May, 1866. It contained the writings of Dr. Ticknor, of Georgia, John R. Thompson, of Virginia, and a few other Southern writers. There was a special department of "Southern Lyrics." The most notable feature of the magazine, however, was some articles written by the editor on education. When we take into consideration the high position held by General Hill, his frank discussion of defects in ante-bellum Southern life and

*In addition to those professedly literary magazines, the Southern Methodist and Presbyterian churches revived their quarterlies, the former of which has maintained ever since an increasingly high standard of excellence.

his plea for scientific and industrial education are most noteworthy.

"We must," he says, "abandon the æsthetic and ornamental for the practical and useful. We need practical farmers, miners, machinists, engineers, manufacturers, navigators, blacksmiths, carpenters. * * * Agriculture must be studied as a science. We want practical learning, not scholastic lore. We want business men, with brain and hands for work. Less attention should be paid to politics, and more to domestic thrift and economy. Let us have a system which will bring a greater duty and glory to our desolate places. Will the flowers of rhetoric plant any roses in our burnt districts? Will oratory benefit those who have no constituents to harangue, no legislative halls to enter?"

He makes a detailed comparison of the South and England, showing how the former had developed only in one direction, that of political power, while the latter had developed every type of man and every interest of society. More significantly, he compares the South with the North in industry, energy and perseverance. The result of the war is explained by the South's want of adaptation of right means to accomplish cherished ends. We must learn from New England the lessons of industrial diversity as well as culture. Only with this spirit shall we be ready to face the future.

The most pronounced advocate of these views, however, was *DeBow's Review*, reëstablished in January, 1866, "devoted to the restoration of the Southern states and the development of the wealth and resources of the country." The outside page of the first number was a picture representing the dawn of a new day in the South—the sun shining on the Mississippi River, alive with boats; on factory smokestacks, railroads, telegraph wires, hogsheads of tobacco, cotton, reapers and sugarcane. With the same old enthusiasm and with an undaunted hope and remarkable resourcefulness, DeBow announces the policy of the magazine as the building up of industry and enterprise rendered necessary under the

new and altered conditions of things. Regarding the
issues of the past as dead, it is the part of the *Review* to accept in good faith the situation. The
editor seems to rejoice in the fact that the United
States is a fixed and permanent government, and
believes that the part of the South in the future of
the nation is to be a commanding one:

> "This section must do everything in her power to throw her immense
> uncultivated domain into the market at a low price and resort to in-
> telligent and vigorous measures, at the earliest moment, to induce an
> influx of population and capital from abroad."

Side by side with these optimistic pictures of the
future there appeared in the *Review* the most pessi-
mistic articles of George Fitzhugh, who could see
only the disappointment and despair of the present,
and in the result of the war the ushering in of an
age of radicalism and anarchy. But the enthusiasm
of the editor was calculated to disarm the criticism
of his contributors. His cry was "Light up the
torches of industry." As before the war, so now
he brings out the resources of each Southern state
under such subjects as the following: *The Failure
of South Carolina; Virginia, Her New Spirit and
Development; The Cotton Resources of the South;
The Vast Resources of Louisiana; The South and
Direct Foreign Trade.* He pleads for diversified
industry:

> "We should not wait for the political and commercial and social re-
> construction of the divided union. We should ourselves commence the
> work of reconstructing our ruined agriculture on the foundation of a
> diversified industry. Begin small if need be, but begin."

Unfortunately the editor did not live long enough
to see the results of his advice on any large scale.
He died in New York Feb. 27, 1867. The *Review* was
maintained by some of his associates for two years
longer, and then met the fate of so many of its predecessors and contemporaries.

The most signal efforts to maintain magazines after the war are seen, however, at Baltimore. Baltimore had always been an almost distinctively Southern city, and now that so many people from Georgia, Virginia and other states removed there, it became the headquarters of publishers of Southern books and of proprietors of Southern magazines. First we find a magazine entitled *Southern Society,* which made promise of fulfilling the demand of Southern readers for the lighter forms of literature. On a far better basis the Turnbull Brothers established the *New Eclectic,* which lasted from 1868 to 1870. Besides containing reprints of the most striking articles in foreign periodicals, it sought to encourage Southern talent. No better idea can be gained of the way in which publishers and editors appealed to Southern writers for support of such ventures than the following extract from a letter written by Margaret J. Preston to Paul Hamilton Hayne in 1869:

"Within the last month I have had various letters from the editor of the *New Eclectic* about the magazine. The proprietors are somewhat disheartened in the attempt to maintain a distinctively Southern journal, and they have asked me to use whatever influence I may have among literary friends, writers and others, in arousing some true interest in their undertaking. I promise for myself contributions *gratis,* and newspaper squibs in their behalf. * * * Now, I beg you will speak a good word for them in one of your Georgia papers. An extended subscription list is all they require to give permanency to the magazine, and to afford them the means of enlarging its attractions. If it fails, through the inertia and apathy of the Southern people, then farewell to any attempt to sustain a magazine south of Philadelphia. The Turnbulls have been men of means (they have lost heavily lately) and during the first year of their connection with the magazine sunk thousands in endeavoring to maintain it. So you see they have been willing to support Southern literature at some little cost to themselves. The editor says that the writers of the South seem apathetic."

In this way were such Southern writers as Simms, Hayne, Lanier, Mrs. Preston and others called upon to support various enterprises in the form of magazines. Simms wrote just before his death in 1870:

"I write for two Baltimore journals, from neither of which have I got my pay. I have balances due by both, which I fear I shall never get a cent of." For the most part they did their work cheerfully, and even at some sacrifice. In the year that Simms died, a successor to the *New Eclectic* was established in Baltimore—the *Southern Magazine,* edited by William Hand Browne, now professor of English literature in Johns Hopkins University. The first number appeared January, 1871, and the last August, 1874. The magazine started off with tributes to Robert E. Lee, who had died a few months before. Besides republishing articles from the *Cornhill Magazine* and the *Contemporary Review,* it had as contributors such conservative writers as Dr. R. L. Dabney, a polemic and reactionary leader in the Presbyterian church; such scholars as Professors Thomas R. Price and Basil L. Gildersleeve, of the University of Virginia, and the more distinctively Southern creative writers Hayne, Richard Malcolm Johnston and Sidney Lanier. Johnston published his *Dukesborough Tales* under the pseudonym of "Philemon Perch," while Lanier contributed his *Prospects and Retrospects, San Antonio de Bexar,* and a number of his earlier poems. One of the cherished objects of the magazine was the encouragement of the writing of a series of Southern textbooks, among which were Maury's geographies, Holmes's readers, Venable's mathematical series, Gildersleeve's Latin grammar, and DeVere's French grammar, and other modern language textbooks. Edward V. Valentine, the Richmond sculptor, suggests a meeting of all interested in Southern literature, science and art as the best means of advancing the cause of Southern culture. There were several articles, notably one by Judge W. A. Cocke, demanding that Southern talent should arise to assert itself:

"We must train up writers to vindicate our cause before the world and posterity and to put on imperishable records the lofty and heroic exploits which we blazoned on our shields and flags in gold and scarlet. We have borne long enough the reproach of having developed no authors whose utterances the world cared to hear. The Southern people must awake to the sense of their duty."

The editor did what he could to establish right standards of literary criticism. Paul Hamilton Hayne in an article entitled *Literature of the South*, wrote some golden words:

"No foreign ridicule, however richly deserved, nothing truly either of logic or of laughter, can stop this growing evil, until our own scholars and thinkers have the manliness and honesty to discourage instead of applauding such manifestation of artistic weakness and artistic platitude as have hitherto been fostered upon us by persons uncalled and unchosen of any of the Muses. * * * Can a people of mental dignity and æsthetical culture be vindicated by petting incompetency and patting ignorance and self-sufficiency on the back?"

The most indefatigable champion of the Southern cause was the *Southern Review,* established January, 1867, by Alfred Taylor Bledsoe, formerly professor of mathematics in the University of Virginia and the author of the noteworthy book entitled *"Is Davis a Traitor?"*. A man of undoubted intellectual power and with remarkable energy and resourcefulness, he had already during the war, by his studies in the British Museum, made himself familiar with the first hand sources necessary for the study of early American history. He brought back into the South the point of view of John C. Calhoun and gave forth the arguments in favor of secession with searching logic and a scholarship that was more exact than that of the great statesman himself. He conceived it to be his duty through the *Review* to give permanent statements to the ideas that had been fought for by the Southern people. His first volume was dedicated "to the despised, the disfranchised and downtrodden people of the South." He announced the subject to be emphasized in this organ as

the causes and consequences of the war and the ideals
of education which had prevailed in the old South.
He would not allow any criticism of his course to
change him in his desire to set forth the Southern
point of view.

"Shall we bury in the grave of the grandest cause that has ever perished on earth, all the little stores of history and philosophy which a
not altogether idle life has enabled us to enmass, and so leave the just
cause, merely because it is fallen, to go without our humble advocacy?
We would rather die."

He quoted with great gusto the words of Robert E.
Lee: "Doctor, you must take care of yourself; you
have a great work to do; we all look to you for our
vindication." None of the discouragement incident
to the management of the *Review* or threatened poverty could for one moment cause him to swerve from
his frequently expressed object. In a long article
in Vol. VIII., in pleading with the Southern people
to stand by him in his fight, he says:

"To abandon the *Southern Review* would be like the pang of death to
me. It is the child of my affections. I have made so many sacrifices
for it. I have bestowed so many fears and anxieties and labors upon it,
that I have often said to myself in the midst of my greatest troubles, no,
it shall not be abandoned! * * * Money is not my object. I am
willing to work for the South; nay, I am willing to be a slave for the
South. * * * Nothing but an unconquerable zeal in the cause of
the South and of the truth, could have sustained us under the heavy
pressure of its doubts, its difficulties, its trials, and its vexations in
spirit."

In spite of all discouragements, then, he rededi-
cates himself to his work, adding, "If, indeed, we
are not very greatly mistaken, the *Southern Review*
has only renewed its strength and plumed its wings
for a higher, bolder, nobler and gladder fight than
ever before."

Not only did Dr. Bledsoe write on political and social subjects, but on all questions of his age, always
from the conservative and reactionary standpoint.
For one number he wrote all but one article, ap-

proximately 250 pages. He nearly always had from three to five articles, generally on some political, mathematical or philosophical subject. He reminds one of a great Titan battling against the spirit of his age. He has no sympathy for modern democracy, for to him it was the child of infidelity. He is opposed to all the tendencies of modern science, for it tends to destroy the faith of mankind. He fights against it now with incomparable ridicule, and now with seemingly unanswerable logic. He is opposed to industrialism, looking upon it as the enemy of all that is chivalric and beautiful in civilization. He will have nought to do with German philosophy or German criticism, for they are both the inaugurators of the reign of radicalism and rationalism. His theological articles, echoes of his *Theodicy*, are concerned with such ancient problems as the mode of baptism, the damnation of infants, and predestination.

As one reads the articles of Dr. Bledsoe, many of them written with glowing style and always with clearness and force, he feels that there is expressed in vigorous language one of the best types in all literature of the conservative point of view. Certainly there is nowhere else where one can see the spirit of those conservative Southerners who before the war and since have battled against the inevitable tendencies of modern life. The articles are frequently long and heavy, but to a student of the intellectual history of the Southern people they are absolutely indispensable.

However important the *Southern Review* may be to one who would understand the conservative South, it did not express the point of view of the men who were to shape the future of this section. The spirit of *DeBow's Review* was to animate the industrial development of the South. The point of view of scholars and men of letters is to be found best expressed in two magazines that have been largely determined by the ideals which prevail in two progressive Southern institutions. It has been noticed that in the furtherance of the ante-bellum magazines, college and university men played an important part, although they never became the animating spirit. Significant of the increasing emphasis put upon education in the New South is the influence of the *Sewanee Review* and the *South Atlantic Quarterly,* the one established in 1892 and the other in 1902, both of them continuing to the present time. We have the definite expression of the ideas not only of the respective communities, but of a large number of scholarly men and publishers who live in the South and in the country at large. For obvious reasons attention is here given primarily to the *Sewanee Review.* While several members of the faculty of the University of the South must be given full credit for their share in the financial and intellectual support of the magazine, to Prof. W. P. Trent, formerly of Sewanee but now of Columbia University, must be attributed its conception and its establishment on a proper basis. While working up the material for his life of William Gilmore Simms, he necessarily studied carefully the ante-bellum magazines of Charleston, and felt that one or two of them did a valuable service in behalf of Southern letters. Hence his resolution to establish a magazine devoted to such topics of Theology, Philosophy, History and Literature as require fuller treatment than they usually receive in the popular magazines, and less technical treatment than they receive in specialist publications. Why should not a magazine, conducted with something of the spirit of the English reviews, minister to the cultivation of sounder criticism both of literature and of life? Professor Trent was well adapted for the work here undertaken. A man of wide reading and remarkable industry, and an exceedingly clear writer and a fearless critic, he conducted the *Review* with marked success. Entering upon his work with the full prestige that came from his life of Simms, which was at once recognized as the most scholarly work done by a Southerner within the decade 1890-1900, he soon attracted as contributors some of the best scholars of the country.

One of the main objects of the *Review* was to maintain the right to think clearly and correctly on all political, social and artistic questions, and then say honestly what was thought. In the discussion of Southern conditions both the editors and the contributors have written in accordance with the demands of truth rather than of sentiment. The industrial movement has been properly interpreted, the spirit of independence in politics has been at once noted and directed, adequate though not over much attention has been given to Southern literature, and a series of notable articles on problems of higher and secondary education have appeared. Furthermore the discussions of ancient and modern literature, and especially of English literature, have rendered the *Review* a potent factor in the dissemination of the spirit of cosmopolitanism, which is one of the prime requisites of the South of to-day. Most notable of all, however, has been its insistence, in season and out of season, on the importance of the national spirit. During the sixteen years of its existence there has been scarcely a note of sectionalism sounded. As Professor Henneman, who succeeded Professor Trent in 1900, has insisted, "The first thought for the Southerner of this generation to realize is the thought of a common union and a national citizenship."

To the same effect has ministered the latest of all

the Southern magazines, *Uncle Remus's Magazine,*
started in Atlanta, May, 1907, edited by the late Joel
Chandler Harris and published by the Sunny South
Publishing Company. For five years Mr. Harris
had looked forward to the establishment of a magazine which should be provincial in the nobler meaning of that word and yet national in its appeal. As-
sociating with him his son and a number of business
men in Atlanta who furnished capital to the amount
of $100,000, he wrought for eighteen months for the
establishment and maintenance of a magazine that at
once attracted the most favorable attention throughout the country. Naturally, Mr. Harris himself contributed the most significant stories and articles.
Whether bringing back upon the stage the inimitable
Uncle Remus, or discoursing in the homely Georgia
dialect of Mr. Billie Sanders, of Shady Dale, on contemporary question of politics and society, or indulging in the quaint and imaginative reflection of
the owner of Snap Bean Farm, he has appealed to a
large number of the American people. Unfortunately, he died before the full fruition of his hopes
and ideals could be realized. On his deathbed he
said to his son:

"If this illness takes me off and they try to start any monument business, don't let them do it. If what little I have done is found worthy of
commemoration, tell the people of the South to let the magazine succeed—to stand back of it with their subscriptions, and if it is not too
much trouble, run a little line somewhere, 'Founded by Joel Chandler
Harris.' Keep the magazine clean and wholesome and fresh with the
best and simplest in life."

Thus ends the story of Southern magazines, a
long record of heroic devotion, of ambitious plans
and in the main of failure to realize in any adequate
way the ideals of their projectors. To bibliographical students the least important of them sometimes
furnish significant points; to the student of social
life they are indispensable for filling in the pictures

of the past; to those who are interested in the South's literary development, they furnish inspiration, even while their failures produce despair. As these words are written, announcement is made of the reëstablishment in Richmond of the *Southern Literary Messenger,* as a memorial to Edgar Allan Poe. Thus the cycle returns and we end the story as we began it, with the name of the best magazine ever published in the South.

BIBLIOGRAPHY.—Harrison, James Albert: *Life and Letters of Edgar Allan Poe;* Ingle, Edward: *Southern Sidelights;* Minor, B. B.: *The Southern Literary Messenger;* Trent, W. P.: *Life of William Gilmore Simms;* and the files of the magazines mentioned.

EDWIN MIMS,
Professor of English Literature, Trinity College; editor South Atlantic Quarterly.

CHAPTER XXII.

SOUTHERN EDITORS.

N any enterprise the pioneer, blazing the way, is worthy of remembrance. William Parks, in 1727, published the first newspaper of Maryland at Annapolis. Its name was the *Maryland Gazette*. The next Southern newspaper to appear was the *South Carolina Journal,* established by a New Englander, Eleazar Phillips, Jr., about 1730, in Charleston. In 1736 Virginia's first newspaper was printed by the same William Parks who had started the Maryland press. At Williamsburg he published the *Virginia Gazette*. North Carolina's first editor was James Davis, a native Virginian, who in 1755 issued the *North Carolina Gazette* at Newbern. At Savannah, Ga., in 1763, a Scotchman, James Johnson, published the first journalistic enterprise, the *Georgia Gazette*. The *Kentucky Gazette* was the first newspaper published west of the Alleghany Mountains. An enterprising Virginian, John Bradford, was its founder and editor. It first appeared in 1787. Four years afterwards a New Englander, George Roulstone, published, at Rogersville, Tenn., the *Knoxville Gazette*. As soon as Knoxville could be laid out the paper was moved to its future home. In the District of Columbia the first editor was Benjamin Moore, who in 1796 issued the *Washington Gazette,* and that four years before the seat of government was moved. In Mississippi a Pennsylvanian, Andrew Marschalk, about 1799 published the *Natchez Gazette*. In Louisiana the first publisher was one Fontaine, who in 1803 established the *New Orleans*

THOMAS RITCHIE.

Moniteur. In Alabama a brace of editors, Miller
and Hood, thirty miles to the northward, published
in 1811, the *Mobile Centinel.* This was at Fort Stoddard, while awaiting the relinquishment of Spanish
control over that part of the territory subsequently
embraced in Alabama. The first Arkansas editor
was William E. Woodruff, a native of New York, who
in 1819, established at Arkansas Post the *Arkansas
Gazette.* The pioneer editor of Texas was Gail Borden, a native New Yorker, who in 1835 published the
Texas Telegraph at San Felipe.

The first newspapers were established under the
patronage of the governors of colonies and territories, who regarded them as the best means for
informing the people as to the laws passed and
the conduct of public affairs. As a rule, the owner
of the newspaper was a practical printer. He sometimes showed himself a shrewd business man and
occasionally a doughty controversialist. His establishment furnished the medium through which politicians, lawyers, ministers and writers expressed
their views or published their productions.

The first Southern editor to have definite convictions and to exercise a positive influence in public
affairs from their expression was Thomas Ritchie
(1778-1854). From 1804 to 1845 he edited the *Richmond Enquirer.* During Polk's administration he
edited the *Washington Union* in connection with
John P. Heiss, who had been transferred from the
Nashville Union to the Washington paper. A native
of Virginia, he was unquestionably the leading representative of the ante-bellum school of political
journalists in the South. Personal defamation was
a weapon used for political advantage. By subter-
fuges or sophistries to win support and to secure advantage, to meet deliberately and to destroy an
antagonist, to remove distrust or suspicion—these

were procedures fully recognized by the journalistic craft, at whose head stood Ritchie.

The journalistic methods of the day served to embolden the partisan, to inspirit the halting, to elate the faithful. With such persistency did Thomas Ritchie ply the arts in vogue that he came to be more abused and despised, more trusted and admired, more courted and feared than any of his contemporaries. Andrew Jackson, though a member of the same party, called him a political renegade and the greatest scoundrel in America. Horace Greeley termed him the Talleyrand of the press. Hezekiah Niles described him as the prince and high priest of weathercocks. John Randolph of Roanoke spoke of him as a man of seven principles—"five loaves and two fishes." On the other hand, he was called the Atlas of state-rights, the Napoleon of the press, next to Thomas Jefferson the most influential of Virginians, and the father of the Democratic party.

To Virginia as the mother of presidents and the intepreter of states-rights, the entire South looked for its political oracles. In his book, *The Flush Times of Alabama and Mississippi,* Joseph G. Baldwin did not overestimate this influence when he said of Virginians living in other states: "They read the same papers here they read in Virginia— the *Richmond Enquirer* and the *Richmond Whig.* The democrat stoutly asseverates a fact, and gives the *Enquirer* as his authority with an air that means to say, that settles it; while the *Whig* quoted Hampden Pleasants with the same confidence." John Hampden Pleasants (1797-1846), as Baldwin intimates, occupied the same relation to the Whig party that Ritchie did to the Democratic party. From 1824 to his death he was editor of the *Whig.*

The manner of Pleasants' death was an illustration of the bitterness that characterized the journal-

JOHN HAMPDEN PLEASANTS.

OF VIRGINIA

ism of the period. The two newspapers, as organs of opposing political parties, occupied through their responsible directors an intensely hostile relationship. Mere differences of personal opinions were settled frequently by the duel with pistols or swords. Both weapons were used in bringing about the death of the gifted Richmond editor. Thomas Ritchie, Jr., and his brother, William Foushee Ritchie, had assumed charge of the *Enquirer* after the father went to the *Washington Union*. In a controversy with the *Whig,* the *Enquirer* had impugned the courage of Pleasants. Such an imputation uniformly meant the wiping out of the stain upon the "field of honor." By agreement the two combatants, Pleasants and Thomas Ritchie, Jr., met upon the field with swords and pistols. Without taking positions, they were to attack upon sight. They advanced firing upon each other. Exhausting their pistols without deadly effect, when they came together, with swords they engaged in a hand-to-hand encounter. The result was that Pleasants received four pistol shots and a cut, while Ritchie had but a slight wound. Pleasants' death followed after two days.

Another great Virginia editor whose career began about the time the Ritchies and Pleasants closed their careers was John M. Daniel (1825-1865). From 1847, with an interim when he was minister to a foreign court, to 1865 he edited the *Richmond Examiner*. He was a native of Virginia. During this period of ten or eleven years he acquired great fame and influence. His paper's politics was Democratic, though it exercised independence in criticisms of party men and measures. Daniel was a representative of the intensely personal journalism of his times and had several duelling encounters. In one of these he received a wound from the nervous

effect of which his death is thought to have been
hastened.

The mother of presidents, Virginia may also be
regarded as having been the mother of editors. To
Washington journalism and to influential party
mouthpieces she furnished some noted men. For
half a century the names of Gales and Seaton at the
masthead of the *National Intelligencer* were familiar
to intelligent readers of newspapers throughout the
Union. They were brothers-in-law. In 1812, when
Joseph Gales (1786-1860) became owner of the *National Intelligencer*, he invited William W. Seaton
(1785-1866) to become his partner. Death alone interrupted the relationship. Gales was born in England, whence as a child he was brought by his father,
a refugee, to America. The father, Joseph Gales,
Sr. (1760-1841), for nearly forty years was editor of
the *North Carolina Register,* published at Raleigh,
which he made a recognized force in Southern affairs.

Besides Seaton, other Virginia-born editors of
note at the national capital were Francis P. Blair
(1791-1876) and John C. Rives (1795-1864), who
from 1829 until 1845 edited with great vigor the
Democratic organ, the *Globe*. That was the exciting,
bitter, eventful period known as the Jacksonian era
in American politics. During it the brilliancy and
fury of the greatest political storms antedating the
civil war culminated. In the stirring events and
amid the party councils, the *Globe* and its editors
were at the front and in the thickest of the fray. In
his young manhood Blair went to Kentucky, where
he was banker, farmer and court official. One day
Jackson saw an article in the *Frankfort Argus*.
Pleased therewith he inquired the name of the writer. The information came that it was Francis P.
Blair. At the time Duff Green (1791-1875) was editor

Jno. M. Daniel

of the administration organ, the *United States Telegraph*. His friendship for John C. Calhoun, whom he wished to make president, caused Jackson to overthrow him and to install Blair in the succession. With Rives as partner, this "court paper" flourished until forced to make way for Ritchie's *Union*.

The *Frankfort Argus* was a power in Kentucky Democratic politics as long as Amos Kendall (1787-1869) was at the helm. When Blair was writing for it, Kendall, as fourth auditor of the postoffice department at Washington, had been rewarded by Jackson for the fight made in a state whose politics was dominated by Henry Clay. Kendall was a New Englander, graduated at Dartmouth College. He was regarded as one of the most astute and helpful of the supporters of Andrew Jackson's administration. His party work was further rewarded when he was made postmaster-general in Martin Van Buren's cabinet.

New England was a great feeder for Southern editors. Thence came a large number of men who occupied high position in journalism. They illustrated the zeal, enterprise, intelligence and enduring qualities of New England. To-day, looking over the list of influential newspapers in the South and marking their longevity, it will be found that while the great organs of parties, founded either by native-born Southerners or by foreigners, have disappeared, many of those of the same class established by New Englanders still exist and are factors in the country's material development. Gales and Seaton and the *National Intelligencer*, Ritchie and the *Enquirer*, Pleasants and the *Whig*, Gales and the *Register*, Pinckney and the *Charleston Mercury*, Fell and the *Savannah Republican*, Penn and the *Louisville Advertiser*, Barksdale and the *Mississippian*, and Bayou and the New Orleans *Bee* are names that live

only in newspaper annals. On the other hand, Aru-
nah Abell and the *Baltimore Sun,* Aaron A. Willington and the *Charleston Courier,* John W. Townsend
and the *Mobile Register,* George D. Prentice and the
Louisville Journal, George W. Kendall and the *New
Orleans Picayune,* William G. Hunt and the *Nashville Banner*—these names attest the enterprise of
New Englanders and the persistency of New England instititutions.

Other contemporaneous journals, prominent and
often quoted, were edited by New Englanders. They
were the *Nashville Union,* edited by Jeremiah
George Harris, and later by Elbridge G. Eastman;
Mobile Advertiser, by C. C. Langdon; *Wilmington
Commercial,* by Thomas Loring; *Carolina Gazette,*
by E. S. Thomas; *New Orleans Crescent,* by J. W.
Frost; *New Orleans Tropic,* by T. B. Thorpe. These
are accompanied by a number of lesser lights. In
their adopted homes, their services were valued
highly and their success was marvelous. With little
or no capital in the beginning, they gave their lives
and influence to every legitimate enterprise of the
section. They encouraged commerce, supported
every educational enterprise, entered unreservedly
into the life of the people among whom they had cast
their lot, owned slaves and defended the "peculiar
institution," fought either upon the duelling field or
in the street encounter, and contributed their part in
every way to the welfare of the South.

South Carolina has been the nativity of some men
who occupied a large place among Southern editors.
Notable among them were the prolific author, William Gilmore Simms, Richard Yeadon, Robert Barnwell Rhett, Jr., John J. Seibels and A. B. Meek. It is
a significant fact that, with the exception of Simms,
these were college-bred men. Rhett was a Harvard
alumnus, Yeadon and Seibels were graduates of the

College of South Carolina, while Meek was a graduate of the University of Alabama. Meek and Simms belong to that large element of Southern men of letters who, either continuously or at intervals, were connected with the press. Simms edited for several years the *Charleston Gazette.* With the New Englander, Thaddeus Sanford, long editor and proprietor of the *Mobile Register,* Meek was associated. Seibels was editor of the *Montgomery Advertiser.* Yeadon was the associate owner and editor with Willington of the *Charleston Courier.* Simms and Yeadon are the best known and remembered of this group. Throughout their long and fruitful lives they were intimately associated by virtue of kindred tastes and high intellectual endowments. Yeadon acquired fame as a lawyer as well as an editor. In 1832 he became editor of the *Courier,* taking up his pen to fight the battles of the Union against nullification. For clearness of treatment and vigor of style, his editorials were widely commended and quoted. His editorial course was not always pleasing to the *New York Herald,* guided by the elder James Gordon Bennett. With apparent pride Yeadon was wont to point to the fact that Bennett learned his first editorial lessons in the service of the *Charleston Courier*—his newspaper cradle.

Besides the Gales, father and son, England gave to Southern journalism another noted editor in Francis W. Dawson (1840-1889). Coming to America to aid in the establishment of a Southern Confederacy, with its downfall he found himself adrift. After some newspaper ventures and experiences in Richmond, Va., in 1866 he went to Charleston, where he became associated with Robert Barnwell Rhett, Jr., in editing the *Mercury.* Soon afterwards he, with a Virginian, R. R. Riordan, founded the *News,* which was merged with the *Courier.* His death came by assassination, but did not grow out of any news-paper quarrel.

Georgia has been the home of many famous editors. In Savannah there were I. K. Tefft, the Rhode Islander, who edited the *Georgian* and founded the Georgia Historical Society; William T. Thompson, who founded the *Morning News* and wrote *Major Jones's Courtship;* and his partner, J. H. Estill, whose death caused an inestimable loss in state affairs. In Augusta there were James Gardner, who as editor of the *Constitutionalist* from 1850 to 1860 proved himself a power in the state's politics; Ambrose R. Wright, who as editor of the *Chronicle and Sentinel* made an influential newspaper. Associated with this journal are the names of Patrick Walsh, a native of Ireland, who became United States senator, and the Maryland poet, James R. Randall, whose editorial writings gave prestige to the paper. In Macon there were Simri Rose, who founded the *Messenger* and took a lively interest in public affairs; the poet, Harry Linden Flash, who wrote for the *Telegraph and Messenger;* and Joseph Clisby, a writer of force and style. In Atlanta the *Constitution,* a post-bellum newspaper, has set the pace for Georgia journalism. The names of Evan P. Howell and Henry W. Grady are suggestive of its quality and influence. Henry Grady's brief career was nothing short of brilliant and phenomenal. Men recall with distinct pride and in eulogistic phrase his illuminating editorials, his winsome oratory, his fervent patriotism, his broad national spirit, his contagious enthusiasm, his superb political management. The services he rendered as a pacificator between the sections long alienated give him a lasting place in the hearts of the American people. From earliest childhood sympathy with the negro race was a marked attribute of his character.

In the South the editor and the man of letters have often been represented in one person. In Georgia, besides Randall and Flash, the late Joel Chandler Harris was for years an editorial writer. Henry Timrod edited the *South Carolinian* at Columbia. James Barron Hope founded the Norfolk *Landmark*. John R. Thompson edited the *Southern Field and Fireside* at Augusta. Albert Pike edited for a time the *Arkansas Advocate* at Little Rock, and · the *Appeal* at Memphis. George D. Prentice gave fame to his newspaper, the *Louisville Journal,* not only by the brilliancy and humor of his editorial work, but by the verses he wrote. Apart from his own productions, Prentice's greatest literary efforts were expended in search for young writers who gave evidence of poetic talents. To give them substantial encouragement was his habit and delight. Among them familiar names are John Howard Payne, L. M. Sigourney, Amelia Welby, Alice and Phœbe Cary, L. Virginia French, and others of equal fame and merit.

After the War between the States it was the policy of Henry Grady to encourage literary expression on the part of Southern writers. He did not restrict the field. He had a genuine love for history. It was his cherished hope and confident belief that a school of Southern writers, handling judiciously and sympathetically the rich literary material in Southern life and traditions, would in time appear as the best interpreters of Southern life and thought. He was familiar with the history of New England's development in letters. He asserted that the writings of Joel Chandler Harris would prove the antidote for noxious teachings and false impressions that had gone abroad. It was a wise impulse that led him to secure Harris for the *Constitution,* and otherwise to encourage literary effort through the columns of his journal. Later it was no immodest

claim when he declared that his paper had been instrumental in filling Georgia with good books.

The most widely known of Tennessee editors was
William G. Brownlow (1805-1877). Editing the
Knoxville Whig, he was designated "the fighting
parson," at the same time being a Methodist minister. His unique personality, combative disposition
and powerful influence had weekly manifestation in
the *Whig,* and finally made him a national figure and
gave his paper a national reputation. The strong
Union sentiment which kept East Tennessee loyal, in
the main, to the Union during the war is justly attributable to the aid and encouragement he gave to
the support of the Federal government.

At Nashville, as editor of the *Union,* Jeremiah
George Harris, who claimed to be an editorial
pupil of George D. Prentice, enjoyed great reputation, and left his impress upon the history of
the state. In 1839 he was singled out by James K.
Polk, who had rare sagacity in the selection of men
for special work, to aid in the restoration of the
Jackson supremacy in Tennessee politics. The leaders who had revolted against what they regarded as
the tyranny of Jackson had once been his strongest
supporters. Harris began by publishing their
speeches in defense of Jackson, and made their opposition appear as fine specimens of political somer-
saults. His foremost antagonist of the Nashville
press was Allen A. Hall, editor of the *Banner,* who
secured files of the paper Harris had been editing in
New Bedford, Mass., and pointed out editorials that
savored of abolitionism. It was one of the liveliest
newspaper wars in Tennessee journalism.

At Memphis Henry Van Pelt and Jesse H.
McMahon were the rival editors who made most
reputation in the era preceding the war. The
former edited the Democratic organ, the *Appeal,*

which he founded, while the latter in the *Enquirer* waged the battles of whiggery. Each was a fine type of the old-school editors, vigorously fighting his party's battles and working unceasingly for the social uplift of his community.

Mississippi having no large cities had no newspapers that circulated outside of the state to any extent. Ethelbert Barksdale edited the *Mississippian,* which, published at the state capital, exercised the largest influence in state politics. He was noted for keen thrusts as a paragrapher and as a forceful writer whose views were accepted as oracles. Volney E. Howard, a native of Maine, was an editor of note, while at the same time practising law. As Democratic editor he had many controversies with the Whig press, always sustaining himself with vigor.

In Louisiana the early influential newspapers were published in the French language by men of French extraction. The first American editors to impress themselves upon their public were John Gibson, of the *True American,* and Peter Wagner, of the *Courier,* each published at New Orleans. Wagner was from Baltimore. He was an excellent illustration of the fiery, fighting editor of the Southwest, and had several duels with fellow journalists. Of gigantic proportions, he was a tempting target, but came out of all his duelling episodes unharmed except in a single instance. He once suffered a slight wound in a finger when he insisted on shortening the intervening distance from fifteen to five paces. Connected with the founding and conduct of the *Picayune* were some men who made a marked reputation in Southern journalism. The founders were Francis A. Lumsden and George W. Kendall (1809-1867). The former a North Carolinian and the latter a New Englander, they were men of shrewd insight and practical judgment. They carefuly abstained from indulging in the virulent personalities so common to Southern editorial policy. They maintained a non-partisanship or independence in politics in strange contrast with their contemporaries. Associated with them later were editors who filled a large place. These were Alexander C. Bullitt, who had previously edited the New Orleans *Bee,* and Samuel F. Wilson, who for sixteen years had been connected with Thaddeus Sanford on the *Mobile Register.* Bullitt was a Kentuckian, educated at Transylvania University, while Wilson was born in Connecticut and a graduate of Columbia College.

The best-known editor of Texas journalism was A. H. Belo (1839-1901), a North Carolinian, who came out of the war penniless. From the battlefield of Virginia he rode horseback to Texas, where he soon became interested in the *Galveston News.* He soon became a partner of the founder, Willard Richardson, and in 1875 became sole proprietor. In 1881 he organized a stock company, and in the publication of the *Dallas News* he practically duplicated the work done at Galveston.

There are few Southern editors who link the old with the new régime. Perhaps Henry Watterson of the *Louisville Courier-Journal* is the only illustration from among those who enjoy any far-reaching reputation. The newspaper of to-day is a distinct entity from what it was of old. The personality of the editor is no longer its overshadowing feature. Long since Southern newspapers in the larger centres have adopted metropolitan methods. In the days of intensely personal journalism, the names of editor and journal were synonymous. In reading the editorial utterances of the *Louisville Journal* it was George D. Prentice who spoke. It was John

HENRY WATTERSON.

Forsyth who after Sanford fulminated in the *Mobile Register*. It was Thomas Ritchie who dominated the *Richmond Enquirer;* it was Robert Barnwell Rhett, Jr., who spoke in the *Charleston Mercury*. Now all is changed, and editorial utterances are veiled in anonymity.

BIBLIOGRAPHY.—Avery, I. W.: *History of Georgia*, 1850 *to* 1881; Brewer, Willis: *Alabama;* Clayton, W. W.: *History of Davidson County, Tennessee;* Hudson, Frederic: *History of Journalism;* Keating, J. M.: *History of Memphis;* King, William L.: *Newspaper Press of Charleston, S. C.;* Piatt, John J.: *Biographical Sketch of George D. Prentice;* Weeks, Stephen B.: *North Carolina Press of Eighteenth Century;* Centennial Edition of *Charleston News and Courier*, 1803–1903; Semi-Centennial Edition of *New Orleans Picayune*, 1837–1887; articles by G. F. Mellen in *The Methodist Review* (Nashville) and *The New England Magazine*.

GEORGE FREDERICK MELLEN,

Formerly Professor of Greek and History, University of Tennessee; now of the Knoxville Sentinel.

CHAPTER XXIII.

LIBRARIES IN THE SOUTHERN STATES.

N the records of the Virginia Company for the date Nov. 15, 1620. occurs the following significant entry:

"After the acts of the former Courte were read, a straunger stept in, presenting a Mapp of Sir Walter Rawlighes contayninge a Descripcon of Guiana, and with the same fower great books as the Guifte of one unto the Company that desyred his name not be made knowne, whereof one booke was a treatise of St. Augustine of the Citty of God translated into English, the other three greate Volumes wer the works of Mr. Perkins' newlie corrected and amended, which books the donor desyred they might be sent to the College in Virginia, there to remayne in saftie to the use of the collegiates thereafter, and not suffered at any time to be sent abroade or used in the meane while.   For wch. so worthy a gift my Lord of Southampton desyred the p'tie that presented them to returne deserued thanks for himselfe and the rest of the Company to him that had so kindly bestowed them."

In some regards this quaint passage from the minutes of the Virginia Company is one of the most interesting bits of information that has survived, touching the beginnings of the nation.   It is a most effective rebuttal to the theory that the purpose of the founders of Virginia was nothing more than exploitation and commercial gain.   The name of Henry Wriothesly, the third Earl of Southampton, alone, carries with it a host of suggestion that leads in fancy to William Shakespeare, his bosom friend, and the whole galaxy of Elizabethan and Jacobean poets and dramatists.   The settlers of Roanoke and Jamestown came bringing with them the culture and the traditions of the England that had created *Hamlet* and *King Lear*.   Indeed, it was but a few years after the production of these master plays that we find George Sandys, in his cabin beside the James, occupied,

PAGE FROM RECORDS OF THE VIRGINIA COMPANY
Referring to a Proposed College and Library in Virginia

when not interrupted by Captain John Smith's innumerable preparations for expeditions against the
natives, in translating into unusually creditable
English verse the *Metamorphoses* of Ovid.

Early History.

Who the founder of the first American library was,
the most minute investigation has been impotent to
reveal, and, however interesting any speculations regarding his identity may be, the establishment of the
same would still be secondary to the facts already to
be gleaned from the passage quoted, that even in the
South's earliest years plans were completed for the
University of Henrico, and the nucleus of its library
already placed in trust with the Virginia Company.
Yet these plans were destined never to be realized;
famine, internal dissention, and the terrible massa-
cre of 1623 brought them all to naught, and it was
nearly three-quarters of a century before James
Blair founded William and Mary College at Williamsburg; New England in this way being permitted to anticipate Virginia by nearly sixty years.

In spite of this, however, it should not be inferred
that the colonists of Virginia were not alive to the
value of books. The gulf between the Southern colonies and England was a matter of space alone; the
life in Virginia and the Carolinas being as closely
modeled on that of the mother country as conditions
would permit. The manorial system, of course, was
the one adopted, and developed as an institution to
such an extent that it has left an ineffaceable mark
upon the manners and traditions of the Southern
people. In spite of its faults and anachronisms, the
feudal system tends to develop a type of culture all
its own. Being based in spirit on the idea of the
family, it discourages the growth of large communities, hence we should expect to find the children

taught by private tutors, and libraries gathered by private collectors.

This was the case in the Southern colonies. It has been more or less a puzzle to some well-intentioned historians that Southern men should have taken such a very prominent part in the formation of the Union. Perhaps the most illuminating light that has been thrown upon this problem has been the publication, of late, by *The William and Mary Quarterly* of private libraries owned by the Virginia gentry. These collections ranged from a half a hundred volumes to five and six thousand; the library of William Byrd and that of Thomas Jefferson approximating the latter figures. In all more than sixty libraries are enumerated, and a very reasonable estimate would place the number of books in the private collections of Virginia prior to the Nineteenth century at 50,000 volumes. What was true of Virginia was equally true of the other colonies, Maryland and South Carolina certainly not lagging far behind the Old Dominion in matters of culture. In North Carolina, Stephen B. Weeks finds traces of nearly forty large private libraries, collected prior to the Revolution.

In these lists of private libraries some very interesting facts are brought to light, not the least of which is the exceeding high quality of the books purchased. It was a small and poor collection, indeed, that did not have its selection from the Latin poets, the Greek philosophers and dramatists, and often works of French and Italian writers. Nor were these merely school texts, for where prices have been assigned for purposes of sale they have been such as would indicate that the editions were of standard library quality. This inference is borne out by such copies as have come down to us in collections still intact, or which bear the autograph or bookplate of some colonial owner. The unusual number of folios, too, which are quoted in these collections are an additional proof of this contention.

The most remarkable collection of which we have knowledge was that of William Byrd, 2d, of Westover. Byrd was one of the most wealthy and influential of the Virginia manorial lords, and is said to have possessed at one time an estate that approximated 200,000 acres. He was educated in England, and in intimate touch with the most cultured men of the time, among them Robert Boyle, Earl of Orrery, the famous physicist; General Oglethorpe; the Duke of Argyle; Mark Catesby, the botanist; the Marquis of Halifax; Sir Robert Southwell, and many others. His extensive learning is clearly shown by the books he purchased which were unusually well catalogued in 1777. They are grouped under the following heads: "History; Voyages; Travels, etc.; Law; Trials, etc.; Physick, etc.; Entertainments; Poetry; Translations, etc.; Divinity, etc.; Classics and other Latin and Greek authors; Miscellaneous." Some of the titles quoted in the list of 5,000 volumes fill the soul of the modern book lover with envy, and he is tempted to speculate regarding the fate of this remarkable collection of books. That they were scattered we know, for copies bearing the bookplate and coat-of-arms of Byrd have turned up here and there, a number of them, it is said being in possession of the Ridgeway branch of the Philadelphia Public Library. The Library of Congress has an exceptionally fine folio, Petit's *Leges Atticæ*, which was one of the books obtained by purchase from Thomas Jefferson. Perhaps other works were purchased by the latter at the sale of Byrd's library, but they have not been identified.

Another early colonial library of especial interest was that of Dr. Charles Brown, a physician who was interested in natural sciences. The books in this collection were mainly devoted to mathematics, chemistry, physics, medicine and kindred topics. Indeed, it is a commentary on the learning of the Southern colonist to find so many books on scientific topics in their libraries; hardly a one of the whole sixty or more listed failing to contain books of that nature. The fate of the collection of Dr. Brown is hinted at in a paragraph in *The Virginia Gazette*, 1738, to the effect that this was "the finest and most copious in natural philosophy and physick ever exposed to sale in the colony." This library contained 82 folios, 128 quartos, 407 octavo, and 6 miscellaneous, and was valued at £108.

In 1719, the library of Orlando Jones was inventoried at £484, which would indicate that his collection was exceptionally large and valuable. The library of Councillor Robert Carter of Nomini Hall, Westmoreland county, inventoried in 1772 more than 500 volumes. The Carters constituted a large and influential group of families, all of them composed of people of culture and possessors of large collections of books. That the art of music was not neglected is evidenced by the inventory of the library of Cuthbert Ogle, which contained a splendid collection of music, including works on the theory of the same. Numerous references to purchases and repairings of spinets and other instruments also prove that music played no inconsiderable part in the life of the men and women of the time.

The most noted collection of books started during the colonial time and indeed, the most interesting private collection from the point of view of content and influence on American library history, was that of Thomas Jefferson. The Southern makers of enfranchised America were all men of unusual learning and catholicity of taste. Madison, Randolph, Mason, we know were not only possessors of splendid collections of books, but also were in intimate touch with statesmen and scholars in Europe. This was particularly true of Thomas Jefferson, who was an insatiable reader and an unusually gifted letter-writer. He was in correspondence with the leaders of the Eighteenth century school of philosophy and statecraft, influencing and in turn being influenced by the men who led in the transformation of Europe. His collection was the fruit of fifty years of patient watchfulness, and at the time of its purchase by Congress as the nucleus of the collection destined to replace the one destroyed by the British, numbered 6,700 volumes. The fact that the Library of Congress was first instituted at the suggestion of President Jefferson made it peculiarly fitting that his collection should be purchased to supply the loss of the original library at the hands of a foreign foe. In addition, the United States gained for a comparatively moderate sum, the most remarkable private collection in America.

This library forms a striking index to the astonishing genius of its owner; his universality, his profundity, his generous sympathy with everything that stood for freedom of the human spirit were clearly revealed in this collection of books still preserved to us amid the 1,500,000 books that constitute the Library of Congress. A goodly number of the works, particularly those in philosophy and statecraft were presented to him by the writers, and the title pages and flyleaves bear the autograph inscriptions of such men as Condorcet Dupont de Nemours, in fact, many of the choicest spirits of the age.

As an evidence of his scholarship a good share of the works, many of them on the most abstruse subjects, are critically annotated by his own hand, the French works often containing the comments in the language of the text. It might also be asserted that

Thomas Jefferson was the father of American library science, for he was unquestionably the first in this country to arrange an extensive collection of books according to a scheme of classification both minute in detail and comprehensive in scope. The scheme was adopted from Francis Bacon's classification of human knowledge, and on the purchase of the collection, was adopted by the Library of Congress as its own arrangement, serving during its growth of a century from 7,000 to more than 1,000,000 volumes.

As has thus been indicated, the earliest development in book collecting assumed the form of private libraries, yet recent investigations have proven that the first endeavor to institute public libraries in America was made in the South. This was due to the efforts of Thomas Bray, the founder of the Society for the Propagation of the Gospel. Indeed, the first systematic plan for the establishment of publicly supported free libraries, as far as we know, in the history of all time must be accredited to this London preacher who flourished during the reign of William and Mary. Thomas Bray has been quoted as a shining example of what may be accomplished by a man of mediocre ability who is possessed of determination. Nevertheless, if the fact of his being some three hundred years in advance of his age and being in possession of an insight enabling him to see the educational potentialities of the library, be not in the nature of genius, then the definitions of the latter quality are all at fault. In addition, he has been criticised in England for establishing nothing but clerical libraries, and in America for not keeping his libraries alive after his death, yet all of these points conceded do not deprive him of the credit due for a work great in conception, and in view of the besetting conditions, equally great in accomplishment. Nor

1. WALSH MEMORIAL LIBRARY, SEWANEE, TENN.
2. COSSIT LIBRARY, MEMPHIS, TENN

should it be assumed that his interests were merely theological; every activity towards social betterment. found in him a worker who stopped at no sacrifice in its furtherance. He was the friend of General Oglethorpe, and allied with him in the movement for prison reform, aiding also the latter's plan for colonizing Georgia.

Thomas Bray's scheme, as outlined in *Apostolick Charity, Primordia Bibliothecaria,* and other pamphlets published during the last decade of the Seventeenth century, involved the establishment of a publicly endowed free library in every cathedral town and important parish in the British Isles and the colonial possessions. More than 400 libraries were proposed in this comprehensive scheme, 160 of which were actually placed in operation, of which a modicum still exist in Great Britain, and 150 in the foreign possessions, all of which have disappeared, or have been absorbed by later collections. The fact however, that none of the Bray libraries still exist in America does not in any wise militate against their historical interest, nor against their contemporary influence.

In Neil's *Founders of Maryland* is given a list of thirty of these libraries established in Maryland alone. Of these the collection at Annapolis was the largest, containing 1,095 volumes. The average volumes to each library were thirty, the whole totaling 3,043 volumes. The books that form these libraries have in large part disappeared, a few, however, still remaining in the Library of St. John's College, Annapolis, bearing the inscription, "De Bibliotheca Annapolitana"—melancholy vestiges of an enterprise worthy of a better fate than the one experienced. The Bray libraries were established in Virginia, in North and South Carolina and Georgia; books valued at £2,400 being sent to the colonies prior to 1700.

It was seventy years after the disastrous failure of the University of Henrico that an institution of higher learning was instituted in the South. This was William and Mary College, founded in 1693 at ,Williamsburg, mainly through the efforts of Commissary James Blair. This was the second college established in the English colonies, the first being Harvard, in 1636. There is good reason for assuming that the nucleus for a library had already been gathered when the doors of the college were opened, for it is recorded that the original selection of books was made by the founder, whose private library in addition was bequeathed to the same on his death.

From the statement of Dr. John Millington, a former librarian of William and Mary, we learn that the library was the recipient of many valuable gifts during its career. "Many books were presented by Sir Alexander Spotswood, Robert Dinwiddie, and the General Assembly of Virginia. Louis XVI., of France, also presented the celebrated *Cyclopædia,* and a number of quarto volumes on natural history, splendidly bound and illustrated. President Jefferson and the Honorable Robert Boyle of Ireland, were among the donors."

Perhaps no institution in America has experienced more misfortunes than this famous old school. During the Revolution, the buildings were occupied by the French, and part of the same was destroyed. Just how much the library was injured it is difficult to estimate; it is not reasonable, however, to infer that it went unscathed. Again, in 1850, it suffered from fire, the main building being destroyed, rebuilt, however, only to meet almost total destruction during the War of Secession. At this time the buildings were gutted and the library numbering more than 8,000 volumes was destroyed. It has only been during the last few years that the college has found renewed life, again taking its place among the institutions of the land. The library now numbers more than 10,000 volumes.

The first public library founded in the Southern states whose history runs undisturbed to the present is that of the Charleston Library Society, which grew out of a library club organized by seventeen young men of Charleston, S. C., in the year 1748. In 1754, in order to permit the development of a public library, a royal charter was applied for. The receipt of this, however, was delayed eighteen months, owing to the fact that the vessel bearing the document was captured by a French cruiser; which incident, as stated by the catalogue of the library issued in 1770, had "almost fatal consequences to the Society." Nevertheless, this temporary backset was soon overcome, and from thence to the Revolution the library prospered; so much indeed, that in 1770 an interesting catalogue was issued, showing that the library at that time was in possession of 2,956 volumes. This catalogue, of which the Library of Congress possesses one of the few copies in existence, is perhaps the earliest library catalogue issued in America. The books listed therein were of high class; many of them, in truth, of greatest interest and rarity to-day, Eliot's Bible being one that may be particularly noted. The esteem in which the institution was held by the citizens may be inferred from the large number of subscribers, who appeared to be undismayed by the severe conditions of membership, and the heavy fees required. According to the provisions of the charter, it was necessary to pay the sum of £50 in order to become a member, weekly dues of five shillings being paid until the sum of £200 in all had been paid. Failure to attend regular meetings subjected the offender to a fine of ten shillings, and failure to serve as an officer when elected resulted in a fine of £5. A salaried librarian and assistant were provided for, their entire time being devoted to the library.

A somewhat interesting detail to be noted in the rules was the one providing for a sliding scale in the lending of books. According to this, the reader was permitted to keep pamphlets out four days; octavos and duodecimos, twelve days; quartos, sixteen days, and folios, twent-four days. In addition, twelve hours were added for every additional six miles traversed by the member in traveling to his home; a very necessary recognition of conditions arising from the manorial system of life then in vogue. A fine of five shillings was assessed for every twelve hours a book was permitted to become overdue. The success of the library may be inferred from the fact that in 1775 the property of the Society was estimated at $20,000.

In 1771, John McKenzie, a lawyer of Charleston, who had long been an active worker for the Library Association, and in addition an ardent collector of books for his own sake, died and left his private library of nearly 1,000 volumes in the care of the Society, to be preserved by it until a college should be established in Charleston, in which event the institution should receive them. These books duplicated, more or less, works already in the Library Society, and on the foundation of the college at Charleston in 1791 were transferred to that instituttion. In the disastrous fire which occurred in 1778, destroying one-half of Charleston, all of the collections of the Library Society, with the exception of 185 volumes were burned. The McKenzie collection, being stored elsewhere, fortunately escaped all damage except that of rough usage.

The long continued war coupled with this disaster,

reduced the library for a while to a state of comparative non-existence. Immediately following the declaration of peace, however, the Society was reorganized and a new collection begun. In 1790, the number of volumes was 342; in 1808, 4,500; in 1811, 7,000; in 1850, 12,000; in 1904, 30,000.

The Society has issued a number of publications, the earliest being "The Rules and By-Laws," three editions of which were printed between 1761 and 1770. The first catalogue was issued in 1770, with an appendix, containing accessions, in 1772. A catalogue of the McKenzie collection was also issued in 1770. Other catalogues were isued in 1790, 1802, 1806, 1808, 1811, 1818, 1826, 1831, 1847, 1854 and 1876. The issue of 1826, compiled under the direction of the president of the Society, Hon. Stephen Elliott, was a most important bibliographical effort, particularly from the point of view of classification, the catalogue and supplement to the same comprehending in all 511 pages.

The collection suffered greatly during the war, the building being used as a hospital. As soon as peace was restored the library was reopened and again took up its activities. In 1874, the Apprentices Library, founded in 1824, which had been partially destroyed by fire in 1870, was merged with the Library Association, the latter thereby broadening its scope and influence.

The second existent public library founded in the Southern states prior to 1800 was that of Alexandria, Va. This resulted from a meeting held at the home of John Wise, July 24, 1794. Its charter was obtained in 1798, and modified in 1799, under which law it has continued until the present. A catalogue of sixty-one pages was issued in 1856, at which time the collection numbered 4,481. The Alexandria Library, however, has been more or less inactive since the war, and now contains fewer volumes than were recorded in 1856.

The first public library to be organized in the valley of the Mississippi was the Lexington (Kentucky) Library, organized in 1795, about fifteen years after the settlement of the region.   The founding of this library and of Transylvania University, so early in the history of that tremendous enterprise, aptly called "The Winning of the West," reveals the temper of the men who made the success of that enterprise possible.   The leader in the movement for the establishment of these institutions was John Bradford, the founder of the first press in the West, and one of the most remarkable figures of his time. The friend of Clay, and of other leaders of pioneer Kentucky, he wielded an influence less widely known than that of those men, but none the less vital. As the editor of the *Kentucky Gazette,* which was the first of a long list of newspapers instituted by him, or through his influence, he was in a very true sense the moulder of political and social ideals for that newly settled region.

When the difficulties of overland transportation in pioneer Kentucky are considered, the wonder grows that a proposition for organizing a public library should have been considered at all.   It was necessary to import the greater number of the books from London, in which case they were subjected to risk from ocean, river and overland transportation, resulting in month-long delays, and often total loss from the elements or from the savages.   In spite of this, a fund of $500 was collected, to which Washington, Adams, Burr and other noted men contributed, and in 1796 the first consignment of books arrived in Lexington.   For a while the collections of the Library Society were united with those of Transylvania University, but in 1799 a separation was deemed essential, and a charter was obtained for the Library Society in 1800, under the title of "The Lexington, Georgetown and Danville Library Association," thus indicating that it was the purpose of the founders to establish libraries in other important communities in the state. An extensive catalogue was issued of the library in 1821, which shows that at that time it was in possession of approximately 8,000 volumes. Another significant fact to be gleaned from this catalogue is the statement that the Lexington library had absorbed the Lexington Juvenile Library in 1810, thus proving the existence of a children's library in the wilds of Kentucky more than twenty years before the foundation of the famous Apprentices Libraries of Philadelphia and of New York. In 1857 the collections numbered 11,000 volumes, which in 1904 had grown to more than 15,000.

During the decade following the outbreak of the Revolutionary War, literary and educational activities, of course, were reduced to a minimum; yet several institutions of learning were founded within the period. These were Hampden-Sydney College (Virginia, 1776); Washington College, now Washington and Lee (Virginia, 1776); and Washington College (Maryland, 1783). These now have libraries of 15,000, 50,000 and 5,000 volumes, respectively. In addition, the following other institutions possessing libraries ranging from 3,000 to 50,000 volumes were founded before 1800: St. John's College (Maryland, 1784); College of Charleston (South Carolina, 1791); University of Tennessee (1794); University of North Carolina (1795); University of Nashville, Tenn. (1796); Washington College (Tennessee, 1795); Charlotte Hall School (Maryland, 1796); Transylvania (now Kentucky) University (1798).

The period following the Revolution was marked by the opening up of the great West, an enterprise whose very conditions forbade much concern with matters of books and learning, and yet we know that many of the pioneers who passed the Alleghanies from the mother states of Virginia and the Carolinas or down the Ohio and the Valley of Virginia, from Maryland and Pennsylvania, not seldom carried with them precious chests of books and indeed, presses and type for the making of the same. John Bradford, one of the pioneers of Kentucky, issued the first number of the *Kentucky Gazette,* the earliest newspaper in the West, in 1787, when Lexington was still a village surrounded by a stockade. Five or six years after that, when William Blount was appointed governor of the territory south of the Ohio, now the state of Tennessee, at the instance of President Washington, he carried with him into the wilderness a complete printing outfit and a skilled printer, George Roulstone, who was destined to become a person of no little influence in the new state. Roulstone issued the first newspaper in Tennesee in 1791, and printed in addition, Public Laws and other works until his death in 1804.

Along with Governor Blount, acting as his secretary, also came his brother, Willie Blount, who published in 1803, *A Catechetical Exposition of the Constitution of Tennessee,* one of the earliest endeavors to teach civics to the youth of America.

We are well aware from the writings of these men and of their contemporaries, and from the advertisements of booksellers in contemporary newspapers, that even at this early time books were ardently sought. There were a number of private libraries of considerable extent gathered together, one of the largest being that of John Haywood, the first historian of Tennessee, and a man of unique genius.

As an additional testimonial to the value set upon education, it is a fact worthy of note that hardly was a settlement established than a school building was erected and a teacher employed. Thus only three years after the settlement of Knoxville, Tenn., Blount College, the progenitor of the University of Tennessee, was chartered, and two years after the establishment of Davidson county, Davidson Academy (now the University of Nashville), was founded.

According to Rhees' *Manual of American Libraries,* 711 libraries were established in the Southern states from 1800 to 1859, the majority being connected with educational institutions. It is interesting, in addition, to note that many valuable collections of books were gathered by the students of these institutions in conection with their debating societies; eighty-three of these society libraries being formed containing collections ranging from 100 to 3,000 volumes. The influences of these collections of readily accessible books upon the young men who were members of these societies is quite beyond estimate.

Commencing with the decade of the thirties historical societies were organized in the Southern states which began a work too long neglected—that of gathering and conserving historical sources. Much of this, because of thoughtlessness and failure to appreciate its value had alreday disappeared, yet through these agencies much has also been saved. Prior to 1855, nine of these societies had been organized, namely: Virginia Historical Society (1831); Kentucky Historical Society (1838); Savannah Historical Society (1839); Maryland Historical Society (1843); Missouri Historical Society (1844); Alabama Historical Society (1850); South Carolina Historical Society (1855); Tennessee Historical Society (1855); Historical Society of Florida (1857).

Until the beginning of the recent movement toward free libraries supported by public taxation,

public libraries were mainly organized on the coöperative, or share-holding plan, the use of the books
being restricted to the members and their families.
Seventy-five such libraries were in activity in the
Southern states at the outbreak of the war, to which
may be added the state and other administrative libraries, the majority of which were instituted during
the ante-bellum period.   The most important collections of this kind were those of Virginia, Maryland,
South Carolina, Kentucky and Louisiana.

Destruction During the War.

It is quite impossible for those who are unac-
quainted with conditions to understand adequately
the transformation wrought upon the South by the
War of Secession. Almost in the twinkling of the eye
the whole social fabric of the South was swept away,
and a half-century has hardly sufficed to produce an
entire readjustment to new conditions, so fundamental was the change.   Whatever might have been
the virtues or the failings of the ancient régime, it
was an anachronism, and as such was repugnant to
the modern spirit, which marked it for destruction
and with it all the memorials and traditions gathered
through the long years.   The libraries and colleges,
indeed all institutions that fostered and conserved
its culture, suffered heaviest.   Almost every school
building in the South was occupied at one time or
other by soldiers as barracks or hospitals, and books
and instruments of unknown value were used as fuel
or served as toys for the idle hours of high privates.
In many of the libraries, broken sets and mutilated
volumes still remain as pathetic reminders of the
days of blood and fire.
   The famous library at Charleston was partially
destroyed, the building being used as a military hospital; all of the Virginia institutions suffered great-

1. Library, University of West Virginia
2. Library, Trinity College.

ly, as did those in Kentucky and Tennessee. The most astonishing episode, however, of the kind, in that most astonishing conflict, was the burning of the library building and collections of the University of Alabama, during the final days of the war. This library, which was one of the largest and best selected in the South, was ruthlessly destroyed at a time when the issue of the conflict had been decided, and no conceivable gain could have resulted from such an action.

Hardly had the war come to an end than the South betook herself to the tremendous work of rehabilitation. The largest share of this labor was of necessity directed towards political and economic reconstruction, yet the social forces were not neglected. The school buildings were rebuilt or sessions held in temporary quarters; libraries were reopened and stock taken of the tattered remnants of once valuable collections. It must be confessed, however, that the library development during the three decades following the war forms a record marked by few encouraging features. The universities found themselves confronted by dismantled buildings and greatly reduced sources of income, the funds from which, of course, were devoted to the immediate exigencies of the institutions. The libraries, being less imperatively needed than buildings and instructors, were allowed, for the nonce, to languish. Indeed, it was not until the decade of the eighties that we find the collections indicating any marked evidences of growth.

Progress Since the War.

The awakening of library enthusiasm in the Northern states, which led to the formation of the American Library Association in 1876, did not reach the South for fully fifteen years. One Southern librarian was a charter member, and several attended conferences prior to 1890, but the representation of the section was exceedingly slight, even to 1895. The first city library club in the South was probably one organized in 1893 at Knoxville, Tenn. A congress of women librarians met at the Cotton States and International Exposition held at Atlanta, in 1895, the success of which showed the awakening of interest in Southern library conditions; and librarians were invited to take part in the educational and literary program of the Tennessee Centennial which was held two years later. In 1897 a Georgia Library Asociation was organized, and in 1899 the American Library Asociation held its first conference in the Southern states at Atlanta. This proved of great benefit in stimulating interest in library expansion, and in encouraging the formation of library clubs and state associations. A library club was organized at Nashville in 1900, which was the nucleus for the Tennessee State Library Association, the first conference of which was held in 1902. Other states have formed associations as follows: Texas and Florida in 1901; Alabama and North Carolina in 1904; Virginia in 1905; Kentucky in 1907. Several inter-state meetings have been held, although as yet no Southern association has developed, notwithstanding the fact that such an organization, if affiliated with the American Library Association, would be exceedingly desirable, for it could institute a propaganda not possible to the national association.

In several of the states, library commissions have been created, and in others the state department of education has been empowered to perform the functions of such commissions. The recognition of the library as an educational force, approximately coördinate with the school is, in itself, a tremendous forward step. The theory that education ceases with the receipt of a diploma has been justly exploded, and the library, at last, has attained in the South, as in other sections, its recognition as the "University of the People." Yet its efficiency would be minimized were it content to remain a passive agent, merely a storehouse of books, so to speak. In this respect, also, the Southern libraries are becoming aware of their responsibilities and grasping their opportunities. In order to reach the people who are unable or disinclined to seek out the main libraries, systems of branch and traveling libraries are being developed, the former for the benefit of the city dwellers far distant from the main library, the latter for those in the rural districts who are cut off from all sources of literature. The pioneer work of this kind was done by the women's clubs of the South, the first traveling libraries being sent out from 1890 to 1895 by the women of the Kentucky and Tennessee Federations to the mountaineers of the Alleghanies and the Cumberlands. Now there are well-organized endeavors in the majority of the Southern states to place well-selected collections in every community of any importance whatsoever.

The most notable expression of this movement is to be found in North Carolina, where legislative enactments promulgated in 1901, 1903 and 1905, had made a systematic plan of campaign feasible. In this state alone there are approximately 2,000 rural and school libraries, aggregating more than 175,000 volumes, and accessible to 250,000 inhabitants, for whom they are the only sources of any literature worthy of the name. South Carolina has followed the example of her sister state, passing a law in 1903 permitting the maintenance of libraries by communities of more than 5,000 inhabitants, and in 1904 passing a school library law under which, prior to 1907, more than 800 libraries had been established. Virginia has also instituted a system of traveling libraries under the direction of the state librarian, more than 500 of these being in successful operation. Prior to 1901, traveling libraries, publicly or privately supported, were also in existence in Maryland, Georgia, Alabama, Louisiana and Texas.

One of the greatest detriments in the development of public libraries in the past has been the lack of specific legislation authorizing the taxation of a community for the support of such institutions. This difficulty, however, is gradually being overcome, and already several states have enacted statutes providing for the same, and in the others legislation is pending.

With the new century the South has entered, as has been indicated, into an era of astonishing library expansion. With regard to this, and in all deference to other forces that have promoted the same, it is no disparagement of the latter to say that this has in great measure been due to the philanthropic activities of Mr. Andrew Carnegie. The munificence of his gifts, and the coöperative conditions usually conditioned on their acceptance, have awakened many Southern men and women to an interest in a work concerning which they had had little previous knowledge and no enthusiasm. The opportunity for obtaining a library building that would be an ornament to the community has in many cases proven a temptation too strong to be ignored, although the gift in most cases has carried with it the necessity for supporting and collecting a library. While it is true that from time to time small towns have accepted gifts upon conditions that they have found somewhat onerous, yet in no case has there been failure to make the best of the opportunity, notwithstanding the sacrifices involved. The existence of the building has often served as a psychologic influence in attracting books from unconsidered sources; the structure

1. Carnegie Library, Atlanta, Ga
2. Carnegie Library, Montgomery, Ala

alone being a permanent and generally wholesome object lesson in architectural taste. It is quite impossible to enumerate more than a few of the donations made by Mr. Carnegie: Louisville, New Orleans and Richmond have received over $250,000; Atlanta and Nashville have buildings costing more than $100,000; and in connection with the former an endowment fund for the support of a Southern library school has been tendered and the school has been in successful operation since 1905. Chattanooga, Montgomery, Jacksonville, Norfolk, Dallas and Worth, have buildings costing $50,000. In addition to donations to public libraries, Mr. Carnegie has been very generous to many educational institutions—Tuskeegee Institute, perhaps, benefiting to the greatest extent.

It must not be thought, however, that Mr. Carnegie stands alone as a benefactor of libraries in the Southern states; indeed, within the last twenty years, gifts to libraries have been numerous, and relatively munificent. The Cossitt library at Memphis, Tenn.; the Howard Memorial Library at New Orleans; Lawson McGhee Memorial Library, at Knoxville, Tenn.; Asheville Public Library, North Carolina; Trinity College at Durham, N. C.; John B. Stetson University, at DeLand, Florida; Vanderbilt University, at Nashville, Tenn.; Tulane University and Sophia Newcomb College, at New Orleans, and others, have large gifts of moneys for library buildings and books.

It was in the universities and colleges that the libraries were first systematically collected, and one would expect a proportional expansion. This, however, does not appear to be the case. It is only of late that the majority of the Southern universities have awakened to the comprehension of the work of the library. Apparently they have found it very difficult to divest themselves of the tradition that the library is more or less secondary to the more strictly academic functions and departments of the university. The policy of placing the library in the hands of a professor or of forcing the librarian to do work of teaching in order to piece out a very inadequate salary has had a deleterious effect upon library expansion in Southern educational institutions. Signs of better days, however, are strongly in evidence, and at last the library is becoming recognized for what it really is—the veritable heart of its institution. This change of attitude has in part resulted from the adoption of the seminary method of instruction, rendering it necessary for the students to gain access to original sources of information, hence requiring the adoption of modern systems of library administration. Nevertheless, there are still not a few colleges that have no regular librarians, or if they have, are paying salaries entitling that official to a rank hardly better than that of an instructor.

The university libraries, too, have been singularly unfortunate. As has already been indicated, war and fire have destroyed some of the largest collections in the South. Nor has the evil star finally set for in 1895 and 1905, respectively, two of the largest collections in Southern colleges suffered almost total destruction; those of the University of Virginia and the Vanderbilt University.

The first named had suffered less from the war than the majority of its fellows and had gathered what was perhaps the largest and best academic collection in the Southern states, numbering 50,000. The library, in the mind of Thomas Jefferson, was the link that bound all of the academic departments of a university into unity, and by his solicitude for the library in his plans for the University of Virginia he strove to realize that ideal. Conditions, of course, have prevented its full attainment, yet the influence of the library on the students of the university and through them on the scholarship of the South is beyond estimate. The famous rotunda has again been restored by skillful architects and the collections therein are being developed along modern lines.

The library of the Vanderbilt University was founded contemporaneously with the university itself, Commodore Vanderbilt setting aside a share of his original gift for the purchase of books. In 1904 the collections aggregated 42,000 volumes. Of these 21,000 were burned in the fire that destroyed the main building in 1904. Some of the special collections, especially those in ancient and modern languages, were especially valuable and were a total loss. The buildings, however, were soon replaced by a new structure and every endeavor is being made to replace the losses on the shelves.

One of the best working collections, particularly in literary criticism and philology, is possessed by the University of the South, at Sewanee, Tenn., and housed in the most satisfactory building, from an architectural point of view, in the Southern states. This library was the especial object of devotion on the part of Prof. John Bell Henneman, and will remain an enduring monument to his scholarship and enthusiasm. The libraries of the university contain approximately 30,000 volumes.

The University of North Carolina has an excellent library of 50,000 volumes housed in a building valued at $55,000. This is one of the few universities that possesses a large endowment for the upbuilding of the library set apart from the general funds of the institution.

Trinity College at Durham, N. C., has a collection of 30,000 volumes, and a library building valued at

$45,000, the gift of James B. Duke, and in 1905, the library of the University of Georgia was moved into its new building, the gift of G. P. Peabody.

The nucleus of the library of the College of Charleston, as has been noted, was the gift of books bequeathed for the purpose by John McKenzie, in 1771, and entrusted to the care of the Charleston Library Society until the institution should be established. It was not until 1791 that this event transpired, at which time such remnants of the original gift as had survived were transferred to the university. In spite of its long career the library has failed to develop in proportion, numbering only 15,000 volumes in 1904.

The following Southern educational institutions have collections numbering 20,000 volumes and upward: University of Alabama (20,000); Alabama Polytechnic (20,800); University of Georgia (30,000); Mercer University, Georgia (27,750); Emory College, Georgia (29,708); Berea College, Kentucky (20,630); Central University of Kentucky (20,099); Kentucky University (20,000); Southern Baptist Theological Seminary (23,000); Louisiana State University and Agricultural and Mechanical College (26,000); Tulane University, New Orleans (36,000); United States Naval Academy, Annapolis (44,000); Mt. St. Mary's College (26,000); Woodstock College, Maryland (67,000); University of North Carolina (42,000); Davidson College, North Carolina (20,000); Trinity College (28,500); South Carolina College (33,783); Presbyterian Theological Seminary (20,000); University of Tennessee (20,000); Cumberland University, Lebanon, Tenn. (21,000); Vanderbilt University, Nashville (36,000); The University of Nashville, Tenn. (20,000); University of the South, Sewanee, Tenn. (26,000); University of Texas (50,-

000); Sam Houston Normal Institute (20,000); Baylor University (20,000); University of Virginia, (60,000); .Washington and Lee University, Virginia (50,000); Union Theological Seminary, Virginia (20,000); Roanoke College, Virginia (23,000); Virginia Theological Seminary (25,000).

No city south of the Mason and Dixon line has a library history longer and more remarkable than Baltimore. Indeed, in this respect, it takes rank with Boston, New York, Philadelphia, Washington and Chicago, as a centre of library activities. Some of its collections, doubtless, may claim their origin in the Bray libraries, while others more recently instituted, have developed to first rank and influence. Of these the most important is the Peabody Institute, founded by George Peabody in 1857, who endowed it to the amount of $1,400,000. The plan of its founder involved the bringing of all cultural influences to the people of Baltimore, hence a share of its activities had been devoted to supporting lecture courses, a symphony orchestra and an art collection, yet the library has more and more overshadowed the other phases of the work of the institute. This splendid reference collection now numbers more than 150,000 volumes.

In addition to the Peabody, Baltimore has the libraries of the Johns Hopkins University, aggregating 125,000 volumes; the Maryland Historical Society collections (41,000); the Enoch Pratt Free Library (219,865); and forty-four other collections ranging from 1,000 to 40,000, aggregating in all more than 1,000,000 volumes.

Louisville and New Orleans are rapidly developing into centres of library activity; the former, by means of the extensive gifts from Mr. Carnegie, has erected a splendid central library building, a $30,000 branch for the negroes of the city, and is expending in addition $200,000 for eight branch libraries. Louisville possesses, in addition, the large collection of books of the Filson Club, numbering over 50,000 volumes.

New Orleans had three libraries prior to 1830, all supported by lotteries, but on the passing of the French influence in 1845, these were supplanted by a school library organized by Mr. Shaw, of Massachusetts, and finally in 1849, by the foundation of the Fisk Free Library endowed with a building which was afterward donated to the Louisiana University. In 1886 Miss Anna Howard, the daughter of Charles Howard, founded as a memorial to her father, the Howard Library, giving $115,000 for the building. It is strictly for reference and numbers 50,000 volumes.

New Orleans, also, has benefited from Mr. Carnegie's philanthropy, he having given $275,000 for a central free public library and three branches.

The social forces are the most difficult of all to measure. Their dynamics are so subtle and so widely diffused that long periods of time alone serve to supply the data necessary for weighing and measuring. Of the influence of his books upon the man of the early South, we are permitted to judge by the work the Southerner did in the forming of the nation. Again the schools and libraries of ante-bellum days surely had a large share in the development of the men who defended, by impassioned speech and heroic deed, social traditions and an ideal of the state doomed by the spirit of progress. Of the influence of the library movements of the present, it is too early to judge, yet it is not beyond reason to prophesy that they are destined to work with power towards a higher culture and a purer democracy.

EDWIN WILEY,
Library of Congress.

CHAPTER XXIV.

SOUTHERN HISTORICAL SOCIETIES.

Early History.

N the region generally known as the South, comprising the states of Maryland, Virginia, West Virginia, North Carolina, South Carolina, Georgia, Florida, Alabama, Mississippi, Louisiana, Texas, Arkansas, Missouri, Kentucky and Tennessee, there have been enumerated some sixty-five historical societies, counting all that formally claimed interest in that study as a part of their purpose in any degree. The titles of their publications of every sort mount up to about 800, equaling, on a rough circulation, 250 volumes, octavo, of 500 pages each. Not one of these institutions is a century old, even if we allow the earliest date claimed. The first step in their chronology goes no farther back than 1819, an honor attributed to the New England Society of Charleston, S. C., which has really been only social, with activities limited to speeches at an annual dinner. It was twelve years later, 1831, before a living one came into being, that finally, after two decades of virtual sterility, developed into a healthy producing organ. It was in keeping with the environment and traditions of the state that to the Virginia Historical Society belongs the credit of this historical primacy in the South. Furthermore, the organizers were in step with the spirit of national leadership in Virginia from colonial days, when they declared for the interests of Virginia in particular and the United States in general. This elevated view has been maintained till the present, and the long series of volumes are permanent additions to the sum of knowledge, both for the locality and for the country at large. Virginians have migrated southward and westward, to the Gulf of Mexico and to the Pacific Ocean, and to their descendants in all quarters it is a matter of deep interest to have the letters, diaries, documents and other original material of colonial times put into print so that all can follow the swelling streams of influence that radiated from that little band at Jamestown. This emphasis on the importance of primary data has been the guide line towards which all the others have tended, furnishing a high example for the rest.

The South shared in the almost universal indifference to study of the past in the United States for some six or eight decades after the adoption of the constitution. Although more than a dozen of those totaled above were formed before 1860; they did but little of lasting value, some, indeed, only gasped and then died to be revived after a lapse of years. Their whole output before that era would scarcely make a dozen dignified volumes. But there were some contributions of weight and significance. The South Carolina Society had begun to feel its way into the mass of colonial archives in English repositories. Virginia was looking in the same direction. She also issued, in 1859, the address of Professor George F. Holmes, of wide vision and comprehensive grasp as he pointed out what a beacon star that little knot of men that settled on the James had been in the world experiment of an English colonial empire. Pathetic, too, he was as he saw the impending storm of fratricidal strife that was soon to break. Almost a dramatic antithesis to his utterances did the Society present a couple of years later when they placed in typographical dress *Washington's Diary,* covering the first two years of his service as President. A fine but vain attempt to allay passions by spreading before all the innermost thoughts and calm words of the Father, at the birth of the republic that was now to be split in twain.

After the War of Secession.

During the four years of gigantic contest, and the subsequent ones of slow and painful readjustment, men's energies were with the present, and there was no leisure or inclination to gaze backwards. But as soon as men had settled in the new order Virginia again took the lead and in 1870 the State Society sent out a circular calling for aid, but it was more than a decade before she began the issue of those solid volumes of colonial and revolutionary data. It was not, however, till well on in the last quarter of the century that the South caught the fever of historical interest that was becoming so general throughout the land. The fires of patriotism began to burn and organizations to be formed based on descent from the formation stages of our civic life. Genealogy was almost a passion, and anxious days were spent in libraries and among public records in trying to trace pedigrees back the required distance. This veneration for the family tree gave a great impetus to the cause. Stimulated by all these forces there was an abundant flowering which soon turned to periodicals. About the dawn of the Twentieth century there were more than a dozen of these magazines, though a few gave only a part of their pages to the subject. There were two in West Virginia, one in Maryland, one in Washington, two in Virginia, two in North Carolina, one in South Carolina, one in Alabama, one in Texas, one in Missouri, one in Kentucky and three in Tennessee. This list includes two limited to the War of Secession, which had grown into an important field of investigation on both sides of the conflict. In a short while every

Southern state had a state society in working array, though many have never got any farther. In this expansion Virginia is again in the front. Her quarterly, now numbering nearly twenty annual volumes, owes a large part of its success to the careful genealogies which compose a considerable fraction of the whole. South Carolina took the same course, though not with such large circulation. A measurable harvest, however, has rewarded all who have been able to afford proper tillage, as there are always some connections who are willing to pay a fair price for this pardonable, even commendable, vanity.

Special Aid of Southern Associations and Institutions.

But once more does the South illustrate the general tendency in the country. It was found that this culture was too elevated for the average run, and that the fees from a restricted but appreciative class came too slowly to justify much publishing. Indirectly, all, in time, got some of the benefits of the wider diffusion of historical knowledge, and it was urged that all should contribute to the cost. Taking the cue from their brethren of the West, the voluntary state organizations in the South commenced to appeal to the commonwealth to carry the burden. The pioneer in this new path was Thomas M. Owen, of Alabama, who has merited unstinted praise. He had been one of the three organizers of the Southern History Association in Washington, D. C., had revived the Alabama historical society, and had been a vigorous worker in other ways. Fortunately, he had held public office and knew how to appeal to politicians and the public. He drafted measures, secured their adoption by the state legislature, and obtained appropriations for advancing the cause. His efforts have resulted in the creation of a state department of history at Montgomery, devoted to collecting and publishing, but with most strength on the former. The museum of relics and manuscripts is rapidly growing, following one of the finest examples in the country, that one in Madison, Wis. Mississippi soon copied the Alabama model with some happy modifications; later South Carolina and West Virginia took the same cue. Virginia is indirectly doing something of the same by enabling her state librarian gradually to put in print the store of original material that has been preserved. Maryland accomplishes similar ends by aiding the State Historical Society in making available the state archives. Virtually all the other states have done something for the cause, either through voting money or by providing quarters, or reaching the same goal in a roundabout way through some of its subsidiary agencies, such as the state university or other school.

Among all forms of civic contributions the city of Charleston is unique. For a number of years, under the inspiration of Mr. W. A. Courtenay, first a book dealer, then a cotton manufacturer, and at one time mayor, the annual volume of municipal reports contained, as an appendix, some historical data. In the main these papers were of the highest value, being original material in the local field. Mr. Courtenay went to personal expense to insure the excellence of the series. Transcripts were obtained from London and other foreign sources, besides the harvest from the homes in the neighborhood. Glances were thus afforded back to the founding of the city. After Mr. Courtenay's removal to the western part of the state to supervise his cotton-mill ventures, less of his time and knowledge could be given to the editing, and the quality and quantity of the historical addendum declined until it practically ceased, but he gave Charleston a distinctive place among American cities in the way of helping historical study.

On these foundations thus rapidly sketched have arisen some features of special interest. Prominent among these is the influence of the War of Secession. Although much bitterness of spirit and harshness of language have been displayed, yet a great deal of good has resulted both in reviewing the past and in quickening the historical sense. The most powerful factor in arousing general interest is the organization known as the Confederate Veterans, while the most solid increment to permanent literature has been the annual volumes, over thirty, of the Southern Historical Society, with headquarters in Richmond, Va. Rev. J. W. Jones and Col. R. A. Brock, successive secretaries, saw the importance of the utterances of the participants in the conflict, and have constructed an imperishable storehouse for the future delver.

But it was the Confederate Veterans' organization that had the popular following. It was not organized until 1889, but through its numerous camps, now nearly 2,000, through general and local meetings, and above all through its monthly organ, the *Confederate Veteran* (Nashville, Tenn.), it has made its influence felt in every corner of the South and to distant points wherever a group of former Confederate soldiers can be gathered. The magazine has over 20,000 subscribers, a figure never approached by any other Southern magazine before its time, and perhaps none since. It is a private enterprise built upon the memories and traditions of the war. Its pages are filled with stories, reminiscences and observations of the actors themselves, and the whole output will be invaluable to revive the setting and recreate the atmosphere of that period. There are also biographies of the dead. The standard is generally high, the tone simple and natural, with little of controversial nature. It is a very worthy attempt, in the main, to portray in plain, straightforward style the facts and deeds of one side of an awful conflict.

A sister association was composed of women, entitled the United Daughters of the Confederacy, usually assembling at the same time and place as the veterans. Their voice was also a monthly, the *Lost Cause* (Louisville, Ky.), of the same general aim and scope as the other, but not so full or so selective. But it ceased after a few years as the field was not wide enough for both. This ladies' auxiliary has also been instrumental in the compilation and publication of books dealing with woman's part in that four years' strife. Notable among such books is the one showing the part of the South Carolina women in the war. A committee of the Daughters did the editing but the state defrayed the expenses of printing. There are other accessory Confederate associations that are beneficial to historical study, but these are the leaders so far, at least, as size and numbers are concerned. Besides these that clearly stated their limitations to the war period, there has been only one historical association that tried to cover the entire section throughout its career, the Southern History Association formed at Washington in 1896. While the constitution included all the past, very little of its strength was put on the years subsequent to 1850. Its activities were confined to the issuing of a magazine, at first quarterly, then bimonthly. There were several annual meetings, but for business purposes only after the first two or three, but the publications mounted to eleven annual volumes and one extra. Emphasis was laid on two lines, original material occupying about three-quarters of the total space, and book reviews and notes the most of the balance, all of a high level. The work definitely closed in 1907 for lack of sufficient

support, but there were no financial claims left un-
paid. The career was never exceeded among historical associations on the business side, as the magazine was maintained eleven years on membership
fees alone, except for a slight assistance during the
last two years. The work was of undoubted influence and won high commendation from competent
judges. The machinery of organization is intact and
the effort can be revived if a way should be opened.

Of the more restricted associations there are some
with special features, though the output of all is of
the same quality substantially. In addition to its
publications, the Maryland Association has something of a social side, as there are large, comfortable
rooms where members can confer, while a bond of
union is furnished by the regular assemblies, monthly, during the winter. There is also a fairly good
library of general works. The Virginia society
has a commodious home used chiefly for a library,
museum and offices. As already said, its energies
are mostly expended on the quarterly magazine,
with much stress on Virginia genealogies, all carefully edited by the efficient secretary, W. G. Stanard.
Much of the success of the Society is, beyond question, due to these pedigrees. In South Carolina an
ethnic element comes to light in the Huguenot Society of Charleston, confined mainly to the state where
the bulk of the descendants of the early French emigrants still reside. An annual meeting and a printed
report, made up in considerable part of valuable
documents, constitute the current of the life of the
Society. Similar interest in the French stock is
seen in associations in Alabama and Louisiana,
though not under that avowed title.

One of the latest of the state organizations, that of
Texas, has a different background from all the
others, as a part of its territory was once under a

foreign flag and then independent. The petty colonial details or the bare legislative enactments of the other states are here replaced by the romance and heroism of the clashes with Mexico, and by the pride in a republic that guided for a short time its own destiny. Around these two centres the imagination can play, and the thoughts can dwell on definite points of interest. Out of these advantages and out of a more extensive constituency has been erected the largest of the state societies, but the printed matter does not yet equal that of some of the others.

Kentucky, in some respects, furnishes the most remarkable of these bodies. A quarter of a century ago, in Louisville, was formed the Filson Club in honor of an early historian in the state. Since then about a score of the most sumptuous volumes have appeared dealing with some phase of Kentucky history, all of quarto size, of fine, heavy paper, with widest margins, handsomely illustrated. Indian struggles, Kentucky soldiers in our foreign wars, Kentucky artists, town histories, etc., have provided themes treated in the series. The moving spirit has been Mr. R. T. Durrett, of breadth of view and of generous nature. The members, several hundred in number, are scattered over the state.

The educational institutions have had no mean part in the general movement. While few have had the means for the establishment of a full professorship of history, in some instances much valuable aid has been furnished by an association in connection with the institution or by the publication of studies by the management. Such subsidiary agencies are to be noted at Randolph-Macon in Virginia, at Trinity in North Carolina, at Vanderbilt in Tennessee, at Washington and Lee, at Lexington, Va., and also at the Normal College in Nashville, Tenn., at the University of North Carolina, the University of South Carolina and other institutions, including, of course, the Virginia University, whose imprint is so plain on the educational field south of her.

But the strongest pedagogical centre for radiating historical influence is furnished by the Johns Hopkins University, in Baltimore. Founded on a fortune whose foundation was laid in Southern trade by a Baltimore Quaker, it was very fitting that his means should thus return a blessing to this section. Under the guidance of Professor H. B. Adams, a man of liberal sympathies who could appreciate the particular circumstances of the region below the Potomac, a strong impetus was imparted to historical study among the more advanced students of the subject in the South. Young men were attracted to Baltimore, which, as a flourishing commercial centre on the borders of both sections, was well adapted to widen their vision and enlarge their charities. Here they were also introduced into the transplanted atmosphere of a German university, and trained in the methods of scientific research. Many returned to their localities to teach, and towards the beginning of the present century the fruits of their culture began to appear in small circles around their institutions. More definite still were their contributions to the historical magazine that Dr. Adams established on the university funds. A couple of stout volumes annually came from the press, of which a very appreciable portion was written by Southern men on Southern topics.

Besides periodicals already referred to as organs of associations, there were several others of value to historical work, either as private ventures or as college journals. The *Gulf States Historical Magazine,* conducted by two enthusiastic young men in Alabama, was an ambitious attempt on a high plane, but the circulation could not be made large enough to be remunerative, though it was devoted entirely to history and geneaology. There are two literary quarterlies—the *Sewanee Review* and the *South Atlantic Quarterly*—that have historical articles of value in nearly every issue.

The religious denominations caught something of the fever, and both Baptists and Methodists formed associations for preserving church history. The Baptists in western North Carolina for two or three years regularly published biographical sketches, but again the financial side was weak. So with the efforts elsewhere of other branches of the Church.

It is the material basis that is insecure in all the Southern historical organizations and efforts. Only three or four societies own convenient quarters, and not one of these has more than a meager income-bearing endowment considering the extent of the work for them to do. Less than half a dozen can afford salaries of any sort, and the equipment in nearly all is scanty. Because of pecuniary troubles, over half of the magazines counted above have ceased. But at present the outlook is more encouraging than ever. The deaths have removed the struggling and made more room for the vigorous. The trend is everywhere towards public appropriations, which can always be made ample enough for legitimate needs. Thus far the legislatures have been generous, and great hopefulness is ahead.

BIBLIOGRAPHY.—Griffin, A. P. C.: *Bibliography of American Historical Societies* (Vol. II of *Annual Report* of American Historical Association for 1905); *Handbook of Learned Societies and Institutions*, published by Carnegie Institution (Washington, 1908); Files of *American Historical Review* and of Southern History Association, especially the latter; Reports and publications of the various historical associations through the South; Files of Southern Historical periodicals.

COLYER MERIWETHER,
Secretary Southern History Association, and Editor Publications of Southern History Association.

CHAPTER XXV.

THE INTELLECTUAL AND LITERARY PROGRESS OF THE NEGRO.

THE present descendants of those Africans belonging to various negro tribes who were imported into the United States between 1619 and the disappearance of the slave import traffic in the earlier decades of the Nineteenth century (the original twenty had increased to 750,-000 in 1790) are the outcome, the most of them, of at least six generations of exposure to the hot-house influences, good and bad, of a white man's civilization entirely alien and imposed. Rudely and utterly cut off from the life of their own race and flung helpless into the midst of another which used them but did not take them in, they have for all these generations, per force, founded their ideals and aspirations more and more, as their native background receded, upon the visible part of the life of the dominant and overwhelming white man whose fields they tilled and whose table they served.

Of this white man's modes of thought they had in the beginning but the dimmest understanding. To his manner of life in vast houses of wood and brick and stone they could have no sort of initial inclination.

Nevertheless, when they sought something better than they had, they could find no other model. They have gone on to this day, therefore, imitating the white man's house and his walk and conversation whenever opportunity offered. As to his modes of thought, they were not so easily got at. One could do as he did. One could not tell why he did it. And consequently the things one did lacked something of coherence and effect.

However, the secret might well be hidden in the mysterious volumes which adorned the white man's shelves, and from which, if one was permitted to touch them at all, it was necessary to remove accumulated dust with care. Since the African's descendant learned to read he has been seeking that secret, and finding it still obstinately eludes him, has been industriously committing to memory the formulas, symbols of the secret, set down in the white man's printed books.

Thus the African's descendant has done the best he knew. And if by reason of the anthropological abyss of twenty centuries or so between the negro and what for convenience we may call the Teuton, he has selected the accidental and the superficial characteristics of his model and missed the essentials, if the formula is a formula merely, and carries no comprehension with it, nobody in his sober senses can blame the African's descendant for that. Acutely observant of manners, he conceives that manners make the man, not man the manners. The man he cannot change. He changes the manners as best he may. The old-fashioned negro major domo copied floridly the best—his master's. The negro of to-day is apt to copy rankly the worst. The selection of the model is a matter of accident in both cases. As a free man the African's descendant no longer sees the best. He must find his level—and that level is naturally the bottom in a civilization where he is the least at home and the worst equipped of all the competitors. The matter is one of economics and dynamics, not of morals or of ethics.

The Negro—Characteristics and Progress.

The American negro, or negroid, to be exact, for by 1860 when he had increased and multiplied to 4,500,000 the proportion of mixed breeds was large, has lost the standards of the black race, its separate race pride, and must borrow, though he cannot understand them, the standards of a population whose evolutionary path has been diverging from that of his own people for centuries. He is a mimic—often a marvelous mimic, but the root of this thing he tries to do is not in him. He is acting a part, not living a life. Off the public stage, that is, when the white man's eye is not upon him, and where he can find a mass of his fellows large enough to allow him to lose sight, for a while, of the white man's overshadowing culture, he promptly reverts to type —reverts even though the actual proportion of negro blood in his veins be small. Partly because the negro blood is younger, nearer to the primordial pithecanthropoid beast; partly because the taint of it bars him from the white man's fellowship and the instincts in him which are those of the white race lie dormant and undiscovered, while the others, which are those of the black race, are nourished by the negro environment into which he is forced.

In no field of the American negro's activity is it so important in order to estimate fairly what he has accomplished to hold these matters of recent history and remote ethnology so clearly in view as in the province of literature and work in what may be called intellectual pursuits. All such progress since the war may be grouped under two heads —that which borrows its formula from the ethnologically indefensible theory of the New England abolitionists that the negro is merely an uneducated sun-tanned white man, and that which continues without any particular theory the process of imitating the dominant white next to the imitator's elbow, which began when the first twenty negroes were dumped among the transplanted Englishmen at Jamestown.

The type of the first is W. E. Burghardt DuBois, born in 1868 in Great Barrington, Mass., educated among white men at Harvard and Berlin, refusing categorically to admit the existence of any real ethnological gap between the two races whose blood he shares. The type of the second, is Booker T. Washington, born about 1858, in Franklin county, Va., of a mulatto slave mother and a white father, laborer in a coal mine, educated by his own efforts at the negro school at Hampton, identified from the beginning with the black race in that peculiar relation to the white population around it which has become second nature to both in the South. Washington bases all his policies upon an instinctive recognition of the gulf between the two branches of the human family to both of which he can trace his descent, but only one of which will recognize him as a member. It will be seen as we proceed that practically all the other notable examples of both of these types also have a share of white blood, that the "intellectual" progress we are viewing is that of the negroid, not of the negro.

This matter apart, however, generally speaking, negroes or negroids who rise to any eminence in their native Southern environment will be found (whatever their expressed theories) allowing in the instinctive manner noted in Washington's case, in all practical matters for the existence of a gulf which nature has made and custom fixed. Speaking generally, negroes or negroids brought up in communities where the negro population is too small for the individual to be forced into exclusive association with other negroes or negroids, where as a child he goes to school with the children of the

whites on a plane of more or less equality, where
the crude fact of the chasm, so evident when the
races meet in masses, is not thrust upon him in his
most impressionable years and made a part of his
habit of thought—such negroes or negroids will
be found trying to ignore the existence of any chasm
in act and denying it in words. The one kind,
which may be called (so far as America is concerned)
the normal, tend, where they have ambition, to
preach thrift and to seek economic improvement
first. These feel instinctively that a negro with
property is in a stronger position to ask for the
political and social equality which, naturally enough,
all negroes desire, and they are well aware from
personal experience that the negro as a field-hand,
servant, or squatter can get neither.

Following their instinct they take the only road
toward their ultimate goal which, though circuitous,
appears practicable.

The other kind, exotics, potted plants of humanity,
cling to the white man's printed book. They have
seen the educated negro, the African grown under
glass as it were, accepted as a social equal in communities where there is no mass of negro population
banked behind him to use him as an entering wedge
for a black invasion—where he is as much a curiosity and an incident as a single monkey at a ban-
quet—and no amount of experience afterwards can
convince them that the royal road for their eager
feet does not lead straight through the white man's
classroom to the white man's dinner table and beyond. These exotics never, or rarely, learn that
while what is called "prejudice" may be lulled to
sleep between individuals of diverse races, the mu-
tually repellant instinct of race masses (an ethnological protective envelope) is not thus to be overcome. Having in fact, themselves lost their own

race instinct they must fail to allow for it in others more normally bred.

Thus negro progress in the United States lies in two divergent lines, both of which produce results which may be called literary and intellectual if you choose; for, while the negro writes little but briefs in his own case against the tendency of the white man's civilization to reject him as unfit, it is here that he uses the best efforts of his Teutonically ''educated'' brain—here that he appears, in fact, as a creature rather of mind than of instinct. He writes to insist that he is fit.

So DuBois writes, the graces of New England culture, the fastidiousness of the Boston literary person, clothing strangely, but not disguising, a passionate aspiration and a fierce resentment. Setting out as impersonal mind to prove his point by argument and cold statistics, he drifts infallibly into the region of primitive personal feeling, bursts into lyrical appeal, invective, rhapsody, loses the white man's logic in the black man's emotion. It is then that he is really eloquent, that what he writes is really literature, though, as there is nothing intellectual about it, nothing analytical, it may be considered to detract from the force of his plea instead of helping it. For these lyrical outpourings argue lack of control, lack of direction.

The case to be proved is not that the negro is a poet—Uncle Remus, in his cornfield, is that, and black Mammy in her nursery, and so, doubtless, was fanatic Nat Turner, at the head of his band of ignorant blacks in the Virginia insurrection of 1831, slaying white women and infants and attacking a lonely schoolhouse and slaughtering all the children. Nat held himself inspired, and his language was quite lyrical. The case to be proved is that the negro is a self-possessed contributing member of the body

politic—a good citizen in a republic of white men
who have most of them outgrown the use of poetry
for the purposes of daily life.

It is otherwise with Booker T. Washington, the
bulk of whose voluminous writings do not pretend
to be literature in any sense, who argues very little
and rhapsodizes not at all, whose language is anything but lyrical, who builds like the bee with concrete material, who accumulates facts to show what
the negro has accomplished as a member of the white
man's economic household—how he has learned to
read and write, how he has made a decent living at
trades and professions, how he has acquired land
and a house and carpets on the floor and a cabinet
organ in the parlor, and, perhaps, a bank balance,
and a fair imitation of the white man's code of
family morals. Washington does show, so far as
these things can show it, that the negro can be
a self-possessed, contributing member of the body
politic, a good citizen. What he fails to show,
of course, what he cannot show, in the nature of
things, is this: that such a good negro citizen has
any proper place in the white man's republic. In
other words whether that republic would not be
better for the substitution of a good white citizen
for each of these good negro citizens. And whether
it should not, with malice toward none, aim frankly
at such replacement.

Washington has written many books and magazine articles. His first book *Up From Slavery*, his
own autobiography, a human document of great
value, is his sole contribution to literature proper,
the rest of his output consists of reports and the
sermon of thrift iterated and reiterated after the
fashion of the schoolmaster who has a class of in-
attentive, half-formed, irresponsible beings under
him, and who conceives that the only way to reach

as many as possible of these beings is to keep patiently at it, dinging the same lesson into their ears. It is not a bad method, but only a very patient man can use it successfully. Washington is a very patient man. He is an instinctive plodder, but he represents the negro's highest intellectual achievement because he has known how to concentrate his mental energies steadily upon a practical matter. His at least is the intellect directed, efficient.

What the negro must demonstrate is that he does possess this intellect efficient, that he can hold his own economically with his white neighbor, not that he can memorize the white man's textbook formulas and get good marks at free school or even capture Rhodes' Scholarships. Thomas Hunter, long president of the Normal College of the City of New York, the apex of the Metropolitan public school system for girls, declared a few years ago, that while nearly all of the many negro girls who had entered this school in his experience of it, had appeared to learn rapidly at first, only one of the lot had ever managed to get through the upper classes, where the work began to call for judgment more than memory. Mr. Hunter was as nearly as possible an observer without prejudice in this case, and his opportunities were excellent.

What he noted, besides agreeing perfectly with the teachings of the ethnologists, is confirmed by the opinion held currently everywhere in the country that the negro high school or college graduate unless he turns teacher or preacher (when all he has to do is to pass his formulas along undigested) is not an efficient instrument—that he rarely builds on the foundation of his learning and discovers practical application for his academic accomplishments. That, in short, he is like the cannibal with the missionary's top hat. The exceptions to this rule among the negroes who stand out from the mass of their fellows are few enough. Booker T. Washington, as already noted, is such an exception. Frederick Douglass has been accepted by some as another, though he owed most of his seeming success to the fact that he was used by the white abolitionists as human exhibit A of the black man's wrongs and was pushed ahead by them, not on his own merits, but on the merits of the cause.

The Maryland slave (born 1817 of a white father and a negro mother) possessed undoubtedly ability and shrewdness which fitted him for better things than the work of a field hand. He rose by his own efforts to the grade of mechanic, but what happened to him after his escape from slavery to Boston, after the Massachusetts Anti-Slavery Society launched him as a lecturer, cannot be set down as his achievement. He was a sign and a symbol held up for men to see. He was floated on the top of the abolition wave into public office. He did not climb there. Nothing that he wrote is literature, nothing need be filed for posterity's reference except his autobiography, *The Life and Times of Frederick Douglass.* That is a document in evidence. As Douglass himself in life was exhibit A of a cause, so his book is historically exhibit A of the true inwardness of the movement in favor of that cause. But it is raw material merely, as much so as is the talk of Mandy to Rufus in the kitchen.

In fact, the genuinely intellectual side of the negro, the power to use the mind independently, to judge, analyze, combine, is not nourished to any very profitable extent on books at all; rather it thrives on everyday practical affairs. In every community in the South and in many in the North, you will find the shrewd, successful negro or negroid who has these powers though he cannot sign his name, and alongside of him the college-bred negro, full of parrot phrases and classroom jargon, utterly lacking the powers which the other daily exercises. The explanation seems obvious. The negro is mentally quite sufficiently developed to use his brain with effect upon the immediate and the concrete. He is not sufficiently developed to start with the white man's generalizations, or more exactly, the formulas in which these generalizations are expressed, and work down to the concrete. He is in the class in arithmetic. He is not fit yet awhile for that in algebra and analytics. The capable Booker T. Washington is in type and in fact exactly like Peter the successful barber and Walker who runs a profitable carrier's business in a certain Southern town, though neither Peter nor Walker can read or write. It is Washington's native shrewdness which has made him what he is, which has enabled him (as did Walker also) to stand well with the white community while he leads the blacks. His knowledge of the white man's books is incidental. Indeed, it is strictly limited to a small set of simple and purely utilitarian chapters. It is the rule of three. Algebra, Washington does not attempt, nor pretend to connoisseurship in the fine art of letters.

Of all the negroes who have essayed books after the white man's pernicious example, the earliest exhibit, Phyllis Wheatley, was a case of the hot-house process pure and simple. This slave girl, born in Africa and brought to Boston at the age of about eight years in 1761, was kept in a house of one John Wheatley of that town, and "educated"—taught the trick of verse. Her verses were printed as a curiosity at the time and her "Poems" have no other interest.

It may be said, in fact, that every achievement, especially every intellectual or literary achievement, of every negro gets, because it is the achievement of a negro and as such a curiosity, an amount of advertising which makes it loom much larger than life on the contemporary horizon; which must be discounted in any calm estimate of the intellectual and literary progress of the race. What is true of Phyllis Wheatley absolutely, or Douglass largely, is true to no inconsiderable extent of Booker T. Washington and DuBois. Both owe a certain part of their seeming eminence to the quality of rarity which is the sole distinction of the man with six fingers. Even Paul Laurence Dunbar (b. Dayton, O., 1872; d. 1906, contributor to newspapers in New York and sometime a member of the staff of the Library of Congress) admittedly a genuine, though minor, poet, has a fame quite disproportionate to his actual place in the catalogue of contemporary minor poets. He, too, is, in part, a curiosity.

Yet Dunbar has put into verse very simply and sincerely that range of the negro's emotions which is not too primitive for public expression in the white man's country. The unrestrained negro poet is heard only where the negro is quite himself— when masses of negroes are gathered together outside the white man's pale, where the suppressed race instinct collected there blazes up and not remote savage ancestors take possession of the bodies of their descendants and break up the veneer of the white man's manners with which they are overlaid. White men have caught the weird and savage note of this poetry at negro night camp-meetings, which are the ancient African religious orgy dressed in a Christian garment as a bushman might wear a white shirt. A negro, if he would be a published poet in a white man's country must be a minor poet. So Dunbar sang—in *Oak and Ivy, Majors and Minors, Lyrics of a Lowly Life* and the rest—of the negro sad and glad

—not of the negro fiery and passionate. He has written prose also—a novel *The Uncalled,* and a volume of stories *Folks From Dixie*—but it is of no significance.

On the other hand, the late Joel Chandler Harris, taking the negro as he seems when he is minstrel in the white man's hall provides in his immortal stories of "Brer Rabbit," better negro literature for consumption in the white man's country, than any literature the black man has ever written for that market. Because the negro, to appear natural to the audience to which American authors look for support, must be the negro as the white man knows him. The negro himself cannot see himself as the white man sees him. What he writes about himself appeals to the white man necessarily much less strongly that what some observant white man writes about him.

All the other well-known negroes of this country are, like Washington and DuBois, teachers or else preachers—disguised sometimes as editors of negro newspapers. Washington is the voice of Tuskegee, reporting progress, conciliating the white man, inviting funds to invest in more progress. also the voice of the leader pointing his people to what they have done and exhorting them to further efforts. DuBois is the voice of Atlanta—of a little band of negroes now marrooned in the Black Belt, who have acquired more or less of the white man's culture and resent bitterly exclusion from the fellowship of the cultured who live across the color line. DuBois in *The Souls of Black Folk,* and from time to time in all that he writes, makes true negroid literature. He speaks with the voice of the outcast from his father's house. The ordinary negro, bred among his kind, has no such voice. For he is not an outcast from his father's house. or if he is. he has never known that house. If, therefore, he prospers among those of his own color he is usually proud and content. DuBois, writing about the negro of the Black Belt, nevertheless always imputes to him his own bitterness. He labors, indeed, to awaken in him that bitterness and to use it as a lever of progress.

DuBois's exhibits of his race's claims and wrongs as *The Philadelphia Negro* and *The Negroes of the Black Belt,* and his many magazine articles on what the educated negro has done or can do, what the white man has denied him or would deny him, are special pleadings not literary in intent. As pleadings, as already hinted, they lose effect in the court to which they are addressed because they ignore the essential circumstance that the question at issue, so far as the country at large is concerned, is not so much how to advance the negro as to how to prevent the negro from retarding the upward tendency of the rest of the population.

Bishop Henry M. Turner (born at Newberry Court House, S. C., 1834), chaplain of colored troops during the War of Secession, official of the Freedman's Bureau, member of the Georgia legislature in the reconstruction period, and afterwards postmaster and detective in the Federal secret service, is now chiefly known as an agitator for the removal of his race to Liberia. He is preacher and politician. He has composed a book on *Methodist Polity,* compiled a hymn-book and written *The Negro in All Ages.* He is a power among his people, but it cannot be said that he stands for any intellectual progress in his race. On the other hand, William Saunders Scarborough (born in Macon, Ga., 1852), a graduate of Oberlin, the first college to encourage co-education of the races, and now professor of Wilberforce University in Ohio, has devoted himself to the scholastic. He is professor of Greek. He has published a book

of first Greek lessons and a translation of *The Birds*
of Aristophanes, and he has written on negro folk-
lore. As Dunbar was the poet of the race, so Scarborough appears as the scholar.

Archibald Henry Grimké (born in Charleston,
S. C., 1849), a graduate of Lincoln University, practitioner of the law, resident of Boston and editor
of *The Hub* newspaper, author of lives of Charles
Sumner and William Lloyd Garrison; and Francis
James Grimké (born near Charleston, 1850), a minister, are both contributors to the negro's side of
his case against American civilization; while T.
Thomas Fortune, lately editor of the negro organ
The Age, in New York City, is another contributor
not without ability to write and think. He has published *The Negro in Politics* and *Black and White.*
Charles W. Chesnutt (born in Cleveland, O., 1858),
schoolteacher in the South for some years and now
a lawyer in his native city, is yet another whose
name is more or less frequently signed to articles
bearing on the problem of which he is an embodied
fraction. He has published the *Conjure Woman*
and *A Life of Frederick Douglass.*

Daniel Murray, in a *Preliminary List of Books and
Pamphlets by Negro Authors,* published for the Library of Congress in 1900, has gathered enough
names and titles to fill a thin booklet. His list contains 182 names of authors and 266 titles of their
writings, and is yet obviously incomplete even as a
summary of negro authorship up to 1900. Analysis
of the titles shows that most of this output consists
of papers on educational or religious subjects, arguments on the negro question, or autobiography. Several writers have attempted poems and some few
fiction, but what has been accomplished in this direction is negligible. The bulk of the 266 titles are titles
of pamphlets merely.

The names of negroes who are credited with more than one title include, aside from those already considered: R. C. O. Benjamin (eight titles, one a *Life of Toussaint L'Ouverture*); Edward Blyden (three titles); William Wells Brown (five titles); Alexander Crummell (four titles); Martin R. Delaney (three titles); Joseph E. Hayne (two titles); James H. Hood (four titles); Edward A. Johnson (two titles); John M. Langston (two titles); Daniel A. Payne (four titles); I. Garland Penn (two titles); H. Cordelia Ray (two titles); John P. Sampson (two titles); C. S. Smith (four titles); T. G. Steward (three titles); Benjamin T. Tanner (five titles); D. Augustus Straker (two titles); Marshall W. Taylor (five titles); George W. Williams (three titles, including *A History of Negro Troops in the Rebellion, A History of the Negro Race,* and *The Negro as a Political Leader*). We may mention besides, Eloise Bibb, author of poems, and Linda Brent, author of *Incidents in the Life of a Slave Girl.*

There are, of course, any number of negro or negroid preachers and teachers whose writings, of no importance in themselves, have found their way into print in church and school bulletins and in similar ways. In a certain sense all these composisions, also, are exhibits of intellectual progress, but they are like the schoolboy's essay which gets into the school magazine, they are to be considered as "exercises," not as achievements. There have been since the war a number of negroes, often negro preachers, who have held public office; some have been members of Congress and have had speeches printed. No one of them, however, has been anything more than a pawn in the political game. It is impossible to use them as sign posts of intellectual progress or samples of literary success.

Negro Schools and Institutions.

The quality of the intellectual progress of the race has been indicated in treating of the negroes who are known as writers, the agents of that progress have been the negro public schools of the South, supported mainly by the white people of the South during a period when they have been hard put to it to educate their own children, the individual efforts of any number of Southern white men and more Southern white women in their several communities, and various schools organized chiefly under the auspices of the American Missionary Association of Northern membership and abolitionist inspiration.

At the close of the war an army of women from the North marched upon the South to rescue the freed slave from his ignorance, and though some men came too on the same errand, the sentimental, even somewhat hysterical quality of the movement— its essential feminist character—has left its mark upon the work, and, in view of the highly hysterical character of the negro himself, has mixed much harm with the good sought to be accomplished. The American Missionary Association, however, founded Hampton Institute in 1861, and the Freedman's Bureau, set up in 1865 as the legal guardian of the emancipated blacks, spent, prior to 1870, $5,000,000, and established or helped in establishing some two thousand schools, many of which have, of course, perished, while others—usually those in which the American Missionary Association or some religious body was also interested—have survived and prospered.

Between 1868 and 1878 twenty-five normal and collegiate institutions, scattered from Virginia to Texas, and mainly or exclusively devoted to negro education were established by various religious denominations—the Congregationalists and Baptists

leading.   Wilberforce in Ohio had already been
founded in 1857—the first negro university, perhaps.
Berea College, in Kentucky, had been opened as a
mixed school before the war also, and it was only
in 1908, after half a century of its existence, that
the United States Supreme Court affirmed the con-
stitutionality of the Kentucky law forbidding the co-
education of the races there.   The years immediately following the war saw after the establishment of
Hampton Institute in Virginia, the model and forerunner of Washington's famous Tuskegee, the foundation in 1866 of Fisk University at Nashville, Tenn.,
of Howard University in Washington (1867), of Atlanta University in Georgia, of Lincoln University
in Tennessee, and of many other colleges for negroes
throughout the South.   Most of the more ambitious
of these institutions had the patronage of Northern
religious bodies, the support of Northern philanthropists and a teaching force in the beginning of
New Englanders or New England educated negroes.
Besides 131 separate public high schools in 1900,
there were 128 secondary and higher schools for
negroes controlled by religious bodies, Northern or
Southern.

    These schools, where they have not been "indus-
trial," have tended to the production of teachers
and preachers only.   Their aim has been to divorce the negro from the soil, as the aim of Washington's school at Tuskegee (founded by him, under
an appropriation of the Alabama legislature in 1881,
and since jointly supported by the state and his efforts), has been to hold him to it—to encourage him
to become its owner.   Eloquent commentary on the
practicality of the two policies is found in the
census figures for 1900, by which it appears that the
negro continues to be more successful economically
in agriculture than anywhere else.   In that year

there were 746,717 farms operated by negroes—187,-
797 by their owners, 557,174 by tenants. The average size of these farms was 51.2 acres, the average
value of the farm products $308. The proportion of
negroes owning farms had increased 3.5 per cent. in
the ten years preceding. Of 3,807,008 negroes engaged in gainful occupations employing at least 10,-
000 negroes in 1900, 33.7 per cent. were agricultural
laborers, 19 per cent. farmers, planters, or overseers
—52.7 per cent. in all. These same returns showed
that the negro mechanic was losing ground, partly
no doubt, on account of the discrimination of trades
unions against him. The census of 1890, which
showed 57 per cent. of negroes engaged in agriculture as laborers or farmers, 31.4 per cent. in personal
service, 5.6 per cent. in manufactures, and 4.7 per
cent. in trade and transportation, showed only 1.1
per cent. in "professions"—mostly teachers and
preachers, with a few doctors and lawyers. This 1.1
per cent. was the result of twenty-five years of
"higher" education.

Before 1870 there were practically no public
schools for negroes in the South except in Memphis,
New Orleans and Nashville. Naturally the care of
the black man in bondage was his master's, not the
state's concern. In 1877 the total number of negro
children of school age in the District of Columbia
and the former slave states was reported at 1,513,065,
and of that number 571,506 were enrolled in the public schools. By 1882-83, when the colored school population of the District of Columbia and the former
slave states was reported at 1,944,572, the enroll-
ment in the public schools in that territory was 802,-
982. So that within two decades the South had
built up a public school system for the blacks, in
spite of the fact that the whites of that section had
in the same period to rebuild their homes and for-

tunes and provide somehow for the education of their own children. By 1901 a million and a half negro children, or 57 per cent. of the whole number of school age, were being educated in these schools.

The higher education so-called, which has affected a few thousands only, has been almost exclusively under Northern direction and has depended largely on Northern support, because only persons at a safe distance from the centres of negro population could fail to recognize that the negro of the South in the present generation, at least, did not need and could not take, with any real profit to himself or the community, any such higher education. He must, his white neighbors saw, if he built at all, build upwards from the foundations, not from the air downward— in other words, do as they had done.

The result of all this education of both kinds—low and high—so much of which is utterly misdirected and none of which is scientifically adjusted to needs which the kindest and wisest white man can under- stand only imperfectly, is this and no more—that the negro has learned to read and write. The amount of the negro's literary and intellectual progress since emancipation is really that he has become more than 50 per cent. literate, whereas be- fore that time he was almost wholly illiterate. That is a long step, considering everything that must be considered. He has spent all his available energy during almost a half century in gaining it. As befits one still in the primary grades, his leaders are still primary teachers and neither he nor they have risen above the purely academic stage in the white man's culture. All negro literature may be described most accurately as classroom exercises by pupils and practice essays by pupil teachers.

H. L. BROCK,
New York City.

ND - #0013 - 160123 - C0 - 229/152/34 [36] - CB - 9780365329855 - Gloss Lamination